IRRESISTIBLE FORCE

THE LIFE AND TIMES OF
GORILLA MONSOON

BRIAN R. SOLOMON

Copyright © Brian R. Solomon, 2025

Published by ECW Press
665 Gerrard Street East
Toronto, Ontario, Canada M4M 1Y2
416-694-3348 / info@ecwpress.com

All rights reserved. No part of this publication may be reproduced, stored in a retrieval system, or transmitted in any form by any process — electronic, mechanical, photocopying, recording, or otherwise — without the prior written permission of the copyright owners and ECW Press. The scanning, uploading, and distribution of this book via the internet or via any other means without the permission of the publisher is illegal and punishable by law. This book may not be used for text and data mining, AI training, and similar technologies. Please purchase only authorized electronic editions, and do not participate in or encourage electronic piracy of copyrighted materials. Your support of the author's rights is appreciated.

Editor for the Press: Michael Holmes
Copy editor: Peter Norman
Cover design: Jessica Albert

LIBRARY AND ARCHIVES CANADA CATALOGUING IN PUBLICATION

Title: Irresistible force : the life and times of Gorilla Monsoon / Brian R. Solomon.

Names: Solomon, Brian, 1974- author

Description: Includes bibliographical references.

Identifiers: Canadiana (print) 20250228092 | Canadiana (ebook) 20250228122

ISBN 978-1-77041-768-7 (softcover)
ISBN 978-1-77852-472-1 (ePub)
ISBN 978-1-77852-473-8 (PDF)

Subjects: LCSH: Gorilla Monsoon, 1937-1999. | LCSH: Wrestlers—United States—Biography. | LCSH: World Wrestling Entertainment, Inc.—History. | LCGFT: Biographies.

Classification: LCC GV1196.G67 S65 2025 | DDC 796.812092—dc23

PRINTED AND BOUND IN CANADA

PRINTING: FRIESENS   5 4 3 2 1

Purchase the print edition and receive the ebook free.
For details, go to ecwpress.com/ebook.

This book is dedicated to the memory of
Mrs. Maureen Marella, true wrestling royalty and a
woman who honored me with her trust and support.

It's also dedicated to the entire Marella family, and I humbly
offer it as a tribute to the man who was so loved by them
and by the world. But especially to Valerie, who was always
around to answer with limitless patience all my pestering
questions about the father who brought her so much joy.

And on a personal note, to my uncle, Peter Purpura, who
motivated and inspired me to become a writer more than
anyone else. He happened to be a theatrical performer and
longtime WWF fan who showed me from an early age that
pro wrestling is one of the purest forms of theater there is.

"One of the best friends I've ever had in my life.
Just an honest, decent man."
—Bobby "The Brain" Heenan

"Gino had a heart as big as all outdoors . . .
he was a really principled guy."
—Cowboy Bill Watts

"A very gracious man. And very intelligent.
He was really a piece of work, I'll tell you that."
—Ken Patera

"He was such a fair character. A legit friend.
Just a big guy with a golden heart. I miss him."
—Johnny Rodz

"He was the most generous person I've ever met in my life."
—Davey O'Hannon

"Gino was just a salt-of-the-earth guy.
You knew where you stood with him all the time."
—Jerry Brisco

"He was quite an athlete. Quite a gentleman.
And a hell of a family man."
—Tony Garea

"There was such kindness that surrounded him."
—Gary Michael Cappetta

"Everybody at that TV studio that had worked with Gino Marella loved and revered him."
—Kevin Kelly

"He was a man's man. A man of his word, of honor and integrity."
—Hugo Savinovich

"He was a hell of a father, a hell of a person and one hell of a stand-up guy, always."
—Mike Chioda

"He was always there to offer advice. And it was never to tear down. It was always to enhance."
—Jimmy Korderas

"It's the ultimate success story in wrestling, when somebody gets in a business, becomes a main event guy . . . and they can pick and choose what they want to do. They get part of the office and end up doing TV announcing and being the figurehead president. I mean, Jesus Christ."
—Jim Cornette

"He was the gentle giant. But boy, if you pissed him off, leave town."
—Mario Savoldi

CONTENTS

Foreword	By Bret "Hitman" Hart	9
Introduction		11
Chapter 1	A Final Bow in Philly	17
Chapter 2	A Secret Heritage	22
Chapter 3	Big Bob	28
Chapter 4	Tiny	39
Chapter 5	Gino	56
Chapter 6	The Manchurian Giant	81
Chapter 7	To the West Coast and Back	119
Chapter 8	Points on the Territory	147
Chapter 9	The Boy, the Boxer, the Bruiser and the Bleeder	189
Chapter 10	The Only Wrestler to Retire for Good	225
Chapter 11	Vinny Makes His Move	260
Chapter 12	Prime Time	302

Chapter 13	The Gorilla and the Brain	344
Chapter 14	Changing Times, Changing Roles	376
Chapter 15	President Monsoon	416
Chapter 16	"Goodbye, My Friend."	435
Chapter 17	History Has Been Made	460

Acknowledgments		477
Appendix	A Glossary of Gorilla-isms	480
Notes		485
Bibliography		501

FOREWORD
BY BRET "HITMAN" HART

Few men have walked in bigger shoes than Gino Marella, especially in the larger-than-life world of professional wrestling, where good men generally die like dogs. Gino was a man's man. A guy who was loved and respected, both in and out of the ring. I had the pleasure of meeting Gino in 1979, when I was just breaking in. He took the time even then to speak of his admiration for my dad and how he held special memories of his time in Calgary. Little did I know that my dad had taken him down to the Hart House basement, soon to be famously known forever as the Dungeon thanks to Gino. That day in 1961 led to Gino getting cross-faced and getting a busted, bloody nose that somehow cemented their friendship. Only in pro wrestling do these things happen.

Gino went on to become a legend of the business. He was as tough as he looked—not only a tough wrestler with a real background, but more importantly, he became a huge draw and made a lot of money. Enough to earn his place as a top man in the grandest wrestling company of them all, WWE. By the time I wound up there, Gino was a made man. He took a shine to me in those early days, when my prospects were low and my future was dim. He always spoke highly of my dad and praised me, privately telling me to hang in there and to make my dad proud someday.

Often it was simply a compliment on my match, but my day would come while teaming up with Jim "The Anvil" Neidhart and the Hart Foundation, when he bestowed upon me the moniker "The Excellence of Execution." I can't explain what a huge boost that was at a time when few even noticed me. One day, I asked him why he dubbed me with such high praise and he simply said, "You execute every move with such precision. It's the truth. You're a great worker. Better than anyone else."

Gino was a real friend to me in those early days. He was a great wrestler, businessman, family man, but more important than anything else, he was a true friend to everyone who knew him. He was famous for his honesty and his big heart; I can think of no man who ever had anything but the highest respect for him in and out of the ring. "Gorilla" was a second father to me, and I'll always be indebted to him for all he did for me throughout my long career. There was only one Gino Marella, and he had a platinum heart right till the very end.

INTRODUCTION

Though it seems like a lifetime ago now, I once worked for WWE. It was an interesting period, what you might even call a dream come true. Truth be told, it spoiled me for any other job and was a seven-year adventure filled with a whole lot of rewards and a handful of regrets. One of those regrets is that I never got to meet Gorilla Monsoon. There were others from his era, the old guard from the territory days, with whom I would have my brushes during my time there: cantankerous old Freddie Blassie, the King of Men; the amiable, gnome-like Arnie Skaaland with his ever-present cigar; the trusted consigliere Pat Patterson, slowly being edged out by the rotating cast of TV writers they'd brought in to do what he used to do all by himself. But not Monsoon. He was gone by then. And what made it tougher to accept was just how close I had come.

■

It was the morning of Tuesday, October 19, 1999, and I was in the unlikeliest of places: sitting in the vaunted, marble-lined lobby of Titan Tower at 1241 East Main Street in Stamford, Connecticut, a folder in my sweaty hand containing a few printed copies of my very short resume.

I had made the drive up from Brooklyn to interview for the position of Creative Services and Publications copy editor, a glorified proofreader role that would hopefully help me get my foot in the door with a company I'd wanted to work for since I was twelve years old. Back then, it was still the good old World Wrestling Federation, under the corporate umbrella of Titan Sports, Inc. But that was about to change in a very big way. In fact, as I sat there in Stamford, the changes had officially begun some forty miles away, on Wall Street.

That's because that very day, the day my journey with the company began, was also the day that the company officially went public, offering shares on the New York Stock Exchange under the new corporate name of World Wrestling Federation Entertainment, Inc. or WWFE (they'd get the "F" out just a couple years later). It was a day of vast, monumental changes, the full effects of which wouldn't be felt or understood for years and perhaps decades to come. What had been run for over forty years as essentially a glorified mom-and-pop family operation was on its way to becoming something very different. The links to the past, which had already been straining ever since Vincent Kennedy McMahon had taken over his father's operation a decade and a half earlier, would soon grow fainter than ever, as a slicker, more corporate entity began to take shape.

Of course, on that morning, I really had no idea about any of that, or what the full implications were. I'm not sure anyone really did, not even the man at the top.

But another bittersweet irony was that this change came just ten days after one of the cornerstones of that company, Robert "Gino/Bob" Marella whose vision, talent and goodwill had helped to build it and nurture it, was laid to rest at Lakeview Memorial Park in Cinnaminson, New Jersey. This family company was still reeling from the loss of one of its most beloved members as a brand-new chapter was beginning—one which would take it so far away from the company he had known. I had seen the heartfelt tributes aired on *Monday Night Raw* and *SmackDown* just the week before.[1] Less than two months earlier, he had still been making the trip in from Jersey to record voice-overs at the TV studio right down the road from where I was sitting. I'd quite literally just missed him.

INTRODUCTION

Nevertheless, his spirit lingered at that place in a very real way, and as I came to work there starting on Valentine's Day 2000, I came to sense it all around me: in the employees who had known and loved him, and who still talked about him like a grandfather or uncle. In the stories they would tell, even the ones tinged with sadness toward the end. I'll never forget the day that a certain manila inter-office envelope crossed my desk. It was one of those with the printed grid where you write the name of the person you're sending it to, and then pass it along so that each recipient can see the names of everyone who had passed along the envelope before. Seeing my name at the bottom, I slowly scanned upward in curiosity, reading all the names, going back weeks and months, of those who had previously used the envelope, until my eyes came to rest at the very top of the list, where just one word was written:

"Gorilla."

It was an odd feeling. There it was, right in my hands. Physical, tangible evidence of the man who had once been a giant in this place, both literally and figuratively. He was real; he had been here. It was also the feeling of knowing that this was as close as I was going to get to him.

■

Fast-forward another year. I'm seated in catering, backstage at Reliant Hall in Houston, Texas, during the WWF's Fan Axxess, a convention being held the weekend of *WrestleMania X-7*. I'm here to collect as many interviews as I can in my capacity as staff writer for the WWF's family of magazines, as well as WWF.com. Given my historical bent, I'm especially interested in tracking down some of the legends who had been brought back that year to take part in *WrestleMania*'s "Gimmick Battle Royal"— essentially, the WWF's equivalent of an old-timer's game.

I'm keeping a close watch on the door, when suddenly, in walks Bobby "The Brain" Heenan, his black leather jacket and jeans a far cry from the glittery, Rodeo Drive character I'd come to know on TV as a kid. But once he opened his mouth, there was no doubt whatsoever who it was. This was "The Brain," who had taught me from a young age that "a friend in need is a pest"; who had insisted we all be "fair to Flair"; who bragged about his credentials as a "broadcast journalist"; and who for seven years had made it his life's work to frustrate and exasperate Gorilla Monsoon at every turn.

I can honestly say that I've never been around anyone in real life who was as genuinely funny as Bobby Heenan. From the moment I approached him and asked for an interview, he was "on," cracking me up with one-liners and jibes. I asked him if he might want to be president, and he said he didn't want to take a pay cut and move to a bad neighborhood. He was as quick as a whip, even though he didn't need to be. There were no cameras, just him and me. But that's just who he was.

As the conversation continued and I got more comfortable, I decided to ask him about Gorilla. Given their professional history, and how millions of fans so fondly remembered their years behind the broadcast desk together, I was eager to get some of his thoughts and memories of his late colleague.

Right there, the jokes stopped. The twinkle vanished from his eye, the smirk fled from his face, as he got quiet and considered for a moment before speaking.

"I was very affected by his passing. He was one of my best friends. We argued, we'd fight each other back and forth, but we had mutual respect for each other. It was a great loss in my career . . ."

He paused, his eyes welling up with tears as his voice cracked.

". . . and in my life."

I apologized, not meaning to have upset him, not realizing how fresh the wound still was a year and a half later. But he continued as he wiped away the tears.

"Some things like that just happen in life. There are some great marriages in this world, and that was one of them. I knew what he was gonna say. I could feed him; he could feed me. Then when I'd get upset with him, he knew what to say, and I knew what to say. We never had to discuss anything. It just worked."

At that, the twinkle returned, along with the smile. Not a snide "Bobby the Brain" smirk, but a genuine smile of warmth and remembrance. The interview came to a close shortly afterward; he thanked me and went out into the hall for a cigarette. Reluctant at first, I chased after him for a quick picture—company policy be damned. He happily obliged, and we parted ways. As I sat back at my table, listening to the playback on my voice recorder, I was a little embarrassed about making Bobby so emotional. It wasn't my intention to exploit him—at that point in my life, I honestly didn't fully understand how deeply close those two men had been.

I had gotten just a glimpse of it, and in later years, I'd learn so much more about what was one of pro wrestling's great friendships. It was another hint of the man I'd never gotten to know, but whose presence was everywhere.

■

Over the course of thirty years writing about pro wrestling, I've had opportunities to speak with a veritable who's who of luminaries and legends of the business spanning decades. During my time with WWE, as well as before and after, I've managed to fulfill personal and professional dreams I could never have imagined. But I know I'll never have the chance to check off that one bucket list name, the narrator of my young wrestling fandom, as he was for so many others. However, what I can do is tell his story—a story that should have been told years ago, but which I'm honored to be able to assemble today. The story of a man beloved and respected by everyone with whom he crossed paths—and sometimes feared, if there was cause to be.

If you're looking for dirty laundry and skeletons in the closet, look elsewhere. This isn't that kind of book. Besides, there's none to be found. He liked to smoke his Kool menthols, he played blackjack like a riverboat card shark, and he probably ate a lot more ice cream and lasagna than he should have, and that's about it. In other words, he lived life. And better than most of us. But what you will find is the story of an inherently decent and loyal man who kicked ass when he needed to, and who left the business better for his having been in it. And that's a story that any author would be proud to tell.

CHAPTER 1

A FINAL BOW IN PHILLY

"Wrestling is a vicious, vicious business. You have to love it.
If you survive, it will be good to you."

The location, unsurprisingly, is Philadelphia, Pennsylvania. This used to be Gorilla's town. But the building isn't the old Philadelphia Arena, or even the good old Spectrum, where he had officially retired from the battles of the ring some nineteen years earlier. It's a brand shiny new building, just three years old. They were originally going to call it Spectrum II, but then the corporate interests got involved, as they tend to do. These days, it's called the First Union Center (which the Philadelphians, in their inimitable way, have taken to calling the FU Center).

The date is Sunday, March 28, 1999. The World Wrestling Federation is in residence for the fifteenth annual edition of *WrestleMania*, an event he helped to put on the map. An event he was the voice of for the first eight years of its existence, and for which, to many fans, he will always be the voice. He is the narrator of their memories. But times have changed. The product has changed. These days, they call it "Attitude." As if they invented it. Nevertheless, it's a whole different kind of show now from the one he presided over, but he's learned to keep that to himself, like the rest of the old crew. Today, he's not in town to call the action at ringside, and his health being what it is, he might not have even been able to if they had asked him.

He's here, ostensibly, to act as a "ringside judge" for something they're calling a "Brawl for All" match—a legitimate mixed-martial-arts-style match, the kind of reckless idea he probably would've tried to talk them out of if he were a slightly younger and healthier man, back when they listened. But really, he's here to make a rare public appearance before the fans, and the reality is that it could be the last one. He hasn't been seen on television in almost two years, and a whole generation of viewers who grew up with him misses him. Beyond the man, he represents something: a flashback to a simpler time in the company. He certainly hasn't been forgotten in these two years since a heart attack took him off the road and off TV. But it definitely has seemed like an eternity.

His old friend, ring announcer Howard Finkel, who has not only been there since the first *WrestleMania* but also named it, stands in center-ring in his customary tuxedo to make the introductions. First, the special referee, Vinny Pazienza, just a couple of weeks away from a super middleweight fight right up I-95 at the Foxwoods Resort Casino in Connecticut. Next, the judges, starting with Kevin Rooney, the 1975 Golden Gloves champ who helped guide the career of Mike Tyson until Don King came into the picture. Then the "Bayonne Bleeder" himself, Chuck Wepner, a boxer who faced both Muhammad Ali and André the Giant.

And then finally, in his booming voice, Howard introduces another person who could make that claim[1]:

"Our final judge certainly needs no introduction. He is one of the all-time greats in the World Wrestling Federation, and I'm proud to say, a Hall of Famer as well: the one, the only, Gorilla Monsoon!"

The crowd of over twenty thousand breaks into a warm and gracious ovation, with many coming to their feet to show respect to the man who stands at ringside between Rooney and Wepner. A black suit and understated burgundy turtleneck take the place of the typical frilly tux or colorful jackets he's known for. The trademark blue-tinted glasses, which he wore for years to protect his sensitive eyes from the glare of the television lights, are replaced with yellow. A shadow of his former self, he looks every bit of his sixty-two years, and at least ten more than that. Pale, gaunt and easily fifty pounds slimmer than he was the last time they saw him, he smiles weakly, then turns to the appreciative thousands and offers a friendly wave. But there's a sadness in his eyes as he attempts to conjure up that energy and excitement they remembered, which always made them believe next week's show would be even better than the one before. He isn't the only one in the building wondering, "Is this a goodbye?" As it will turn out, it is.

He takes his seat just outside the ring, right next to Wepner. A lifetime ago, he had to put the Bleeder in his place at Shea Stadium, one of the few times anyone actually dared to test his unspoken reputation. But that's all water under the bridge. Right now, they are just friendly ring luminaries there to bear witness to a sorry spectacle between the rotund king of the four-rounders, Butterbean, and poor Bart Gunn, a tough but untested WWF talent who had the gall to spoil the company's plans by becoming the wrong person to win their original "Brawl for All" tournament last year and is about to be punished for it by being tossed headfirst into a human buzzsaw.

A couple of years ago, Butterbean agreed to take part in a worked boxing match for the WWF. This time, it's very much the real thing, as Bart Gunn finds out after just thirty-five seconds of the first round, when he gets rocked with a right cross to the jaw that swivels his head like a weather vane before sending him to the canvas. Just like that, it's over. In the ensuing chaos, those watching very closely might spot Gorilla getting up from his ringside seat. A concerned (and maybe slightly disgusted) look on his face, he reaches out and puts a comforting hand on the arm of the stunned Bart Gunn, struggling to sit up in the corner, and asks if he's alright. Once they can get him out of the ring and to his feet, Gorilla helps the young wrestler to the back. The absurdist spectacle rolls on as someone in a San Diego Chicken costume passes them in the aisle on his way to the ring to kill some time with Pazienza due to the extreme brevity of the fight.

It's an understated moment of kindness amidst all the ruckus that gives a glimpse of the true character of Gorilla Monsoon, a man who has always done his best to look out for the boys, and who tried to put their needs ahead of the needs of the office whenever possible, even when he himself was part of that office. That hasn't changed, even in the face of illness and infirmity. But other things have.

■

The prematurely old and tired man who made his final public appearance that day was not the same one fans remembered from just a few years earlier. In fact, given the young age of many fans watching both live and at home, as well as a high fan turnover rate, there may have been some who didn't remember him very much at all. At least not for what he had accomplished in the best years of his career. Maybe they remembered him as the figurehead WWF president. They might have remembered him as an announcer, but it had been a good six years since he'd been phased out as one of the company's lead microphone men, and he'd been slowly fading into the background ever since. The memory of wrestling fans can be notoriously short.

The fans on that day could be forgiven, perhaps, for being unaware of how much he had contributed to the company. After all, a lot of what he had done had been shrouded in the secret code of kayfabe, a code he took so seriously that he had the word put on the license plate of his car. Time, the ravages of diabetes, not to mention a heart irrevocably broken at the loss of a beloved son, had dimmed the power of the man who had once been known by multiple generations of fans for different reasons. For one generation, he had been a massive, rampaging monster who tore through their favorite heroes until becoming one of them himself. For a later generation, he became the friendly voice of the company, his call of the action linked to some of the most memorable events in WWE history.

He spent his career working for the McMahons, becoming a trusted member of the inner circle and even owning a piece of the company at one time. His presence behind the scenes was so valued, and so powerful, that the area right behind the curtain, where he would see wrestlers off to the ring and greet them when they returned, is literally named after him to this day—and not just in WWE but in all of wrestling.

To his friends, he would always be Gino. His social security card said Robert Marella. But to the rest of us, he was Gorilla Monsoon.

He was one of the industry's most adored figures—remembered fondly by fans of the '60s and '70s as much as by fans of the '80s and '90s. Remembered fondly by everyone who worked with him, including Vince McMahon himself, even if their relationship had been a bit more complicated than the company's version of history might indicate.

For legendary WWWF world champion Bruno Sammartino, with whom he secretly shared a great friendship, not to mention ethnicity, he had been an archrival, battling the champion more times than any other challenger, from that blustery day in Roosevelt Stadium to their epic time limit draw in Madison Square Garden and beyond. In those days, he'd been the stark raving mad and mute All-Asiatic champion from the wilds of Manchuria, led to the ring by his devious handlers Bobby Davis and Wild Red Berry. Later on, he'd find his voice, not to mention the admiration and trust of the fans. He'd tangle with them all, from Killer Kowalski and "Cowboy" Bill Watts to "Superstar" Billy Graham and even Hulk Hogan, the man he'd help lionize behind the mic in later years. He'd make national headlines going toe to toe with Muhammad Ali. Behind the scenes, he'd ascend to power, becoming one of WWE founder Vince McMahon Sr.'s most trusted advisors. As an announcer, he'd form classic commentary teams with Jesse "The Body" Ventura and Bobby "The Brain" Heenan and coin some of wrestling's most recognized vernacular. And he'd become one of the first inductees to the WWE Hall of Fame, an accolade he earned more thoroughly than nearly anyone. His story is unlike any other in wrestling history.

Just six months after *WrestleMania XV*, Bob Marella was gone. The people who cheered politely for him on that day in Philadelphia could indeed be forgiven for not knowing the whole story of who he had been.

Now it's time to fix that.

CHAPTER 2
A SECRET HERITAGE

"No, my mother didn't name me Gorilla."

It should go without saying by this point, but the legacy of Gorilla Monsoon most certainly does not trace its origins to Manchuria, that sometimes amorphous region encompassing parts of present-day eastern China and Russia. It was certainly not on the banks of the Amur River that his family originated, nor the seaports of Vladivostok, the snowy climes of the Changbai Mountains, nor anywhere else within five thousand miles. In fact, the family history of Gorilla Monsoon is far less Manchu than it is *mangia*.

Perhaps the worst-kept secret in all of pro wrestling was the fact that Robert Marella, the man known to fans as Gorilla Monsoon, was actually an Italian American. And not only that, but a very proud one. And yet, far from the many other Italians and Italian Americans in wrestling, who embraced their heritage as an essential part of their persona and appeal, he had to keep his heritage to himself for most of his career. Certainly not in the very beginning, when promoters changed his name to "Gino Marella" to actually further emphasize his ethnicity and make him sound less American. But beyond those first couple of years—and despite continuing to be called "Gino" behind the scenes—he had to hide his true family origins.

Even in later years, when the whole Manchurian pretense was dropped and he spoke perfect English as a television announcer, the ring name of Gorilla Monsoon was never dropped, and he was never directly acknowledged as being an Italian American, although there were certainly lots of fun hints and Easter eggs galore for those astute fans who looked and listened for them, such as when he'd rattle off the names of Italian meats and cheeses as only someone who'd grown up eating them would. However, for the most part, it was far more ambiguous than it was for other of his great friends like Dominic DeNucci, Ilio DiPaolo, Tony Marino, Gino Brito and of course "The Italian Superman" himself, Bruno Sammartino, who were able to wear their Italian-ness on their sleeve like a badge of honor.

■

Yet indeed, the Marella family can be traced entirely, and only within one generation, to the Southern Italian region of Apulia, in the province of Foggia. Although he was born in America, both of his parents came from the tiny rural community of Faeto, nestled in the Daunian Mountains in the southernmost expanse of the Apennines, not far from the "spur" of the Italian boot that juts into the Adriatic Sea. With a population of only a few hundred, the town was founded in the thirteenth century by French-Provençal soldiers who had just finished annexing parts of Southern Italy for Charles of Anjou, and the isolated municipality even boasts its own unique language of Faetar, formed by the blending of the extinct Provençal tongue with the regional dialects of surrounding Italy.[1] This was the kind of provincial town with a great church steeple right in the square, and where flocks of sheep and goats could be seen wandering across the road from the surrounding hilltops.

It was Gino's grandfather, Angelo Marella, who at the start of the twentieth century made the decision to leave this country lifestyle behind and come to the New World, a place of opportunity where many of his countrymen were flocking in those days. On February 4, 1905, at sixteen years of age and with twelve dollars in his pocket, he boarded the SS *Perugia*,[2] a Scottish steamer that specialized in ferrying Italians to New York and back, crammed in with over a thousand other third-class passengers. The clerks at Ellis Island would classify the young man on their harbor entry logs as a "peasant"—a typically blunt descriptor for a boy with no English, no job and almost no money.

But young Angelo was far from an aimless nomad. Rather, he'd come to America on a temporary basis, to visit his older brother Vito, who had already settled with his family in the industrial town of Emporium, Pennsylvania, where he worked in the lumber yards. It was his first time visiting the United States, and it must have certainly made a great impression on him, because it was where he'd soon choose to build his own family and spend the rest of his life.

First, in order to build that family, he needed to do the sensible thing and find a nice Italian girl. Preferably from his own hometown, as his own forefathers had done for centuries. The New World wasn't going to change that Old World tradition. At least not yet. So Angelo would soon return to Faeto, and in fact, later that very same year, he would find that girl in the form of sixteen-year-old Amelia Galluci. Not uncommon for the time and for the place, the two adolescents would marry, and on November 10, 1906, they brought a son into the world, named Leonardo after Angelo's father.[3] That son would grow up to be the father of the man who became Gorilla Monsoon.

Looking for work to support his new family unit, Angelo temporarily left his wife and two-year-old son behind in Faeto, but this time with a more permanent plan in mind. On November 25, 1908, he boarded the *San Giorgio*, a sleek new armored cruiser that was the pride of the Italian navy but also doubled as a transport ship.[4] Its steerage section loaded with a slew of other Faetani laborers with similar ideas, the *San Giorgio* left the Bay of Naples and spent fifteen days crossing the Atlantic before reaching New York City on December 10. This time, Angelo was headed to stay with his sister (also named Amelia), at 60 Ward Street[5] in the upstate city of Rochester, New York, already then becoming a destination site for clusters of Faetani and residents of adjacent Foggia villages due to the enticing promise of both industrial and farm work. In the case of Angelo, he had a job lined up working for his brother-in-law, Antonio Spinelli, as a railway laborer.

Once his employment situation was secured, Angelo sent word home to Amelia and the baby, who followed suit in early 1909 and made the journey for a new life in a new country. Amelia Americanized her name to Mary, baby Leonardo became Lenard, and they took up residence in a rented apartment down the road from Angelo's sister and brother-in-law, at 10 Ward Street. Before long, the family started to grow. Over the course of the next decade and a half, Lenard would become the oldest of eight siblings: The first born in America was his sister Columbia, proudly named for the Italian discoverer of their new country, although they'd later call her Sally. Next were Antonette (1911), Joseph (1916), Julia (1918), Mary (1921), Angelina (1923) and Carmela (1924).

Despite the growing number of mouths to feed, prosperity followed. While Lenard was still a little boy, the family saved up enough money to buy their first home, about two hours east in Rome, New York, where Angelo worked for a time on a local farm, along with a lodger, Joseph Contrada, who was renting from them at the time. While Mary could speak English, Angelo still spoke little to none, although that didn't make much difference due to the high concentration of Italian immigrants that created a support system throughout those upstate communities. Nevertheless, in families of that size, they could use all the help they could get, and so in 1921, with only one year of high school under his belt, Lenard was pulled out of school in order to help support the family. This was a common practice in those days for immigrant families who had come to the United States, prevalent among the working-class Italians who often valued hard, manual work over higher education. This was also why the Italians were among the immigrant groups who would earn the reputation for helping build the very infrastructure of America with their sweat and determination, with men like Angelo working on roads, railways and sewer systems, constructing buildings of all kinds in the country's ever-growing cities. What they lacked in education they made up for in grit and resilience.

■

In those days, acquiring a skill was the key to success for the children of immigrants, and so Lenard took on an apprenticeship in carpentry, an industry that would one day help him support a family of his own. By 1925, the Marella family had moved back to Rochester, where they lived at 813 Jay Street. It was still a community with a lot of other Italian families, including many who even hailed from the same region as the Marellas did. Among these were neighbors Domenico and Maria D'Ainto, whose daughter Marie would take an interest in Lenard, a situation welcomed by the family, at least in part because the D'Aintos had also emigrated from the village of Faeto. Although they had been living in America for nearly two decades, the family would be able to preserve its heritage for at least one more generation in the face of the Great Melting Pot.

By the age of twenty, Lenard had taken on a job as a cabinetmaker for the Hopeman Lumber & Manufacturing Company at 569 Lyell Avenue, in one of Rochester's major industrial districts,[6] while eighteen-year-old Marie worked nearby for the Rochester Gas & Electric Company. On November 19, 1927, Lenard Marella took Marie D'Ainto as his bride, and the young couple moved in with Marie's parents at 819 Jay Street. He was not the first of Angelo and Mary Marella's many children to marry, as his younger sister Columbia had already moved out with her new husband the previous year at the tender age of sixteen. At the time Lenard left his family's home, his other siblings still living there ranged from sixteen-year-old Antonette down to three-year-old Carmela.

In contrast to the fruitful and multiplying Angelo and Mary Marella, Lenard and Marie Marella remained childless for the first seven years of their marriage, although it's not entirely out of the question for the time period that there may have been very young babies who did not survive past infancy, which was sadly a common aspect of immigrant family life in America during the Great Depression. However, the first confirmed record of a child being born to Lenard and Marie Marella would come in 1934, when their son, Lenard Jr., later affectionately called Sonny, came into the world.

The 1930s was a trying time for working-class Americans, especially those who had only been in the country less than a generation. Supporting a wife and son could not have been easy for a cabinetmaker still in his twenties, but by all accounts, the Marellas got by. They may not have been a prodigious family, the likes of which Lenard had grown up in, but nevertheless, it was soon about to grow by one more. And that would be the one who would go on to make the family name famous, even if he achieved that fame while using a different name.

CHAPTER 3
BIG BOB

"I was in constant pain when I was growing that rapidly. I felt like my body was being stretched on a rack."

Robert Marella would enter the world during a time of great strife for Americans, but especially for working-class immigrant families. The country was struggling to crawl its way out of the effects of the Depression, with the shadow of impending war across both the Atlantic and Pacific Oceans growing ever longer. Even still, the optimistic American spirit helped keep those families afloat, their loving households ensuring they could get through even the worst of times. Franklin Roosevelt had just been elected for a second term on the promise of happy days being here again, and hardworking families like the Marellas would be the bridge the country would eventually cross to get there, with the bringing of new life into the world being the most optimistic gesture of all.

In some ways, Lenard Marella was a little more fortunate than others. A part of that forgotten generation too young to have served in the First World War and too old to serve in the coming second one, he dedicated himself to his profession and to his community, taking part in

Italian-American civic organizations and even serving as a scoutmaster in his local Boy Scout chapter, Troop 171. Like the many other Italians putting down roots in Rochester in those days, it would be the next generation, born in the United States, that would benefit the most from the groundwork their parents laid, moving away from the traditions of the old country and embracing Americanization and the prosperity that came along with it.

It may have seemed a tall order at twenty-five dollars per week, but that was slightly better than the average workingman's salary in the fall of 1936, when Lenard and Marie learned that Sonny was soon to become a big brother. Robert James Marella was born on Friday, June 4, 1937, at 6:47 in the evening at Rochester Municipal Hospital.[1] Only six pounds at birth, he would more than make up for that in time, thanks to a twist of fate and biology. In those early years, he began to show signs of the man-mountain he would one day become. He would go through the first of the two unthinkable family tragedies of his life, then rebound from the loss by hurling himself at a very young age into the sport that, in one disparate form or another, would come to define the rest of his life. It would also make him the most prominent member of his family and arguably the most famous athlete to ever come out of Rochester, not to mention one of the most well-known wrestlers who ever lived. And it would be a bizarre journey to success that could never have happened if his family had remained in a tiny village in the hills of Italy.

■

In the beginning, it was a happy childhood like any other, and young Robert (only those outside the family called him "Bob") applied himself to school, showing a high scholastic aptitude right from the start, as well as an interest in athletics. He was fluently bilingual, as Italian was regularly spoken in the home, thanks in part to his grandmother, who lived with them for a time. He attended Rochester Public School No. 1, Martin B. Anderson Elementary,[2] starting in 1942—a little boy in a country at war, but he was somewhat insulated from those realities by the protective bubble of family life. In fact, it's likely that one of his earliest memories of the world at large would've been the Japanese attack on Pearl Harbor just a few months earlier—a defining national trauma that remained in the minds of all Americans of his generation and which he'd famously refer to quite often during his time as a TV commentator several decades later.

However, that family bubble would be harshly burst in the second grade, with the shocking and untimely loss of his mother, Marie, to a chance household accident. While changing a lightbulb in the basement of their home at 63 Joiner Street, she made a quick turn and jabbed herself on a rusty nail. As was common in those days in immigrant families distrustful of modern medicine and accustomed to home remedies, she didn't have it looked at. In fact, at the advice of her mother, she kept the wound a secret from Len, and the two of them tried to clean and dress it on their own. Unfortunately, the puncture became seriously infected, with gangrene eventually setting in. By the time the situation had been disclosed to Len and the kids, it was too late to do much about it. On February 1, 1945, Marie Marella died, just one month before her thirty-sixth birthday.

It was a bitter and rueful memory that would remain with Robert for the rest of his days.

"He said it was stupidity, that's what he called it," remembers his wife, Maureen, recalling the way he'd described the story to her.

At the ages of seven and ten, Robert and Sonny found themselves without a mother. And Lenard found himself a widower at thirty-eight; a single father with two young boys to raise, no mean feat for a working man in the 1940s. It was tough enough in a two-parent household, as was evidenced by the ravaging bout of rheumatic fever that struck Sonny—a common childhood illness of the time that caused permanent heart damage. In that era of traditional gender roles, it was expected for a widower with young children to seek out a new young wife as soon as possible, and that's exactly what Lenard did, before long meeting twenty-two-year-old Concetta Mary Gullo on a blind date. On June 15, 1946, he made her his bride. Her family was from Sicily, which was apparently close enough to Faeto for Lenard.

By all accounts, Connie took to her two new stepsons right away and accepted them no differently than if they were her own. In fact, Robert would always think of Connie not as a stepmother but as a mother. She had stepped in during what had to have been a low point for their family, and for that, he was eternally grateful.[3] Before long, the family was expanding again, with the first of Robert and Sonny's three half-sisters, Rosemary, being born in 1947. Two more, Angela and Amelia (Amy), would come along in 1950 and 1954, when both boys were already teenagers.

Despite the change and upheaval in his young life, Robert redoubled his dedication to academics and to athletics. He became known in school for his exceptional penmanship. In the third grade, he won a prize in an essay contest put on by the Society for the Prevention of Cruelty to Animals (SPCA), demonstrating a love of animals that would stay with him throughout life and giving a glimpse of the gentle nature he'd become known for in spite of his intimidating presence. And like many boys of his generation, he would gain an introduction to sports through the local YMCA. Beginning at the age of eight, he would start to love the sport that would buoy him through the rest of his academic life and take him in directions he couldn't possibly have imagined.

■

Robert began trying his hand at wrestling at the YMCA, and immediately took to it. And yet there were significant disadvantages he'd have to overcome. He had always had very weak vision and was quite near-sighted, necessitating thick glasses from a young age. By his own description, he was "small and puny."[4] There wasn't much he could do about the vision, but the "small and puny" was about to change through forces over which he had no control. Starting at the age of ten, due to a sudden secretion of the pituitary gland, he would quickly grow a foot taller in just the span of one year, going from about four foot eight to about five foot eight by the time he was eleven. The dramatic growth spurt would go on for one year more, so by age twelve, he stood about six foot four—almost a foot taller than the 99th percentile for his age.

It's impossible to know what could've caused this painful and freakish explosion in size, which ended just as abruptly as it began. After that initial two years of extreme growth, Robert would only grow about another inch or two before adulthood. His father was just under five foot eleven. His grandfather was only five foot nine. It clearly wasn't anything hereditary, and although it put him through hell for those two years in the late '40s, it would also change his life forever. But along with the height would also come weight struggles that would dog him for life as well. He was a heavy kid, but he would use sports to channel both his height and mass into something productive.

By the time he started as a freshman at Thomas Jefferson High School in the fall of 1951, he was ready to do something special. He already loved wrestling. He'd also been dabbling in basketball at the YMCA, a natural fit with his height. Plus, at his size, football was a no-brainer—he was every coach's dream. High school would be a kind of awakening for him, when he discovered his natural calling as an athlete, but also when he began maturing into a thoughtful and responsible young man, as he gradually became one of the school's shining lights and most popular students over the next four years. He was becoming a kid with a really good head on his shoulders, a quality that would serve him well above all others throughout what was soon to be a remarkable life.

Over the course of four years at Jefferson, he'd letter in three sports, including football and track and field, but especially wrestling, which was the only one of the three that he went out for beginning in freshman year. At that time, he was still quite literally growing into himself: A tall, awkward, even gangly teenager despite being easily already over two hundred pounds. He was raw material for Jefferson wrestling coach Roger Bunce, a former Jefferson alum himself who'd recently got back from naval service during World War II. Bunce was building a reputation as a great mentor to young athletes, but it didn't take much vision to realize the potential of someone like Marella.

What he lacked in experience and technique, he made up for in raw power and size, and he still proved an asset to the Jefferson Statesmen even in that first year while still a backup member of the team in the heavyweight/unlimited class. There were nine high schools in the city of Rochester at that time, and Jefferson was not really considered one of the most athletically competitive. Each year, the wrestling season led up to the Rochester Interscholastic League Championships. Marella made it as far as the semifinals in the heavyweight class his freshman year, where he suffered a disappointing pinfall loss in five minutes and fifty-two seconds to Dave Sharp of John Marshall High School. Lesson learned, Marella would see to it that this would be the only time he would ever be pinned in a championship tournament match for the remainder of his high school career. Even still, he had little to be ashamed of, as the day had been a rough one for the Statesmen, who saw only one of their six semifinalist participants make it into the finals of his weight class.

Ironically, it was just as Bob Marella was getting involved with amateur wrestling in high school that the vastly different professional version was gaining massive popularity nationwide thanks to the new medium of television. The early 1950s was one of pro wrestling's golden ages, with seemingly everyone watching it on the tube, and it wouldn't be hard to imagine that Marella was very much aware of it. In fact, to capitalize on the popularity of pro wrestling as a way of recruiting new students to the Statesmen, the squad would even refer to itself as the "Grunt and Groan Team"—a reference to pro wrestling's nickname at the time as "the grunt and groan game," owing to the wailing, over-the-top histrionics of its participants. Little did young Bob know that some of the very men appearing each week on TV were individuals he'd be sharing rings and locker room with in just a few years.

In addition to wrestling, the other activity Marella took part in from the beginning was the school choir, called the Jeff Singers. From his barrel chest came a rich baritone voice, and he had enjoyed singing very much since childhood, being raised in a musical family in which his brother and father were also singers and his stepmother could play piano by ear. A love for Neapolitan folk songs and Italian opera in general had been fostered in him as part of his Italian-American upbringing. It was the music commonly heard around the home, and he would continue to indulge in singing it his whole life. In his freshman year, in fact, he got to participate along with Sonny, who was a senior at the time and also a member of the Jeff Singers. Bob's teammates even came to expect to hear his mellifluous voice coming from the showers after a tough meet or game.[5]

The towering youngster was starting to turn heads in the halls at Jefferson, not the least of which were among the athletic coaching staff. By sophomore year, he had been recruited for the football team under Coach Paul Fauth and the track and field squad under coaches Anthony Merlino and later George Baird. A natural for the offensive line, Marella became Fauth's left tackle, and players on opposing teams soon came to learn about and fear the kid often called "The Jefferson Giant." In track and field, he gravitated toward the shot put, once again a natural fit for his pure power. And yet, showing that he was far from a lumbering behemoth, Marella also competed in the high jump, adding dexterity and speed to his impressive physical arsenal.

Hitting the weights and packing on the muscle and mass to fit his enormous frame, Marella had already started bulking up by sophomore year. He became known not only for winning but for winning a significant portion of his matches by pin—typically uncommon in high school wrestling. But with his smothering size and the overwhelming way in which he was learning to wield it, opponents more often than not found themselves looking at the ceiling.[6] After another strong season, he would make it to the semifinals of the Rochester Interscholastic League championships again, where he suffered a 4–0 loss to Paul Kantsampes of West High School. It would be all the defeat he would care to taste during his high school career.

By junior year, Marella was willing himself from promising student athlete to a force of nature. And not just in athletics, either. Joining the executive student council, he'd parlay that into a landslide election as student body president the following year, with over a thousand students voting. Everybody loved the guy with the oversized physique and the personality to match. The Jefferson Statesmen football team remained an outlier, amassing a 3–2–1 record for Marella's '53 junior year season. With the city championship in sight, they sustained a notoriously humiliating defeat to West High that ended their season in a disappointing manner. It was proof that even a six-foot-five, 250-pound offensive lineman can't carry a team on his shoulders alone. In the shot put, he came in second place in the interscholastic championships, with the winner throwing a distance of forty-seven feet and nine and three-quarters inches. Marella would respond the following year by demolishing that distance, as well as all distance records in the city.

The Bob Marella who hit the mats as a junior was a determined individual who plowed through his competition, piling up wins in his unlimited weight class even when his team as a whole continued to struggle against other schools. Often, he would lift the Statesmen out of defeat on his own, such as when he scored a pin in forty seconds on February 2, 1954, handing his team a 24–17 win over Edison Tech. Seven weeks later, he closed out the regular wrestling season with another pinning victory over Mike Stelljes of Marshall High School, pushing Jefferson to a 20–18 triumph. This time, when it came to the Rochester Interscholastic Championships, he would not be denied, pinning the massive Aldo Frediani of defending city champs Madison High in the semifinals, then outpointing Raymond Jobes of Edison Tech 6–2 in the finals. Madison would still win the meet convincingly with 45.5 points to Jefferson's 29.5, but Marella was off to the sectional championships.

Organized by the New York State Public High School Athletic Association (NYSPHSAA) starting in 1947, the regionals were and are divided into eleven sections governing public high school sports throughout the state, excluding New York City. Rochester falls into Section V, covering the entire Genesee Valley. On April 3, 1954, at the ninth annual NYSPHSAA Section V Wrestling Championships, Bob pinned Gary Speer of Bath Haverling High School in just one minute and five seconds to win the ultimate prize, the sectional championship in the heavyweight class. It would be the first major achievement of an outstanding amateur wrestling career.

His athletic achievements had helped make him a very popular figure in school, and his senior year would be a whirlwind of opportunity. It was a textbook example of a promising student on the rise. And it was a great time to be an American teenager, a time often idealized through a lens of nostalgia in years to come: *I Love Lucy*, Davey Crockett and Jackie Gleason on the television; "Mr. Sandman," Pérez Prado and the McGuire Sisters on the radio, with the rock 'n' roll explosion of Bill Haley & His Comets just a few months away. Bob was student president, and student treasurer was his high school sweetheart, Mary Jo Giancursio[7]— the couple was voted as having the "Most School Spirit" at senior prom.

Between working on the school paper (*The Jeff Journal*) and the yearbook committee, organizing fundraising and social activities and performing with the Jeff Singers, Bob was a busy young man. His singing was in demand in talent shows and at school dances. He was even a member of Jefferson's air raid squad, a stark feature at many schools in those duck-and-cover Cold War days. In February of '55, he and other student government members even got the chance to participate in "Students Day in Government," a civics project put on by the Junior Chamber of Commerce that saw the kids get an inside glimpse of Rochester City Hall.

Bob was named "Chief of Police," but in the midst of being briefed on his responsibilities, ironically realized that he'd left his car in a no-parking zone. Rushing down to Aqueduct Street just as the cop was writing him a ticket, he shouted out, "You can't give me a ticket! I'm the Chief of Police!" The officer looked him over for a moment and said, "Well, get it out of here." So he did. The amusing interaction even made the local paper,[8] only further adding to Bob's growing legend in the school.

The varsity football squad went 5–2, its best season in years, tying for second place in the league, with No. 55, 275-pound offensive tackle Bob Marella, one of eighteen lettermen on the team, dominating team photos like he dominated on the gridiron. Along with thirty-eight of the other best high school players in Rochester, Bob was invited to the annual awards dinner held by the local Touchdown Club at the Chamber of Commerce, sponsored by the *Times-Union* and the *Democrat and Chronicle*. After a rousing speech from Naval coach (and future first coach of the Oakland Raiders) Eddie Erdelatz, the players received their honors, including Marella and his teammate, star player Dominic Bianchi, both of whom had been voted the Statesmen's two finest players by the sportswriters of both newspapers.

In shot put, although the Jeff squad lost every meet that year, he won his event every time, including one meet in which he hurled the twelve-pound iron ball fifty-two feet, setting a new all-time high school record for the city of Rochester that would stand for twelve years. Needless to say, he won the interscholastic title that year for the shot put. He'd come in second in the sectional championship, held at the University of Rochester's Fauver Stadium in June.

The best word to describe him on the mat that year would be "unstoppable." The ever-growing Marella, by this point approaching 285 pounds, went completely undefeated in his senior year, finishing up the wrestling season in March with a typically quick pinfall victory over Will Heineman of Marshall High School, giving the Statesman a 25–21 win at their last meet of the season. Marella then went on to duplicate his post-season success of the previous year with apparent ease. In enemy territory at Madison High School, he bulldozed through the quarterfinals with a 51-second pin; then came a semifinal rematch with Frediani in which he outpointed the tough Madison grappler to become one of only three Statesmen to make it to the finals in their weight class. He then pinned Alex Ferguson of Madison in three minutes in the finals of the Interscholastic League to win the Rochester championship once again. The Madison team would retain their city championship that day, but the unlimited weight class title belonged to the Jefferson Giant.

Two days later it was the NYSPHSAA sectional championships at Brockport State Teachers College. Jefferson students came in droves to cheer on the only member of the Statesmen who had made it to the championships, and they wouldn't be disappointed. His opponent was Ray Griffee, a stout and solid junior for the Geneva Panthers. Marella took Griffee down in the early going, but Griffee managed to make it through the first period. He'd only make it another minute, as halfway through the second period, Marella brought all his weight to bear with a body press, and it was all over. For the second year in a row and to close out his high school wrestling career, Bob was the Section V heavyweight wrestling champion.

In what should have been of no surprise to anyone, Bob was selected "Boy of the Year" for Jefferson High School's Class of 1955. In the yearbook it was written of him, "Bob is in all ways Jefferson's big man," along with the inscription, "Always happy, spreading cheer, 'Big Bob' is 55's Man of the Year." Just as he had done in the high jump, he truly stuck the landing on his tenure as a Jeff High student. In fact, his academic achievements had earned him a scholarship to Ithaca College, just ninety miles southeast of Rochester, where he'd be able to continue to excel while still having the option of an occasional weekend visit with the family back home.

Lenard and Connie had to feel as if they'd raised a young man of boundless potential, who was achieving great things in the country that only a generation earlier had been new to them. He had bounced back from the loss of his mother at a young age and had harnessed the unusual hand that nature had dealt him. As an athlete, but especially as a wrestler, he had all the tools. Soon, he'd take that skill from a regional stage to a national one. And while there's only so far that amateur wrestling can take you, he'd even find a solution for that problem when the time came.

CHAPTER 4

TINY

> "I think the United States should subsidize its athletes.
> After all, a man can't eat amateur trophies."

For all that he would later do in the world of professional wrestling, it was during his time at Ithaca College that Bob Marella would first gain a measure of notoriety on the national stage, distinguishing himself as an athlete of note and cultivating a high profile. He was the big man on campus, both literally and figuratively, in spite of the ironic nickname that the nearly 300-pound and six-foot-six student had already received as a freshman. To those who were there when he was, he would always remain a local legend, remembered warmly and fondly by those who had the good fortune to interact with him or witness his amazing achievements. Just as he'd done at Jefferson High, he would make waves in track and field and football, but especially in wrestling.

It would also be a time when he would learn all too well the limitations of amateur athletics—a time of some disillusionment, in which it became apparent that even being an athlete of superb size and skill could only get you so far. He would eventually taste the frustration of defeat, as well as the harsh realities of economics, which meant that as great as he was, he would have to find a way to adapt as he entered full adulthood. It would be a lesson he would always take with him as he went on to seek success and prosperity fiercely, both for himself and for those he needed to support. With a college romance and hasty marriage quickly bringing the responsibilities of adulthood, the laurels of the athlete would have to take a back seat—at least for the moment.

Nevertheless, he'd turn into one of the greatest sportsmen in the history of Ithaca College, setting records in discus and shot put, as well as wrestling, where he'd become an NCAA finalist and Ithaca's first heavyweight All-American with the fastest pin in school history. He was one of only thirteen Ithaca wrestlers to ever go undefeated in a season, one of only five heavyweights to do so, and the only heavyweight to duplicate the feat in multiple seasons. And he'd do it all with a smile on his face and a spring in his step, delighting spectators with the unlikely feat of cartwheeling on his way to the mat, already indicating that he was not just an athlete but a performer who knew how to keep people entertained. Since 1980 and to this day, the Bob "Tiny" Marella Award has been given out at Ithaca to the most outstanding wrestler of the year—as sure a testament as any to his enduring legacy there.

When the big kid from Rochester first arrived on the old Ithaca campus heading into the fall of 1955, he turned the heads of football coach Art Orloske, track and field coach Isadore "Doe" Yavits and acclaimed wrestling coach Herb Broadwell, who had been delivering some of the Ithaca Bombers' greatest mat accolades since he'd gotten started at the beginning of the decade and would continue to do so for nearly twenty years. In fact, the *Ithaca Journal* of January 5, 1956, described Marella as a "297-pound bundle of joy to Broadwell's hopes," as was confirmed by Broadwell having snatched him up for the varsity team the month prior, in the middle of his freshman year. The problem, which would remain the case throughout his college career, was that it was impossible to find anyone of comparable size and skill to practice with him or give him any kind of workout.

Fellow Ithaca alum Curtis Raymond remembers just how much Marella stood out in those days, a student truly in a physical class by himself:

> My first sight of him was in a gymnastics class... And we were doing different things on the parallel bars. I couldn't understand why he wasn't doing any of the other exercises that we were doing. But when a kid would get up on a piece of equipment, he would walk over and stand next to him. Come to find out he was so big and so strong that if he got on the parallel bars and started rocking back and forth, he'd break them... So he would just stand there, and if a kid started slipping or falling, he'd put out one hand and hold the guy up.

He lettered in all three sports starting in his freshman year, with Orloske first putting him at right tackle, then moving him to center, especially when he got a real sense for what he could do. This was a kid who could run the 100 in eleven seconds flat in full gear, and who once slammed an opponent on the gridiron to the ground by grabbing him by the collar at arm's length. He'd also come to be known for duplicating this feat with large and heavy objects. His teammate Jack Stanbro once recalled seeing him holding a 150-pound weight straight out at arm's length and keeping it there, with his football teammates once reporting a similar feat with a giant 110-pound can of milk during one training session. As a freshman, he hurled a shot put some forty-seven feet and seven and a half inches at one particular meet, coming within two inches of breaking the college record that had been set before World War II. Which was OK, because he'd wind up eventually smashing that record before he was done.

Athletes have admittedly gotten bigger on average over time, but in the mid- to late 1950s, Marella was a marvel to behold, towering over his teammates in every sport and commanding attention everywhere he went. Add that to his natural, innate skill, and you had one formidable young man. "I used to high-jump 6-feet-8, 6-feet-10 on a real good day," he once recalled. "I used to attract large crowds when I high jumped. People used to say, 'Let's go over and watch the elephant jump.'"[1] Although he never joined the school team, he was even fond of dabbling in basketball, and Stanbro recalled the sight of Marella barreling down the court like a runaway train and hitting slam dunks.

Early in his college career, Broadwell was already declaring that Marella had the makings of a top-notch wrestler, adding that "several coaches who have seen him in action believe he has as much potential as our Olympic heavyweights."[2] And although that bold prediction didn't quite come true, Broadwell was pretty damn close to the mark in his assessment. As a freshman, he was a diamond in the rough, a raw piece of talent who had been seasoned as an athlete by his high school experiences, but who would take that to a different place entirely over the next few years. It also didn't hurt that he was continually getting more massive, breaking the 300-pound mark by the end of his first year, then working to rein himself in to 270. The back-and-forth weight oscillation would become a lifelong theme.

He was "like a god" on campus, as Raymond and others would describe him, and he took to the new environment with ease. He continued to indulge in his love of singing, joining the school vocal chorus and even forming a barbershop trio with two other prominent school athletes, John Larsen and Ted Wiltsie.[3] He'd perform in school musical productions of *South Pacific* and *Oklahoma!*, among others. His academic performance even improved further from where it was in high school, and he remained on the Dean's List throughout his college career. Unsurprisingly, he took an interest in Ithaca's School of Health and Physical Education, eventually choosing a phys ed major with a biology minor meant to prepare him for a career as a coach and gym teacher, but also had the inadvertent effect of supplying him with an array of arcane anatomical references that would characterize his TV announcing career much later in life.

In his freshman year on the mat, he'd win seven out of nine matches, and that would be the lowest win ratio of his entire Ithaca career. The first of only three losses he ever suffered in dual meet college competition took place on February 5, 1956, and demonstrated how inexperience was the only thing holding him back. Outweighing his opponent, King McLean of State Teachers College, by nearly one hundred pounds, Marella made the mistake of overenthusiasm, lunging at McLean to try to tie the match in the third and final period, only to stumble and wind up underneath the quicker McLean, who had been cautiously lying in wait. Nevertheless, the match was described as the "crowd-pleaser of the evening," with Marella and McLean "butt[ing] around the mat head-to-head like two bull elks in mating season."[4]

Ithaca College was certainly a competitive school when it came to sports, but not considered one of the elite sports schools in the country, even during those days before the institution of NCAA divisions and Ithaca's classification as a Division III school. The Bombers wrestling squad had enjoyed some winning seasons since Broadwell had taken over, but during all four of Marella's years there, this would not be the case. Still, just as in high school, very often Tiny's performance outshone the team's performance, and he remained dominant throughout. His wins were usually quick, and usually by pinfall, and sometimes the only taste of victory the Bombers would get the entire meet, such as December 10, 1956, when he pinned Charles Dinkelmeyer of Syracuse University with a cradle in four minutes and forty-two seconds on the occasion of Ithaca's first-ever meet against Syracuse, for his sophomore season opener.

Marella suffered the only other two regular-season losses of his college career during sophomore year, amassing a 9–2–1 record, before going totally unbeaten for the next two years. And one of those losses came on a technicality during a meet against Lock Haven, when the referee ruled that Marella had illegally locked his hands. In late winter of 1957, he made it to the championships of the Eastern College Athletic Conference, representing Ithaca in the Interstate Intercollegiate Individual Invitational Wrestling Tournament, otherwise known as the 4-I's. After decisioning Joe Farmer of Oswego 5–0 and Dan Nash of Ohio University 6–3 in the opening rounds, Marella was shut out 2–0 in the heavyweight finals, losing to Dick Bruneman of Miami University, who never took Marella down but rather scored his points on an escape and riding time.

Although he continued on to greater successes in track and field and wrestling as an upperclassman, Marella walked away from the gridiron after sustaining a knee injury at the end of his sophomore season. This would allow him to focus even more strongly on his remaining two sports, as well as his academics. During the summer months, he took some work in construction, taking part in the building of the Rochester War Memorial, an arena in which he would later appear during his pro wrestling career.

As time went on, the legend of Tiny grew. Students would turn out in droves to see him flatten guys in seconds. In fact, he usually had to hold back to avoid causing serious bodily harm, even if he wasn't always successful. In those days, the Ithaca College campus was modest, located in downtown Ithaca with a couple of small rented theaters serving as gymnasiums. Stanbro recalled a training session with Marella in one of those gyms, during which Marella accidentally dislocated Stanbro's shoulder and was mortified at having done so: "I tried to get 'Tiny' to pull my arm back out and he wouldn't do it. He cried like a baby. He felt terrible. That's how strong he was, but also what kind of a heart the guy had."[5] Not even Coach Broadwell himself was safe, as Marella once accidentally snapped his collarbone like a twig during another training session.[6] From then on, the 165-pound coach forbade his other students from even sparring with Tiny.

Wrestlers from opposing schools would be known to even drop out of a meet if they knew they were matched up with Marella. Raymond remembers an occasion of a wrestler learning the hard way not to underestimate him, during a special exhibition in which athletes from the much larger University of Buffalo came to modest Ithaca to mix it up with the Bombers:

> There was a heavyweight wrestler, who was also a tackle on the UB football team, and he knew about Tiny Marella. People were telling him this is a big fat guy, you're going

to kill him . . . They had this kid all piped up, ready to go. And he looked over and there was Tiny sitting on a little bench, eating oranges. He must have eaten a case of oranges watching him . . . They say to this kid, the thing to do is to go out fast and tackle like you've been practicing in football. So they start, and all the kids stand up and scream in this little tiny theater. The kid goes running across the mat, and he tackles Tiny; Tiny picks him up, pulls him over his head, slams him down on the mat and pins him in about five seconds. And the crowd goes crazy.

And although the exact time frame is not known for certain, it also appears to be during junior year that Marella first got to know Inez More, a senior at Alfred Agricultural Technical Institute, a school that was a regular sports opponent for Ithaca. It's easy to imagine the prim and bespectacled More—a farmer's daughter from the little hamlet of Hobart on Route 10 in New York, population 585—marveling at the power and charisma of this star athlete, just as everyone else did. Studying to be a medical secretary, she was, like Marella, a Dean's List student and shared a love of public speaking, singing and performing in school musicals. The two began a relationship that would eventually turn serious.

Marella went undefeated in dual college wrestling meets in his junior year, piling up a record of eight wins, no losses and one draw, which occurred on January 15, 1958, when he and Bob Benson of Lock Haven went even at one point apiece. Just three days prior to that, Marella had performed in more typical fashion against Syracuse, when he smothered Syracuse wrestler/footballer Al Benecick in just thirty-five seconds in what was called the most exciting match of the meet, with the *Syracuse Herald-American* describing Marella as handling the 220-pound Benecick "as though Al was just a feather floating by," taking him down with an armlock and body press in a flash and pinning him with "brute force." The last three victories of his junior season came by way of pin, and it probably would've been even more if he hadn't had to miss at least one meet due to an injured ankle.

It was also during his junior season, at a meet against Clarkson, that he vanquished his opponent in just eighteen seconds. It would remain the Ithaca wrestling record for fastest pin for the next thirty years and remains the record in the heavyweight division to this day.

His relentless training included daily two-hour workouts and a close eye on his diet, although as he approached the end of junior year, it was clear that he was destined to break through three hundred pounds and stay there. A renewed drive and focus, and a determination not to be denied, led him once again to the Eastern Intercollegiate championships—and this time, he won. One of only two Bombers representing Ithaca on March 15 at the 4-I's in Cleveland, Marella first beat Charles Stenho of Toledo University 7–2 in the semifinals, then went on to outpoint Les Nader of Kent State 2–1 to snare his first conference championship. Tiny was no longer a star wrestler on the Ithaca squad—he was now *the* star wrestler on the Ithaca squad.

■

And yet he was such a standout athlete that, at the time, wrestling was not even considered his primary sport. That was track and field, and it was his aspirations in the discus throw and shot put that led him to sit out the NCAA wrestling championships junior year, which he most certainly would have qualified for if he had chosen to. But he had a lot to prove, hurling heavy objects great distances and with relative ease. That year, he set the school discus record with a throw of 134 feet and eight inches against Lock Haven, as well as the school shot put record with a distance of forty-eight feet and three inches against Alfred, very likely achieved as an approving Inez looked on. Both these records would only stand until he smashed them the following year, setting new records that lasted nearly to the end of the 1960s, ensuring the name of Tiny would be remembered on campus long after he had moved on.

But before moving on, he still had a dominant senior year ahead of him, in which he would be named co-captain of the wrestling team and during which the mat sport would finally take front and center in the young man's ambitions. To that end, he leaned into packing on the mass, to the point where they took to weighing him on a meat scale. Coach Orloske badly wanted him back on the football team, but Marella politely declined. Instead, with a look to the future, he began teaching at the high school in nearby Brighton, working as an assistant gym instructor and assistant to the football coach, all while remaining among the top 10 percent of students in Ithaca's health and physical education program. Meanwhile, Inez had already graduated and had taken up work as a stenographer in the town of South Kortright, just down the road from her home in Hobart.

The Bombers went 5–5 in the 1958–59 season, but Marella remained undefeated, finishing with a 9–0–1 record, with a draw breaking up what had been a seventeen-match winning streak dating back to junior year. Closing in on 350 pounds, he steamrolled over dual meet competitors: pinning 240-pound Ken Klaus of RIT in a quick 2:45 using "beef and experience," as the *Rochester Democrat and Chronicle* put it; landing a 36-second fall on Oscar Jansen of Syracuse; followed the next day by a 28-second fall over Bill Riley of Clarkson, leading the *Ithaca Journal* to describe him as a "wrestling prodigy"; ending the three-year undefeated streak of Oswego's Joe Farmer with a 6–2 decision in the season closer.

"Ithaca College's colorful, undefeated heavyweight grappler"[7] was never pinned in collegiate competition and went on to successfully defend his heavyweight crown at the 4-I's in March of '59. One of 107 wrestlers representing thirty different schools at the event, he pinned Bob Hall of Kent State in 1:20 in the semifinals, then outpointed Herman Lederberl of Alfred 11–2 in the finals to capture his second consecutive Eastern Intercollegiate heavyweight title. He was one of three students representing Ithaca that day, but make no mistake—the one that everyone was watching was Tiny, who even then could hold a crowd in the palm of his hand while making it look easy.

Ithaca had finished with a number-sixteen ranking, and Marella was the sixth-ranked heavyweight wrestler in the country. This time, nothing was stopping him from the NCAA national championships, and at the end of March, Tiny Marella made his way out to Iowa City for the twenty-ninth annual competition, with Ithaca's hopes pinned upon him, the only Bomber to make it. It was the largest-ever NCAA championship tournament up to that point, with 274 entrants representing sixty-seven schools and 303 matches held. Looming large over the proceedings was the shadow of Oklahoma State. With thirty-four titles to its name in various weight classes, OSU won the meet almost every year, and in the heavyweight class, it had Ted Ellis, a 255-pounder from Blackwell, Oklahoma, who was the top-seeded heavyweight in the tournament.

Marella wouldn't be the only future professional wrestler taking part that year. Dale Lewis, a heavyweight contender from the University of Oklahoma, had previously competed in Greco-Roman wrestling at the 1956 Olympic Games in Melbourne and would do so again in 1960 in Rome before embarking on a twenty-year career in the squared circle. Over in the 191-pound tournament, you had Big Ten champion George "Tim" Woodin of Michigan State, who would change his name to Tim Woods, later donning the trademark white trunks and mask to become the original "Mr. Wrestling." Meeting him in the semifinal match that year at 191 pounds was Iraqi transplant Adnan Kaisy of OSU, who was immortalized first in the 1960s and 1970s as make-believe Native American Billy White Wolf and later embraced his roots in the 1980s and 1990s as the villainous Adnan Al-Kaissie—a sheik or a general, depending on what company he was working for.[8]

It soon became apparent, as if it wasn't already, that Marella and Ellis were on a collision course. After getting past Pete Veldman of Minnesota 6–1 in his opening match, Marella lambasted Iowa State's Jan Schwitters 11–1 in the quarterfinals to advance to the semis, where his opponent was Walter Goltl, undefeated All-American from Northern Colorado and number-two ranked seed. Marella and Goltl went 1–1 in regulation time, then deadlocked 1–1 again in overtime, with the referee judging the match for Marella. He'd made it to the finals by the skin of his teeth, but now found himself face to face with the big Oklahoman Ellis, who'd gotten there with much greater ease. The number-one-ranked heavyweight was not just the only wrestler in the tournament to score multiple pins, but he'd pinned all four of his tournament opponents in a total match time of thirteen minutes and twenty-six seconds.

Despite a nearly one-hundred-pound advantage, there was no question Marella found himself on the mat with a truly superior wrestler, perhaps for the first time. And yet, that day at the Iowa Field House, Tiny took OSU's best to the limit. This would be no easy win. The two behemoths had one point each at the end of three grueling periods. In overtime, a desperate Ellis, sensing Marella's power waning, did all he could to keep the big man down on the mat and scored two points for riding time in the process. It was enough to win the day for OSU's heavyweight, with OSU also winning the entire meet with a total of seventy-three points—a record twenty-two points ahead of the second-place team, that other grappling powerhouse, Iowa State. Ithaca came away with only ten points, naturally all courtesy of Tiny Marella.

He'd come close—just about as close as anyone could come—to being the NCAA heavyweight wrestling champion for 1959. He'd have to settle for first runner-up. It was a taste of disappointment for a competitive athlete like Marella, but it only whetted his appetite for more. What he didn't realize at the time was that his amateur wrestling career had just peaked. Unlike what he'd experienced prior to the NCAAs, there would be more disappointment and frustration on the way, and he'd have a tough time adjusting to it.

■

For a wrestler of Tiny's caliber, the next logical step was the AAU national championships in April—the highest amateur sports accolade in the United States, open not just to college athletes but to all qualifying competitors. With the backing of the venerable New York Athletic Club, Marella entered the competition, held in April in Stillwater, Oklahoma. This time, he'd be competing in two tournaments, one for Greco-Roman and one for freestyle. And both times, he'd have to again settle for second best. In the first round of the Greco-Roman tournament at Stillwater's

Gallagher Hall on April 15, he lost via decision to fellow future pro Dale Lewis. In the second round, he eliminated Japanese entrant Kanji Shigeoka by pin. The third round featured a fluke injury that gave Marella the duke by default: His opponent, Ted Holmes of the Los Angeles YMCA, came at him when he wasn't quite ready, and Marella instinctively threw him down, accidentally breaking his arm.

But in the fourth and final round, Marella had to contend with the 303-pound Bill Kerslake, a bona fide phenomenon and future National Wrestling Hall of Famer out of Cleveland. The twenty-nine-year-old Kerslake had already represented the U.S. twice in the Olympics, was a gold medalist in the 1955 Pan American Games and achieved a four-second pin at the 1956 AAU tournament that remains the fastest pin in national tournament competition to this day. In the end, Kerslake decisioned Marella to win his seventh AAU Greco-Roman title, with Marella finishing second.[9]

Three days later at the freestyle AAU tournament, Marella once again hit the Kerslake wall, this time even harder. After eliminating Shigeoka once again, and decisioning Bob Gutmueller of the First Army and Dan Sayenga of Tulsa in earlier rounds, Marella made his way into the round robin finals, where he was joined by Kerslake and by Ted Ellis, the very man who'd vanquished him in the NCAAs. First, Kerslake did what Marella couldn't and pinned Ellis, then Ellis and Marella wrestled to a draw, which eliminated Ellis from the competition, and set up a Kerslake/Marella rematch for the heavyweight freestyle championship. Nine brutal minutes later, Bill Kerslake became the first opponent to pin Tiny Marella's shoulders to the mat since his freshman year of high school.[10]

Nevertheless, Marella returned to Ithaca a local hero, having placed second in both NCAA and AAU competitions, and finished out his college athletic career with one more triumph, winning the discus championships in May in the finals of the New York State Track and Field Association. By the time he graduated with his bachelor's in physical education, he had a great deal to be proud of. His final dual meet college wrestling record stood at 31–3–3 over four seasons, leading to an easy selection as MVP senior year. He had amassed twenty-one first-place finishes in shot put, and eighteen in discus. His forty-eight-foot-eight-inch record in shot put and 142-foot-2.5-inch record in the discus would stand for years, as would his campus legend.

■

After his graduation on June 8, Marella was offered a unique opportunity. A team of eight elite American amateur wrestlers was being put together to go on a tour of Europe and the Middle East, taking on the elite wrestlers of seven foreign countries, kicked off by a four-city tour of the Soviet Union, making them the first American wrestling squad to cross the iron curtain. AAU national heavyweight champion Bill Kerslake had dropped out due to personal commitments, and the spot was offered to Marella, the first runner-up. The newly minted graduate Marella accepted the offer to be the team's heavyweight, bid his family and his girlfriend Inez a fond farewell and went to New York City, where he'd spend a week training with his teammates at the New York Athletic Club under two-time Olympic medalist Henry Wittenberg, before leaving for Russia out of New York City by plane on June 17.

The tour was intended as a gesture of international sporting goodwill and to pique interest in wrestling leading into the 1960 Olympic Games. But for Marella, and in fact for the entire U.S. team, it turned into a sobering, exhausting and extremely frustrating experience. It would play a part in souring Marella completely on wrestling and amateur sports in general. After years of riding high as the beloved and unbeatable Tiny, he was about to embark on a four-week wake-up call that he was in no way ready for. In later years, looking back, he would try to downplay it, and promoters would either dance around or just fudge the details when discussing his amateur background, but the truth was that Marella endured the shellacking of his life, coming up against human machines who ate, breathed and slept wrestling for the honor of their countries. And nowhere was this truer than in the USSR, where resounding humiliation awaited the Americans, setting the tone for a miserable month ahead. The trip would change Bob Marella forever.

Thanks to a flat tire on their plane, it was five hours later than scheduled when the team finally arrived in Moscow to take on their Soviet counterparts in front of a crowd reported in different places as anywhere between twenty thousand and sixty thousand, in a meet televised across the entire Soviet Union. Those patrons had waited patiently to see their wrestlers prove their superiority over their Cold War rivals, and in that regard, they most certainly were not disappointed. The USSR won the meet 7–1, with 123-pounder and two-time NCAA champion Terry McCann the only American to win his match.[11] The nervous Marella refrained from cartwheeling to the mat before that booming Moscow crowd, and with good reason: He was trounced by the formidable Savkuz Dzarasov, the 238-pound 1959 world champion who secured the pin despite giving up more than 75 pounds. His next match, in Leningrad, against 1956 Olympic silver medalist and USSR champion Boris Kulayev, was a little bit closer but had the same result, with the thirty-year-old Kulayev pinning Marella's shoulders to the mat.

While there, the team met up with some of Henry Wittenberg's family living in Moscow, and the coach was so appalled by their living conditions that he wound up giving them most of the money, gifts and other items that had been allocated to the team for the entire twenty-day trip. A gesture of great empathy, if perhaps not of the greatest foresight for the team. Thankfully, the Soviet sports authority was able to provide the Americans with food, often watching with awe and shock as the hungry athletes consumed what would be considered there to be half a week's wages' worth of food in a single sitting.

The U.S. team would go on to lose all four of its meets against the Soviets, with things going much the same way in Kyiv, Ukraine, and Tbilisi, Georgia, where they wrestled outdoors in the rain before a drenched crowd of ten thousand. In none of them did the Americans succeed in getting more than two wins. Marella was pinned in all four outings, although he did dominate the Tbilisi match before being stunned and pinned in the final minutes. To say the boys were in a state of shock would be an understatement, but this was just the beginning. Competition awaited them in Warsaw, Poland; Tehran, Iran; Istanbul,

Turkey; Sofia, Bulgaria; Prague, Czechoslovakia; Paris, France; and Dublin, Ireland. At least Marella could claim that he made it all the way to the end, battered and bruised as he was—four of the eight American grapplers were so banged up halfway through the tour that they were unable to even compete.

The next stop after the Soviet Union was Warsaw, with two of the six competitors already too hurt to take part in the proceedings. Both the team's and Marella's losing ways continued. They traveled south to Istanbul, where at the Mithatpasha Soccer Stadium, they deadlocked with the Turkish team twice—first 3–3 on July 7 and then 2–2 on July 8. Marella lost on points in his first outing against Ismet Atli, then scored one of his rare victories of the trip the following day, outpointing Suleyman Bastimir. And while the USSR was certainly the worst of it, by the remaining outings in Czechoslovakia, Bulgaria, France and Ireland, the Americans were mere shells of the enthusiastic athletes who had departed New York the month before. By the time they boarded their homebound KLM Royal Dutch Airlines plane in Amsterdam on July 14, they were a dejected and soundly defeated bunch.

In later years, looking back, Marella would try to rationalize what happened over there. In an effort to minimize his Russian losses, he'd exaggerate the sizes of his opponents, describing them as biblical-style giants, while they were typically smaller than he was. He'd tell enraptured listeners that none of them could even get him off his feet. In more candid moments, he'd put part of the blame on a deficiency in American collegiate programs in preparing wrestlers for the differences between freestyle and Greco-Roman wrestling, and especially in preparing them for Greco-Roman, which is far more popular in European and Asian countries. He'd blame stricter rules in international competition, which gave less leeway in counting pins. He'd blame a lack of proper government financial support—the American squad was backed by the independent USA Wrestling Foundation—but had to face finely tuned athletes who had the full financial backing of their respective governments, a factor he claimed made them, for all intents and purposes, professionals. "Without subsidization, it's impossible, unless you happen to be loaded with money," he told the *Rochester Democrat and Chronicle*.[12] "We won't win the Olympic wrestling, simply because we are not sending our best in the US." Whatever the excuse, it was clear that the experience had severely disillusioned the young man and given him a quick crash course in the realities of life. As he once caustically observed, "All of those medals and trophies are fine, but all of them and a dime will get you a cup of coffee."[13]

■

Five days after his return to the United States, on July 19, 1959, in Ithaca, New York, Robert James Marella took Inez Mary More as his wife. At twenty-two and twenty-three years of age, respectively, it was a young marriage but not terribly out of the ordinary for the place and time period. Inez already had work as a stenographer, and Bob intended to continue what he started as a physical education instructor and football coach for Brighton High School in the fall. In the end, it would turn out to have been a mistake of youth, but as with all such mistakes, they couldn't recognize it at the time. The life that awaited Bob just wasn't going to be something Inez was ready for, but for the moment, her new husband was still priming himself to make one last-ditch effort to prolong his amateur wrestling ambitions.

The 1960 Summer Olympics, set for the following summer in Rome, was looming on the horizon, and there was one opportunity that could still afford Marella a ticket to Italy: the III Pan American Games, which were taking place at the end of August in Chicago. Held among summer sport athletes in North and South America, the intercontinental competition is a gateway to the Olympics for many, and Marella most certainly saw it as such when he headed to Michigan State University for the tryouts just two weeks after his wedding, along with 150 other hopefuls. After making it to the heavyweight finals of the tryouts, with a spot on the United States' Pan American team hanging in the balance, he went up against Dale Lewis, who had already decisioned him in the first round of the Greco-Roman AAU Championships the previous spring. And despite his 190-pound weight, the once and future Olympian was able to defeat Marella again. Perhaps it was the physical and psychological toll the world tour had taken on him, or perhaps Lewis was simply the better grappler—either way, Marella was forced to accept a spot as heavyweight alternate for the Pan Am team instead.

However, prior to the team's pre-game training session on August 19, Marella made the decision to forfeit his spot and was replaced by Dave Behrman, an incoming freshman at Michigan State. He had officially had enough of what had to be the humiliating experience of spending years as an unbeatable force, only to come up short time and time again in such a brief period of time. His Olympic hopes finally dashed, he had taken amateur wrestling as far as he was willing to go. It was time to embark into the real world. The pressures of life were already upon him, and it was time to start earning a living. "You have to be independently wealthy to compete in amateur athletics at the international level after you leave college," he would later ruefully say. "I wasn't."[14] But although it may have seemed like a crushing blow, destiny wasn't through with Marella just yet. Far from it. Dale Lewis would go on to capture the gold medal at the Pan-Am Games and represent the U.S. in Greco-Roman wrestling at the 1960 Summer Olympics, while Bob Marella would settle into young married life and become a teacher. However, while both men would "turn professional," in the realm of pro wrestling, Lewis would be a mere footnote, while Marella would ascend to the highest of echelons and attain a level of power and influence few wrestlers could ever dream of. It was a whole different world, and he would soon be entering it.

CHAPTER 5
GINO

> "I got a call from wrestling promoter Frank Tunney, who asked me if I wanted to turn pro. I asked him how much it would pay... He said he could give me $500 a week, and he asked if I wanted a couple of weeks to think it over. I said, 'I'll be there Monday.'"

The end of 1959 represented a real shift in the life of the young Bob Marella, but where that shift was eventually leading wasn't yet clear. On the surface, twenty-two years old and fresh out of college, he seemed to be settling into normal, domestic adult life with his new wife at 356 Avenue B on the corner of Hollenbeck Street, back in his hometown of Rochester. The whirlwind dream of national and international amateur athletic competition was over, and a slightly rattled and disappointed Marella was instead focusing himself on something he seemed to genuinely enjoy: educating and working with young people. Despite his setbacks, he had made a great showing for himself, was already by far the most accomplished individual his family had produced since coming to America, and had a lot to be proud of. There was nothing wrong with pivoting to become a productive citizen and humble member of society, the expected course taken by many a successful college athlete after school.

Except not only was his time in the spotlight far from over, it could be argued that it hadn't yet really begun. Marella was soon to become known to legions of people, most of whom would have no idea he had even been an amateur athlete, although that was the initial hook used to help get him there. The strange, wonderful, sordid, glorious, surreal, lucrative, mysterious business of professional wrestling awaited him, and his accomplishments on the mats of Ithaca, the NCAA and AAU would help provide his ticket into that world. It also didn't hurt that there weren't many people walking around who were 310 pounds, six foot six and not only in shape but able to slam dunk a basketball and do a mid-air split, touching their feet to their hands. Marella was an athletic freak of nature in the best sense possible, and it was going to pay off for him in a big way.

But it still wasn't going to be easy. He was going to have to work for it. At first, it would seem like just another exercise in frustration, a nut he couldn't crack. In those early years, he'd have to earn every dollar he made with sweat and determination, to a degree that made everything that followed seem more than deserved. He'd travel all across North America trying to make a name for himself, chasing success and losing his marriage in the process. But like all the work he was putting into his new ambition, even that would turn out to have been overwhelmingly for the best. With the right connections and a little luck, he'd start building his legend on the other side of the world, and when he returned to America, it was not as a man but as a monster. It would take more than amateur success. His name would only carry him so far—in fact, his name itself was going to change in the end, not once but twice. But it was that first change that really stuck. Because even long after the world got to know him as Gorilla Monsoon, those close to him continued to call him Gino. And that would never change.

■

It's debatable whether Marella still had any hope of making the 1960 U.S. Olympic wrestling team after failing to make the Pan American team, but it's clear that even in the unlikely event he might have been selected as an alternate, he was done waiting around. "I'd love the trip and the glamor of the Olympics," he'd later tell sportswriter George Beahon of the *Democrat and Chronicle*, "But tell me, what working man with any family at all can afford to give up nearly two months out of his work schedule?"[1] There were some offers from the Cleveland Browns, Green Bay Packers and San Francisco 49ers, but Marella's knees had already taken enough of a beating in college football that he wasn't sure the sport was a good idea for a man of his size, and declined. Although he didn't have a family to support yet, he did have a household, and so he took up teaching at Brighton High School, just a fifteen-minute drive from home. For extra money, he also continued taking on construction work, putting his massive frame to good use.

But fresh off his high-profile summer, Marella's was still a notable name, especially around town, where many people still admired their local sports hero. One of those people was a certain Ignacio "Pedro" Martinez, although in his case, the admiration had a lot to do with dollar signs. At a time when the professional wrestling business was divided into dozens of regional territories across North America, Martinez was the boss of the Great Lakes Athletic Club, a promotion based in Buffalo that mainly presented events all along the I-90 corridor, from Syracuse in the east all the way down to Cleveland, including other towns in Ohio and New York like Canton, Akron, Toledo, and Marella's hometown of Rochester. Having been pushed out of New York City in a power play during the early 1950s, Martinez had made his way upstate, eventually buying out promoter and former world heavyweight champion Ed Don George to carve out his slice of the wrestling pie far north of the Big Apple.

In those days, the pro wrestling business was all about ticket sales, and promoters were always on the lookout for the next great angle that would help draw fans to the arenas. Sometime in the beginning of 1960, Martinez hit upon an idea he hoped would do just that. A supporter and benefactor of amateur wrestling, as many promoters were in those days, Martinez had donated money to help support the AAU team on its world tour the previous year and knew all about Marella's accomplishments. Hoping to do some business, Martinez contacted the young gym teacher and pitched an idea that would perfectly suit the show business world of pro wrestling, where it was all about showmanship: Marella, an accomplished "real-life" wrestling star, would come down to the Rochester War Memorial and "challenge" the pro wrestlers to a fight, insisting that an amateur champion could defeat any phony pro. It was the kind of "worked shoot" angle, based in real life, that would appeal in almost any era, even being used in the twenty-first century with amateur greats like 1996 Olympic gold medalist Kurt Angle.

Marella was intrigued and perhaps a bit amused by the proposition and decided to give it a shot. But before he could take part in any such plan, he'd have to be prepared and broken into the world of professional wrestling, which was an entirely different animal from the amateur stuff he'd been doing up to that point. First and foremost, he'd have to be taught how to "work"; that is, how to make a performance look like a legitimate competition, how to engage the paying fans, and also how not to hurt your opponent while doing so. This was no longer about trying to win, but rather trying to put on a show, so it required a different skill set and mindset. But the rigorous discipline and athletic prowess built up during his years on the mat would still be a fine place to start and give him an advantage over the average wannabe pro wrestler who didn't know a wristlock from a wristwatch, as he'd later be fond of saying.

Martinez put Marella in touch with Hungarian journeyman wrestler Sandor Kovacs, who worked for the promotion at the time as a trainer and a booker, helping to make the matches and craft the storylines or "programs" that would help draw crowds and money. As booker, Kovacs had helped concoct the plan to bring in Marella in the first place, and now he'd help get him ready to go from wrestler to "rassler." The inner workings of pro wrestling were completely closed to the public, unlike the much more transparent world of amateur wrestling, but it's safe to assume that Kovacs and Martinez were just as impressed with Marella's size and skill as his previous coaches had been.

With an athlete of Marella's natural prowess, it didn't take long to get him reasonably ready for the ring. By February, it was time to put the plan into action. In a carefully orchestrated publicity stunt, Marella came down on February 10 to the Rochester War Memorial, the very arena he'd worked construction on while still in college, and "crashed" the proceedings, making a scene and demanding a match with one of the professionals, whom he ridiculed for their alleged fakery. Martinez played the outraged promoter, afraid of the challenge from a "real" wrestler, and had Marella escorted from the building by security.

The incident made the local papers, and Marella did all he could to help play it up. "The only conclusion I arrive at is that they are afraid to give me a match because I can beat their hippodrome artists,"[2] he wrote in a letter to the *Democrat and Chronicle*.[3] "I would appreciate your printing this letter, as it would help my cracking this wrestling monopoly." The newspapermen saw right through the theatrics but seemingly went along with a wink and a nudge to help give some publicity, as they often did in those days. The promotion ran weekly cards at the War Memorial, and so Marella continued to show up for the next couple of weeks and continued to get "kicked out." Martinez set himself up as the heel, reluctantly granting Marella a chance to see if he'd fall flat on his face. Playing up Marella's local appeal, it was announced that he'd be stepping into the ring for the next War Memorial card, scheduled for March 2.

When the night arrived, Marella was nervous. Maybe not as nervous as he'd been stepping on the mat in Russia, but this was something entirely new for him. The show had drawn over three thousand spectators, more than a typical War Memorial card, with many who didn't normally attend wrestling coming down to see the Rochester boy make good. He could be seen that night warming up in the middle of the locker room, jiggling his hands and waving his forearms as a reporter interviewed him about his impending professional debut and giving up his Olympic standing. "I'm not waiting for the Olympics," he responded. "I need the money I can make as a pro, and right now I still need my construction job."

A voice came from across the room: "Hey, Marella. Don't you worry. Pretty soon, you'll be able to tell 'em to keep that job."

On the other side of the locker room, oiling his six-foot-six, 270-pound body to gleaming perfection, was Houston Harris, the African-American grappler from Benton Harbor, Michigan, who, as Bobo Brazil, had become pro wrestling's equivalent of Jackie Robinson. Brazil was in the semi-main event that night, teaming with Yukon Eric against the outrageously villainous Gallagher Brothers, and had taken notice of the locker room newcomer. The two would go on to become the best of friends, but on that night, Brazil was the veteran star recognizing the potential of an impressive rookie. His prediction would turn out to be a prescient one.

Martinez was less complimentary. Playing the scornful wrestling promoter role that would become all too familiar to wrestling fans of later generations, he first bragged about his luxury apartment and other riches, then turned his attention to Marella: "Take a good look at him, because you won't see him any more . . . I gave the AAU $3,000 to help finance that team's trip. Now he's biting the hand that fed him. He's ungrateful. He's colorless. He's got no chance to make it big . . . Besides all that, he lacks humility . . . Next time, I'll make him work in a curtain-raiser, if I use him at all."

For Marella's opponent that night, Martinez and Kovacs had chosen Ramon Lopez, a twenty-year undercard veteran whose job it was to make others look great, which he'd been doing for Martinez for the past eight months up to that point. And this night would be no different, as Marella made short work of the Puerto Rican journeyman, putting him away in just four minutes, much to the appreciation of the fans.[4] There wasn't much razzle-dazzle to Marella's work that night, but that was exactly what Martinez wanted, in keeping with his new rookie's legit reputation. If there was any Olympic hope left, it was gone now—Bob Marella had gone professional.

■

Contrary to what he told that reporter, Martinez was interested in bringing Marella back and would do so a few more times. It was common in those territorial days for promoters to run angles specific to particular marketplaces, and that's exactly what he did in Rochester. Looking to avoid overexposing the inexperienced newcomer, he waited three weeks before bringing him back, this time as a substitute for Kovacs against Baron Gattoni, a rugged and wooly Milanese whom Marella once again dispatched with relative ease. Brazil would be there again to witness the proceedings, as would another young wrestler, Billy Red Lyons of Hamilton, Ontario, in the main event that night against the goose-stepping Fritz Von Erich (who was really Jack Adkisson of Jewett, Texas). Although Lyons had been in the game a few years, he and Marella were of similar age and became fast friends.

Martinez gave Marella two more shots, one in April against "Dancing" Dick Nelson and then in early May against Marcel deParee, and he was booked to go over both times, as he had been before. But there was a problem. Martinez's in-character denigrations had turned out to be not entirely inaccurate. Once the novelty of seeing the NCAA and AAU finalist in a professional ring had worn off a bit, Marella came across a bit bland in the ring, not to mention that his immense size and power made his matches seem predictable and uncompelling. He had no persona or "gimmick," that certain something special a good promoter or booker can hang on a wrestler to help get them over with fans—and that seemed to be how Martinez wanted it.

Marella liked picking up the extra money, but he was definitely looking to make more and wasn't going to as long as Martinez insisted on booking him so sporadically. Inez doesn't seem to have been thrilled with her husband doing a little moonlighting in this odd world, but she tolerated it as long as it didn't take away from his more dependable work in the classroom and on the construction site. Understandably, he felt that he was being ignored, as though Martinez had gotten as much from him as he wanted, which may have been true. Marella had some training and his wrestling license, but for the time being, had no choice but to keep on with his day jobs. His brief taste of the business, however, had given him the idea that he could be earning a whole lot more.

Although Martinez seemingly had nothing else for him, Marella was fortunate in that there was someone else who had also moved on from the Great Lakes promotion—his trainer Sandor Kovacs. In those days, North America's territorial pro wrestling system was largely controlled by the National Wrestling Alliance, a conglomerate of regional promotions across the continent that agreed not to compete with one another, and for each to stay in its respective corner of the world. Wrestlers benefited from the system in the sense that they could move relatively freely from one territory to another with the right opportunity. That opportunity came over the summer of 1960, when Kovacs was able to bring Marella with him for a card up in Quebec for promoter Eddie Quinn. This was a more high-profile territory than Martinez's and could afford Marella some of the exposure for which he was hoping.

Another benefit to working Montreal was the sizeable population of Italians. Ethnically Italian wrestlers could do well in a place like that, appealing to the local fan base. Marella already had the right last name; it was the first name that needed work. "Bob" simply wasn't a very Italian-sounding name. It's not clear who came up with it (possibly Quinn himself), but Marella was given the much more ethnic-sounding name of "Gino." One story has it that the name originated from Marella's fondness for patronizing a restaurant owned by veteran wrestler Gino Garibaldi, but Garibaldi was a California-based wrestler, and Marella wouldn't make it out west as a wrestler for several years. Whatever the reason, when Marella hit the ring in Montreal on July 28, it would be as Gino Marella. He'd be known throughout the business that way for the rest of his life, with even close friends and associates sometimes not remembering it wasn't the name on his birth certificate.[5] From then on, he was Gino.

The show was to be held in Delorimier Stadium, an open-air baseball park that had been the home of the top farm team of the Brooklyn Dodgers. Before a crowd of nine thousand fans, three times the size of the gatherings at the Rochester War Memorial, Kovacs walked his protégé through the opening match, a handicap tag team encounter in which Gino singlehandedly won out over both Kovacs and partner Maurice LaPointe. It was a big-time affair, and even more important than the match would be the people he'd encounter that day for the first time. In the main event, teaming up against former NWA World champions Lou

Thesz and Édouard Carpentier, was the hated duo of Hans Schmidt and the fearsome Killer Kowalski.

Born Edward Władisław Spulnik in Windsor, Ontario, and first known in the business as Władek Kowalski, he insisted his friends, of which Gino was destined to become one, call him Walter. He was even taller than Gino and had been a major attraction in Montreal for years, having made his villainous name off an accident in the ring in 1952, in which he'd torn off the cauliflower ear of Yukon Eric with an unfortunately placed kneedrop. A major headliner with a lot of pull at the time, he'd get his first look at Gino Marella in the opening match that day, and he wouldn't forget it.

Also sharing the locker room with Gino that day for the very first time, wrestling in the semi-main event against Reggie "Crusher" Lisowski, was another newcomer to the business who would one day become inextricably linked with Gino for all time to come. Bruno Leopoldo Francesco Sammartino had only been in the business a couple of months longer than Gino, but his rise had been much more meteoric, and he'd been a major hit in New York from his very first appearance, in which he'd bodyslammed the 601-pound Haystacks Calhoun in Madison Square Garden. A hulking powerhouse who'd made his way into the business by way of competitive weightlifting, unlike Gino, he had been born and raised in Italy, making his way with his family from the town of Pizzoferrato, Abruzzi, to Pittsburgh as a teenager in the years after World War II. On that day in Montreal, Gino was a curtain-jerker while Bruno was one of the top attractions, but that would change in years to come. They wouldn't meet again for a while, but eventually would get to know each other quite well, sharing the ring with more often than with anyone else. Out of that rivalry and a shared ancestry would grow a friendship that, in more than one way, would be one of the defining aspects of Gino's career.

■

Just a couple of weeks later, Marella got a phone call that would change his life. One province over from Quebec, a few hundred miles from Montreal down the A-20 to the 401 and a stone's throw across Lake Ontario from Rochester, was another Canadian wrestling hotbed, Toronto. Running an Ontario circuit based in the Maple Leaf Gardens, promoter Frank Tunney had gotten wind of the new young giant from upstate New York and had an interest in using him that went far beyond a handful of appearances. Tunney envisioned the newly christened Gino Marella as an ongoing attraction. Toronto and its environs had an even stronger Italian presence than Montreal, and as luck would have it, included in that population was an enclave of immigrants from Faeto, the very village from which Gino traced his lineage.

Hoping to tap into that market, Tunney reached out to Marella one Sunday morning in August 1960, with an offer that was simply too good to pass up. At a time when the average American's salary was $110 per week, with a new teacher's salary probably falling somewhere below that average, Tunney was offering him nearly five times as much for weekly appearances at the Maple Leaf Gardens. Gino in later years would say that if he could have made as much teaching as he could wrestling, he wouldn't have become a wrestler, and while he truly enjoyed his job, he accepted Tunney's offer without hesitation—which also was likely not taken too well by Inez, who could see this crazy wrestling stuff taking up more and more of her husband's time and encroaching on their quiet newlywed life. Toronto was hours away, even if it would only be on Thursday nights. With his feet on the ground as always, Marella would continue with his day jobs for the time being, just until he was sure this wrestling thing was really going to work out.

To ensure Gino got over with the Toronto faithful, a little more showmanship was needed. He'd have to be more than just an amateur champion, and when Tunny learned that Gino could sing, he struck on just the idea, which could be witnessed from his very first appearance against rough-and-tumble "Butcher Boy" Lee Henning at the Gardens on August 18, 1960. Standing in the center of the ring, his opponent anxiously waiting for the match to get underway, Gino took the ring announcer's microphone, and from his lips, a sweet bel canto baritone rang out over the crowd of five thousand:

Vide 'o mare quant'è bello!
Spira tantu sentimento,
Comme tu a chi tiene mente,
Ca scetato 'o fai sunnà . . .

The song, "Torna a Surriento," recalled the beautiful Southern Italian town of Sorrento, nestled on the blue-green Bay of Naples, and as Gino sang it, one can imagine more than a few less-than-dry eyes in the house. His quick win over Henning was a foregone conclusion. Gino Marella had made an impression.

The singing gimmick continued throughout Gino's five-month run in Toronto. The Neapolitan songs he had been immersed in growing up, as well as the operas of Verdi and Puccini, came in handy, and he would draw on many of them each time he stepped through the ropes. It was a time of ethnic heroes in wrestling, and Gino fit right in. As his experience grew week by week, he started to be put in longer matches—no more weekly squashes, but sometimes matches that would even go to the twenty-minute time limit. He was getting in ring shape, becoming a better worker with each match. And he was rising up the card. By September, he had been put in the semi-main, defeating the four-hundred-pound Mighty Jumbo on a show headlined by the Tolos Brothers against Yukon Eric and Toronto legend "Whipper" Billy Watson. Less than two months later, Tunney booked him in his very first main event, as he teamed with Watson against Edmonton's Gene Kiniski and supposed "Soviet" baddie Ivan Kalmikoff. After tangling with the real thing back in Moscow, a pretend Russian was a piece of cake for Gino. And working with the top star in the territory helped give Gino "the rub," as they call it in the business.

As eager as he was to climb the ladder, the only match he refused was when Tunney tried to put him in the ring with Terrible Ted, the wrestling bear that regularly toured all the circuits with his trainer and frequent "opponent," Canadian wrestler Gene DuBois. Ted and DuBois happened to be making their way through Toronto in the fall of 1960, and it seemed a natural fit to pair him up with the gigantic Marella, but Gino politely turned down that dubious offer.

Wrestling one night a week, Marella continued to teach at Brighton in the fall semester. And as always, he still had time for family. On Saturday, October 22, his big brother Sonny got married at Holy Apostles Church back in Rochester, and he was there to serve as an usher, their little sister Rosemary as one of the bridesmaids. Sonny and his wife Zhan would remain in Rochester for a time, with Sonny taking a job with his father at the lumber company until it shut down a few years later, then relocating to Texas to take a job working with his brother-in-law.

Tunney kept Gino around Toronto into 1961. He had improved quite a bit but was still pretty green, and one match a week was only going to get him so far. If he wanted to succeed in the business, he had to commit to it fully. Tunney promised him more work down the road, but in the meantime, put him in touch with another Canadian promoter who could give him more dates, if he was willing to go on the road full time. The catch was, it was over two thousand miles away, in the frozen tundra of Alberta and Saskatchewan. In other words, if he was going to do it, it would mean leaving the classroom, giving up the day job and relocating out west for half a year.

It was a huge decision, and needless to say, not what Marella's wife wanted at all. As pro wrestling became more a part of her husband's life, Inez wanted less and less to be a part of it. Growing up on a farm in a tiny hamlet in upstate New York, she likely found the whole thing completely hair-brained and impractical, not to mention that she had zero interest in such a drastic relocation. Bob and Inez had met when they were very young, and the marriage had been a hasty one. Now his life was starting to change, and in order to keep her, he'd have to remain a schoolteacher and construction worker. When given the choice, the twenty-three-year-old Marella chose wrestling. The call of the business drove a wedge between the college sweethearts, and when Bob flew out to Calgary, Alberta, on the morning of Saturday, January 6, 1961, Inez would not be with him. It's possible that they never lived under the same roof again.[6]

The precise end of the marriage, like most everything else about it, is shrouded in mystery, although on a Kansas State Athletic Commission application for a wrestler's license dated November 1961, Marella listed himself as unmarried[7]. In less than three years, Gino would meet someone new who would accept him for who and what he was, and who would know him as Gorilla Monsoon before she knew him as Bob Marella. Eventually, he would remarry, and this time it would be for keeps: a loving marriage that would survive all the tests of the wrestling industry like almost no other. But that was all still some time away. For now, Gino had a name to make for himself.

■

On the way out of the Toronto territory, Gino performed the time-honored wrestling tradition of doing the job before he left, taking the very first loss of his professional career in a match against Stan "Krusher" Kowalski (no actual relation to Killer) before hopping a plane for Calgary. It was there that he first arrived at 435 Patina Place SW in the residential neighborhood of Patterson Heights. A red brick mansion of 5,600 square feet, sitting on 2.17 acres of land, it was home to the Hart family, led by patriarch Stu and his wife, Helen, with seven sons ranging in age from one to twelve years. Stu Hart was a tough character that only the wrestling business could've produced—a man of steel, with gravel in his voice, who had pulled himself up from a childhood spent living in a tent on the prairies of Alberta, started wrestling during the Great Depression and had become one of the leading power brokers of the business, reigning over a territory that spanned a large swath of Western Canada, and even extended south into Montana. It was hard, cold country, and other promoters were more than happy to leave it to someone like Stu Hart to run.

The territory was known as Stampede Wrestling, and it would be Gino's first full taste of the pro wrestling business, hitting the snowy roads, making the towns and wrestling four or five times a week in places like Edmonton, Saskatoon, Regina and Lethbridge. He would never forget the hospitality and kindness shown to him during those months. He'd come away from it with great respect and gratitude for Stu and his family, and many years later when Stu's son Bret, whom Gino first met at the tender age of three years old, arrived in the WWF, Gino would still remember and became one of the young second-generation wrestler's greatest advocates and supporters.

But before he experienced that kindness, Gino would have to survive a baptism of fire that in a way was typical of the wrestling business in those days—even if there was nothing typical about the small wood-paneled room in Stu Hart's basement where Hart would take great pleasure in testing the abilities of young wrestlers. In later years, it would become known as the Dungeon, but whatever it was called, many a man found himself tied up in knots in that room, stretched to the limits of his endurance by Hart, a renowned "shooter" who knew many ways to break a human body. And so it was with great interest that Stu sought to test himself against an elite amateur champion and one day lured the unsuspecting Gino downstairs for a workout.

Of course, Marella's reputation preceded him, and Hart knew it wouldn't be the usual stretching session with the typical green recruits who found themselves at his mercy. However, Hart also knew a few things they were never going to teach you on the mats of Ithaca College. After locking horns with Gino for several tense moments, Stu somehow got him down to the mat in a double grapevine position, his arm behind Gino's head with his legs wrapped around his massive thighs. Hart then took a liberty with the youngster to test his reaction, in the spur of the moment grabbing his head in a cross-face, running his left forearm across his face until his nose burst. Blood was suddenly everywhere, and as Gino tried to rear up like a wild beast, Stu Hart came to the frightened realization that he may have made a grievous error in judgment.

"He was terrified," says Ross Hart, who was only about twelve months old at the time but heard the story repeated many a time in family lore. "He thought if he got up, he didn't think he could have contained him. He obviously had pissed him off and gotten him enraged. My dad just kind of held him there a couple of minutes until I think they were both blown up by that time. And my dad always had so much respect for him, but I don't think he ever took that kind of liberty with him again." Adds Ross's brother Bret, "I don't think Gorilla quite knew what he was dealing with with my dad, and I don't think my dad knew what he was dealing with with Gorilla. I think they both remembered the occasion quite well, that they were both quite lucky to get out of it the way they did."

Hart admired his new recruit's background and so billed him as Bob "Gino" Marella to capitalize on his name. Gino made his Stampede debut on January 6, 1961, with a win over "The Alaskan" Jay York in the semi-main event of a card at the venerable Victoria Pavilion, Stampede's home arena. During his time in the territory, he would more or less be kept at the semi-main level, with the occasional main event such as on February 3, when he teamed with top attraction and future Hawaii promoter Ed Francis to take on John Smith and the Mighty Ursus. On some of his early Stampede cards, he'd share the locker room with Lou Thesz, who was always on the lookout for a legitimate shooter and who was impressed with Gino's amateur resume. In fact, he was so impressed that he saw fit to bring Gino out further west to the British Columbia territory for a single main event at Vancouver's PNE Garden on January 23. It would be Marella's only known match with the legendary former world champion, and he happily did the honors in two out of three falls before Thesz brought him back to Stampede with him the next day.

It was a sign of respect that Gino had gotten noticed by someone of Thesz's caliber. "You could tell he was fairly inexperienced, but he knew his way around the ring a little bit," explains Ross. "Because of his size, guys didn't take advantage of him. Nobody really wanted to mess with him. I don't think guys took liberties with him in the ring because he had so much size, he would just overpower you and could wrestle, too." In a legit shoot, Gino could manhandle an opponent if he had to, and he had no problem letting people know that in the ring, including old-school shooters like Thesz. In fact, because of his size and power, it started making sense to play him up as a bully, and it was in Stampede that he first started playing around with the role of heel, arrogantly offering an ever-growing pot of hundreds of dollars to anyone who could pin him within ten minutes. No one ever collected.

It was in Stampede that Gino worked with midgets for the first time; promoters would later enjoy teaming their largest wrestler with some of their smallest throughout his career. He also took part in—and handily won—his first battle royal, at Exhibition Auditorium in Regina, Saskatchewan, on February 23. He returned to Toronto in June a more seasoned, formidable professional than he had been when he left, not to mention having gotten his first TV exposure thanks to Stampede's weekly show from the Victoria Pavilion. It was a crucial learning experience in the early stages of his career.

■

This time, Gino was able to fully take part in the Toronto circuit, appearing at the Maple Leaf Gardens as well as places like Niagara Falls, Hamilton, Oshawa and St. John's, Newfoundland. Picking the singing gimmick right back up where he left off, he remained popular with fans, who would often throw money in the ring during his pre-match performances—a significant supplement to his income, as he would later tell it. And now that he had really started to pay his dues and put in his time, he began to be fully accepted by the boys in the locker room. He especially fell in with a clique of other ethnically Italian wrestlers who shared a love of the same food, the same music, the same culture. Chief among these was Ilio DiPaolo, an eleven-year veteran from Introdacqua, Abruzzi, who was something of the godfather of Italian wrestlers at the time, respected and admired by all. He also happened to be married to Pedro Martinez's stepdaughter, Ethel, which meant that he was heavily pushed throughout the upstate New York territory where Gino came from. The Italian circle in the area also included Tony Silipini, who wrestled as Tony Marino and also hailed from Rochester.

"They had an admiration for one another which was pretty evident, and I saw that when they were together," remembers Dennis DiPaolo, who still runs his late father's Italian restaurant in Blasdell, New York. "My father always said that he was very impressed with him. He was a special individual, a true wrestler, as my father would say."

In addition to the locker room, Marella was also very popular with the front office. Frank Tunney obviously recognized his intelligence and savvy, not to mention his level of education and athletic accomplishment, as could be observed by the fact that in late August he chose him among the handful of his wrestlers to accompany him to the fourteenth annual convention of the National Wrestling Alliance, which was being held in Toronto that year.

It was likely there that he first met former (and future) longtime NWA president Sam Muchnick, who shortly after made him a very important offer. In addition to corralling the collection of scorched cats that made up the NWA's membership, Muchnick also ran his own promotion based in St. Louis. A former sportswriter with many connections in the St. Louis community, Muchnick prided himself on presenting a relatively clean, scientific brand of pro wrestling and had gotten wind of Marella from some of his colleagues. He brought in Gino in November for a six-month run.

Muchnick's was essentially a one-city promotion, but wrestling for him also meant a chance to work for his sister promotion, the Heart of America company, also known as Central States, covering parts of Missouri, Kansas and Iowa. Then owned and operated by Orville Brown, who had been the inaugural NWA world champion before his career was cut short by a car accident in 1949, the concern also involved a partnership with established Kansas City promoter George Simpson, as well as retired Greek wrestler Gust Karras, who'd been running Friday night shows in St. Joseph since the 1930s. And so Gino made his way to the Midwest, right into the heart of the NWA.

St. Louis wasn't quite the most lucrative promotion in wrestling, and it was far from the biggest, but under Muchnick's control, it was the most prestigious and offered those who worked there a chance to be noticed by all the other NWA promoters. Gino made his debut at the legendary Kiel Auditorium on November 10, defeating Karl Von Schober via disqualification. It was his highest-profile area to date, which also meant he'd have to start out again in opening matches and work his way up. But he'd also have a chance to appear on *Wrestling at the Chase*, a then-new weekly TV program that would go on to become a St. Louis institution, presented in the elegant ballroom of the Chase Park Plaza Hotel before a dapperly attired audience that looked more like they were there for a wedding than a wrestling show.

St. Louis also wasn't a place where Gino could expect to win all his matches like he usually did. This was a territory packed with major stars, as was evidenced by the November 24 Kiel show that saw him go down in defeat to the six-foot-six, 320-pound "Mormon Giant" Don Leo Jonathan. That would also be the first time he found himself on the undercard of a world heavyweight title match, with rugged Washingtonian Johnny Valentine challenging for the NWA world championship against the man who'd held it since July, the bleached blond and perfectly tanned "Nature Boy" Buddy Rogers. Not only a gifted performer, the wily Rogers was also a locker-room lawyer par excellence, skilled in the backroom politicking and chicanery on which much success in the business was based. Gino got to know Buddy during his time in the Midwest, as well as some of his assorted cronies and hangers-on like Buddy Austin, who went wherever Rogers went, and whom Gino would dutifully do a job for while working in St. Louis.

Gino was getting seen and making all the right connections. By January 1962, he'd transitioned over to Central States, where he was especially appreciated by Karras, who made him a highlight of his weekly cards at the St. Joseph Auditorium. Never without his trilby hat and briarwood pipe, Karras effusively sang the praises of Marella to anyone who'd listen, including *St. Joseph News-Press & Gazette* sportswriter Bill Scott, to whom he said, "He's a natural. He has youth, size, speed, skill and most important, heart. They know they've had a fight when they tangle with Gino."[8] Upon his St. Joseph debut, the *News-Press & Gazette*, likely with material fed to it by Karras, declared, "Close observers of the pro mat action expect the big fellow to have a long tenure in the business and to make his way to the top within the next few years."[9] Ballyhoo or not, the claim would turn out to be more of a prophecy.

Getting in good with Buddy Rogers's crew was no doubt a positive for Gino's career, but there could also be a downside to being in the champ's orbit, such as what transpired in the early morning hours of Monday, January 25, 1962. Gino was riding with Buddy Austin and a fellow newcomer to the business, twenty-four-year-old Croatian-Quebecois George Stipich, who had just started wrestling under the name Stan Stasiak, in tribute to a prominent Polish grappler of the 1920s. They were making the four-hour drive from St. Louis to Kansas City when they stopped off at the one gas station in the one-gas-station town of Kingdom City, Missouri. While Gino slept in the back seat, Austin and Stasiak had some tense words with the attendant and wound up roughing the guy up pretty good, getting themselves arrested. No charges were filed against Marella, who apparently slept through the whole thing and also made sure to describe himself as a "former Olympic wrestler" (not the only time he would do this) when questioned by the authorities. Now, whether Gino was actually sleeping through the altercation happening right outside the car, or just being very smart, can be left to the judgment of the reader. In any event, Austin and Stasiak were released on $100 bail, and Austin was wrestling Marella that very night at the Memorial Hall in Kansas City.

In a sign of how well-regarded Gino had become by the NWA power brokers like Muchnick and Rogers, just one week later at the next Memorial Hall card, he'd be granted a title shot against the Nature Boy. In the two-out-of-three-falls affair, the resourceful world champion scored the first fall after a bodyslam and questionable elbow to the throat. Marella pinned Rogers in the second fall, using the finishing combination he was already coming to rely on: a "giant swing" in which he'd lift his opponent off the mat by the legs and spin him around repeatedly, followed by a smothering body press splash. And finally, Buddy pinned Gino in the third and deciding fall after his opportunistic flunky Austin had bashed Gino in the jaw while the referee, retired Kansas City fireman Lou Spindle, was otherwise occupied. It was Gino's first shot at a world title in pro wrestling. He'd have many, many more down the road, but this would be his only shot at the NWA version. His destiny lay on a different path.

Gino was a big attraction as a babyface in Kansas City for a few months, acting as a thorn in the side of Rogers and Austin, even coming close to defeating Austin for his Central States heavyweight title. It was also in the Memorial Hall that he locked up with Happy Humphrey, who, at nearly three times Gino's weight, was the heaviest pro wrestler to ever step through the ropes. Before heading back to Toronto in May, he'd make a slight detour through Nebraska and Minnesota in territory that was then affiliated with the American Wrestling Association. On May 14, he'd be matched up with the comparably sized Dr. Bill Miller, another fellow former amateur wrestling, discus and shot-put standout, who'd been an All-American and Big Ten heavyweight champion for Ohio State University. The two erstwhile collegiate greats met in the ring in the studio of TV station KETV for the televised wrestling program put on by Omaha promoter Joe Dusek. Five days later, Dusek sent him to St. Paul, Minnesota, where he made his one and only appearance in the AWA proper for promoter and owner Verne Gagne, a two-time NCAA champion and 1948 Olympian in his own right. Coincidentally, that night, Marella would lose to Bob Geigel, who would take over the Central States territory from Orville Brown the following year.[10]

For the next ten months, from the summer of 1962 through the winter of '63, Gino would rotate between the Ontario territory and the Missouri / Central States territory, two areas where fans had come to know and love him. While in Toronto, he was reunited with Bruno Sammartino, who had been temporarily exiled from New York through a series of Machiavellian machinations (more on that later) and was being pushed to the moon by Frank Tunney. This would be the first time the two men would regularly share locker rooms, even though Bruno was already the bigger star. In fact, Gino made a couple of undercard appearances at the Maple Leaf Gardens on nights when Bruno would challenge Buddy Rogers for the NWA world title. While not on the road, he managed to work a few shots for Pedro Martinez in Rochester and Buffalo. The promoter who'd given him his first break was finally interested in using him again, but by that point, Gino had become a big enough attraction that he had options.

In November 1962, he and Sammartino were brought in by Eddie Quinn for two big shows, one at the Ottawa Coliseum and the other at the Montreal Forum. Also on those shows was Killer Kowalski, recognized as world heavyweight champion by the Montreal Athletic Commission. But Marella wasn't brought in to wrestle either of them; rather, on both nights, his opponent would be a six-foot-ten, three-hundred-pound Japanese monolith by the name of Shohei "Giant" Baba. The young Baba, a former pitcher for the Yomiuri Giants of Tokyo, had been touring North America for over a year—more than half his wrestling career at the time—on loan from his mentor Mitsuhiro "Rikidozan" Momota, who controlled all of professional wrestling in the Land of the Rising Sun. Baba, already a major touring attraction, won both encounters, pinning Marella in the second one; but more importantly, the Japanese contact Marella would thank for his showings would prove to be a crucial turning point in his career very soon.

Gino was starting to come into demand as something of an attraction himself, as could be seen when he was invited by Detroit promoters Johnny Doyle and Jim Barnett to take part in a twenty-man one-night tournament at Cobo Arena that featured an array of talent from far-flung promotions. That night, he was included among major stars such as the white-meat babyface from Buffalo, Mark Lewin and the Arabian madman himself, The Sheik, known to his mom and dad as Eddie Farhat. There were familiar faces like Billy Red Lyons, Dr. Bill Miller and Don Leo Jonathan. And then there was Fred Blassie. A tanned and bleached blond villain like Buddy Rogers, Blassie was much rougher around the edges than the foppish Rogers. A sailor who had served in World War II, he was almost twenty years Marella's senior, and in his middle age, had recently made a sensation of himself as the most hated heel in California. They would meet backstage at Cobo that night for the very first time. But their paths would certainly cross again.

Meanwhile back in Toronto, Gino was witness to history the night of January 24, 1963, when he wrestled in the opening match at the Maple Leaf Gardens against the hirsute and loincloth-wearing Beast (Sicilian-Canadian wrestler Johnny Yachetti) the night that Lou Thesz defeated Buddy Rogers to win the NWA world heavyweight title for the final time—the extent to which Rogers was a willing participant in that outcome still being a somewhat open question. Bruno was also there, facing Buddy Austin on the undercard. That night, both men were outranked by the main eventers. That would not continue to be the case for much longer. In fact, the two were both getting so popular with Toronto fans, and with each other, that two weeks later at the next Maple Leaf Gardens show, with Rogers getting his rematch against Thesz in the main event, the semi-main featured Sammartino and Marella sharing a wrestling ring for the very first time, as they'd join forces in a tag team affair against Bulldog Brower and Taro Sakuro (aka the original "Great Kabooki" Rey Urbano).

■

By March 1963, Gino could confidently consider himself a seasoned professional. Three years into the game, he was a reasonably polished and dependable worker, combining speed and agility with his size and power to show that he was more than just another hulking giant of wrestling. Life on the road had taught him about showmanship, and at a firm and fit 325 pounds, he could throw dropkicks, not to mention his usual splits and cartwheels, making himself a marvel to behold. He was getting attention from the right people, which would lead to his being selected among a roster of American and Canadian wrestlers to be brought over to Japan for a major world-spanning event. The fifth annual World Big League was going to be a fifty-one-day tournament to take place in Japan from March through May, presented by Rikidozan's Japanese Wrestling Association.

Professional wrestling was the most popular sporting event in Japan and had been since taking shape there during the American occupation following World War II. It had become far more popular than it was in the United States, and Rikidozan was then, as he still is considered now, the greatest sports sensation of any kind in the history of Japan. In those days, recent geopolitics being what they were, American wrestlers (*gaijin*) were usually presented as the bad guys, and Rikidozan and his later followers particularly gravitated toward *gaijin* of great physical size or possessing some other quality such as blond hair or cowboy attire that would emphasize their oddity and exoticism to a Japanese audience. Gino had a few things going for him. For one, he was being vouched for by Killer Kowalski, a veteran of the Japanese tours whose influence carried a lot of weight and who had seen enough to know Gino could hold his own. Plus, the World Big League would mark the triumphant return to Japan of Giant Baba after a year and a half of traveling abroad, and Baba knew firsthand what Marella could do in the ring.

In the third week of March, Gino made the long trip to Japan, joining a North American contingent that included the likes of Kowalski, Haystacks Calhoun, former NWA world champ Pat O'Connor, Gino's old trainer Sando Kovacs, Frank Townsend, "Cowboy" Bob Ellis, the Great Togo and Fred Atkins. He'd spend the next two and a half months living and working there, and in later years, it could be looked back on as the turning point of his career, between mid-carder and main eventer. His size and athleticism would immediately grab attention, but Rikidozan also wanted Gino to become more intimidating, and in line with most of his other *gaijin*, to work fully as a heel, something he hadn't really done before. Simply put, Gino was a decent, likable, good-hearted guy with a friendly, cherubic face, and playing the frightening bully didn't come naturally to him. To help get it across, he had to look scarier, and so he started growing out his facial hair, before long sporting bushy sideburns and a scraggly beard, sure to stick out in the buttoned-up world of 1963.[11]

It would be no picnic. Gino would wrestle in over fifty matches over the course of eighty days. And Japanese fans expected more athleticism and fewer shenanigans in their wrestling, meaning that the Western wrestlers would have to push themselves a little further than they might have to back home. He made his Japanese debut in Tokyo on March 22 against Korean wrestler Kintaro Oki, another Rikidozan protégé. He'd later tag up for the first time with Kowalski, forming a formidable team of feared *gaijin* giants that would later be replicated with great success in the States. A couple of those tag matches would go a full sixty minutes, pushing Gino to previously untested limits. He'd meet Baba again in a series of six highly anticipated one-on-one matches, never getting the win, but lasting to a forty-five-minute time limit draw in one of them, and helping Baba to instantly become a major attraction in his homeland just as he'd been in the U.S. Gino would do better against Rikidozan's third major protégé of the era, the twenty-year-old Antonio Inoki, whom he defeated both times they met. He'd even mix it up with the mythic Rikidozan himself in tag team matches where Rikidozan usually teamed with Baba or his longtime tag team partner and associate, former sumo Toyonobori.

Gino glowered, he scowled, he grimaced—he did all he could to intimidate the more demure and respectful Japanese fans. Hooking up with Kowalski was a gift: The two seemed like a natural pairing, and Marella's status was lifted just by association. In the press, he became known as Shiroi Zou ("The White Elephant") and Ningen Taifu ("The Human Typhoon"). But away from the ring, the twenty-five-year-old Marella, the youngest foreign wrestler on the tour, was having the time of his life. He fell in love with Japan, and despite the grueling schedule, he was able to relax and have fun, without the pressure and angst he had experienced when he had last toured abroad as an amateur. He became deeply enamored of Japanese culture, starting a collection of trinkets, clothing, décor and other souvenirs that he'd continue to bring back home throughout what would become several tours of the Far East. And he certainly had no trouble doing that, as he was making the best money he'd ever made in his life.

Kowalski wound up winning the entire World Big League tournament, amassing 13 points, while Marella tied with Fred Atkins for third place with 7.5 points.[12] Toward the end of the tour, the North Americans were joined by Dick Beyer, former wrestler and footballer for Syracuse University, who was in the midst of achieving his greatest notoriety as the masked Destroyer. The Destroyer had become a sensation in Japan, and on May 24, 1963, he battled Rikidozan for the NWA international heavyweight championship at the Metropolitan Gymnasium in Tokyo before a crowd of twelve thousand, in addition to seventy million more watching at home on TV, making it the most-watched program in the history of Japanese television. Gino was there that night, taking on the Great Togo on the undercard before the largest audience that would ever see him wrestle in his entire career.

Japan made Gino more confident and more comfortable performing in front of large crowds than ever before. He had all the makings of a wrestler who was on the way up in the business. He was making some serious money. The relationships he was building were paying off, and were about to pay off to a greater degree than he had probably ever hoped to achieve when he was dreaming big dreams back home in Rochester. Kowalski in particular was a good man to know, because he had friends in high places throughout the business—not just in Canada and Japan but also in the United States and, as it turned out, in the most high-profile and lucrative promotion of them all. As May drew to a close, Gino was preparing to head back to the States. He'd left the country as a gentle giant. But he'd be returning as a monster.

CHAPTER 6

THE MANCHURIAN GIANT

*"At one time, I was a very hated individual.
It was my trademark. But it's better than teaching school."*

Meanwhile, as all of this was happening, a powerful wrestling empire was taking shape in the northeastern United States. And as with all great empires, it had more than its fair share of intrigue, political maneuvering, and all manner of backstabbing and double-dealing. It would benefit from encompassing some of the nation's most lucrative and populous markets, including control of what was then the mecca of ring sports, Madison Square Garden. Not only was it becoming one of the geographically larger territories in the business, it was also without a doubt the most profitable—and that was even the case in New York long before the territory had taken its current form, even before anyone named McMahon had ever gotten the keys to the Garden.

The company was the Capitol Wrestling Corporation, but the boys just called it "New York." To go there meant you had really and truly made it in the business. And Gino would not only get a chance to go there, but he would play a crucial role in helping to establish the promotion, becoming the first in a long tradition of "monster heels" that would become a trademark of the company for decades. While there, he would go from a promising up-and-coming wrestler to a bona fide main event superstar virtually overnight, becoming a made man in the business in the process. It would become his home, and the place where his legacy would truly be born, in more ways than one. Everything up to then had been a dress rehearsal.

At the time Gino arrived, the territory included not just downstate New York but also New Jersey, Connecticut, eastern Pennsylvania and, of course, Washington, DC, where Capitol Wrestling had been born. It also had a hold in Baltimore and its surrounding environs, with inroads made into Rhode Island, Ohio and most recently Massachusetts, where a promotional war was underway that would see the Capitol organization take over Boston within the next year.

Spearheading the whole operation, with already more than a decade of promotional experience under his belt, was Vincent James McMahon. A second-generation Irish American who had grown up in relative comfort in Far Rockaway, Queens, he had been around the ring his entire life. The son of Roderick "Jess" McMahon, who had been involved in the promotion of boxing and wrestling in the New York area going back to the 1910s, as a child he'd roamed the very hallowed halls of Madison Square Garden, where he'd eventually wheel and deal as master of all he surveyed. After serving in the Coast Guard during World War II, he'd taken to the family business but managed to exceed even the success of his father. Unlike Jess, who mainly served under the major New York power brokers, working as matchmaker for boxing impresario Tex Rickard and promoting wrestling in the suburbs under the shadow of promotional czars like Jack Curley and Rudy Dusek, Vince rose to be top man on the totem pole in his specific corner of the wrestling world, and respected appropriately throughout the rest of it.

Starting in the early '50s, Vince McMahon the Elder promoted wrestling in the nation's capital, having purchased a ramshackle 1,800-seat arena at 1341 W Street from the widow of longtime DC promoter Joe Turner. It wasn't far from the mid-Atlantic region where McMahon had been stationed during the war and was an uncontested territory, far enough away from the tumult of the New York wrestling scene that Jess knew all too well, which is partly why he'd seen fit to help set up his son there. But not long after Jess's sudden passing in 1954, things were already afoot that would see his son dive headlong into the very shark-infested world from which his father had thought to protect him.

Still using Washington, DC, as his base of operations, he renamed his building the Capitol Arena, wiring it for television in order to take advantage of the mass communication craze that had been turning pro wrestling into a household word, bringing it into the homes of millions of potential paying customers. By mid-1956, his weekly TV show from the Capitol Arena, *Heavyweight Wrestling*, began airing on the nationally broadcast DuMont Network as a summer replacement on Thursday nights. The show was a hit and started getting McMahon's name on the national radar as a promoter to be reckoned with. He was gaining strokes behind the scenes, and the talent featured on his show was suddenly in great demand in other places.

McMahon built a crucial alliance with Philadelphia promoter Aurelio "Ray" Fabiani, a Naples-born violin virtuoso who presented both pro wrestling and opera in the City of Brotherly Love. Fabiani had been a veteran of the promotional wars for over thirty years, and promised to help elevate McMahon into a major player on the Northeast scene. A major obstacle on that path was one Joseph "Toots" Mondt, the grizzled and bespectacled brick wall of a man from Greeley, Colorado, who had been a formidable shadow shaping the development and promotion of professional wrestling for nearly half a century, navigating its treacherous waters with cunning and brute force when called for. A dangerous grappler in his own right, a student of the fabled Farmer Burns correspondence course, he had been, along with Ed "Strangler" Lewis and Billy Sandow, one-third of an infamous wrestling trust that would in later years be known as the Gold Dust Trio, establishing what was in some ways pro wrestling's earliest national promotional network and helping to transform pro wrestling from a mere worked sport to a viable live entertainment business.

Mondt is often credited with innovating wrestling as a touring attraction, with a troupe of "heels" and "babyfaces" working angles and matches that incorporated exciting action and explosive "finishes"—basically everything it would come to be known as to later audiences—but it's hard to tell even if any of those claims were true. That was all part of the mystique and ballyhoo of the man who had been maneuvering behind the scenes of the New York wrestling scene since before the Great Depression. He'd spent some time in California in the '30s, but only in an attempt to establish his dominance on both coasts simultaneously. Maintaining a luxury suite in the ornate Warwick Hotel on the corner of West 54th Street and Sixth Avenue from almost the time that William Randolph Hearst had first built it, he had by the 1950s orchestrated a series of power plays that saw him sitting atop the Big Apple's wrestling scene. This included establishing Manhattan Wrestling Enterprises, an outfit he initially ran with Buffalo's Pedro Martinez until a disgruntled Martinez laid him out backstage at the Garden in 1954; forming a key partnership with Garden matchmaker Charley Johnston; and gradually pushing out Rudy Dusek, who had been NYC's grappling kingpin before him.

By the time Vince McMahon came knocking on his door, Toots was in his sixties but still grasping the reins of power for all he was worth. When it came to Madison Square Garden, he had the promotional muscle and all the connections. But now, thanks to the power of TV, that technological marvel still somewhat distrusted by the old-school impresarios of Mondt's ilk, McMahon had the talent that fans wanted to see. With the wheels greased by Fabiani and Toots's old California associate Johnny Doyle, Vince and Toots worked out a partnership in the summer of 1957, officially incorporating to become the Capitol Wrestling Corporation, with fifty-fifty ownership between the two men. McMahon would be the man in charge, with Mondt as his advisor and fixer. It didn't hurt that even on social security, Toots could still kick the crap out of half the locker room if needed, as he'd done to world heavyweight champion Dick Shikat in his Warwick suite when he once got out of line in 1933.

Capitol Wrestling presented its first card at the Garden in November 1957 and promptly set business on fire with the winning attraction of

Mondt's longtime headliner Antonino Rocca and his young tag team partner Miguel Pérez, appealing to both New York's Italian and Latino fan bases in much the same way Toots had been plugging into the immigrant demographic since the days of "Golden Greek" Jim Londos in the 1930s. The promotional wars continued, but by 1961, the dust had settled and Capitol held full sway over the most coveted venue in the industry. They also had their new golden goose in the form of Buddy Rogers, whom McMahon and Mondt had pushed all the way to the NWA world heavyweight title.

As champ, the Nature Boy delivered a record-setting string of sellouts at the Garden that would forever put Vince in awe of him, but this also caused waves of dissension and acrimony throughout the NWA. The other regional promoters accused McMahon of monopolizing the NWA world champ (which he was), preventing him from fulfilling the full touring obligations of the titleholder that was one of the main benefits of NWA membership. For their part, McMahon and Mondt had grown impatient with putting up with the whole charade—frankly, they were doing astronomical business and didn't need anyone else anyway. So why share Rogers at all? They consented to allowing Buddy to drop the NWA title to Lou Thesz in January 1963 in Toronto, then promptly pretended it never happened—easy to do in those arcane days of isolated territories in which promoters controlled what got printed in newspapers and wrestling magazines. Next, McMahon and Mondt seceded from the NWA, coming up with their own fictional sanctioning body, which they called the World Wide Wrestling Federation, or WWWF. Thus, Capitol Wrestling continued to recognize Buddy Rogers as the world champion.

■

However, by the time Gino Marella got to the territory in the summer of 1963, Rogers was no longer the WWWF world champion. That distinction belonged to someone Gino already knew pretty well from the Toronto days: Bruno Sammartino. While Gino was in Japan, the humble Abruzzese expatriate had become arguably the biggest star in the business, squashing Rogers in forty-eight seconds at the Garden on May 17, 1963, to claim the world title for the throngs and throngs of Italians and other working-class fans in the Northeast who had accepted him as their hero and champion in an overwhelming groundswell of support.

But the journey to get there had been anything but smooth. Although they were destined to make a lot of money for each other, Sammartino and McMahon never really got along, and this antipathy would color Bruno's relationship with the McMahon family from day one. For one thing, the main reason Bruno had been in Toronto in the first place was that he had been on the outs with Vince due to the promoter's insistence on backing Rogers, a man for whom Sammartino reserved the closest thing to true contempt that his generous heart could muster. Bruno had long felt that Buddy was holding him back, that he was a bully and a backstage politician—an opinion borne out by a host of others who lost patience with his locker room manipulations. Mondt had always backed Bruno, maybe because he had been a discovery of Rudy Miller, Mondt's business partner in the Pittsburgh territory. But Vince seemed to view him only as a popular upper mid-card attraction. In fact, when the naïve rookie Sammartino had chosen sides against McMahon in a brief New York City promotional war with old Russian warhorse Kola Kwariani, McMahon had seen fit to have him blackballed, resulting in a humiliated Bruno having to come crawling back to Capitol with his hat in his hand.

By the time he was in Toronto wrestling for Frank Tunney, Bruno had had enough of McMahon's untrustworthiness and Rogers's manipulations. In fact, on the way out, he'd even reportedly let Rogers have it in a brief but explosive locker room brawl before leaving New York for Ontario. Sammartino had washed his hands of the whole mess, but McMahon soon found that he might have made an error. Rogers's health issues, including a serious heart ailment, had left McMahon wondering how long he could count on Buddy as his champion after all. Then there was Buddy's notorious politicking, as it started to become apparent to McMahon that the Nature Boy might just be trying to steal the whole territory out from under him. Vince's buyer's remorse was setting in. If he was going to make this whole WWWF experiment work, he needed a hot attraction to build it around. He needed Bruno Sammartino.

Needless to say, Bruno now had the leverage in the negotiations. He not only wanted the title, but he wanted to humiliate Rogers in convincing and explosively quick fashion, both of which he got. The coronation of Bruno Sammartino had ushered in a new era of dominance and big business in the Northeast. But as with any great champion, he'd need convincing threats to his position to rally the fans to his side for repeat performances around the horn. Like any great hero, he would need a villain. And in the case of a powerful, imposing hero like Bruno, he'd need an especially imposing and intimidating villain. That's where Gino would come in.

■

While Bruno was becoming the toast of the Big Apple, Gino was finishing up for Rikidozan in Japan. After weeks of sharing locker rooms and rings with him, Killer Kowalski got a distinct sense that Gino would be a perfect fit for Capitol Wrestling and the New York territory, with its larger-than-life characters and personalities. Kowalski had been wrestling as a top heel attraction for Vince McMahon on and off going back to the beginning of Capitol and had a lot of connections there. After the end of the Japan tour, Kowalski headed directly to Massachusetts, where he was scheduled for the main event at the Boston Garden. It was a special night because the WWWF had finally pushed Tony Santos's Big Time Wrestling out of Beantown and added it to the regular Capitol circuit, installing promoter Abe Ford in Santos's place. While there, Kowalski talked up Gino. One chief connection was Wild Red Berry of Pittsburg, Kansas, once one of the best light heavyweight champions of all time, now a loyal lieutenant of McMahon's who, with the aid of the pocket dictionary he carried everywhere he went, had also set the standard for the fast-talking, know-it-all wrestling manager. Also on hand that night as part of the main event was Bobo Brazil,[1] who could certainly vouch for Gino, having known him since his very first match back in Rochester.

Another contact was the brash wunderkind Bobby Davis of Columbus, Ohio, who had been a hit as an obnoxious wrestling manager before his twentieth birthday, but had walked away from the business to get into real estate after a falling-out with Buddy Rogers. Davis had been Rogers's manager and helped bring him to the Northeast in the first place, but had refused to keep working with the Nature Boy once he insisted on continuing to wrestle despite his heart condition. Kowalski reached out to the now twenty-six-year-old Davis and coaxed him to come back to New York with the idea of managing Marella, whom he viewed as a can't-miss prospect. Davis agreed.

While the Killer was advocating for him with McMahon and company, Gino was soaking in the sun in Hawaii on a six-week stopover, living off some of the copious money he'd made in Japan. While there, to keep the money coming, he managed to work a handful of dates for the local territory run by Ed Francis and Lord James Blears, taking part in a battle royal and two main events against Honolulu's own King Curtis Iaukea. By the time he left Hawaii in mid-July, he'd presumably already gotten the call from Capitol to come in for a look. On his way across the country and back to the East Coast, he made one last stop in St. Louis for an appearance on *Wrestling at the Chase*. It would be the last time he would ever wrestle as Gino Marella.

■

After arriving in Manhattan, he made his way to the Holland Hotel, a somewhat seedy flophouse at 341 West 42nd Street in Hell's Kitchen. The Capitol Wrestling Corporation had its offices on the second floor, and Vince McMahon was waiting. In those days, McMahon had a circle of trusted advisors and partners around him. In addition to Toots, there was Willie Gilzenberg, the wizened ring sports impresario who'd been deeply involved in the New Jersey and New York boxing scene since the 1920s, and who'd been working with Toots in wrestling promotions almost as long. Gilzenberg had used his influence to help install McMahon as the new boss of wrestling in New York and had fought many of McMahon's behind-the-scenes battles while Vince was still stationed down in Washington, DC. For his role, he'd been named the official president of the World Wide Wrestling Federation, acting as Vince's buffer in an often chaotic promotional landscape. As far as the public knew, the official headquarters of the WWWF was Gilzenberg's dingy sixth-floor office above a drugstore in the Kinney Building, on the corner of Broad and Market in Newark, where he did business (and spent many nights) when he wasn't home with his family down in Miami.

There was Phil Zacko, the squat and ornery son of Lebanese immigrants who had been with McMahon and Mondt since the beginning of Capitol Wrestling. Zacko had proven his loyalty to McMahon by helping him get a foothold in Baltimore, turning on his former associate and previous Baltimore kingpin, Ed Contos. Zacko had since become a crucial lynchpin in Baltimore and was also positioned to take over Philadelphia from Ray Fabiani as Fabiani stepped away from wrestling to focus on his great promotional love, opera.

There was also Arnold Skaaland, a son of White Plains, New York, and journeyman of the Northeast who had become a wrestler on the New York scene after serving his country in World War II, back in the days when Rudy Dusek still ruled the roost. Arnie had been a fixture on the undercard of Capitol shows from the very beginning and was a loyal foot soldier of the McMahon operation who also helped behind the scenes, promoting shows in his hometown, as well as being in charge of the precious cashbox in the Garden and other places, clenching his ever-present cigar between his teeth as he counted the tickets. With an eye to the future, the middle-aged Skaaland had also transitioned into the role of "manager" to Bruno Sammartino, enjoying all the benefits of high-profile big city life at the side of the beloved world champion.

And it may not have been on his first day at the office, but it's likely that, at some point in the summer of 1963, Gino also met the younger son of his new boss for the very first time. Vincent Kennedy McMahon was a brash, charismatic eighteen-year-old at the time, heading into his final year at Fishburne Military School down in Virginia, where his father had boarded him to try and keep him on the straight and narrow. With his primary residence still with his mother, Vicki, in North Carolina, young Vince would often spend much of the summer with his father and stepmother, Juanita, at their seasonal home in Rehoboth Beach, Delaware. Only in the last few years had he gotten to know his dad, who had abandoned the family and moved back to New York shortly after he was born, leaving him to be raised in a trailer park with a series of abusive male companions of his mother, most notably Leo Lupton, whose last name young Vince had used right up until he first met his father in the late 1950s. It was Juanita, in fact, along with her mother-in-law, Rose, who had worked to smooth things over and reconcile the boy with his father.[2] Since then, he'd gotten a taste for his father's high-powered urban lifestyle, and more importantly, the outlandish and subversive business that made it all possible.

But on this particular day, it was the father that Gino was intent on meeting. There was business to be conducted. The WWWF was already developing a reputation for outlandish gimmicks and characters, and Gino was about to be bestowed with a whopper of one. The company had no need of another Italian babyface to appeal to the Northeast fans, as that was already its stock-in-trade with wrestlers like Argentina Apollo and, of course, Bruno Sammartino, as well as a rotating cast of others. In fact, Vince didn't want him as a babyface at all. The reasoning was, a wrestler of his size and power was difficult for fans to identify with, as they generally gravitated to the underdog, and it was also less convincing for such a big man to have to "sell" the offense of his opponents for sympathy. This meant that Gino's happy-go-lucky opera-singing persona wasn't going to cut it.

McMahon and Mondt had already heard all about the heel work Marella had started doing in Japan. They loved the beard and asked him to grow it out even more, in addition to letting his hair grow out just a bit to create a wild, unkempt look, especially in a pre-Beatles era, when more than two inches of growth on a man's head pegged him as either a bohemian or a lunatic. As Gino himself would tell the story, Vince took one look at him and said, "You're gonna be Gorilla Monsoon." There might have been an initial inclination to simply call him "The Gorilla," which would make sense in a time of calling wrestlers things like "The Beast," "The Brute" and "The Shadow." But in the end, McMahon took inspiration from "The Human Typhoon," one of the nicknames the Japanese had bestowed on Gino. It also didn't hurt that "Gorilla Monsoon" had the same initials as "Gino Marella," meaning no expensive change in ring gear would be required.[3]

It was a much more distinctive name. And it was more than that. It was a gift: a monicker that would stick in the minds of fans, that would be catnip for newspaper reporters, a sensationalized name that was absolutely iconic almost from the very start. Like "Gorgeous George," "Killer Kowalski" or "Haystacks Calhoun," it would transcend the business, and in some ways, transcend Gino himself. It was also a sure sign that Capitol had big plans for him. With Bruno as the newly crowned world champion, they needed threatening and credible challengers for their Italian Superman. Buddy Rogers, the former champion, was the first logical choice—but Buddy Rogers was making trouble, and even then, they knew it could be more than he was worth. Throughout its many name changes and incarnations over the decades, the company would become known for developing and elevating what are known in the business as "monster heels." Gorilla Monsoon was about to become the first. He would be billed as the "All-Asiatic Champion"—a rather hazy accolade that he'd never really lose since he had never really won it and never actually defended it. But it would add to the mystique.

■

Gino was scheduled to debut immediately on Capitol Wrestling television. At the time, the company presented two weekly programs—one from the Capitol Arena in Washington, DC, and the other at the Bridgeport Arena, run by local promoter Joe Smith, on Washington Avenue in Bridgeport, Connecticut, where Gino made his first appearance as Gorilla Monsoon on a show that aired live on Tuesday night,

July 30, 1963. Touting the upcoming show, the *Bridgeport Post* described Monsoon as "a newcomer bound to make a powerful impact on the local wrestling scene"[4]—a statement that inevitably originated from the Capitol Wrestling PR machine but nevertheless proved quite true. In the opening match, he made short work of perennial WWWF journeyman Eugenio Marin. Also appearing on the card that night were some familiar faces: In addition to Arnie Skaaland, who wrestled on just about every Capitol show in those days, Gino ran into Tim Woods, the former Big Ten champion from Michigan State, now a fellow professional in the midst of a modest push. Also appearing that night was a twenty-year-old newcomer from the verdant Puerto Rican island of Culebra, the fiery young Pedro Morales, who would begin a long, fruitful friendship and professional relationship with Gino that would come in handy a decade later.

Gorilla Monsoon was a snarling, animalistic beast in the ring, showing no mercy to his much smaller opponent. Despite the real Bob Marella's eloquence and high level of education, Gorilla Monsoon was a mute monster who spoke no English. Violence was his only language. When it came time to speak, that's where his manager Bobby Davis came in. Just as important as the match itself, Davis was on hand with his brand-new protégé to extoll his fearsome abilities and unique background, reportedly the brainchild of Davis himself: The former manager of Buddy Rogers claimed that after Rogers had lost the WWWF world title to Bruno Sammartino, he had gone on sabbatical to find a new challenger to help him avenge Rogers's loss and get the title back. He had traveled all the way across the globe to the wilds of Manchuria, following the legend of a Neanderthal man, six-foot-six and 365 pounds, whom he had finally found bathing nude in a stream. Born on an isolated farm, Monsoon had traveled with a gypsy caravan of wrestling bears. He ate only raw meat and was rumored to drink the blood of his poor victims. Davis claimed to have brought Monsoon to the United States, where he had destroyed Antonino Rocca in less than three minutes in a match down in Florida. Of course, the match had actually never taken place. The point was to put over Gorilla Monsoon as having easily defeated the man who had been Capitol Wrestling's beloved hero prior to Bruno Sammartino.[5]

■

Two days after his WWWF television debut, Gorilla Monsoon came to the mecca of not only Capitol Wrestling but the wrestling world, making his first of what would be ninety-five appearances at Madison Square Garden when all was said and done. In under four minutes in the second match of the night, he manhandled and pinned Karl Steif, who normally wrestled under a hood as the Shadow, but was prevented from doing so by Madison Square Garden's strictly enforced rule against masked wrestlers (his real name was Clyde Steeves, by the way). Gino was able to reunite with and thank Killer Kowalski, who had an easy night, beating a rookie Ron Reed (who'd later go on to greater fame down in Florida as Buddy Colt) in two minutes in the semi-main event.[6] On top that night, Sammartino teamed with Bobo Brazil in a losing effort against Buddy Rogers and "Handsome" Johnny Barend. Rogers had been allowed to pin Sammartino in that best-of-three-falls encounter, with the idea of building up to what was then considered the looming rematch between the two.

Right away, Monsoon was programmed into a series of quick squash matches against hopelessly outmatched wrestlers all around the Capitol horn: Pete Sanchez, Manny Soto, Bobby Boyer, Jack Miller, Gene Kelly, Buddy Rosen, Skaaland, Reed. To up the ante, he was put in handicap matches against two wrestlers at a time, with much the same outcome. He quickly became known for short, shocking victories—a subtle callback to his similar reputation in the amateur ranks. For a brief time, he was paired up in Davis's stable of wrestlers with Rogers himself. Children in particular were enthralled by the villainous Monsoon appearing on their black-and-white TV sets. Among them was then-eleven-year-old Mike Omansky of Upper Saddle River, New Jersey, who recalls another tall tale Davis told, which said a lot about the mindset of Capitol's promotional strategy at the time: "Rogers and Monsoon were in the gym, when they were briefly tag teaming, and Davis told Rogers to put the figure-four on Monsoon. He does it. Davis turns around. He hears screaming. He figures Monsoon is in pain. Turns back around. He sees Rogers is in pain. And Monsoon had broken the figure-four. He was the first man to break the figure-four."

Gino was on the fast track in the most high-profile, big-money territory in the business. He watched with great interest how the big shots in the company reaped the benefits of being the kings of New York. After Garden shows, Vince would invite a select few out to dinner at Jimmy Weston's, a swanky supper club and jazz bar that had just opened on East 56th Street and was already gaining a buzz thanks to clientele like Sinatra, Howard Cosell and Johnny Carson. Although the main business office was in the Holland Hotel, about twenty minutes away from that dilapidated structure, Toots Mondt still maintained the luxury suite he'd had at the Warwick since the days of the Wrestling Trust back in the '30s, and that was where he, McMahon, Gilzenberg, Zacko and the rest of the inner circle did their most private business and enjoyed their time neatly tucked away from the bruisers who worked for them.

Although he wasn't exactly moving in those circles yet, Gino was quickly making friends. One of them was Italian-Canadian wrestler Louis Gino Acocella, who wrestled as Gino Brito, a Montreal native barely two years in the business. Bonding over their shared heritage, the two Ginos would sometimes travel together, sharing cars and hotels. They'd take turns singing the Italian opera they both adored, and Gorilla would talk about his love for the great tenors like Franco Corelli and Beniamino Gigli, as well as the great old Neapolitan songs. "One time he sang, 'Innamorata,'" Brito recalls. "We were in some small town in the hotel room. He had a very good voice. I don't know if he ever took voice lessons, but he could hold all the right notes and his diction was good, much better than I, especially in Italian." As their car sped down the highways, it would often be filled with the sounds of Frank Sinatra, Tony Bennett, Nat "King" Cole, playing on giant eight-track tapes as they dreamed big dreams about their future in the business.

In the case of the bigger Gino, that future was all but at hand. Political intrigue meant that he'd be getting plugged into the world title picture sooner than anticipated. Buddy Rogers had been angling to regain the championship from Bruno from the moment he'd lost it, but the heart ailment he'd been trying to hide from the athletic commissions had slowed him down. He'd taken on a road agent position promoting for Capitol in his hometown of Camden, New Jersey. He'd also finally managed to secure that rematch, which was being planned for the WWWF's first open-air stadium show out in Jersey City, Willie Gilzenberg's domain. The twenty-four-thousand-seat Roosevelt Stadium had been the site of the 1946 minor league ballgame that first saw Jackie Robinson break pro baseball's color barrier. It had housed the Brooklyn Dodgers for a few games during their last couple of seasons before moving to Los Angeles. Gilzenberg had a bit of a history in the building as well. Back in 1940, he'd orchestrated a match there between his meal ticket, "Two-Ton" Tony Galento, and former heavyweight champ Max Baer. He'd also brought the Marcel Cerdan vs. Tony Zale middleweight title fight there in 1948, and two years later, brought in Sugar Ray Robinson to defend his welterweight title against Charley Fusari. Willie and Toots Mondt had also previously partnered up for a wrestling show there back in 1952.

The Capitol trust had envisioned a major crowd for such a hotly anticipated rematch. On August 29 on *Heavyweight Wrestling* from the Capitol Arena, Sammartino and Rogers had taken part in a public contract signing with Gilzenberg presiding. But then things started getting complicated. From the beginning, Rogers's understanding was that the belt was coming back his way. But Bruno was drawing much better than anyone could've dreamed, and McMahon started to balk at the idea of taking the strap off his new gold mine. Bruno was also younger, healthier and worked for less money. Add to that Buddy's lingering health concerns and the fact that he'd become a royal pain in the ass, and the decision was clear. Bruno would stay on top, and Rogers was out. Naturally, he'd be expected to put over Sammartino in the rematch, which was more than someone with a Buddy Rogers–sized ego could stand.

Then, on September 16, with less than three weeks to go before Roosevelt Field, Buddy no-showed Madison Square Garden, where he'd been scheduled to team with Monsoon against Sammartino and Brazil as part of the big build. Switching gears, McMahon put Gorilla over strong in the match, having him pin Brazil in the first fall and come perilously close to doing the same to the world champion, only for the eleven p.m. curfew to bring an end to the match. For the Nature Boy, the no-show was the last straw. He was suspended indefinitely by the New York State Athletic Commission. Rogers associate Ron Reed would later recall a heated telephone conversation between Vince and Buddy, where all the disagreements came to a head, and where the relationship between Buddy Rogers and the Capitol Wrestling Corporation came to an end.

With the big date on the horizon, McMahon decided to take a risk and give Gino a shot to run with the ball, as the replacement for Buddy Rogers. His simmering monster heel push would be accelerated. Fans were told that Rogers had retired and that a tournament was being held, sponsored by *The Ring* magazine, to determine Sammartino's new challenger. Like most wrestling tournaments in those days, it was largely fictional, especially due to the limited time that was left to scramble and set up the new match properly. But Monsoon did manage to easily trounce that Rogers crony Buddy Austin in the "final" to officially be named as Bruno Sammartino's new number-one contender and his opponent for Roosevelt Field.

The newspapers ate it up. Perhaps owing to the fact that Gino was quite obviously not ethnically Chinese, in some reports he was played up as a "Russian"—which wasn't too much of a stretch, given that the Manchurian region encompassed parts of China and what was then the Soviet Union. In this way, the match had a bit of a Cold War "USA vs. USSR" flavor to it, with the immigrant Sammartino defending not just the title but the honor of his adopted country against a Soviet barbarian. The *Jersey Journal and Observer* wrote that Monsoon taking Rogers's place was "like telling a condemned man that the gas chamber will be substituted for the electric chair," but maintained confidence in Sammartino, "whose popularity among Italian-Americans is exceeded only by spaghetti."[7] With concern over the turnout among fans who wanted to see the Rogers rematch, Capitol was in damage-control mode, trashing Buddy to the press for no-showing the Garden, with an incensed Bruno doing his best to bury the former champ: "Rogers will have to wait a long, long time before he gets a shot at the title. And that may be never . . . As long as I am champion, I'll be calling the shots, not Rogers. I don't like people showing up for matches only when they feel like. The fans don't like it, either. They've put up with Rogers long enough. This is the start of a new era . . . If Rogers thinks we can't get along without him, let's prove him wrong."[8] It might as well have been Vince McMahon himself speaking—which it probably was, through his champion.

Ten days before the match, on the Bridgeport television show, the stage was set. Monsoon had crushed none other than Tim Woods in a match that took place right before Sammartino was set to wrestle in a non-title main event. Gorilla took to bullying and assaulting Woods after the match, leading an outraged Bruno to hit the ring and promptly lift the 365-pounder and slam him to the mat, marking the first time the big man had ever been taken off his feet since arriving in the territory. A stunned Monsoon fled the ring to lick his wounds. The die had been cast. For the first time ever, Bruno Sammartino and Gorilla Monsoon were on a direct collision course.

■

It came down to a breezy, clear evening in Jersey City. October 4 was a cool night—perhaps a little too cool, which was partly blamed for the somewhat lackluster turnout of 8,103 (less than half the typical attendance at the Garden), despite the brave face Gilzenberg would put on to the press. There was also the fact that many fans had been hoping for the promised Sammartino/Rogers rematch that had been canceled weeks before, which was still printed on the tickets that night. As fearsome as he was, Gorilla Monsoon was a relatively untested and unproven newcomer in the eyes of Capitol fans. But that was no matter, because Gino was about to change their minds. This was the chance of a lifetime, what his career had been building toward, and he knew it. Face to face with the heavyweight champion of the world, on a high-profile stage, with the media watching.[9] He and Bruno were going to give these people more than they bargained for.

The champion came out of his corner at the bell fast and furious, trying to stun his much larger opponent with a display of raw brutality. Mike Omansky was there that night, just a wide-eyed kid taking it in from the safety of his seat: "These were like two superhumans against each other. And as a fan, I didn't know who would budge! Each one had dominant moments. So we were kind of in awe over that. In awe when Bruno could push him around. In awe when Monsoon could chop Sammartino down." The fans had come that night to see the monstrous villain get finally put in his place and knocked down a peg by their hero, and Gino knew that. Vince knew it as well. But he also knew there was money to be made with these two that could stretch beyond this one night.

Enraged at his opponent's ability to absorb punishment like no one he'd faced before, Monsoon hurled Sammartino into the turnbuckles, causing his head to collide with the metal ring post as the beloved champion tumbled from the ring to the outside. The Italian powerhouse crumpled to the floor, face down, as the crowd held its collective breath. When he lifted his head, a sheet of scarlet framed his face in a portrait of fury. The image, and the blood, had exactly its desired effect, whipping the crowd into a further frenzy. A little old lady at ringside scurried over to wipe down Bruno's face with her handkerchief, like Christ on the road to Golgotha. But the champ waved her off as he ascended back into the ring, both fire and blood in his eyes as Gorilla Monsoon backed off toward a corner, only now realizing what he'd done.

After scooping up the Gorilla for a few jaw-dropping bodyslams, Bruno penned him into the corner and started raining down forearm smashes and punches. Referee John Stanley demanded that he stop, which only caused the incensed Sammartino to lift up Stanley and toss him across the ring like a toy. As Monsoon hung helpless across the ropes, Sammartino continued his assault, with the surprisingly game Stanley continuing to get in the middle and get tossed for his troubles. Finally, the ref had no choice but to call for the bell. After twelve and a half minutes, the champion had been disqualified. He would keep his belt, but Monsoon got to claim the victory in this, their first encounter.

Disregarding the bell and the efforts of Stanley and some wrestlers who came out from the back in street clothes to help break it up, the battle continued for another five minutes. Fred Cranwell of the *Jersey Journal and Observer* described it as "like having a ringside seat at World War II and seeing the Japs win."[10] It was then that the fans, who "sounded like a bunch of ancient Romans rooting for the lions," decided to take matters into their own hands, as they sometimes did back in those days. Some tossed their folding chairs into the ring. Amidst the chaos, one intrepid fan actually made it inside the ring with his chair and smashed it over Gino's head, breaking it in half.[11] With the help of a mounted police escort, Gino was able to finally get out of the ring and make his way to the back, where he took shelter in the locker room until the place cleared out.

Shell-shocked, he cleaned himself up until he was ready to jump in his car and head back to the Holland Hotel, where some of the boys stayed while wrestling in the area. What he didn't realize was that unlike his hellacious war with Bruno, which had been executed perfectly as planned, that final rogue chair shot to the head had left him wounded—concussed, in fact. "As I was pulling out onto the highway, I felt that I had four flat tires," he'd later recall. "But I looked at them and everything seemed OK. That's the last thing I remember. At nine in the morning, two wrestlers found me behind the wheel of my car in the parking lot of the hotel. I don't know where I went before then, or how long it took me to get there. It'll always remain a mystery to me."[12]

Gino hated hospitals and never bothered to have himself checked out. The mystery of how he'd driven the forty-five minutes from Roosevelt Stadium to the Holland Hotel remained just that. Anyway, he was too busy basking in the glow of a job well done at the highest level. Despite falling far short of the crowd that had been hoped for, the attendance set a new Jersey City wrestling record, and the gate, at $23,236, was just $1,246 short of the all-time state record for wrestling. In reports the next day, Bruno put Gino over strong to the press, calling him, "the toughest wrestler I have ever faced. I don't think there is anyone in the ring today who is stronger." Ballyhoo or not, it was pretty close to the truth. And what he said next was most important of all, expressing his desire to wrestle Monsoon again, "so I can prove that I can beat him cleanly." The seed was planted, which had been the goal all along. McMahon and company had given the fans just a taste and in doing so had turned Sammartino vs. Monsoon into the hottest wrestling feud on the continent. And thanks to word of mouth, the power of the New York / New Jersey press, and the far-reaching influence of the all-important wrestling magazines, it became the match that made Gino into a major league professional wrestling attraction, virtually overnight.

Gorilla Monsoon had truly arrived.

■

Just like that, the general consensus went from, "We want Rogers!" to "Buddy who?" But that's how it goes in the wrestling game, and Gino was riding the wave. Vince and Toots shifted gears accordingly and promptly plugged in Gorilla as Bruno's number-one rival of the moment. Seventeen days after Roosevelt Stadium, they brought the battle to Madison Square Garden for the first of what would eventually come to seven times that the pair would meet center-ring for the heavyweight title at the most famous arena in the world, and this time, a sellout crowd of 18,969 rabid New Yorkers paid $58,049.39 to witness it. Watching from the highest balcony that night was a teenaged Bill Apter, who would one day come to befriend both men as the industry's leading journalist and photographer with the best seat in the house: "There was no doubt in my mind at that age that that was a real fight. Nothing. Nothing. And it wasn't only that—the fans in attendance . . . You know, a lot of people might have said wrestling is fake back then. But not that match. [We believed] those guys legitimately hated each other." They would wrestle to a wild twenty-one-minute double-disqualification that night, fanning the flames even further.

And although the hatred was what sold the tickets, behind the scenes, Bruno and Gino had become fast friends, bonded by their shared ethnicity and similar age. But more than that, Gino looked up to Bruno—figuratively, if not literally. Although Bruno had only been in the business for less than a year longer than Gino and was less than two years older, he had reached the top much faster and already commanded the respect of being the guy who drew the house. Gino understood that almost as much as Vince McMahon and Toots Mondt. Bruno Sammartino had given him this opportunity by agreeing to work with him, deeming him worthy of such an enviable spot. It was something he'd never forget. In those days of strict kayfabe, it was forbidden for faces and heels to be seen in public together, so their growing friendship was kept secret from anyone outside the business. They rarely were able to travel together, but Gino would sometimes be known to crash at the Pittsburgh home of Bruno and his doting wife, Carol, which would have left any wrestling fan quite gobsmacked in those days for sure.

A rematch was set for the next Garden show the following month. Capitol continued to feed Gorilla Monsoon a steady diet of hapless enhancement talent. Along the way, he'd sustain the first loss of his WWWF career when he dropped a match via count-out to his old mentor Bobo Brazil at the Washington Coliseum in DC on November 4, in a match refereed by Tony Galento, whom Gilzenberg was still trying to keep fed. But that did nothing to slow Monsoon's momentum, which was further strengthened on November 14, when in a TV main event from the Capitol Arena, he paired up once again with Killer Kowalski, this time to win the WWWF United States tag team championship from the surly duo of Skull Murphy and Brute Bernard in a heel vs. heel encounter not uncommon for the time.

It was the WWWF's only tag team title at the time, and the first championship of any kind in Gino's professional wrestling career. And best of all, he got to do it with the man who had been partly instrumental in hooking him up with Capitol in the first place.[13] Fans already bought

Monsoon as a verifiable menace to society, but seeing him paired up with Kowalksi, whose reputation for evil and sadism already greatly preceded him, made Monsoon that much more menacing by association. But when it came time for that next Garden show, it was Kowalski who worked the undercard, as Monsoon had another date with Sammartino for the world title. And this time, the Gorilla had a belt of his own to show off as well. The crowd had swelled for the rematch, with standing room opened up and 19,706 squeezed into a building whose regular seating capacity was about 18,500. It was the largest crowd that would ever witness the two men go to war. The gate that night was $59,806.82—the biggest the Garden had seen since the Rogers salad days a year and a half earlier. It was also their longest battle to date, coming in at nearly twenty-five minutes. Bruno got his first win of the feud, but it came by way of count-out, which again settled nothing. They had sold out the Garden twice, but it would be their last match there for a little while.

One of the reasons the November 18 Garden show would mark an attendance peak was that four days later, while riding in a motorcade through Dealey Plaza in Dallas, Texas, President John F. Kennedy's life would be cut short by a bullet from the 6.5mm Caracano Model 38 rifle of deranged ex-Marine Lee Harvey Oswald, throwing the entire nation into an extended period of shock and mourning. It is impossible to overestimate the impact this historically tragic event had on the American populace. Setting aside the years of trauma inflicted on American society at large, it took months for anything like normalcy to return to public life in general. People just were not in the mood to gather for public events, and understandably so. The following month, the Garden attendance saw a drop of more than 40 percent, and it wasn't until early the following year that numbers started to edge back to where they had been.

■

But the train roared on. Gorilla Monsoon had become Capitol's top-level bad guy, which had been the point, and he was quickly becoming one of the hottest heels in the business. In fact, he was probably the single biggest star Capitol Wrestling had created since breaking away from the NWA and establishing the WWWF, aside from Sammartino himself, of course—although Bruno had already been a main event star even before returning to New York. Due to the magnitude of the territory, news was spreading through the business, with the other promoters and wrestlers taking note of what was going on. Even some who had known Gino on the way up, before the Manchurian days, marveled at his newfound success, including Ilio DiPaolo up in Buffalo, which his son Dennis would later remember: "Gino switched over and became Gorilla, and my father would always go, 'Madonn', that goombah, what is he doing?' But it worked out well for him, changing who he was, instead of trying to compete with Bruno for the Italian following. It was a great move."

And if the upward trajectory of his career wasn't enough, away from the ring, at the end of 1963, Gino crossed paths with the person with whom he was going to spend the rest of his life. Maureen Joan Hess was a beautiful young woman of German-Irish stock who had grown up on the west side of the city in the aptly named neighborhood of Hell's Kitchen. The youngest of five children born to Frank and Helen Hess, she had wanted for so much all through her life, which is probably why Gino would one day see that she'd never have to want for anything again. Her father, a construction worker and taxi driver, had tried to provide as well as he could, but it was a life of struggle.

For twenty-four-year-old Maureen, matters were even further complicated by the fact that she had two children—three-year-old Sharon and nine-month-old baby Joseph. Like Gino, she had married very young and very impulsively, and it had not worked out. "My ex-husband had walked out," she remembers. "And he did me a big favor, believe me." Nevertheless, being a single mother of very young children was no easy road for a woman in the early 1960s. She had taken a job at the McGraw-Hill publishing company in mid-town and had gone back to living with her parents, which also happened to be right around the corner from the Holland Hotel. For a time, in fact, one of her in-laws had been babysitting the son of Bobo Brazil, who was living in the hotel while working the New York territory. And that was how Maureen came to know Kathleen

Wimbley, wife of Bobo and one of the pioneering African-American women of professional wrestling in her own right.

When Maureen took Sharon and Joey to the playground, Kathleen would often be there with her son, Randall. Afterward, they would sometimes go to the coffee shop inside the Holland Hotel. And that's where she met Gino: "I was not intimidated by him whatsoever—even though when I first met him, he wasn't supposed to be speaking English!" In fact, Gino talked a lot with Maureen in that coffee shop, and before long, they were dating. Maureen had some awareness of wrestling thanks to her association with the Brazil family, but also just from living so close to the hotel and being a New Yorker in those days, she knew the name Gorilla Monsoon. She had also seen enough of the Holland, and the denizens who hung around the bar across from the coffee shop, to know it was far from an orthodox life the wrestlers led. Nevertheless, the two hit it off immediately.[14]

■

At the time he met Maureen, Gino was the top contender for the world heavyweight title and one half of the tag team champions. After their two matches at the Garden, he and Bruno had started to take their act on the road, with a trio of consecutive matches over a three-day period: First a match in Philadelphia at the Convention Hall; then in Pittsburgh, at the time a satellite territory of Capitol run directly by Mondt and Rudy Miller; and finally at the Baltimore Civic Center for Phil Zacko. Gorilla won all three by disqualification. On December 16 at the Garden, with Sammartino for the moment having moved on to Dr. Jerry Graham as a challenger, Monsoon took on Brazil—a guy he was probably sharing quite a few coffees with at the Holland Hotel—in a match that went seventeen minutes to the curfew without a winner.

He and Kowalski had also been defending their own gold against teams like the Fabulous Kangaroos, the pairing of Gino Brito and Klondike Bill, the super-team of Sammartino and Brazil and others. But just three days after Christmas, they would drop the straps to the swarthy and imposing

Greek-Canadian tandem of Chris and John Tolos at the Teaneck Armory, a brick cathedral-like National Guard base in New Jersey that was a regular Capitol stop. Although the Tolos Brothers were technically also heels, they were cheered as they won the title in two straight falls—that's how hated Monsoon and Kowalski were. Mike Omansky was there that night as well, having made the twenty-minute trip down from Upper Saddle River: "It was packed for this show. Because there were good matches on top. Dr. Jerry Graham was being pushed against Bruno, Argentina Apollo was popular, and the tag title match. Back then, the tag titles were a big deal. They could main event."

Two days after the title loss, Gorilla Monsoon also suffered what was not only his first pinfall defeat to Bruno Sammartino but his first pinfall loss of any kind since coming into the territory. With the disqualification rule waived, in a match where anything went, the champion finally got a decisive win over his challenger in Philadelphia, arguably Capitol's second-most important town at the time. But it wasn't a TV match, and in those days, fans really didn't know what was happening in other cities, so the feud could still keep going. Perhaps it was done as an experiment, to finally give Bruno a clean win over Gorilla and see how it went over, while hedging promoters' bets by keeping it away from New York for the time being. Whatever the reason, the Sammartino/Monsoon war continued to rage across the Capitol circuit into 1964, with more matches in January in Washington, DC, and White Plains, as well as return matches in Pittsburgh and Baltimore.

As the two young lions continued their rivalry, into the territory came another exciting newcomer who'd become fast friends with both. Cowboy Bill Watts was a six-foot-three, three-hundred-pound former offensive guard for the Oklahoma Sooners who'd turned down an offer from the Minnesota Vikings when he realized he could make more money wrestling. While taking a sabbatical from the Northeast to spend some time with his wife back home in Kansas, Wild Red Berry had passed through the Oklahoma wrestling territory to pay a visit to the promoter, his old friend Leroy McGuirk, the treasurer of the NWA, who hadn't let a little thing like blindness stop him from making a living in a business full of untrustworthy cutthroats. While there, Berry laid eyes on Bill Watts, just a year in the business, engaging in a series of very physical challenges to NWA world champion Lou Thesz. Berry liked what he saw and brought Watts to the attention of Vince McMahon, who brought him in to be built up as the number-two babyface in the WWWF, partner and ally of Bruno Sammartino.

At the time, Monsoon and Kowalski were on their way down as a team, failing to regain the title in their rematch with the Tolos Brothers in Paterson, New Jersey, then losing to the duo of Bobo Brazil and Argentina Apollo at the Garden in both January and February. In fact, at the February show, the team had their unofficial breakup (although they would still occasionally team), when an angle was shot in which miscommunication during the match had caused the two behemoths to come to blows themselves, knocking each other cold, much to the confusion of Brazil and Apollo and the ecstasy of the 14,764 Garden faithful. None other than Tom Wolfe, bastion of the New Journalism movement and known for his colorful turn of phrase, was on hand covering the event for the *New York Herald Tribune* and described the moment thusly: "The noise is unbelievable. There is nothing in the whole world of sport that approaches the complete visceral satisfaction of this exultation."[15] Meanwhile, on top that night, Bruno was defending against Gino's old foe Shohei "Giant" Baba, who had been brought in from Japan, and whom Gino had even gotten a chance to tangle with once again, this time as Gorilla Monsoon, in a couple of matches in Washington, DC, a few weeks earlier.

Also in February, Monsoon was hooked up in a few tag team matches with a new partner, Dr. Jerry Graham, just to make sure fans knew he was still in the main event mix. Which wasn't a hard sell anyway, as he continued to clash with Sammartino in places like Hamburg, Pennsylvania, Camden and Elizabeth, New Jersey, and back again in Pittsburgh for a third time for Mondt and Miller—all with indecisive finishes. The following couple of months saw them matched in Teaneck, New Haven, West Hempstead at the Island Garden, Trenton, and back in DC. A dislocated shoulder sustained during an eight-man tag team match on March 9 in DC, pitting himself, Kowalski, Jerry Graham and his "brother" Crazy

Luke against Bruno, Apollo, Don McClarity and Brazil, put Gino on the shelf for ten days. But then he was back on the road, clashing with Bruno.

■

After a couple of months of bouncing around, Bill Watts had started to really make a splash in the territory after going to a time limit draw with Kowalski in DC, and it made sense to put him in the ring with Monsoon next. They first battled on April 3 in Pittsburgh, where Toots Mondt was over the moon for the rugged Oklahoman with the legit athletic pedigree, just as he'd been for Bruno and Gino. And Toots's endorsement went a long way. The Gorilla and the Cowboy also met in Bridgeport for TV on April 7 and May 9 in Altoona, Pennsylvania. It was a wild double-disqualification every time, establishing Watts as a major star in the area, and just as importantly, reinforcing Monsoon as still a serious threat.

Speaking of the Cowboy, he was also getting pulled into some shady backroom dealings that would wind up indirectly having a most fortuitous effect on Gino's career. The specter of Buddy Rogers had never fully disappeared, and the Nature Boy was hatching a plan to take back the title and possibly even the territory itself. He'd pitched a concept to McMahon that would involve Watts turning on Sammartino and taking on Rogers as his manager. Watts would win the world title, but then, naturally, Rogers would turn on him, come out of retirement and win the title back. So essentially, to avoid having to deal directly with his hated nemesis, Bruno, Rogers would use Watts as a transitional go-between champ to help him get back on top. And because McMahon always had a soft spot for Rogers, he went for it.

The young and still somewhat naïve Watts was brought into the discussions. "I was sent undercover to meet Buddy by Red Berry, working in proxy with Vince and them in the home office, that Bruno could not know about," remembers Watts. The problem was, Watts and Sammartino had become close friends and workout partners, and Watts felt guilty about double-crossing the man who'd welcomed him into the territory with open arms. Watts secretly went to Bruno and spilled the beans about the plot to discard him: "I didn't trust it. So I had a conference with Bruno and told him about it, but said you can't trace this back to me because I don't want the office on me." So instead, Bruno sent his fan club president, Georgiann Mastis, who also happened to be close friends with Buddy's wife, Terry, to go to Jersey and feel her out.

Once Georgiann confirmed the information, knowing his friend Bill wouldn't be singled out as the informant, Bruno confronted Vince and downright refused to get back in the ring with Rogers. He'd worked too hard to prove himself and get over to allow the Nature Boy to strut back in and take it all away. "He told Vince he wasn't gonna work with Buddy," recalls Watts. "If he put him in the ring with him, he'd kill him or cripple him." McMahon was forced to back down. With the Rogers deal blown up, he had to regroup, and decided to go back to Gino, who had worked well with Bruno the previous fall, and drew well at the Garden. Besides, the Sammartino/Monsoon feud had never really had a decisive winner, especially as far as the New York fans were concerned. And for his loyalty, Bruno rewarded the Cowboy by suggesting to Vince that Watts eventually turn on him so they could work their own series of big-money matches around the territory, which would happen the following year—without Rogers's involvement, of course.

■

But for now, Bruno Sammartino vs. Gorilla Monsoon was once again headlining Madison Square Garden, in what would turn out to be perhaps the most talked-about of all their matches. For the rest of their lives, both men would cite it as the greatest match of their careers, and it remains a part of WWE lore to this day. The date was May 11, 1964. Broadway may have been right down the street, but in the parlance of the wrestling business, Sammartino and Monsoon were about to have one right in the Garden.

It had been half a year since the two men had given the New York crowd something to talk about, and this time they were bound and determined to top themselves. They came into the ring well before ten p.m.—pretty early for the main event, but it had been announced that the usual one-hour time limit for world title matches had been waived, meaning the match would go as long as it took to decide a winner. To this day, it's not entirely known why they were given so much time that night, going so long that two advertised matches had to be canceled.[16] Sammartino had never been tested like that before, and only one time in his storied career would he ever have a title defense that exceeded it in length.[17] For Gino, it was an ultimate test of endurance—as much stamina and conditioning as he had in those days, he'd never been part of anything like this; and amateur matches, as grueling as they may be, never go longer than seven minutes. It represented Gorilla Monsoon at the peak of his physical powers—a mountain of lightning-fast physicality and an irresistible force if ever there was one.

Within the first five minutes, the champion came out of his corner in a furious explosion of motion. Similar to what he'd done in Roosevelt Stadium, he attempted to stun Monsoon right out of the gate, this time with a high dropkick aimed right at the head. But Bruno lost control of the move in mid-air—instead of keeping his feet close together, as is standard form, they came apart. One landed as intended, with Gorilla blocking it with his hand. The problem was, the other foot landed flush in Monsoon's unprotected side, cracking two ribs. A painful injury that makes every breath a dagger, it might have stopped a lesser man cold in his tracks. But with 16,300 people watching, Gino wasn't about to quit, despite the fact that he knew the finish was nowhere near in sight. "There was considerable danger involved," remembered the champ in his 1990 autobiography. "Gorilla could have punctured a lung, but he never gave up. Even though I thought he was more on the defensive that night than usual, it never occurred to me how much pain he must have been suffering."

Referee John Stanley, who'd worked their Jersey City match and was thankful to sit this one out, told a reporter of Gorilla before the match, "I'd have to say that with his weight advantage of 100 pounds, and as the fastest 365-pound man I've ever seen, he could do it."[18] In later years, reports would vary on the exact time of the match, but contemporary reports put it at seventy minutes. To this day, it remains the second-longest singles match in WWE history.[19] The two titans battled under the lights until they could battle no more, and the only thing that brought it to an end was the fact that the Garden, then as now, is beholden to the Teamsters, IATSE Local 1, IBEW and the other labor unions that charge heavily for any show that goes past 11:01 p.m. No one crossed the unions unless they wanted to pay exorbitantly, which meant that the bell brought things to an abrupt conclusion, with Johnny Addie's unmistakable voice making the disappointing announcement to the crowd.

"Tireless to a point of amazement,"[20] clutching his side and bathed in sweat, Gino nevertheless seemed disappointed as well. In a rare breaking of kayfabe, he even vented some of that frustration to the press, stating to Lester Bromberg of the *New York World-Telegram* after the bout, "I had no idea that time was going so fast." The crusty veteran Kola Kwariani, on hand that night as an adviser to Vince and Toots after losing the New York wrestling war, concurred, calling it "the fastest long match ever." And Kwariani would've known, as the Sammartino/Monsoon war turned out to be the longest wrestling match Madison Square Garden had seen in nearly thirty years, since the time "The Irish Whip" Danno O'Mahony had defended the undisputed heavyweight crown against former champ Ed Don George for nearly an hour and a half in the same building, back in the days when old Kola was still donning the trunks.

But whether the curfew draw had been planned that way or called on the fly for some reason lost to time, whatever disappointment there may have been swiftly subsided. Gino had put on a performance unlike anything Vince, Toots, the media, the fans or anyone else there had ever seen, and one that would stand as the pinnacle of his in-ring career. More impressed than ever with his colleague and rival, the champ knew he'd been in a fight: "I walked into the dressing room after the match, and just sat for over an hour. I was fatigued. I never was so tired in all my years wrestling as I was after that match."[21] Many years later, Gino would recall, "It was the greatest match that I was ever involved in, no question in my mind . . . [We tried] to eliminate any possibility of going to the eleven p.m. curfew, and we did anyway," adding with his typical hyperbole, "I lost twenty-two pounds of water weight during that match. I was wasted for three days following that match. It was a real education for me."[22] In reality, he would be back in the ring the very next day for a TV squash match in Bridgeport, only making the feat that much more impressive.

The Garden broadway changed things. If he didn't have it already, he'd won the permanent respect of everyone. From that moment on, Gino was a made man in New York.

All that remained was for Gino to demonstrate one final act of loyalty that would bring an end to Sammartino/Monsoon as Capitol's top feud, at least for the moment. It was time to do the job. At the next Garden show on June 6, Bruno and Gorilla would be matched one more time, this time in a best-two-out-of-three-falls affair intended to determine a decisive winner. The crowd was slightly inflated from the previous month's barn-burner, and 16,781 customers paying $52,178.59 witnessed Bruno Sammartino putting Gorilla Monsoon down for the three-count in shocking fashion, just twenty-four seconds into the first fall. Bruno then returned the favor, with Gorilla pinning him in fourteen minutes and twelve seconds to take the second fall. Tied up at a fall apiece, in the third and deciding fall, after eleven minutes and thirty-six seconds, the champion pounced on his mammoth challenger and secured the pin once and for all to retain the title. They would continue to lock up around the horn as the heated feud was blown off in all the other Capitol cities and towns, but that brought an end to the iconic original run of Sammartino/Monsoon matches on the grand stage of Madison Square Garden.

Also on the card that night, losing to Puerto Rican sensation Miguel Pérez in the opening match, was another fellow countryman Gino was getting to know: one Louis Albano, the thirty-one-year-old son of an obstetrician and concert pianist from Mount Vernon who'd been away from the territory for a couple of years but had recently returned and found his way into New York's Italian clique. Best-known for his mafia-inspired tag team, the Sicilians, with Tony Altomare ("The Stamford Stomper" to his friends), Lou was toughing it out as a lower-card heel. A tad short for a wrestler in the land of the giants, he was a little off-kilter, with an inspired gift for gab that wasn't quite being tapped into. Bigger things awaited him.

Life was good at the top in New York. Gino started to gain access to the inner circle and would sometimes be invited to those swanky gatherings at Jimmy Weston's after the show. The money wasn't anything to sneeze at either, as wrestlers in the Northeast stood to make more of it than those almost anywhere else, and if you were drawing the houses in the main events, that much more so. We don't know exactly how much Gino was pulling in, but we do know Bruno was clearing well over one hundred grand a year, and regularly working with him was an enviable spot to be in. Around this time, Gino began to indulge in his love of slick automobiles—the bigger, the better. The high-toned, sporty Buick Special was first, with Gino extending the track of the driver's seat just to make sure he could fit inside. In later years, however, he'd be a Cadillac man through and through. Away from the ring, his sharp duds painted the perfect picture of a 1960s hipster, complete with ever-present prescription black shades that helped protect his sensitive eyes from the sun.

The press took greater interest in him than ever, and even at that early stage, he demonstrated an ease with being interviewed and being a spokesman for himself and his business. Unlike on television and in his matches, he seemed perfectly willing to break character to the degree that he would speak English, even if he dutifully stuck to the whole Manchuria backstory. "In the ring, he is an awesome spectacle of unleashed fury," wrote George Bernet of the *Newark Star-Ledger*. "Out of it, he is a well-spoken, quiet-voiced young man who does not confine his remarks to business."[23]

Things were also getting serious with Maureen. They were in love, and they were inseparable. Importantly, that love also extended to Maureen's young children. "He said, 'I know I want you as my wife, so would you like to live together first?'" she remembers. "And I said, 'I don't know how my parents are gonna feel about this, and I don't want my kids thinking they have a man coming and going in their life. How do you feel about two children? You're taking on the responsibility.'" Rather than be a hindrance, he accepted them as part of the package. On any given afternoon off, park patrons might spot the hulking Gorilla Monsoon pushing little Sharon and baby Joey on the swings. He took Joey for his first haircut.

He knew he'd found a long-term home with Capitol and felt secure putting down some roots. But the Holland Hotel was no place for Maureen and the kids. This was reinforced in the early morning hours of June 23, 1964, when an eighteen-year-old girl was senselessly murdered in the parking lot by yet another unhinged ex-Marine, this one firing a .38-caliber Smith & Wesson from one of the rooms of the hotel. The shooting took place shortly after some of the boys had gotten back from a show out in Waterbury, Connecticut, and some had even witnessed the crime.

Gino took Maureen and the kids, and they got an apartment in northeast Philadelphia. Nevertheless, it was a tough transition for Maureen: "I was crying every night. I missed New York. I missed the stores . . . And I didn't drive, so that was hard." Living with a pro wrestler was also hard, especially being so far from family: "He would come home late at night, sleep till noon, get up, eat, and back on the road. I wasn't sure I was gonna make it, to be honest with you. But when you love somebody and you trust somebody, and it's both ways, it works. It was no picnic for him out there, either."

In the ring, there was still plenty for Monsoon to do off the steam of the Sammartino feud. He challenged Bobo Brazil for the United States championship he perennially carried. He began teaming with Kowalski again, facing off against babyface super-teams containing various combinations of such heroes as Bruno, Bobo, Ernie Ladd, Red Bastien and his newest road partner, Bill Watts. Amidst the stench of sweat at the venerable Sunnyside Garden on Queens Boulevard, Monsoon and Kowalski battled Luke Brown and Jake Smith, the amiable Kentuckians, on loan from Big Jim Crockett in the Carolinas. At the end of the summer of '64, in Forbes Field, home of the Pittsburgh Pirates, they teamed with their manager Bobby Davis in a six-man against Watts, Chief White Owl and Ace Freeman, the semi-main event of a card headlined by Sammartino defending the belt against his newest threat from the West Coast, Freddie Blassie.[24] And of course, Bruno and Gorilla would continue to take their own show on the road, blowing it off in Philadelphia, Washington, DC,

West Hempstead and White Plains, bringing the action to fans from Scranton, Pennsylvania, to Newark, New Jersey, to Commack, Long Island, to Norwalk, Connecticut. With the edges of the territory continually growing, they could take the main event to new Capitol cities like Providence, Rhode Island, Steubenville, Ohio, and all the way out to Fairmont, West Virginia.

Philadelphia was a short-lived experiment for Gino, Maureen and the kids, and before long, they had relocated across the Delaware River to the town of Paulsboro in South Jersey. There was a little more support there, living amongst an enclave of Capitol talent that included Waldo Von Erich, Wild Red Berry, Fred Blassie, Smasher Sloan, Haystacks Calhoun, Gene Kiniski and Bill Watts. It was also centrally located between Washington, DC, and Bridgeport, where Capitol's television was taped. Gino and Bill had gotten quite close by this point, and once the office finally pulled the trigger on turning Bill heel in February 1965, it became easier for the two of them to be seen in public, which meant traveling together became even more common. This also meant that the Cowboy found himself in the unlikely situation of having to listen to Gino sing his opera in the car. But all in all, the memories were positive: "I worked with Gino a lot, and I really liked him. I thought he was really a principled guy."

Watts got his own trio of main events against Sammartino at the Garden over the winter and spring of '65, and Monsoon was present for every one. On the first occasion, February 22, he'd have the second of two consecutive twenty-minute time limit draws with Bobo Brazil at the Garden in as many months. On the night of the final Bruno/Cowboy confrontation, May 17, Gorilla's match was scratched for time. Which was a shame, because he had been scheduled to take on twenty-seven-year-old Wahoo McDaniel, then linebacker for the New York Jets, in what would've been their only one-on-one encounter—truly one of wrestling's great missed opportunities. Thankfully, they did face off in a few tag team matches, including the first time Monsoon was teamed up with Watts, to take on Wahoo and Bruno on February 18 in Washington.

Bruno, Bill and Gino had become a clique of their own, but Bruno and Gino shared the extra bond of their ethnicity. Watts could readily see how close they were, which could also include breaking each other's chops; and sometimes he got to see when, like all great friends, it went a little too far, as it did one time at the National Guard Armory in Fredericksburg, Virginia. It was a little spot show in front of a thousand people, and Bruno and Gino found themselves in the main event again for what had to feel like the thousandth time. Ever since their string of Garden epics, Gino had enjoyed ribbing the champion just a little bit about the role he'd played in establishing Bruno's relatively new title reign. "Gino liked to pop off," Watts explains. "And he would always say something like, 'I made you champ.' And he said that in front of Bruno's wife, and it really pissed Bruno off." Jump ahead to that night in Fredericksburg, and as they're getting ready to go out to the ring, he did it again. From across the locker room came Gino's voice, in Italian:

"Andiamo, Bruno, mostrerò loro ancora una volta come ti ho reso campione." ("Let's go, Bruno, I'll show them one more time how I made you champion.")

Apparently, it was one time too many. Bruno bided his time till they got to the ring. From the curtain, Watts watched them closely, the only one who knew what was going on. The moment they locked up, Bruno made himself perfectly clear, grabbing Gino tightly by the balls and informing him in no uncertain terms—in Italian as well—that he'd had about enough of his jabs, good-natured though they may have been. The message was received. "Gino was a good athlete, but Gino was not a street fighter," Watts explains. "He would wrestle you, but he didn't wanna be in a fight. And Sammartino was the strongest man in the world at the time and had the heart of a lion . . . So anyway, Gino wanted no part of that. But Bruno didn't brag about it. He and I talked about it later, but only because I'd seen it."

Nevertheless, it was an anomaly in an otherwise harmonious and fraternal relationship between two men believed to be mortal enemies by most of the eastern seaboard. And as long as Gino was in the territory, their matches continued. On June 19, 1965, they finally brought their war to the Boston Garden for the very first time. In fact, Gino had been in the territory for two years, and this would be his first time appearing in Boston at all. After a couple of years of wrangling, Capitol had finally started running the "other" Garden on a somewhat regular basis. As it turned out, Boston only got one Sammartino/Monsoon main event on this go-around, with the champion going over cleanly.

■

By that point, Monsoon was once again a co-holder of the WWWF United States tag team championship, this time joined by Cowboy Bill Watts, Capitol's newest public enemy number one. Monsoon and Watts had won the title in a Washington, DC, televised match on April 8 in yet another heel vs. heel title switch, defeating the nefarious team of Waldo Von Erich and his partner Gene Kiniski, who was leaving the territory after a six-month run to go split his time between St. Louis and the Indianapolis-based WWA. The win happened with Watts riding high as Bruno's top contender, just as Gorilla's initial U.S. tag team title reign with Kowalksi had happened for him—making for another true supervillain tandem.

Unlike the Kowalski team-up though, Monsoon and Watts got a more significant run, holding the title for nearly four months. Two young, hungry, big hosses, they had more in common than their disparate backgrounds might indicate. Legitimate athletes, and formidable ones at that, both had also gotten a strong sense of their position in the pecking order now that they were proven draws. It's not that they were difficult to control, but more that they didn't always have to go along with things they disagreed with. In the lead-up to a big Madison Square Garden semi-main event on August 3 that had them defending against Bobo Brazil and fellow African-American wrestling sensation Sailor Art Thomas, they became displeased with what Watts describes as the "stupid matches" the office was putting them in.

The unfortunate targets of their frustration would be the mid-card babyface duo of Chief White Owl and Argentina Apollo, their opponents at the rinky-dink Ocean Ice Palace in Brick Township, New Jersey, three days before the Garden. The orders from the office were to put over White Owl and Apollo in some kind of disqualification finish, but that just wasn't going to happen. "I couldn't stand White Owl, and Gino couldn't stand Apollo," Watts remembers. "So we changed everything in the ring, and we clobbered them." Scared to death once they realized what was happening, White Owl and Apollo could do nothing but go along with it. Usually in a match like this, the heels' job would be to allow the babyfaces to get their big comeback, to give the crowd some hope. Not this time. There was no comeback on this night; instead, Monsoon and Watts went over in two straight falls in front of a stunned audience.

Three days later at the Garden, they willingly put over Brazil and Thomas with the disqualification finish as planned. And three days after that, they lost their United States tag team title to another pairing of villainous brothers, Dan and Bill Miller, in a TV match on *Heavyweight Wrestling* from Washington, DC, just the fifth installment broadcast from the National Arena, where McMahon had relocated after the demolition of the dilapidated Capitol Arena the previous month. It would be the last title Gino would ever hold while working for the McMahon organization. The truth was, he didn't need them.

And while it would be tempting to assume that the title switch was the result of Monsoon and Watts's insubordination in Jersey the prior week, in actuality, Gino was getting ready to move on, at least for the time being. No matter how great a heel was in those days—and Gorilla Monsoon was a truly great one—they usually had a shelf life in any territory. The fact of the matter was, Monsoon had lasted a lot longer as an effective attraction than most. But in the end, the job of a bad guy is to lose to the good guy, and once that starts happening often enough, the bad guy loses his heat. Gino finished up with Capitol Wrestling with a semi-main event at Madison Square Garden on August 23, losing to trusted friend and former tag team partner Bill Watts in convincing fashion in under seven minutes—the time-honored tradition of putting someone over on the way out.

Nevertheless, Gino had proven himself, and it was understood that he'd be coming back. He and Vince agreed that it was time to take a break, to leave the area just long enough for his absence to be felt; to freshen himself up a bit, make some money elsewhere, then come back when the time was right to raise some hell again. Besides, he and Maureen had their families in New York and had greatly enjoyed their time living in New Jersey. Also, they had just learned that Sharon and Joey would soon have a sibling. The plan was always to come back and set up their family long-term. For the time being, McMahon and Mondt would use their connections to make sure Gino landed on his feet out on the West Coast. A year in California would be just the change of scenery needed.

After five years in the business, it was all paying off, and then some. As Gorilla Monsoon, Gino could write his own ticket. Now when he came into a new territory, he came with the reputation of what he'd accomplished back east. He was a proven commodity. At just twenty-eight years of age, he was in the prime of his career. And in ways he couldn't foresee, the best was yet to come.

CHAPTER 7

TO THE WEST COAST AND BACK

"We had some classic confrontations that will live in the annals of wrestling history... Bruno and I are the best of friends today and many times laugh at the way we tried to maim each other in the 1960s."

Gino had had a great run in New York—a run that had made his career, in fact—but nothing lasted forever in the era of territorial wrestling. Vince McMahon and Toots Mondt had made the wise decision to send Gorilla Monsoon out west, and a few phone calls was all it would take. McMahon's name already carried a lot of weight in the industry thanks to his conquest of the Northeast, and of course, Mondt had been running the wrestling rackets in California when McMahon was still dating cheerleaders, back in the days of Los Angeles impresario Carnation Lou Daro. It was a different era now with the Eaton-LeBell family running things in Southern California, but the two territories still had a special bond, partly due to the many New York–Los Angeles connections and also because both groups were sticking it out at the time without the support of the NWA system.

Gino's time in California would become a turning point in his life in several ways. He would solidify his new family while out there, becoming a new father and remarrying. It would also be the last real period in which he'd spend significant time outside the McMahon family umbrella that had protected him from so many of the pitfalls of the business. Before too long, he'd be back—freshened up, more fearsome than ever and ready to help out Capitol Wrestling at a pivotal time by rekindling his epic in-ring war with WWWF world champion Bruno Sammartino, still in the midst of his historic, generation-defining run. Once there, the pieces would start to fall into place, soon seeing him become so much more than just a valuable wrestling attraction. He'd pretty much never leave again, and who could blame him?

He'd once told himself that if he wasn't making $40,000 a year by his third year in wrestling, he'd know he was in the wrong business. With twice that much time under his belt now, he'd exceeded that amount to the degree where he was quite sure he was doing exactly what he was meant to do. One of the biggest stars in wrestling, he'd make his money up and down the West Coast on the other side of the country, not to mention the other side of the world in Japan and even Australia, before settling down back home again for one last monster heel run. After Los Angeles, San Francisco, Tokyo and Sydney, he'd put his roots down in humble Willingboro, New Jersey, where he'd grow his personal and professional life to the greatest heights of prosperity.

•

At the end of the summer of '65, Bob "Gino" Marella flew out to Los Angeles and reported for duty at the Olympic Auditorium, a gritty structure of brown-painted concrete on the corner of 18th and Grand in downtown L.A. Originally built back in the '20s in anticipation of the 1932 Olympic Games, it had in the intervening years become a West Coast mecca for wrestling and especially boxing. Its close proximity to Hollywood meant that movie stars of Tinseltown's golden age were known to rub elbows there with the hoi polloi amongst the clouds of cigar smoke on a regular basis to take in the fistic extravaganzas. Upstairs on the second floor were the offices of Worldwide Wrestling Associates, run by former California state athletic commission inspector Cal Eaton and his wife, Aileen LeBell-Eaton, with help from Mike, Aileen's son from a previous marriage, and to a lesser extent, Mike's younger brother, Gene.

In the office in those days, there was also the mountainous Jules Strongbow, who'd retired from the ring in the late 1940s and become the Eatons' formidable booker and announcer, as well as Charlie Moto, a Hawaiian doing a sneaky Japanese heel gimmick who helped manage the talent behind the scenes, including getting them lucrative bookings out in Hawaii and brokering talent exchanges with Japan. Ironically, Freddie Blassie, whom Gino had already gotten to know quite well in New York, had been a major attraction for the L.A. office in the early '60s and would later become a crucial part of the front office. But during the window when Gino was out there, Freddie had stepped away from the business and, due to a renal failure that had cost him a kidney, was down in Georgia selling cars—another calling to which he was eminently suited.

Gino was scheduled for an eight-month run, after which he'd head up Interstate 5 to work the Northern California territory run by San Francisco–based promoter Roy Shire. But for now, he located a nice spot to live, a furnished apartment near the ocean in Santa Monica, then sent word back to Maureen. Three months pregnant at the time, she'd taken five-year-old Sharon and two-year-old Joey and moved back in with her parents in Manhattan for the moment. They eventually came out to join him later in September, once everything had been settled.

He wasn't the only one who'd been sent out from the New York office as he was joined by Wild Red Berry, who'd be working as his new manager and mouthpiece. After successfully launching Gorilla Monsoon in the WWWF, Bobby Davis had decided once again to walk away from the business for the time being, focusing instead on the growing real estate and fast-food franchising interests that would make him independently wealthy. In later years, Monsoon would become even better known for his association with Berry than he'd been with Davis, and in fact, would typically refer only to Berry when talking about who managed him early in his career. It was a different dynamic, but it worked: Berry in his houndstooth hat and coat, looking for all the world like a crazed college football coach, a walking thesaurus who used his arsenal of five-dollar words to talk up his charges and put down his rivals in a manner that would be copied by many in later years. Berry would also be there as a representative of the New York front office, helping to look out for Gino's best interests.

At the time, Jeff Walton, who'd one day become Mike LeBell's right-hand man after Mike took over the L.A. office, was just a high school kid and a dedicated wrestling fan who'd gotten a job as a ring attendant, taking the jackets and other accoutrements from the wrestlers during shows at the Olympic. Yet even then, he remembered Gino well: "He was a friendly guy, and he would talk to you. A very knowledgeable guy. And you could see that he knew the business really, really well. And he knew a lot about other things as well. So, it impressed me quite a bit. He even worked all the little clubs. And he got over tremendously."

In addition to weekly shows at the Olympic, the Southern California circuit in those days also included regular stops in San Diego, Bakersfield, San Bernardino, Pasadena and Long Beach. Sharing the locker room at the time was "Crazy" Luke Graham, then the world heavyweight champion as recognized by Worldwide Wrestling Associates, as well as Pedro Morales, both of whom had been sent over earlier from New York. Other familiar faces included the Kentuckians and Billy Red Lyons. There were also the masked Assassins, Jody Hamilton and Tom Renesto, as well as another masked wrestler, Don Jardine, then working as the Butcher, but later gaining greater fame as the Spoiler. It was also there that Gino met thirty-year-old Nicky Bockwinkel, a handsome and popular second-generation star, already ten years in the business.[1]

■

On September 8, 1965, Gorilla Monsoon made his debut at the Olympic Auditorium, smashing preliminary wrestler Jack Allen before a sellout crowd of 10,224 on the undercard of a show headlined by Luke Graham defending his WWA world title against Toyonobori, on loan from Japan. His elevation on the card was quick, and by the end of the month, he was already starting to team with Graham, taking on Pedro Morales and Alberto Torres at Strelich Stadium in Bakersfield. Occasionally, Red Berry would even dust off his trunks and boots, as he did on October 8, when he joined Monsoon in the ring at the Olympic against Morales and Torres. Gorilla began battling Pedro in singles matches, as well as his old friend Bobo Brazil, a perennial superstar in California who'd taken a break from waging bloody war with The Sheik in Detroit to make two special Olympic dates with Monsoon in October and November, even putting Gorilla over in the latter.

Thanks to the wrestling magazines that were sold across the country, Gorilla Monsoon's exploits battling Bruno Sammartino and others were already well known by some of the more knowledgeable fans in California. Now they could see the guy in the flesh who they'd been reading about for the past couple of years. "If you felt that the guy was gonna draw really well, à la Gino, you built him up to the hilt with what you knew or what information you had," Walton explains. "And wrestling fans out here to a big degree, they had heard of these people, but they hadn't seen them. I mean, he was known. The guy was from Manchuria, the guy was a giant, the guy was unbeatable . . . you believed that stuff."

The pairing of the hated Monsoon and Graham was a success, with the duo winning the WWA world tag team title from the Kentuckians at a TV taping in the Olympic on October 27, defeating the scufflers in a best-of-three-falls encounter in which they controversially won the deciding fall via count-out. It had been less than three weeks since Graham had dropped the WWA world heavyweight title to Pedro Morales, and Monsoon and Graham were soon programmed in title defenses against Morales and Nick Bockwinkel, as well as singles matches. However, booker Jules Strongbow saw to it that it wasn't a very long-lived pairing: just four weeks after winning the tag belts, Monsoon and Graham found themselves at each other's throats after a routine TV squash match.

In the aftermath of the team's breakup, the status of the tag team title came into question, with Graham choosing as his new partner the rookie Lonnie Mayne from Salt Lake City, while Monsoon was paired up with another faux Asiatic, Mexico's Raul Molina, who wrestled as El Mongol. The two teams claimed the title for several weeks until Gorilla Monsoon and El Mongol emerged as the undisputed champs after beating Graham and Mayne in Los Angeles on January 23, 1966. They'd eventually drop the gold on February 9 to the popular team of Alberto Torres and another rookie, Claude "Thunderbolt" Patterson of Waterloo, Iowa.

It was a chaotic time for Worldwide Wrestling Associates, with Cal Eaton having passed away suddenly on January 10 at the age of fifty-eight after over a decade and a half of running wrestling at the Olympic with Aileen. By this point, Aileen had become so established and successful in the realm of boxing that she handed over control of the wrestling operations to her son Mike, who'd remain in control of the L.A. wrestling office for as long as there was one.[2] Mike could be a little more stand-offish and seemed to have less of a true love for the wrestling business, but he loved the money that could be made in it. He got along fine with Gino, but even more so, Gino's connection in the office was Moto. "This is a guy that got along with everybody," says Walton. "I remember that distinctly. Laughing and joking with Moto, and Mike really didn't have that much interaction with them. Because Moto was the one mainly that handled the dressing room and [booked] all the shots. Everybody really got along with him."

Like many in the Southern California promotion, Moto had been able to take advantage of the Hollywood connection to land the occasional acting job, most recently on the Western TV series *Wagon Train*. Studios often liked employing pro wrestlers for their unique looks. Gino certainly had that, and he would take his shot, showing up for a few auditions around town, but nothing ever came of it.

Gino still had a few months to go in his Los Angeles run, but the groundwork was already being laid for his transition to head north to the San Francisco Bay Area to work for Big Time Wrestling, an upstart promotion run by the prickly and combative Roy Shire, who was making up for whatever he lacked in popularity with an enormous amount of business acumen and success. Yet another outlaw promotion, which had ousted the National Wrestling Alliance–affiliated group previously in control of Northern California, Shire's company had formed an informal working relationship with the Eaton-LeBell outfit, as the two promotions attempted to keep the West Coast free of NWA control.

As a way to introduce him to Bay Area fans, Gorilla Monsoon was brought in for three monthly shots at the Cow Palace, a sixteen-thousand-seat arena in Daly City, right on the outskirts of San Francisco, which served as the home base of Shire's promotion. The first of these shots took place on February 19, when Monsoon debuted with a strong win over French-Canadian fan favorite Rene Goulet in just seven and a half minutes. Gino would get to know Goulet well in later years during his lengthy time in the WWF, as he would another French-Canadian grappler, Terry Garvin, who was also on the card that night. Topping the bill were the flamboyant and obnoxious Blond Bombers, Shire's cash-cow tandem of San Francisco's top attraction Ray Stevens and his masterful tag team partner Pat Patterson, yet another Montreal native whose power and influence in the WWF would one day rival Gino's. And as if that wasn't enough, Gino was reunited with Cowboy Bill Watts, who'd returned to his babyface ways and held Big Time Wrestling's top prize, the United States heavyweight title, defending that night against former champ, the evil Kenji Shibuya—treacherous heel from Japan by way of Utah.

Meanwhile, on Monday, March 28, 1966, Gino and Maureen welcomed a beautiful baby girl, Valerie, into the world. There was no doubt the relationship was as serious as it could be by this point, but this would be something that would bond them forever. Gino already knew that he wanted to make Maureen his wife and had already raised the subject back when they had first moved in together. Having both been married before, Maureen had wanted to be positive that this was something Gino wanted to take on, particularly the two children who'd also be entering his life permanently. Now that they had added a third, it was all the more apparent that Gino had no intention of being anywhere but by her side. He had kept his wrestling schedule relatively clear for the week leading up to the birth, ensuring he'd be right there with Maureen in Culver City when it happened. But just two days later, he was back in the ring for the regular Wednesday night TV taping at the Olympic, where he had not one but two matches.

Gino finished strong in Southern California, morphing into the role of a "tweener" who would face both the good guys and the bad guys. In fact, after the inevitable split in his tag team with El Mongol, the Los Angeles fans sided with Monsoon in the ensuing feud. Gorilla may have even won the WWA brass knuckles title in an ultraviolent affair against El Mongol at the Olympic, but the specifics are lost to time. He had his final match at the Olympic Auditorium on April 27, losing to Thunderbolt Patterson, then dropped a "loser leaves town" match to Buddy Austin in Bakersfield to finish up in the territory.

■

At the end of April, with baby Valerie barely a month old, Gino, Maureen and the kids packed up and made the trek 350 miles north to the city of Hayward, on the eastern shore of San Francisco Bay. This would be their home for the next five months, while Gino went to work full time for Roy Shire. He had his first match as a regular in the territory on May 6, defeating Ricky Hunter at the Uptown Arena in Modesto. The next day, he'd officially burst upon the scene at the Cow Palace, making short work of the original masked "Spoiler," Vince Montana. In addition to Patterson, Stevens, Watts and Shibuya, Gino shared the locker room with other San Francisco regulars, including African-American sensation Bearcat Wright; Pepper Gomez, Mexico's "Man with the Cast-Iron Stomach"; sinister strongman Ciclón Negro; and Puerto Rican rookie Victor Rivera. Also on the card that night was a fellow Italian-American from the Northeast, one Joe Scarpa of Nutley, New Jersey. Scarpa had attained reasonable success up to that point in the southern territories, but like Gino, he'd later achieve his greatest fame in the WWWF by abandoning his heritage, taking on the feathered war bonnet to become Chief Jay Strongbow.

In addition to Modesto and the red-hot shows at the Cow Palace, Shire was bringing Big Time Wrestling to places like Oakland, Richmond, San Jose and Sacramento on a regular basis. Ever expansion-minded, he had even started getting his feet wet all the way out in Phoenix, Arizona, with monthly cards at the brand-new Veterans Memorial Coliseum, no doubt raising the hackles of NWA affiliate Rod Fenton, who'd been running twice weekly in Phoenix for over a decade.

Perhaps owing to their familiarity from the New York days, Monsoon and Watts were almost immediately programmed with one another, and on June 4, with some handy interference from Wild Red Berry, Gorilla beat the Cowboy two falls to one for the United States title in front of thirteen thousand fans at the Cow Palace. Due to the nature of the win, the status of the title was sent into limbo, with both Watts and Monsoon defending it in the days afterward. Watts would defeat Monsoon three weeks later to confirm his claim to the belt, but the two bruisers would be programmed against each other for the U.S. title throughout much of Monsoon's remaining time in the Bay. Watts remembers one particularly wild and wooly encounter on one of the Phoenix shows: "He hit me with the ring bell. That damn thing was heavy and almost planted me."

One benefit of working for the ambitious Shire was that in addition to Phoenix, he was also sending talent out to Hawaii, where he'd worked out a tenuous agreement with local promoter Ed Francis and his lieutenant, Lord James Blears. After trying and failing to put Francis and Blears out of business a few years earlier, Shire instead went into business with them, initiating a talent exchange program, which was more than welcomed by guys like Gino, who got to spend a lot of time on the beach in between having a few wrestling matches. Gino had been there before in '63 and was more than happy for the change of scenery it provided, returning for the first time on June 29, 1966, for a time limit draw against Nick Bockwinkel. At the end of July, he even got to spend a ten-day stretch with the family and wrestled in only one known match during that time, a six-man tag pitting himself, "Handsome" Johnny Barend and Ripper Collins against the Blond Bombers and Haystacks Calhoun.

By this point, Gino had taken steps toward making his relationship with Maureen quite permanent, obtaining a marriage license from the Alameda County courthouse on June 21. They made it official when, before a judge on August 23, Robert James Marella took Maureen Joan Hess to be his lawfully wedded wife. The jitters ran understandably high for both, as Maureen remembers well: "We were at the judge's place in California, and he was walking back and forth. I said, 'Are you sure you wanna do this?' He said, 'Yeah.' I was a little bit nervous. We got married, and I said, 'Did you give the envelope to the judge?' He said, 'No, I forgot. Do you wanna go back in?' I said, 'No. We're married!'"

This time, it would stick. Much more than that, it would become a model marriage in the dysfunctional world of professional wrestling—the Paul Newman and Joanne Woodward of wrestling, one might even say. A true love story in a business that encouraged anything but. And it wasn't just Maureen who Gino had fallen in love with—it was also her two children, Sharon and Joey, who looked at him as a father, which he would also make official by adopting them both as his own. To call him a stepfather would not only be inaccurate to their family experience but legally inaccurate as well. Gino became Sharon and Joey's dad, just as he was Valerie's dad. And that's all there was to it. The love and care he would lavish upon them would be to a degree that many could only hope to get from their biological parents.

Speaking of the kids, Sharon was six years old and ready for first grade by this point, and so Gino and Maureen knew it was time to return home. California had only ever been a temporary thing, and it was time for Gino to take advantage of that open-door policy he'd established with Capitol. Which was all well and good, because there was still plenty of money to make back on the East Coast. In fact, they might have even gone back sooner, but a massive machinist union strike had put 60 percent of the airlines out of commission during July and August, finally lifting on August 19, just four days before Gino and Maureen were married. Gino finished up in the Northern Cali territory over the course of September, taking his last bow at the Cow Palace, losing a handicap elimination bout against Buddy Moreno and Joe Scarpa on

September 17. He'd then lose around the rest of the circuit in tag team matches, with his final date being September 23, right where he'd begun in Modesto, teaming with Ciclón Negro in a losing effort to Ray Stevens and Haystacks Calhoun.

■

But before he'd return to the WWWF, Charlie Moto down in Los Angeles had gotten Gino booked for a lucrative two-month run back in Japan. This time, he'd be able to work as the fearsome Gorilla Monsoon, whose exploits in Madison Square Garden and elsewhere were known thanks to the early Japanese wrestling magazines and newsletters that were already proliferating. Maureen and the kids stayed in California, awaiting his return at the end of the tour to plan their move back to the Northeast. Also returning to New York was Red Berry, who'd go back to his role in the Capitol front office and lay the groundwork for Monsoon's return to challenge the still-reigning WWWF world champion, Bruno Sammartino.

The Japanese wrestling scene had been thrown into a bit of turmoil since the last time Gino had been there less than three and a half years earlier. A few months after Gino had originally returned to the United States to become Gorilla Monsoon, Rikidozan, the godfather of Japanese wrestling and founder of the Japanese Wrestling Association, had been stabbed in the stomach during a senseless bar fight with a member of the Sumiyoshi-kai yakuza family, dying a week later from his injury. After the unthinkable loss of the biggest wrestling star Japan had ever and would ever produce, his two top protégés, Giant Baba and Antonio Inoki, had filled the void to become the new superheroes of the JWA. Something else that would've been unthinkable while Rikidozan was alive was also happening, as the JWA was about to get its first taste of competition from disgruntled former JWA exec Isao Yoshihara, who was in the midst of forming International Wrestling Enterprise to go to war with his former employers.

The JWA was in need of some American stars, and Moto put together a crew that included Gorilla Monsoon as the top attraction. He also booked Fritz Von Goering and Bob Boyer, two more wrestlers from the San Francisco office, as well as Mike Paidousis from his own Los Angeles office, and added George "Man Mountain" Cannon (aka "Crybaby" Cannon) from the Detroit territory, which had by that point been taken over by Eddie Farhat, The Sheik. The group took part in what was being called the Diamond Series, a new autumn tour that would continue annually through the rest of the '60s. Monsoon wrestled more than thirty matches while there—mainly tag team matches against Baba and partners like Kim Il, Michiaki Yoshimura and Yoshino Sato. He challenged Baba on at least two occasions for the JWA's top prize, the NWA international heavyweight title, losing the first by count-out and the second by disqualification. He even had four matches against the powerful Korean rookie Pak Song Nam, who made his debut on that tour, and who'd later shorten his name to Pak Song, becoming one of the top heels of the 1970s in Texas, California, Georgia and especially Florida.

Gino would never pass up a trip to Japan, but by the end of the Diamond Series in early November, he came back to California, determined not to miss Thanksgiving with his family. Immediately after Thanksgiving, he returned to Tokyo for just one more match. Once he'd returned from that, all wrestling would be put on hold for the next four weeks in order to manage the logistics of moving back home—not just for a short run but permanently. Gino had saved up quite a bit of money, and it was time to buy a home for the Marella family. In December, just before Christmas, they flew back to the East Coast, hunkering down for the time being in a motor lodge in New Jersey. They had decided that Jersey would be a solid central location for working the northeast Capitol territory, just as it had been when they left.

Gino was able to see his parents and siblings now and just in time for the holidays. His young sisters, Rosemary (nineteen), Angela (sixteen) and Amy (twelve) were now all aunts. Lenard and Connie were grandparents and happily embraced all the new additions to the family.[3] In later years, Maureen had nothing but fond memories of them: "They were wonderful. They welcomed me and my children with open arms. Really nice, local people. Nothing fancy about them. Very open and loving."

They were also quite proud of how their son was excelling at his chosen profession and what success he had achieved before his thirtieth birthday. He was, as they say, settling down.

Specifically, he had his sights set on the township of Willingboro in South Jersey. With a population of a little over ten thousand, it was a quiet and cozy suburb developed in the 1950s by the fabled postwar real estate mastermind William Levitt.[4] It was just across the Ben Franklin Bridge from Pennsylvania, and in fact, was considered a suburb of Philadelphia, which made it all the more appealing to Gino since that was arguably Capitol Wrestling's number-two city, not to mention one of the locations of weekly TV tapings. "We came into Willingboro," remembers Maureen, "and asked this guy at the gas station where the real estate was. He told us—and that guy became one of our best friends." They settled on a brand-new, two-story, four-bedroom Cape Cod at 11 Hancock Lane, a 1,800-square-foot home with a nice yard and patio, sitting on 6,500 square feet of land. In short, it was the American dream, all wrapped up with a bow.

And so the Marellas put down roots in New Jersey, but Gino still made sure to see his extended family any chance he got. Amy still remembers vacation trips down to Jersey with her sisters and parents to stay with Gino and see the new place. She also remembers how, even though Gino was so much older than her and living a grown-up life while she was still a young girl, he made time for her whenever he would visit: "Our relationship was good, but I wish I could've seen him more. When I was younger, he'd take me around with him when he'd visit Rochester. Once, he took me to a sporting goods store and bought me a mitt and a baseball, and we went in the backyard and played catch. I was a good catcher, but if I didn't catch it and it hit my hand . . . oh my God. He threw that ball hard!"

In fact, not long after Gino had returned from the West Coast, while she was only in the seventh grade and Gino was at the peak of his fame as the fearsome Gorilla Monsoon, Amy asked her brother if he would come and talk to her class, and he agreed. This led to what surely had to be one amusing day in school, as the hulking and hirsute Gorilla stood calmly in his horn-rimmed Coke-bottle glasses before the stunned group of seventh graders: "He was the highlight of the year! Probably of their whole lifetime, these kids. He answered a lot of questions and put on a demonstration. Nobody ever bothered me again, I'll tell you that!"

■

Settling into the new home and reconnecting with family was important, but it was also important for him to get plugged back in on the East Coast and start making money again. As before, there was a lot of it to be made in New York. He'd been gone only a year and a half, but it was a dynamic territory, and things were always in flux. Vince McMahon still ruled the roost, with partner and advisor Toots Mondt and promoters like Phil Zacko and Willie Gilzenberg. Zacko, McMahon's longtime secretary and treasurer, was in the midst of getting full control of Philadelphia and its environs, as Ray Fabiani had finally decided to sell up and was in the process of retiring. The company had pushed further into Pennsylvania, Ohio and Maryland, becoming more of a presence than ever in Baltimore. Operations in Boston had strengthened under promoter Abe Ford, and the promotion was even adding regular stops further up the I-95 corridor in New Hampshire and Maine.

Rejoining the inner circle was Angelo Savoldi;[5] like Red Berry, he was a well-tenured light heavyweight wrestler, having won the NWA world junior heavyweight title on five occasions, tangling with the likes of Danny Hodge and Dory Funk Sr. down in Oklahoma for years. Despite his southern successes, Savoldi had grown up in Hoboken, New Jersey, alongside Frank Sinatra in the 1920s. He'd gone back to the beginning with the McMahons, breaking into the business back in the 1930s in Brooklyn and Queens on shows promoted by Vince's father, Jess McMahon, and his associate Rudy Dusek, then the boss of New York wrestling. He'd been with the Capitol Wrestling Corporation since it first started in the late '50s, but was down south during much of Gino's original WWWF run. Now back in the fold, he wrestled mostly in opening matches but played a valuable role with the front office in promotions.

Still a couple of years from getting involved in the business himself, McMahon's son Vincent Kennedy McMahon—even then known as "Junior" to the boys—was still spending much of his time near his mother, Vicki, and was in his third year at East Carolina University, pursuing a business degree that he'd one day come to apply in ways his father and his associates couldn't have possibly seen coming. He was also a newlywed at age twenty-one, having married his high school sweetheart, Linda Marie Edwards, a straitlaced girl from a Baptist family whose mother had been friends with Vicki. (In fact, by sheer coincidence, young Vince and Linda had been married just ten days before Gino and Maureen.)

Bruno Sammartino was now nearly four years into his history-making reign as WWWF world heavyweight champion. Capitol Wrestling had firmly established its hold on the Northeast from a territorial perspective. But despite that, managing such a vast territory and maintaining robust business numbers was always a challenge, even with the tremendous drawing power of Sammartino. The trajectory of the WWWF in the 1960s was a little more complicated than is often remembered today. While Bruno had been the unquestioned top draw in the business from 1963 through 1965, in 1966, that drawing power had sagged just a bit. Attendance at the Garden had been trending downward from the end of 1965 to the point that the company had paused its monthly shows at the arena—the heart and soul of the promotion—for eight months in 1966. Capitol's New York TV deal expired at the end of April that year, and the company wasn't able to secure a new one with WOR Channel 9 until August. That helped a bit, with Garden shows resuming in November. But Sammartino needed strong, credible challengers on top, and who better than the man who had lit the Big Apple on fire with the champion a few years prior?

With Capitol up and running at the Garden again, Wild Red Berry returned to the WWWF scene with a pair of challengers for Bruno in the form of Tank Morgan and Bull Ortega—two capable wrestlers, to be sure, but that was only to be a warmup, as Berry was in the midst of bringing his secret weapon back to the scene to take aim at the titleholder. Gorilla Monsoon made his triumphant return to WWWF television in January 1967. Bigger and more intimidating than ever at an awe-inspiring four hundred pounds, he steamrolled the hapless Ricky Sexton on the 12th in Washington, DC, followed later that week by Smasher Sloan on Philadelphia TV and Tony Nero on Baltimore TV. For his return to Madison Square Garden on January 30, he'd originally been matched with Gino Brito, who'd been repackaged by McMahon as "Louis Cerdan" due to the overabundance of Italian names on his roster. But for whatever reason, Cerdan's return to the territory had been pushed back by a month, and so Monsoon found himself in the Garden ring that night against poor Lou Albano, who lasted exactly twenty-three seconds against the Manchurian Giant.

In reality, Gino was glad to be back in the company of so many Italians in the New York territory and fell right back in with the clique, which in addition to Sammartino, Albano and Cerdan now included Angelo Savoldi and his son Mario, as well as amiable babyface Antonio Pugliese (billed as Bruno's "cousin") and Baron Mikel Scicluna, whom Gino had known since he'd been wrestling as Mike Valentino back in the Rochester and Toronto days. Famously a native of the lush island nation of Malta, seventy miles off the coast of Sicily, the ethnically Italian Scicluna had arrived in the WWWF in the fall of 1965 and had even headlined the Garden twice against Sammartino. He'd form another supervillain team-up with Monsoon during this period.

■

But it was all building toward the second and final outbreak of Monsoon's epic in-ring war with the world champion, which would be highlighted by three consecutive main events at Madison Square Garden over the winter and spring of 1967 that combined would draw over $133,000 and more than forty-three thousand people. Monsoon would be the first to get a three-match run at the Garden with Bruno since Bill Miller in 1965, and it wouldn't happen again until The Sheik did it in late 1968. Those three main events, combined with the money they'd draw throughout the circuit in Capitol's other major cities, would help restore Bruno to his number-one position among pro wrestling's box office attractions—not to mention place Gorilla Monsoon firmly on the list as well. The second Monsoon feud would be Sammartino's hottest not only of 1967 but of the entire late 1960s.

In the build-up to the first encounter, Monsoon was given an important win over Bobo Brazil, the territory's number-two babyface, in Washington, DC, on February 20. A week later, he'd be standing in the Madison Square Garden ring across from Bruno Sammartino once more in front of 13,837 New Yorkers. Years before he'd ever get into the business himself, a teenaged Davey O'Hannon was there, having begged his mother to make the trek with him from central New Jersey to see his hero do battle against the hated Gorilla Monsoon. Davey had been following the exploits of his favorite pro wrestlers since the age of seven and was there the night Bruno had won the belt from Buddy Rogers in '63, using his dad's connections in the newspaper business to get around the Garden's strict over-fourteen policy. "We walked up to 48th Street, and there was the old Garden," he remembers. "The excitement and the anticipation in a place like that . . . the old Garden had a lot of character to it, although I probably didn't appreciate it at the time. We had really good seats. And it was just incredible."

The match was a return to form for the two titans. Monsoon was booked very strong, battering and bloodying the champion, eventually tossing him out of the ring after thirteen minutes of action, with the stunned Sammartino unable to get back inside before a twenty-count, leading to a count-out victory for Gorilla. "I had been at several wrestling matches, but it was the first time I ever saw blood in the ring," O'Hannon recalls. "And the place was an absolute frenzy. I mean, it was unreal . . . Gino was a big, big guy. And he was also a phenomenal athlete, even if he didn't look like it. He could fly . . . Everybody in the place was so invested in it. It was unbelievable. You'd see people in tears thinking, 'What's going to happen now?'"

The rematch was set for March 27, but something amazing happened before then. During a TV interview to hype the match, Berry was doing all the talking for his charge as usual but then walked out of the frame, leaving only Gorilla standing there with TV announcer Ray Morgan. Just as he was leaving, Gorilla turned to the camera and bellowed in his best vaguely foreign put-on accent, "Next time . . . I break his back!" Morgan was just as shocked as the fans watching live and at home. It was the first time that Gorilla Monsoon had ever spoken on television.

When the night of the rematch arrived, 17,395 fans—a near sellout—filed in from 49th Street under the unmistakable Garden marquee between the Adam Hats shop and Nedick's orange drink stand. One of them was young Richard Kraemer, another teenage fan from New Jersey whose dad had taken him through the Port Authority that night to witness his first Garden show. "Monsoon was quick; he was agile," Kraemer remembers from that night. "He wasn't just one of those hulking guys like Bull Ortega that Bruno would face, although he was bigger than they were . . . He really showed a lot of emotion. It was a give-and-take match. It almost was like a contest; they would do the finger grips, and he had height, and he would tie Bruno up in the ropes." Monsoon was just too big for Sammartino to get up in his usual standing backbreaker submission finisher, but he did manage to get his massive arms around him for a bear hug. When he finally got the challenger down for the count, the referee counted one, two . . . only for the bell to suddenly ring. Fans initially thought that Bruno had won, only to find out from ring announcer Johnny Addie that the eleven p.m. time limit curfew had been reached. Sammartino and Monsoon had battled for thirty-nine minutes and fifty-two seconds to a draw, much to the frustration of the crowd.

Of course, the closeness of the finish had been booked by McMahon (and Bruno, who had a lot of control over his booking by that point) to maximize interest in the third and final encounter, the blow-off, which had been scheduled for the next Garden show on May 15. Nevertheless, despite Sammartino/Monsoon doing well at Capitol's flagship venue, the company's television struggles continued. WOR began shuffling the show around, dumping it on Saturday nights at 12:30 in the morning—predictably, ratings began to plummet, with viewers at the time being used to a prime-time program.

The burial of the TV show was partly blamed for a comparatively lackluster showing for Bruno and Gorilla's final bow at the Garden. Some also felt that the last-second curfew finish of the previous match had backfired, causing fans in New York to sour on the feud. That might have contributed to the noticeably smaller crowd of 11,804 for the climactic Texas death match to close out the trilogy.[6] After nearly fifteen minutes of battle, Sammartino and Monsoon wound up tussling outside the ring, with no fear of the count this time, as Texas death rules eliminated disqualification or count-out. They eventually made it back in the ring, only for Gorilla—described tactlessly but not inaccurately by the *New York Times* as "blubbery but acrobatic"[7]—to trap Bruno in a crushing waistlock, lifting him off the mat. For the finish, Sammartino kicked off the ropes while in the hold, falling back and landing on Monsoon to achieve the deciding pinfall.

In brilliant fashion, the match had finally sent the fans home satisfied, but at the same time, the champion had not dominated his opponent. In other words, Monsoon was kept strong and could still be presented as a dangerous force to be reckoned with, without losing too much of his heat—the worst fear of any heel. One of the reasons for this was that following the conclusion of the Sammartino Garden feud, Monsoon would be immediately paired up with a brand-new villain being brought into the territory, the devious, salt-throwing Prof. Toru Tanaka. Born Charles Kalani Jr., Tanaka was a judo master and former U.S. Army sergeant who'd become one of the many Pacific Islanders and other vaguely Asiatic-looking individuals to find a lucrative career playing a Japanese pro wrestling villain straight out of Emperor Hirohito's palace. While he was being groomed as Bruno's next number-one contender, Tanaka would be paired up with Gorilla Monsoon in a tag team managed by Wild Red Berry. Each sporting a traditional judo gi outfit, they would, in true pro wrestling fashion, be known as the Orientals—a Hawaiian and an Italian-American from New Jersey. They would remain a top-level heel team attraction, tagging on and off for the next fifteen months. The Orientals debuted in Baltimore on May 20, 1967, taking on the team of Sammartino and Capitol's new promising young ethnic babyface, the towering Spiros Arion from Athens, Greece.

The other reason Gorilla Monsoon would have to be kept strong was that the New York trilogy had, in some ways, only been phase one. Now that the prime market had gotten its fill of the feud and it had been decisively concluded there, the rivalry would be taken back on the road, where it could continue in other markets through the fall, with fans throughout the Northeast getting their chance to witness it live, in those days when you had to buy a ticket to see the good stuff. Bruno Sammartino vs. Gorilla Monsoon became the biggest money-making feud of 1967.

Bruno had by this point bought into the Pittsburgh satellite territory himself, with Toots Mondt selling his points in that business to him and trusted journeyman wrestler Ace Freeman, which may have been why that was the first place Bruno and Gorilla wrestled after the New York run—first on May 29, followed by a rematch one month later.

Perhaps as one last hurrah for Ray Fabiani, Philadelphia got not three but four consecutive Sammartino/Monsoon main events over the "Summer of Love," built around an angle that appears to have been largely lost to time. In the first match, on June 3, Monsoon actually pinned Sammartino, with referee John Stanley "missing" the fact that he'd used a foreign object. Willie Gilzenberg then came out to dispute the call, but the referee insisted his decision was final and Monsoon was the winner and new champion. Gilzenberg's "ruling" was that the title would have to be held up, with the champion decided, naturally, by a rematch at a later date. This title vacancy would only be acknowledged in the Philadelphia market; Bruno remained champ everywhere else. The rematch three weeks later resulted in Sammartino getting himself disqualified, with no champion decided. Finally, a Texas death match in July saw Bruno decisively beat Gorilla to be reinstated (in Philadelphia) as the world champion. Still, that didn't stop them from squeezing one more encounter out of it—a stretcher match in August, which Bruno also won.[8] The angle was such a success that they duplicated it almost exactly later in the fall of that year in Scranton.

The Boston Garden got the match on July 1, with fans there having to wait until September for the Texas death blow-off. After the summer, Phil Zacko in Baltimore got his own trilogy in September, October and November. And there were one-shots all over the territory, including Johnstown and Hershey in Pennsylvania; Providence, Rhode Island;

Morristown, New Jersey; and all the way up in Bangor, Maine. In short, they were milking the big-money feud for all it was worth, and everyone was getting a taste.

Meanwhile back in New York, the rivalry was kept alive in the form of tag team action, with Monsoon and Tanaka taking on Sammartino and Spiros Arion at Madison Square Garden in July and August. Nevertheless, numbers at the Garden were starting to lag again, and by late summer, the TV ratings were so poor that WOR dropped the TV show entirely. It got so bad that by October, the Garden was two-thirds empty for Bruno's title defense against Hans Mortier, with Monsoon and Tanaka facing Dr. Bill Miller and Al Costello in the semi-main. Willie Gilzenberg would swoop in to save the day, using his Newark connections to arrange for Capitol programming to air in the New York area on WNJU Channel 47. WWWF wrestling was the only thing in English on the Spanish-language UHF station, but it was better than nothing.

■

Nevertheless, McMahon and his associates were pleased with Gino and the juice he had helped bring back to the territory with him. He was also quite popular in the locker room and a total pro to work with in the ring, although still more than capable of taking care of himself and someone you most certainly did not want to mess with in that regard. Gino Brito, whose role was usually to put him over strong in either singles or handicap matches, is one of the only ones left to have shared a ring with Gorilla Monsoon in that era. "He was easy at times, and other times, not so easy," Brito remembers. "There were a few wrestlers that he didn't get along with too good. And he could rough you up if he wanted to, because he knew what he was doing in the ring. I don't think he liked it when a guy just came in there and thought he knew the business inside out when he didn't. He could give you a very rough fifteen minutes! But he was still a pro. I forget which town, but him and Baron Scicluna made me and Antonio Pugliese look like champions." Still deceptively quick and agile for his size, he could even do a kip-up, leaping to his feet from a supine position on the mat, which very few half his weight could do.

Away from the ring, he was even easier to get along with. His home in Willingboro was fast becoming a welcoming place for talent working in the territory, and it wasn't uncommon to find the Savoldi family there, or Bruno and his wife, Carol, with their young son David and baby twins Daniel and Darryl, or the young Puerto Rican wrestlers that proliferated in the New York territory in those days and to whom Gino was becoming a great friend and mentor, including Pete Sanchez, Manny Soto and John Rodriguez, known in the ring as Johnny Rodz. It also wouldn't be uncommon to find Gino manning the grill in their yard, cooking up more food than any of them could eat in a week.

And yet it was right at home that Gino and the entire Marella family wound up having a less-than-pleasant experience thanks to what was supposed to be a pleasant afternoon. *The Wrestler* was a brand-new magazine that had just been started up by boxing and wrestling pulp-mag publisher extraordinaire Stanley Weston, who had dispatched his lead photographer Bob Verlin to 11 Hancock Lane in Willingboro for what was supposed to be a feel-good pictorial feature in the fourth issue, intended to be a bold step in humanizing the fearsome Gorilla Monsoon. And it did result in some wonderful, out-of-character and candid photography, as Gino and Maureen posed in front of their home with seven-year-old Sharon, four-year-old Joey and baby Valerie in her father's arms. Even included in the proceedings was King's Ransom, the family's Great Pyrenees, so massive that when he stood on his hind legs, he could put his paws on Gino's shoulders.

In fact, there was one particular shot of the dog looking over his master's shoulder as he showed off part of his gun collection for Verlin. That was the shot that caused all the trouble. When it ran in the October 1967 issue of *The Wrestler*, Gino appeared menacing, a half-smoked Kool menthol hanging from his mouth as he loaded a hand-pistol, with the caption above reading, "Sometimes I could almost shoot that guy Sammartino . . ." It was intended to tie into the Gorilla Monsoon character, to preserve kayfabe even as the curtain was being pulled back somewhat. But the Sammartino and Marella families were close in real life, and both Bruno and Gino were hurt by the depiction, feeling that Weston and company had gone way too far, an opinion even shared by Vince McMahon. The incident severely strained the relationship between the Capitol office and the Weston family of magazines. Wrestling promotions had a love-hate relationship with the wrestling magazines and were sometimes downright distrustful of them. It would take years for the relationship to be mended, thanks in large part to the efforts of Bill Apter, who came on board the magazine staff a couple of years later. But Gino would always remain somewhat skeptical of wrestling magazines in general, occasionally dismissing them with some derision. He was a congenial individual, to be sure, but also someone with a long memory when it came to his trust being betrayed.

Garden attendance perked up on January 29, 1968, with the largest crowd in ten months filing in to witness Bruno defending the belt against Toru Tanaka. But perhaps even more than that, the reason for the heightened interest was that this would be the final wrestling event presented at what would soon be affectionately remembered as "The Old Garden." The grand old building, which had housed wrestling and boxing for over forty years, since the days when Jack Curley still reigned supreme as the Big Apple's grappling kingpin and Jack Dempsey was the heavyweight boxing king, was being demolished. In its place, a larger, more modern stand-alone building of steel, concrete and glass had been constructed over the bowels of Penn Station one mile south, down 8th Avenue. Capitol Wrestling would soon be moving there for a big debut show on February 19, 1968, that saw Sammartino defend against Bull Ramos.

■

But Gorilla Monsoon would not be included in either of those historic shows. In fact, at the time, he was over ten thousand miles away in Australia, where he had been booked for a twelve-week tour of duty. The tenacious and enterprising James E. Barnett, the eccentric wrestling impresario who had been making his mark on the North American wrestling scene since his days in the Chicago office back in the early '50s, had staked his claim Down Under, setting up a promotion he called World Championship Wrestling (a simple yet effective name he'd later employ while promoting in Georgia in the 1980s). The reality was that Barnett was alleged to have fled the country and high-tailed it to the other side of the planet in the wake of a tawdry sex scandal involving everyone from Rock Hudson to the University of Kentucky football team.

In the intervening years, he'd set up this original WCW and turned it into one of the most successful wrestling companies in the world, even if there wasn't much awareness of its existence among fans outside of Australia and New Zealand. As far away as he was, Barnett still had a lot of pull throughout the business and was known to book wrestlers from the United States and Canada on a regular basis—in fact, he'd even gotten Vince McMahon to send him Bruno Sammartino himself for a series of title defenses a few years prior. This time, McMahon was sending over Monsoon and Antonio Pugliese, along with Spiros Arion, who had been there before and was well-established with the Australian fans. Barnett had contacted other promoters as well, with Roy Shire in San Francisco sending Pat Patterson, Ed Francis in Hawaii sending Billy White Wolf (Gino's old college competitor Adnan Kaisy), The Sheik in Detroit sending Killer Karl Kox, Big Jim Crockett in North Carolina sending Tex McKenzie and Fritz Von Erich in Dallas sending Brute Bernard.

Gino had gotten a nice two and a half weeks off at the end of 1967, spending the holidays with his family—something that was always of paramount importance to him—before hopping on a plane for the twenty-hour voyage to Sydney. He made his debut on January 5 with a win over Australian wrestler Larry O'Day in Sydney Stadium, a crumbling sixty-year-old venue affectionately known as "The Old Tin Shed." The circuit at the time included weekly shows there, as well as TV tapings in Sydney and semi-regular shows in Perth.

The promotion was not a member of the National Wrestling Alliance and featured its own world heavyweight championship, sanctioned by a supposed governing body that Barnett had almost vindictively named the

International Wrestling Alliance. Gorilla Monsoon won the title from Italian-Venezuelan grappler Mario Milano on February 2 in Sydney Stadium. He would hold the IWA world championship for seven weeks—the remainder of his time in Australia—defending it against the likes of Milano, McKenzie and Arion. Perhaps it was a favor to Vince McMahon: a thank you from Barnett for sending over such a prized main event talent. Whatever the reason, despite it being virtually unknown to North American fans for decades, it would be the only singles world title that Gino would ever hold in his illustrious career.

Despite that, the Australia tour was, by all accounts, nothing short of a frustrating and uncomfortable ordeal for Gino. "He found that very hard," recalled Patterson years later in conversation with his biographer, Bertrand Hebert. "He was a big man, and it's hot over there. He was not much into going out, and he was completely faithful to his wife . . . He was always missing his family."

Monsoon dropped the title on March 22 to Spiros Arion, who would remain down in Australia for another five months before returning to Capitol. But for Gino, the tour was over. He headed home, relieved as he always was after a long time away. However, his relief was tempered by a health scare that would keep him away from the ring for another few weeks. Up until that point, throughout both his amateur and professional career, Gino had always worn contact lenses while wrestling. He was near-sighted in the extreme—virtually blind, as his friends would kid—and the Coke-bottle glasses he wore outside the ring would never do inside of it. But the problem was that wrestling rings, and wrestling mats in particular, could be very dirty. This was an issue that promoters had become very aware of over the years, and steps had been taken to make sure mats were as clean as possible and free from the dirt and bacteria that could cause things like trachoma, a once dreaded disease of the eyes that had cost a few old-time wrestlers their sight.

But mileage varied from territory to territory, and the cleanliness protocols in Australia may have been a little behind the times. During a match late in the tour, some dirt from the mat had gotten under one of Gino's contact lenses. It festered, quickly resulting in a terrible infection.

Doctors had treated him before he came home, and so when he arrived back in New Jersey, it was with half his face bandaged up. Maureen remembers little two-year-old Valerie crying in fear of her father when she first saw him come through the door. She also remembers how close he had come to actually losing the eye. It was a frightening ordeal that left him shaken.

After the eye infection, Gino swore off wrestling with lenses entirely. Of course, this would have a massive and permanent effect on his working capabilities in the ring. It would be difficult to overstate how bad his vision was, as could be attested by the wrestlers who would be terrified to ride in the car if Gino was driving. Without the aid of lenses, Gino would have to dramatically restrict what he could do in the ring. The acrobatics would have to be phased out; the action would have to be in close quarters at all times, as Gino would have trouble seeing anything or anyone that wasn't directly in front of him. The days of marathon athletic contests that tumbled all over the ring and ringside area would, out of necessity, be over. This would cause many in later years to shortchange him as a worker, unfamiliar as they were with what he had been capable of in his prime.

But none of that mattered to Gino. His health and well-being came first—besides, he always understood that the name of the game in wrestling was to make money any way you could. The matches had been a means to an end. Besides, by that point, the legend of Gorilla Monsoon had grown to such a degree that he'd become one of the biggest draws in the business. The fans would come to see the massive spectacle of a man who'd taken Bruno to the limit. The aura would be enough. He'd keep his giant swing / big splash combination finisher, but much of the rest of his repertoire would transition to more ground-based maneuvers like reverse knife-edge chops. He was still more than capable of throwing his weight around and reminding fans of who was boss, and that was enough, too. He was an attraction, regardless of how much more limited he'd become in what some insiders termed "workrate."

■

He finally returned to WWWF TV in mid-April, making a big splash at the weekly tapings in Philadelphia, Washington and Baltimore, starting with a couple of handicap matches to help re-establish his dominance. One of these would involve a new young enhancement talent, nineteen-year-old Carlos Colón. Brought in at a time when Vince McMahon was looking more and more to populate his cards with Latino wrestlers to capitalize on his programming being carried on WNJU, the Puerto Rican youngster had been in and around the New York wrestling scene since he was a kid cleaning up at the Manhattan gym frequented by Antonino Rocca and Miguel Pérez. He'd get to know Gino well over the course of his next year in the territory, and that friendship would certainly bear fruit in the years to come—some sweet and some bitter.

Back on the scene, Gorilla still had a lot to do throughout the remainder of 1968. Although it had more or less run its course in all the big cities, the rivalry with Sammartino would be kept alive throughout the spring and summer in some of the more out-of-the-way places on the circuit, with return matches in Scranton, Johnstown, Bangor and Steubenville, as well as places like Manchester, New Hampshire and Reading, Pennsylvania, getting a first taste. McMahon even brought the match to Rehoboth Beach during his summer residence there.

On May 20, Monsoon made his first appearance at the gleaming new Madison Square Garden, reuniting with Prof. Toru Tanaka to take on Bobo Brazil and chiseled former bodybuilder Earl Maynard. The Orientals would continue to be featured at the Garden, including an August main event in which they faced the team of Sammartino and the WWWF's newest Latino sensation, Victor Rivera. Apart from Tanaka, Monsoon, one of the company's most established villains by this point, was given the task of teaming with other villains being groomed for shots at Sammartino to help give them "the rub." That included Baron Scicluna, but also the likes of Virgil the Kentucky Butcher and Rocky Fitzpatrick, also known as Cowboy Bob Orton Sr.

Even The Sheik, who by that point had become the hottest heel attraction throughout the entire pro wrestling business, was paired up with Gorilla Monsoon in the fall as a way to present him to Northeast fans when he was brought in for a legendary three-match run against Sammartino at the Garden. Monsoon teamed with the Arabian madman on four occasions, including a TV match in Washington pitting them against Sammartino and Brazil, two TV matches in Baltimore against Sammartino and Haystacks Calhoun and another Washington match that saw Monsoon, Sheik and the Kentucky Butcher take on Calhoun, Spiros Arion and Victor Rivera.

By the end of the year, Monsoon and Sammartino were taking their final bows against each other, and the feud was briefly revived in some of the big towns like Philadelphia, Pittsburgh and DC. But it was clear that they had taken it as far as it would go. In fact, Gorilla's entire run as a main event heel seemed to be on its last legs. Which was no knock against Gino, as he had lasted as a formidable threat in the Northeast for years, an accomplishment that was rare for any wrestling bad guy in any one territory.

If it were anyone else, it might have seemed that the writing was on the wall, and it was time to pack up, hit the road and take the act somewhere new. But for Gino, that was anything but the case. Not only was he not done with the Capitol Wrestling Corporation, but big things were on the way that would dramatically change how fans would view him, and more importantly, would even more dramatically change his position within the company. He'd continue to wrestle, but for the first time in his career, the wrestling itself would take a backseat. Gino was about to become much more than a wrestler—he was about to become a partner.

CHAPTER 8

POINTS ON THE TERRITORY

"That's the name of pro wrestling: money."

In the United States, the end of the 1960s was a time of upheaval and change, and in a way, that upheaval and change was mirrored in Capitol Wrestling. As 1969 dawned, there was much uncertainty. Over the course of the ensuing months and years, a great deal would shift within the McMahon organization. From TV contracts to live attendance to the very ownership structure of the company, big things were looming. And Gino would benefit greatly from the changes, working his way at last right into the inner sanctum of professional wrestling's version of Camelot. If his proven track record as a top heel attraction at the Garden and elsewhere had cemented his status in New York, then what he would next accomplish would translate that respect and drawing power into real power and all the benefits that come with it.

And yet almost at the same exact moment, along the way someone else was working his way into the company through sheer persistence, if not any proven ability as of yet—Vince McMahon's son Vinny. All grown up, Vinny was starting to become a part of his father's business in small ways. But he was still an outsider looking in, as his father and cronies like Gino, Bruno, Willie Gilzenberg, Arnie Skaaland, Phil Zacko, Angelo Savoldi and Lou Albano, and soon others like "The Grand Wizard" Ernie Roth, steered the ship and wielded the reins of power. Gino and Vinny weren't too well-acquainted at the time; but that, like so many other things, would eventually change.

For now, Capitol Wrestling, under the auspices of the World Wide Wrestling Federation, was about to experience its greatest successes yet, soaring headlong into the 1970s with more momentum and popularity than ever. Gino's business savvy and level-headedness—both true rarities in any wrestling locker room—had placed him among Vince McMahon's most favored and trusted individuals. And that would also translate into Gorilla Monsoon's role as an actual professional wrestler changing quite drastically, including a shift to the once unthinkable: becoming one of the "good guys." After all, it's easier to just play yourself, rather than playing a fictional character, when you also have to worry about helping to run the company as part-owner.

However, at the start of 1969, Gorilla Monsoon was still one of the WWWF's most fearsome villains, even if his most effective years in that role were already behind him. He made his final runs at Bruno Sammartino's world title through the winter, off the beaten path in places like Trenton and Scranton, with what would turn out to be their final WWWF championship match taking place March 18 up in Portland, Maine. He was also paired back up with his former championship tag team partner Killer Kowalski, who had returned to the territory and would soon help to facilitate the plan to turn Gorilla Monsoon "babyface."

In fact, the earliest tease of any kind of change for Monsoon occurred during the main event at Madison Square Garden on January 27, 1969, in which Monsoon and Kowalski were facing Sammartino and Victor Rivera in a best-of-three-falls affair. Kowalski was being set up for a run at Bruno's title, and Rivera was in the midst of a hot babyface push, which could be seen by the result, where Monsoon pinned Rivera in the opening fall, then Rivera returned the favor on Monsoon, and then the Killer actually scored a pinfall over Bruno in the final, deciding fall. On the way to that finish,

Monsoon and Kowalski crossed signals as they had during their earlier Garden run years earlier, resulting in some dissension between the two heels. The same result occurred soon after in Boston and Philadelphia. With Kowalski being prepped for another run at Sammartino, it was clear where they were going with Gorilla. The waters were being tested.

In fact, in Philadelphia on March 22, in what would be Gorilla's last match in the Northeast for almost half a year, the tension between the two terrors came to a boil when they actually faced off one-on-one in the ring. Gino did the honors for Walter that night, as was customary from wrestlers taking a break from the territory—not to mention that a win over Gorilla Monsoon would be the ultimate feather in Kowalski's cap if he was going to be positioned again as a serious threat to the world champion. As he had in 1965, Gorilla Monsoon once again needed a freshening-up—but this time it would be a much more drastic one. In some ways, it was the end of an era. Much would happen while Gino was away through the spring and summer of '69, and there would be no turning back—not that he'd want to.

■

For now, he was headed to Japan for another tour, after which he planned to temporarily relocate his family to Hawaii for the summer for an extended work vacation. After spending some time at home in New Jersey, then making the big trip over to Asia, he joined a group of foreign wrestlers that included his old friend Bobo Brazil; a crew out of Los Angeles that featured Tom Andrews, Pepper Gomez, Yugoslavian-American Chris Markoff and the masked Chicano tag team Los Medicos;[1] as well as Cowboy Bobby Duncum from the Florida office. They were all there to take part in the eleventh annual edition of the World League, the JWA's most prestigious annual tournament, which pitted *gaijin* against native Japanese stars. Gino was thrilled to be reunited with Brazil, as can be witnessed in surviving film footage that shows the two taking questions from the Japanese press, Gino wearing his jet-black prescription shades to protect his eyes from the flashbulbs.

He was also reunited with JWA headliner Giant Baba, whom he dealt a rare defeat in his first match of the tour on April 5 in Tokyo. Antonio Inoki, who had also risen to become one of the JWA's major superstars, faced Gorilla twice in singles competition, coming out on top in their initial April 16 encounter in Osaka, then losing to Monsoon in their April 25 rematch. Baba and Inoki formed Japan's ultimate main event tag team at the time, and the duo even battled Monsoon and Brazil on two occasions during the tour, going to a double-disqualification on April 17 in Hyogo and defeating the *gaijin* super-duo on May 5 in Fukuoka. Monsoon faced a wide array of Japan's best during the tour, including another rising star, Seiji Sakaguchi, whom he wrestled four different times in the round robin tournament. By the end, he came in third place among *gaijin* in the World League tournament and fourth place overall. Brazil and Markoff made it as far as the semifinals, while Inoki walked away with the top prize that year, much to the delight of the Japanese.

Maureen and the children missed Gino terribly during the six weeks he was away in Japan, and in June, were thrilled to join him in Hawaii, where they would spend the next three months living near the beach, the longest time they would ever spend away from their New Jersey home. It was a leisurely existence, with Gino having to work only a handful of matches for Hawaiian promoter Ed Francis while his family enjoyed their time basking in the tropical sun—a far cry from the urban Manhattan existence to which Maureen was most accustomed ("What a lazy way of life!" as she'd describe it). Nick Bockwinkel knew that way of life well, as he'd already been there since the previous October and was in the midst of a year-long residency, still a year and a half away from joining Verne Gagne's AWA, where he'd spend the remainder of his career as one of the industry's elite stars. Gino was also able to catch up with Pedro Morales, who'd been making a major name for himself out on the West Coast since leaving the WWWF some four years earlier. In fact, the last of the eleven known matches Gorilla had out in Hawaii that summer saw him challenge Pedro for the North American championship, the top prize in the territory.[2] The working relationship between Ed Francis and San Francisco's Roy Shire even allowed Gino and Pedro to hop on a plane and do a quick one-off at the Cow Palace on August 9, with Gino taking on Klondike Bill while Pedro challenged Pat Patterson for the United States heavyweight title.

■

Meanwhile, there was a whole lot going on back home while the Marellas were away that summer. On June 4, WNJU Channel 47 switched *Heavyweight Wrestling from Washington* from its plum Saturday night time slot to Wednesday afternoons, which proved disastrous for live attendance. The June 30 show at Madison Square Garden, featuring Sammartino defending the title against Michigan high school gym teacher Jim Myers—who went by the name of George "The Animal" Steele—drew only 5,527 fans to the Garden's hallowed halls. It was the smallest crowd for the arena since McMahon had started promoting there and an all-time low for the company in that building that would not be equaled for the next twenty-five years. It got so bad that the July show was canceled altogether, and shows for August and September were not even booked. It was a rough summer, and things didn't turn around until WNJU finally agreed to put Capitol Wrestling back on Saturday nights with a brand-new show starting August 30. *Wrestling from Philadelphia*, later known as *Championship Wrestling*, was also the first WWWF program to broadcast in color.

Pittsburgh newsman and popular TV personality Bill "Chilly Billy" Cardille, long the commentator for the Steel City's *Studio Wrestling* program, was brought in to serve as the amiable host of the new show. The ring announcer would be none other than the younger Vince McMahon, making his first official appearance in his father's promotion. Vinny and Linda had just graduated East Carolina University, and Linda was pregnant with their son, Shane. Leaving North Carolina for good, they had moved up to Gaithersburg, Maryland to be close to Vince and Juanita. Vinny was struggling. He'd just graduated by the skin of his teeth, begging his professors to edge him past the required 2.0 GPA needed to get him out the door. Attempting to put his business degree to decent use, he became a traveling salesman, hawking adding machines, paper cups and ice cream cones, while Linda attempted to help make ends meet, working as an assistant in a law office. What Vinny truly loved was his dad's business—he'd been in love with it since he was a teenager—but the problem was that his dad didn't want him to be any part of it. The ring announcing gig was meant to be a way to shut Vinny up, but what it turned into was a foot in the door.

That wasn't all that Vince McMahon the elder had on his plate that tumultuous summer. In June, the crusty and grizzled seventy-five-year-old Toots Mondt, his trusted advisor and partner for the past decade, decided it was finally time to retire after fifty-seven years in the business and wanted out. Toots owned half of Capitol's one thousand shares, so now Vince had to find someone to buy him out. The first choice was Bruno Sammartino, who had been almost single-handedly buoying the fortunes of the Capitol Wrestling Corporation for the past six years in his role as the indomitable world champion and top draw. The idea of cutting in the headliner for a piece of the action was nothing new in pro wrestling. Ed McLemore had just done it in Dallas with Fritz Von Erich, as had Cowboy Luttrall with Eddie Graham in Florida and Bob Geigel with Pat O'Connor in Kansas City. In addition to a reward for services rendered, it was a good way to keep your top attraction loyal and make sure they stuck around.

However, Bruno had always kept the boss at arm's length. He and McMahon had never quite seen eye to eye, going back to the early '60s, when the old man had blacklisted him. From the beginning, their relationship had been a mutually beneficial one of convenience. Sammartino did business with Vince McMahon, he respected Vince McMahon, but he never trusted Vince McMahon. More than most wrestlers then and now, Bruno was always keen to look out for his own interests first, because he knew no promoter ever would. Before he accepted any kind of deal, he insisted on having everything looked over by lawyers and accountants. McMahon balked at the idea of bringing outsiders into the situation, and so Sammartino rejected the offer.

McMahon and Mondt decided instead to split the shares. Half of Toots's shares, or 25 percent ownership of the company, would go to the loyal and faithful Phil Zacko, who had been one of Capitol's top promoters of record and the point man at television tapings since the founding of the organization. "Phil was also the treasurer, so you had to keep the money guy happy," remembered the younger Vince McMahon of the deal his father made, in a 2003 interview with the author. For the other half of the shares, Vince Sr. had considered Red Berry, another crucial member of the front office and a man with over three decades of experience. At sixty-two years of age, he wasn't much older than Zacko, but his health was failing, and a heart condition was prompting him to retire from the business himself and head back home to his Kansas ranch.[3]

It was Sammartino who suggested his good friend and *paisan* Bob Marella for the other 25 percent, and McMahon and Mondt quickly agreed that it was a terrific idea. Gino was young and vital, only thirty-two years of age. Unlike many of the boys, he had a great head on his shoulders. He was college-educated, which was also very rare for a wrestler in those days. In his dealings with McMahon, he had always shown a great head for the business, both the promoting side of things and the booking side of things. He had demonstrated loyalty, homesteading in the territory for years, and with a family settled down and a home bought and paid for in the area, he didn't look to be going anywhere. The boys all respected him. It didn't hurt that he was six foot six, over four hundred pounds, and knew how to take care of himself in a physical situation if called upon to do so. The choice seemed obvious. It was right in front of their faces.

■

The Marellas returned home at the beginning of September, at which point the offer was made to Gino. He quickly accepted. "I think they knew he was loyal," explained Maureen. "That was the most important thing in this business. He wouldn't go behind their back and do things. He was lucky that he got that."

"Gino got along better with Vince than Bruno did," remembers Bill Watts. "He had no reason not to. There was no nefarious scheme that would affect him, so he just went along. It was a great business decision. It was a good thing for Gino, who had Bruno's approval."

Just two days before the deal was finalized, Charley Johnston, the official promoter and matchmaker for Madison Square Garden, who had been working with McMahon to book talent at the arena for years, and the last of the four Johnston brothers who had had a hand in boxing and wrestling at the Garden for decades, passed away at the age of seventy-four. That meant, after more than a decade of wrangling, Vince McMahon finally found himself the one and only uncontested promoter of pro wrestling at Madison Square Garden, fully consolidating his power as grappling boss of New York City. More than ever, it was crucial to nail down the ownership structure of the CWC.

On September 18, 1969, either at the Washington, DC, offices of Capitol at 1332 I Street NW or backstage at the Washington Coliseum where that day's television taping was being held, Vince McMahon and Toots Mondt sat down with Phil Zacko and Bob Marella and put pen to paper. For the purchase price of $24,400, Marella and Zacko now each owned 250 common stock shares of the Capitol Wrestling Corporation, or one-quarter interest in the company ("twenty-five points"). Per the deal, starting October 15, they would each make monthly payments to Mondt of $203.33, interest-free, for a duration of ten years. Zacko would remain as treasurer and secretary, while Marella would replace Mondt as vice president of the CWC, second-in-command to McMahon himself.

"The guy was very sharp," remembers Gino Brito, who was splitting his time back then between Capitol and the Montreal territory run by Johnny Rougeau and Bob "Legs" Langevin. "He could read somebody pretty good; he knew his business. People respected him because besides being big and strong, he wasn't dumb. He brought a lot to the business. Vince McMahon the father must have seen that in him. And so, they brought him in. He wasn't just a yes man, you know what I mean? He wasn't afraid to give his opinion about anything."

Not even four months past his thirty-second birthday, Gino owned a sizeable chunk of the most high-profile, lucrative wrestling company in the business. It was an entry into a whole different echelon of the industry. He still carried himself as one of the boys—and always would—but he was more than that now. He was part of the office. It meant invitations to dinner at Jimmy Weston's after a Garden show; it meant an office at Capitol's headquarters at the Holland Hotel; it meant access to that luxury suite at the Warwick Hotel that Toots Mondt had also passed on to the corporation after he and his wife, Alda, packed up their apartment in Jackson Heights, Queens, and moved out to St. Louis to care for Alda's ailing mother.[4] Gino was now amongst the inner circle.

And most importantly, it wasn't some honorary title. There were real responsibilities that came with his new position, which he was expected to fulfill. First and foremost would be that new TV show in Philadelphia. While Zacko was the promoter of record, with his name on the license as far as the state athletic commission was concerned, Gino would be the one actually running the show on a weekly basis and calling the shots at the behest of Vince. It would be Gino's first taste of essentially producing television, making sure everyone hit their time cues, was ready to go out to the ring, knew when to wrap things up, understood all the high spots, angles and finishes. He'd even have a hand in determining those angles and finishes, assisting McMahon in booking the undercards especially, conferring with Vince and Bruno on the main event programs that would be counted on to pack in the fans at arenas all across the circuit and would typically be booked out ten months to a year in advance. "You could tell that along the way he gained a lot of power with the office," Brito recalls. "He knew what the wrestling game was. He could read the guys that would get over and draw you money or not. Vince McMahon was the promoter, but he had never wrestled. Sometimes he had to rely on a guy like Monsoon to tell him, yeah, that guy can make it, that guy can draw you money, he's got charisma and all that. That's what Monsoon brought to the office."

In addition to the television tapings, Gino also got his own towns to run. Capitol Wrestling was run almost like a miniature version of the National Wrestling Alliance in those days, stretching out across the entire northeastern United States. Vince McMahon was the boss of all bosses, but different guys held sway over different parts of the territory, using WWWF-booked talent and relying on the TV angles and storylines to drum up interest.

Gilzenberg had Newark and other parts of North Jersey, for example; Skaaland was given White Plains to run; Zacko had Baltimore and Philadelphia; Abe Ford had Boston (for the time being). As part of his deal, Gino was given South Jersey, right in his own backyard, as well as Delaware and some towns in eastern Pennsylvania. Those areas would be his to promote, a revenue stream that would live or die based on his own business acumen and natural instincts.

There was also another role that came with the job. In those days, many promoters, especially those who were not former wrestlers themselves, would have an enforcer in the locker room, sometimes referred to as a "policeman." This would typically be an intimidating wrestler with legitimate wrestling skill, who made sure everyone stayed in line. He might be called upon to test a newcomer in the ring, to make sure he was going to do business; he might on occasion be called upon to discipline someone in the ring who had run afoul of the promotion, to give them what was sometimes called a "receipt." Or maybe he might be someone whose very presence in the locker room was enough to keep people in line when needed, settle locker room disputes and even make sure that notoriously disgruntled wrestlers would never even think of putting their hands on the boss. All of that fell under Gino's purview. In short, he was someone not to be messed with. And the greatest testament to how much respect (and maybe fear) Gino inspired was the fact that he was very rarely, if ever, even tested in that regard. His being there was enough.

McMahon held him in such high regard, in fact, that he had begun to look at him as someone who might take over his own shares in the company someday and become the boss if and when he ever decided to step down. Many wrestlers had transitioned into becoming promoters, and the ones who combined genuine wrestling knowledge and insight with genuine business know-how tended to do well for themselves. It wouldn't have been unprecedented. He had all the tools to thrive if ever called upon to do that and stood out from the rest of the boys for much more than his size. "My dad really had some high hopes for Gorilla to succeed him," confirmed the younger Vince, then just a twenty-four-year-old ring announcer forbidden from even setting foot in the locker room.[5] Jeff Walton, assistant to promoter Mike LeBell in Los Angeles, also remembers hearing the rumor: "Mike was talking to me and he was saying, it looks like Gino's going to be the number-one guy once Senior gets out of it. And I said, that's a great idea."

"Some guys just went there to wrestle, pick up their pay and go home and that was it," explains Gino Brito. "That was our business being a wrestler. Him, he went beyond that. And it paid off for him."

As part of his job running the television in Philadelphia, Gino took up a regular position at a fold-out table located right behind the curtain, making him the last person wrestlers would see on their way to the ring and the first person they would see when they came back. For the rigidly timed tapings, it was a crucial role. He was the one who would brief the wrestlers on their matches and their time, make sure everything was running smoothly, and certainly let a guy know if he'd stunk up the joint as soon as he got back through that curtain. In the days before headsets, he would give visual or sometimes verbal cues to the timekeepers, referees, ring announcers and wrestlers from his position. They would watch him from the ring for any of these cues. Sometimes wrestlers and refs might be signaled to "go home"—or end the match—by a simple gesture like Gino taking off his glasses. And if they didn't get the hint, he wasn't above getting up from the table and approaching the ring to let them know in a more obvious fashion.

It started at the Philly tapings, but soon Gino would be filling this role at all the tapings, at the shows he personally promoted and even at the WWWF's other major shows in the circuit, including the Garden itself. With someone as trusted as Gino manning the position in a hands-on capacity, Vince was free to focus on the broad strokes, holding court in his office in his tuxedo, conferring with whoever needed to be conferred with, secure in the knowledge that he had someone he could trust minding the store. Sometimes in the past and in other territories, this role was simply referred to as the "cue man." But over time, Gino would become so associated with it, so ever-present in that location, that it came to be known as "the Gorilla position."

■

With Gino becoming part of the front office, a drastic change would also take place with his wrestling persona—one that, in some ways, would erase everything he'd done before and remake him in a very permanent way that would carry over to the rest of his active career. It was pretty rare in those days for good guys to turn bad, and even more rare for bad guys to turn good. But Gorilla Monsoon was about to do exactly that. The reasons were fairly obvious. For one thing, with him now taking long-term residence in the territory as an officer, it would be next to impossible to preserve his heel heat forever—and Gino had no intention of slipping down the card to become a jobber. He certainly didn't want to give up those big-match paydays that he'd gotten used to and that his proven ability as a draw had made possible. He wanted to stay in the mix, maybe no longer in the title picture, since only heels got title shots against the long-term babyface champ, but at or near the top as an attraction. To do that, he'd need to court the good graces of the fans. Top babyfaces had a much longer shelf life. With so much more on his plate now running television and fulfilling other duties, he no longer wanted to have to carry the heavy load of working the top program anymore; but as a heel, if he wasn't in the main event, his ability to draw money would become limited fast. Much less of a problem as a face. "Berry had retired, and he was on his own," recalls longtime fan Rich Kraemer. "Tanaka had gone on to team with Mitsu Arakawa. So, Gorilla was like a man without a country."

Another important reason was that Gino had frankly gotten very tired of all the abuse from fans that a heel in wrestling must endure. Over the years, fans had thrown chairs and bottles and whatever else they could get their hands on at him, spit on him, put out their cigars and cigarettes on his broad back, tried to knife him, even threatened Maureen at times when she had been leaving arenas with him. It was one thing if it was his only way to make big money in the business, but Gino had now found another way and had no interest in being the lightning rod of vicious hatred any longer. Plus, he'd finally get to shave off that damn beard.

The manner in which they actually pulled off the face turn of Gorilla Monsoon, believe it or not, is a matter of some debate, and sorting it out becomes a kind of exercise in archaeology. Part of the problem is that virtually no WWWF television from this period survives. Little was covered in the press, and wrestling magazines were notorious for their fabrications. Virtually everyone directly involved with the promotion at the time is gone. Even Gorilla's own recollections of the turn, relayed in various newspaper interviews many years later, appear to be incorrect or mixed-up. So essentially, what we have to go on is the reliability of the memories of fans who were watching that television more than fifty-five years ago, some of which conflict.

So how did Gorilla Monsoon turn good? There had already been hints of it before he even left for Japan, thanks to his brief feud with Killer Kowalski. But the turn began in earnest on the September 18, 1969, edition of *Heavyweight Wrestling from Washington*—held the very same day Gino had signed his ownership papers for Capitol. What appears to have happened is this: Bruno Sammartino was making a rare television appearance, defending his WWWF world title against Canadian wrestler Walter Nurnberg, whom McMahon had given the name "Dynamite" Joe Cox, after a tough-guy wrestler of the 1930s.[6] Cox was a capable scrapper, but Bruno's title was in no danger. Either frustrated at his inability to defeat the champion, or enraged at having been defeated by the champion, Cox grabbed a four-by-four from ringside and started attacking him. Another villain then ran in and joined in on the attack—believed most likely to have been the sinister Waldo Von Erich, just returned to the territory and being positioned as Sammartino's next big threat.[7]

That's when Monsoon hit the ring, initially to the horror of fans, who assumed he was there to join in on the beating. But instead, he grabbed the four-by-four from Cox and chased off Bruno's attackers, saving the champion in unexpected fashion. Monsoon saving Sammartino seemed to come out of nowhere, although it may have been later explained that it was out of gratitude for compassion that the champion had shown to him in one of their brutal, bloody encounters of the past, in which Bruno had checked on his condition after the match and seen to it that he was given proper medical attention—almost certainly a totally fabricated incident that nevertheless served the storyline. After the rescue, Monsoon was gone from the ring as quickly as he'd arrived. "I looked for the man, I want to thank the man, I appreciate what he did. I couldn't believe it was Gorilla Monsoon," said a stunned Sammartino during a promo after the match, as remembered by Mike Omansky, watching at home.

His opportunity would come two days later, on the next episode of *Wrestling from Philadelphia*. This time, Gorilla was wrestling his old tag team partner from the California days, "Crazy" Luke Graham—a heel vs. heel match that already raised a red flag that something was up. The exact details of the finish are not known, but Graham appears to have gotten himself disqualified for some tactics that lived up to his nickname. In the ensuing post-match melee, who should come to Gorilla Monsoon's aid but the WWWF world champion, showing his gratitude and returning the favor. The main event that night saw Bruno and Victor Rivera battle Killer Kowalski and George Steele to a disqualification, and it's possible that Gorilla got involved with that one as well, on the side of the faces. "It shocked me when I saw him become friends with Bruno Sammartino," says Bill Apter, who had witnessed some of their battles firsthand. "It was incredible, I couldn't believe it. I was happy, but back then, not a lot of people made turns like that. That was totally dramatic."

In those days, the process of a full turn could be gradual. Monsoon was immediately plugged into matches on the circuit against the hated Kowalski and Scicluna, both former allies. On the next installment of *Wrestling from Washington*, he faced none other than Waldo Von Erich, the man he'd chased off the week before, battling the pseudo-Nazi villain to a time limit draw. Fans had heard him utter a few words here and there on interviews as of late, but now he just started speaking in a completely normal way, seeming to ditch the old Manchurian schtick with absolutely no explanation, in typical pro wrestling fashion. Fans didn't need an explanation. On October 1, at the first Madison Square Garden show in three months since prime-time television had been restored, Gorilla Monsoon shocked the Garden faithful, coming out in a suit and tie, completely clean-shaven, before a heel vs. heel match between Kowalski and Bulldog Brower. He shook the hands of both participants and politely issued a challenge to the winner, which turned out to be Kowalski, whom he'd battle to a quick disqualification win later that month in his first match at the Garden in over half a year, and the first one ever in which he got to hear the New York fans cheering him on.

But the ultimate sign of Gorilla's complete shift to the good side was seen on the October 16 TV from Washington, when the unthinkable occurred, and Gorilla Monsoon actually teamed up with Bruno Sammartino for the first time in the WWWF. In a non-title match, they defeated Monsoon's old partner Toru Tanaka and Tanaka's new partner Mitsu Arakawa, collectively known as the Rising Suns, holders of the brand-new WWWF international tag team championship. The alliance between the former blood enemies Monsoon and Sammartino was complete, and fans fully embraced the former Manchurian monster into their hearts, a location from which he would never depart.

■

Much would change about Gorilla Monsoon the wrestler following his turn and heading into the 1970s. For one thing, his gear would change, as he ditched the short trunks and took to wearing long tights, typically black with a red stripe, along with a glittery green ring jacket—a hint at the natural affinity for colorful clothing he was never allowed to indulge during his heel years. Later, a black tank top would be added—a concession to his growing girth. But more than just his appearance, more fundamental changes were taking place. His increasing size, combined with his vision issues, would continue to limit his working style in the ring. His peak years as a top performer were really already behind him by the time he turned face—it was a much shorter prime than most top wrestlers get, which, in addition to the wear and tear he had put on his body as a big man was also down to the simple fact that the wrestling aspect of his career was now taking a backseat to the business aspect. Going forward, what went on in the ring would become less important than what was going on outside of it.

To be sure, Gorilla Monsoon was still a top attraction, as he'd always be, but his role on the roster was not what it used to be. Now, he'd become a fixture of the semi-main event on the big shows of the circuit, typically in a handful of positions, whether it be tag teaming with other top attractions in fan-pleasing encounters, teaming with new up-and-coming babyfaces in the territory to try and give them "the rub," or very often tangling with heels who were either on their way up to challenge the world champion, or on their way down after already having done so. Although he rarely lost cleanly, he might be called upon to make a bad guy look suitably formidable, as he first did with Waldo Von Erich and "The Big Cat" Ernie Ladd, another giant of the ring who had recently turned to wrestling full time after leaving his defensive tackle position with the Kansas City Chiefs. After they were done as world title contenders, Monsoon might be called upon to deal them a decisive loss, thereby indicating to fans that their time in the territory was coming to an end. It was a formulaic role that allowed him to focus on his new responsibilities as vice president, both running the shows from the back and working in the front office.

As Gino's role in the company exploded heading into 1970, Vinny still found himself a relative outsider. In January, he and Linda would welcome Shane into the world. Eager to make ends meet and provide for his growing family, Vinny would take a job as a truck driver for a rock quarry. His relentless requests to his dad to allow him to help with the family business had led to his ring announcer role, as well as random odd jobs, but that was it for the moment. "Come on pop," he would implore. "You know I love this stuff."[8] While Gino was running the locker room for the old man, Vinny found himself barred. Remembers Mario Savoldi, "The father's instructions to Gino, to Zacko, to my dad, to everybody, was, 'I don't want him in the dressing room. I don't want him to be a part of it. He's going to sell tickets. That's his job.'" Savoldi even recalls one incident in New Haven when the ban was put to the test: "My father said, 'Vinny, please stay out of the dressing room. You're gonna get me in trouble.' He wanted to be around the guys, but the father would really get really upset. 'I told you to keep him out of the fucking dressing rooms!' At first, the father really didn't want him to be that involved. Because he had graduated college. He had other hopes for him."

Meanwhile, business in the territory was heating up again. Monsoon continued to team with top babyfaces like Bruno, Victor Rivera and Cowboy Bob Ellis. One of the first newcomers to get the Monsoon tag team rub would be the new Italian babyface Mario Milano, who had been brought in for a run in 1970 after Monsoon had spoken highly of him from their time together in Australia. They'd team together on the March 3 show at Madison Square Garden, topping Ladd and Tanaka. Gino would miss about three weeks of action in the early spring of 1970, which may have been the result of a broken shoulder he sustained thanks to a freak accident at the March 12 Washington TV: "Somebody had a microphone stand sitting outside the ring apron, and as I went out of the ring, I could just see myself being skewered by this microphone stand, and I kicked my head the other way, and when I did I lost all conception of where I was going."[9]

By the time he was able to get back in the ring, Gino found himself locked into a nearly year-long program with a new tag team act that had just been brought into the Northeast from Montreal. The fearsome Mongols were made up of veteran wrestler Newton Tattrie (who would soon be tapped to run the Pittsburgh end of the territory for McMahon) and his protégé Josip Peruzović (who would later achieve greater fame as Nikolai Volkoff). Together they were known respectively as Geto and Bepo Mongol, and for the next ten months, they would be "married" to Monsoon, who opposed them in various encounters with partners including the likes of Arnold Skaaland, Victor Rivera, Milano, rookie John L. Sullivan (the future "Luscious" Johnny Valiant) as well as Gino's old San Francisco associate Joe Scarpa, who made the leap to New York in the summer of 1970 to reinvent himself as the enormously popular Chief Jay Strongbow, complete with a feathered war bonnet, beaded leather vest and tomahawk. Like Gino was years before, Scarpa had been repackaged by McMahon, who had no need for another Italian but was in need of an Indian. So, he just created a fictional one—a member of the "Woppaho tribe," as Lou Albano was fond of quipping.

Speaking of Albano, with Wild Red Berry out of the picture, McMahon had reinvented Lou as a heat-seeking manager, christening him "Captain" Lou Albano—a reference to his role in an earlier lifetime as captain of his high school football team in White Plains. The Mongols would be among Albano's earliest charges as a manager, as would the 290-pound Spaniard Oscar "Crusher" Verdu. Together, the loudmouthed Albano and the massive Verdu would light the territory on fire, drawing 20,819 fans to Madison Square Garden on June 15, 1970, for a title match against Sammartino—the largest Garden crowd seen to that date in the new building and the largest in either building since McMahon had started promoting there. They exceeded that number the following month. After the two-match series with Bruno at the Garden, Verdu was given a quick count-out win over Monsoon in August to keep his heat going a while longer. Despite his near-total immobility, Verdu came across as a legitimate threat to Bruno's crown, and Albano almost immediately came into his own as arguably the most hated heel in the company. He was a natural fit, even if his unreliability and penchant for boozing made him tough for everyone to handle, especially Gino, who was often tasked with wrangling him.

■

Another of Gino's important roles started to develop around this time, which saw him as the unofficial public relations man for the company, helping coordinate access to the press, as well as providing well-spoken and articulate quotes whenever necessary. This was how the young Bill Apter, coming into his own as a wrestling journalist and photographer, first got to know him. At first, there was still bad blood between Bill's employer, Stanley Weston, and Gino and the Capitol office, thanks to that article in *The Wrestler* magazine with the gun. But Bill's persistence won out, as well as the assurance that he had no intention of exposing the business. He won over Gino so much, in fact, that sometimes Gino would give him little tidbits ahead of time to leak to the magazines: "He'd just say, three or four weeks down the line, maybe you can print in the magazine that you know, so-and-so might be wrestling so-and-so. So, he started telling me things once he started trusting me."

Trust was always important to Gino, and one of the reasons he'd been given the keys to the kingdom. When he was backstage, it was clear that he was in charge. And yet he was still one of the boys, and he would still often be found—especially at untelevised house shows which required less of his constant attention—sitting at a table somewhere, a cigar in his mouth, intently playing cards, and typically taking everyone's lunch (Arnie Skaaland was a long-suffering victim of Gino's winning ways, which became a widely shared locker room joke). His love of cards, and especially of winning at cards, started in the locker rooms of arenas, armories and high school gyms throughout the Northeast, eventually making its way to the tables of Las Vegas and Atlantic City.

The Capitol inner circle became a tightly knit collection of business associates and friends, which included, on social occasions, their wives. Usually this would be in New York, but it could also mean down in Miami Beach, visiting with Willie Gilzenberg, who made his official residence down there and would frequently entertain and do business with luminaries of both the wrestling and boxing worlds. Willie's daughter Holly, then just a teenager, remembers a particular trip up to New York, dining out with everyone and stopping off at the luxury suite at the Warwick beforehand: "It was as big as the hotel, the entire floor. And then we went to Jimmy Weston's after that. When these people went out to dinner, it was always to the nines. But I'd never been in a place like that [suite] before . . . it was like a house. And I was like, 'Wow, this is what they do?'" Holly also recalls having the Marellas, the McMahons, the Sammartinos and others down at Miami Beach: "I can just see it. My dad would be off with whomever, whether it was Bruno, whether it was Don King, whether it was Bob and Maureen . . . She always called him Gino. The kitchen was where the women always hung. While the guys were talking business, Maureen would be with my mother. They had a bond. That was my life as a child. I knew them all, and they all were so sweet. But my friends would say, 'Oh, are they in the mafia?' And I'd say, 'No, no, it's not the mafia.'"

By this point, Capitol Wrestling and the WWWF firmly controlled the entire region, from Maine to Maryland, as they used to say. Gino's South Jersey portion included places like the resort town of Asbury Park, the middle-class suburb of Cherry Hill, and starting in December 1970, he even got an opportunity to hold an annual fundraising show at the JFK High School gym right in his hometown of Willingboro, an event that everyone in the area looked forward to each year, with Gino typically hosting many of the wrestlers before and after at his home right down the road.

■

His role as the man who got guys ready to face Bruno was played once again in October. But this time it was different, and more important than ever. Because the man who defeated him via count-out at the Garden that night wasn't someone who'd get his typical two- or three-match series with the world champion and move on. This time, Gino was helping to groom the person who was actually going to defeat Bruno Sammartino right in the middle of the Garden ring and take the WWWF world heavyweight championship from him. His name was Oreal Perras, and he was the son of an Ontario dairy farmer, but he wrestled as "The Russian Bear" Ivan Koloff, Soviet scourge of Cold War–era fans everywhere.

Sammartino was burnt out, worn down to the bone with the burden of carrying the fortunes of the company on his back for nearly eight long years. During much of that time, he'd been headlining nearly every single Capitol show on the circuit, from major arenas to VFW halls, appearing five, six, sometimes even seven times a week and defending his title many hundreds of times. For the past couple of years, he'd been fighting McMahon to limit his schedule a bit more but was still generally out there three to four times a week. He wanted time with his family, time to heal, time to maybe even take a sabbatical from the Northeast and tour some of the territories that never got to see him. Finally, McMahon had relented, and the call was made to take the title off Bruno at the January 18, 1971, Madison Square Garden show. After sixty-three successful title defenses there, this time, when Koloff came down from the second rope with that kneedrop and made the cover, there would be no kickout. A shocked pall infamously came over the stricken crowd of 21,106 (a new Capitol record at the Garden). Some wept. Koloff was not even announced to the crowd as the winner and new champion for fear of a riot—which did not stop a contingent of angered fans from tearing up the restaurant across the street later that night. In an attempt to diffuse emotions, there would be one last match that night to follow the title change, and it would see Monsoon and Strongbow battle the Mongols for the international tag team title, all the way to the eleven p.m. curfew to try to keep fans satisfied and in the building as long as possible.

Bruno's contributions to the Capitol organization were vast, and no one appreciated and understood that more than his great friend and long-time in-ring rival, Gino. Truth be told, he had always been in awe of the champion, whom he'd known since they were both rookies together. His respect for Bruno's accomplishments was summed up in the commemorative plaque he had made up, which would hang in Sammartino's home for the rest of his days. It was a sign of ultimate admiration between two men who had spilled blood and sweat together for years. Incorporating the actual championship belt Bruno had defended in the ring, the plaque also bore an inscription that read:

IT GIVES ME GREAT PLEASURE
TO PRESENT THIS
WORLD CHAMPIONSHIP BELT
TO
BRUNO SAMMARTINO
WHO OVER THE PAST EIGHT YEARS
HAS PROVEN TO THE WORLD
THAT HE HAS BEEN

THE GREATEST CHAMPION IN THE
HISTORY OF PROFESSIONAL WRESTLING

WITH DEEPEST RESPECT
GINO

But Ivan Koloff was never going to be the new long-term champion. His reign would be purely functional and transitional. For a long-term solution to the Bruno problem, they needed another popular babyface who could carry the banner and bring in the fans, and Gino would have a strong hand in the selection. It was decided to continue to go the ethnic route, only a different ethnicity this time around. New York and some other northeastern cities had strong Latino populations; Capitol Wrestling had already been airing on Spanish-language Channel 47 for years, and now Mike LeBell's Hollywood Wrestling had begun a Spanish-language broadcast on WXTV Univision Channel 41. To capitalize on the fandom among these populations, Vince wanted a Latino star. Pedro Morales, the Puerto Rican sensation and a fresh-faced rookie for Capitol back in the '60s, had made quite a name for himself since, and he came highly recommended by Gino, who had gotten to see his progress while working in California, Hawaii and Japan.

In preparation, McMahon had organized a meeting with Morales at McMahon's new home in Plantation, Florida, a gorgeous suburb of Fort Lauderdale that was also about an hour and a half north of Willie Gilzenberg's Miami Beach home. Pedro had flown in from Los Angeles, where he'd been working at the time and where he'd also caught the eye of Fred Blassie, likely another trusted Vince compatriot who'd put in a good word for him. It was decided that to help Pedro get over, he'd be presented with Gorilla Monsoon as his manager, the role Arnie Skaaland had played with Sammartino, taking him under his wing and even tag teaming with him.

Morales made his Capitol return in November 1970 and was paired with Monsoon as a mouthpiece who could speak fluently in English, while Pedro would address his Latino fans in Spanish. In his official return to WWWF television in Philadelphia in late December, he teamed up with Monsoon in a match against the Mongols. They would do it again in Washington a month later, on the same show that saw one of the very few defenses of the WWWF world championship that Koloff actually got to make in his mere three weeks with the title, as he took on Gene DuBois (aka "Bear Man" Dave McKigney). Another of that handful of defenses happened to be against Monsoon himself, who got his first title shot in two years when he challenged Koloff at a Philadelphia television taping in a match he lost via count-out. With a heel world champion for the first time in years, it meant that some babyfaces would finally get a crack at the title—but that wouldn't last long, as Morales got his official coronation as new WWWF standard-bearer with a win over Koloff in under eleven minutes at the Garden on February 8, 1971, with yet another record-breaking crowd of 21,812 rejoicing as Morales was joined in the ring by Sammartino, who embraced the new champ and gave his official blessing.

■

Just as he'd been doing for Bruno for the past couple of years, Gino would also help to get new heel challengers ready for Pedro, which included the likes of the Wolfman (Hungarian-Canadian Vilmos Farkas), Bulldog Brower and the rangy Texan Bob Windham, whom McMahon had transformed into Blackjack Mulligan. He also continued his other role of teaming with young babyfaces, and one of those would be Jim Fanning, who had gotten the name "Handsome" Jimmy Valiant while wrestling in Texas and first came to the WWWF in the spring of 1971. "I loved him, he was a gentle giant," remembered Valiant in a 2022 interview.[10] "He took me under his wing right away and helped me." Valiant would rent a home from Gino, where he'd stay for over a year while working the territory.

Gino played a big role in welcoming new guys into the fold, and Handsome Jimmy was a great example of that. He remembered first arriving in New York, where he was picked up at the airport by Lou Albano and taken up to the offices at the Holland Hotel:

He knows I'm one of the boys, I follow him up to the third floor. I looked on the door, WWWF world headquarters, Lou opens the door, and the first guy to greet me was Monsoon. He was in the waiting room . . . He says, welcome Jim, Vince is expecting you, and he introduced me to Arnold Skaaland, Savoldi was there, and the president was there. I go in, and Vince is doing some paperwork, looks over his oval glasses at me. "Come in, Jimmy, come in." Because they respected me. He said, "You come from a man I admire very much, Fritz Von Erich. Welcome to the WWWF. This is gonna be your home for the next year."

Gino took the still-green Valiant back to New Jersey with him and helped get him settled with a place to stay. The next day, he went down to Washington with him and introduced him around the dressing rooms. "All the big stars are there, and the job boys are there. He says, 'Guys, this is Jimmy Valiant, make him welcome.' . . . That's the type of guy Gorilla was. A real sweetheart."

Valiant also tells a legendary story that would be repeated often by other wrestlers who witnessed it, a sure sign that it would be a regular occurrence on the road. Gino, who was always very free with money, is traveling in his Cadillac Fleetwood with his good friend Chief Jay Strongbow, who was quite the opposite, clenching the first dollar he ever made with gusto. They're taking turns paying tolls on the way back to New Jersey, and Strongbow reluctantly hands Gino a twenty-dollar bill for a three-dollar toll. "Monsoon looks in the rearview, he gives me the nod," remembers Valiant. "We get to the booth, Strongbow says, 'Get my change.' Monsoon gets there, hands the toll guy the twenty and says, 'Keep the change!' and takes off. [Strongbow] went crazy! When [Gino] started laughing, the whole car would shake. He looks at me and I'm cracking up. He says, 'I thought you said *keep* the change!'" Adding insult to injury, Valiant then recalls Gino peeling a $100 bill out of his own hefty bankroll, rolling it up inside Strongbow's empty soda bottle and, to the Chief's shock and dismay, casually tossing it out the window and into the median. Strongbow tries to get out of the car and go after it, but Gino says, "Chief, someday some poor soul is gonna be out there picking up bottles, broke, and he's gonna find that bottle. And it's gonna make his day."

■

Business was booming in New York with Pedro as champion, with record crowds at the Garden becoming a regular occurrence. In October, he headlined against Stan "The Man" Stasiak in front of the largest Garden crowd in forty years—and then broke the record again the following month against his old friend Blassie, putting 22,089 in the building.

Starting in March, Vince and Gino had welcomed a new manager to the territory on a part-time basis, who would later become another member of the trusted circle. Ernie Roth had been riling up crowds for years in Detroit as Abdullah Farouk, colorful manager of the noble Sheik, and McMahon would repackage him as the Grand Wizard of Wrestling, pairing him up with Blackjack Mulligan and feuding him with both Monsoon and Morales. Along with Roth came his boyfriend, "Beautiful" Bobby Harmon, whom he'd first met back in the Motor City and would eventually become a business partner as well as a romantic one.

So good was Roth at drawing heat, in fact, that on at least one occasion, it overflowed into a situation of real peril in which Gino had to think on his feet. The date was May 15, 1971, and Morales was defending the title against Mulligan before a typically rabid crowd of drunken reprobates at the Boston Garden. When the Wizard discreetly passed a pair of brass knucks to Mulligan, which was then used to cold-cock the champion, it was too much for the Beantown faithful to bear. Naturally, it was all part of the show, but there was no telling that to the crazed fan who jumped the guardrail and, as Mulligan was climbing back into the ring, stabbed the big Texan in the leg, slicing it open like a carp.

Immediately breaking character, Gino—ostensibly the manager of Blackjack's opponent—jumped in the ring to tend to Mulligan with towels that turned crimson almost as soon as they made contact. He also managed to nab the guy who did it. "God bless him, Gino can't see thirty feet," remembered Mulligan of the incident in a 2016 *Slam Wrestling* interview. "He can hardly see the guy. But he did grab the guy to get rid of him." He also dumped the attacker right at the feet of the Boston police officers, present as usual to help control the crowd, and who infamously laughed it off because they thought it was all part of the show, allowing the guy to slip back into the crowd and get away. Mulligan was rushed to a Boston hospital that night, where his leg was just barely saved by fast-acting surgeons. Security checks were instituted at the Boston Garden going forward, and promoter Abe Ford installed plexiglass barriers around the ringside area to keep any other would-be murderers out.

Although the outcome of that night may have been more than they bargained for, the name of the game was generating interest and excitement by any means necessary. But although Morales's fans, Latino and otherwise, were consistently turning out in New York, in other areas of the territory, things were simply not going quite as well as they had been with Sammartino. As a little insurance policy, Vince McMahon made the much-considered decision to have the Capitol Wrestling Corporation rejoin the National Wrestling Alliance and brought Gino down with him to the NWA's annual convention, held that August in Mexico City. It was the first time either man had attended the convention in years, and the last time Gino had been there, it had been as a rookie wrestler invited by Frank Tunney. This time, he and Vince worked out a deal that would enable Capitol to make use of the NWA's rich talent pool, bringing in top stars to the WWWF from all over the territorial system on a regular basis to help draw. NWA President Sam Muchnick was more than happy to have McMahon back in the fold, with all the power and influence of New York coming along with him. Other than paying dues, there was just one thing Muchnick asked. Because all NWA territories recognized only one world heavyweight champion, who was Dory Funk Jr. at the time, the WWWF title could no longer be officially promoted as a "world championship." That had been the crux of the rift between the two parties, going back to the Buddy Rogers / Lou Thesz days. McMahon agreed, largely because he knew that regardless of what he called the title, as far as his customers in the Northeast were concerned, the WWWF heavyweight champion was the real world champion anyway.

Still, the money was coming in, and as a partner, Gino was making more of it than ever before, entering that rarified air of the "$100,000-per-year man," at a time when the median household income in America was about a tenth of that. He sold the house at 11 Hancock Lane and moved his family about two and a half miles across town to a 2,500-square-foot house sitting on 10,800 feet of land at 58 Crestview Drive, complete with a beautiful in-ground pool, in the idyllic Willingboro neighborhood of Country Club—named for its location right alongside the Rancocas Golf Club. The Marellas would spend the next fourteen years building a life there and becoming pillars of the community, not to mention a center of neighborhood life and a home-away-from-home for countless wrestlers over the years.

Longtime WWE ring announcer Tony Chimel remembers befriending Gino's son, Joey, in those days, first encountering him while he and his friends were playing street hockey in the neighborhood, not even yet realizing who his dad was. He was certainly reminded of it on one particular occasion after he and other boys had taken to teasing Joey about his dad being a "fake wrestler." That night, when Tony's father answered a knock on the door, it was Gorilla Monsoon filling the doorway from top to bottom:

"Hi, I'm Gino Marella. Your son Anthony hangs out with my son, Joey. He came home crying today, saying he's giving him a little bit of a hard time. Could you just ask Anthony to be a little bit easier on him?"

Later, Tony's dad had a talk with him and told him to "cut it the hell out." And that was that. "I thought it was so nice of Gino," says Tony, "to come to the house to stick up for Joey, and not kick the shit out of me or my dad."

It was also in this period that the Marellas got closer than ever with the Savoldis, who also resided in Jersey. It wasn't uncommon, if there was an event happening in Philadelphia, that Angelo and Mario might head down, drop the rest of the family off at the Marellas', then head to the show with Gino, come back later that night and all have a big Italian dinner together before driving back home. There were trips to Boston, which usually included stops in Little Italy after the show, often with Bruno, as well as Coogie McFarlane, a timekeeper who, despite his name, was 100 percent Italian. "Whenever we did Boston, the trip home from Boston, there'd be a gallon of wine," remembers Mario. "Coogie's aunt in the north end in Boston owned a delicatessen, and he would bring a big bag to the Boston Garden full of sandwiches. And that would be our dinner from there back to New York. I'd be driving, and they'd be drinking the wine and eating the sandwiches. I mean, the car smelled like provolone."

■

Gorilla Monsoon was kept busy in the summer of 1971 challenging for the brand-new WWWF world tag team championship, which had just been bestowed on the recently returned "Crazy" Luke Graham and his partner, the French-Canadian Tarzan Tyler, under the tutelage of Lou Albano. On July 24, Monsoon and Morales tagged up to take on the champs and wound up drawing the first $100,000 live gate, not just in Garden history but in the history of pro wrestling in New York. The next month, it would be Monsoon and Strongbow making a run at the belts. Into the fall, he'd continue to battle Graham and Tyler, teaming with everyone from Valiant, Strongbow and Haystacks Calhoun to Rene Goulet, Victor Rivera and Manny Soto.

Gino's television responsibilities would expand in the fall of '71, when McMahon decided the time had finally come to move his weekly TV tapings out of Washington, DC, due to dwindling crowds at the National Arena and the roughening neighborhood that was blamed for it. Starting on September 29, what had once been *Wrestling from Washington* was shifted to the Hamburg Field House in suburban Pennsylvania—a kind of giant Quonset hut owned and operated by the volunteer Hamburg Fire Department that could hold a couple thousand people. The new show would launch as *All-Star Wrestling*, with Phil Zacko as the official promoter but Gino actually running things backstage, just as he had already been doing for *Championship Wrestling* from Philadelphia.

Another major change would take place on the second week of the new show. Capitol's longtime TV commentator, the bespectacled, chain-smoking Ray Morgan, had taken the opportunity of the new assignment to demand more money and enlisted the broadcaster's union to help him—a move which, predictably, had the opposite effect of what he was hoping for. McMahon fired Morgan and replaced him with his son Vinny, even paying him the higher amount Morgan had been asking for in a maneuver of exquisite spite.[11] Employing a family member had enabled McMahon to escape union regulations thanks to a handy loophole, plus his son had been begging for such an opportunity for years, and his father had likely gotten tired of hearing it. The twenty-six-year-old Vincent K. McMahon made his commentating debut on the October 6, 1971, edition of *All-Star Wrestling*. Eventually, he would even replace Bill Cardille on *Championship Wrestling*, becoming the new voice of Capitol TV. As he continued to prove himself, and as he refused to give up, his father would begin to give him more responsibilities, installing him as the promoter of events in the furthest northern region of the territory, up in Maine, where he'd had to remove the previous promoter for skimming too much off the top. It was a promotion just as much as it was a banishment, as McMahon the elder privately hoped his son would be discouraged and give up. He would not. Instead, he and Linda, along with two-year-old Shane, moved from Maryland up to West Hartford, Connecticut, to be more centrally located.

With the new taping schedule in place, the WWWF crew would run the Philadelphia Arena every three weeks on a Saturday night, taping three weeks' worth of TV episodes of their primary show. Then, every third Wednesday, it would be the Hamburg Field House to record three episodes of the B-show. And Gino would oversee it all from his immutable perch in the Gorilla position.

In the ring, he'd spend the remainder of 1971 challenging for the world tag team title and also working to get another new heel tandem over, the Rugged Russians, Ivan and Igor. That feud would stretch into 1972, as he teamed with Soto and Strongbow as well as new babyfaces like Strongbow's popular African-American tag team partner Sonny King and the brutal technician from Germany, Karl Gotch.

However, before the end of the year, in a testament to how big of an attraction he still was, he'd make two rare stops outside the Capitol territory. It all had to do with a raging promotional war that was about to explode in Detroit between The Sheik's established outfit, Big Time Wrestling, and the upstart invading WWA, an outlaw group led by Dick the Bruiser and Wilbur Snyder. In order to fend off the invaders, who were running their first show in the Motor City on October 23, the same night as Sheik's scheduled event at Cobo Arena, Sheik had put out the call to the NWA to assist him. Various member territories would send in their talent to help build a super-show at Cobo, and as part of being a newly reinstated member, McMahon was called upon to do the same. For his part, he sent Monsoon and Luke Graham to do battle on the undercard, with Gino making his return to Cobo for the first time in nearly a decade.

That night, he was included among a collection of luminaries who'd been brought in from throughout the wrestling landscape. Florida promoter Eddie Graham and his business partner Buddy Fuller, both respected ring veterans in their own right, flew in to work a match together. Johnny Valentine came up from the Houston-Dallas circuit to take on the chiseled ex-boxer Rocky Johnson, who had come in from San Francisco. The Funks of West Texas had sent Ciclón Negro to take on Pat O'Connor, who owned a piece of St. Louis. Even Freddie Blassie and the dazzling masked luchador Mil Máscaras had come in from Hollywood to renew their rivalry. In the main event, Dory Funk Jr. came in to defend the NWA world heavyweight crown against Ernie Ladd. The result was a crowd of 8,700, which, although smaller than usual, more than doubled the throng Snyder and the Bruiser had drawn that night across town at the Olympia Stadium, where apparently 4,100 more of Sheik's usual customers had decided to go instead.

That was a crazy week for Gino, as he went back to New York for a Garden show, then hit spot shows out in Portland, Maine, and Lowell, Massachusetts, only to head back to Detroit to be in Cobo the following weekend, this time along with Baron Mikel Scicluna, who'd be his opponent for the second engagement, and The Sheik running unopposed, as Bruiser and Snyder had thought better of running opposition two weekends in a row (they'd be back in full force the following weekend). Also coming in for that show from Pedro Martinez's territory would be Gino's old friend Antonio Pugliese, now going by the more American-friendly name of Tony Parisi, along with someone Gino would soon get to know quite well: the towering Dominic DeNucci, from the little Italian village of Frosolone, north of Naples, who would become a WWWF regular in years to come.

Speaking of Scicluna, the new year brought new heel WWWF world tag team champions, with the Baron joining forces with the newly arrived King Curtis Iaukea from Hawaii to take the belts from Karl Gotch and Rene Goulet. Gorilla Monsoon would oppose them throughout the circuit, with Strongbow in Boston and Philadelphia and with Morales in Scranton. He'd also drop a singles match to Curtis by count-out in Madison Square Garden as the bellowing Hawaiian was readied for Pedro.

■

Now settled into his family life in New Jersey, plus having additional responsibilities as part of the Capitol office, Gino was more hesitant to make trips to Japan than he'd been in the past. But the big-money offers continued to roll in, and in the spring of 1972, it was just too much to pass up. Plus, the Japanese Wrestling Association was on its last legs, with Antonio Inoki having jumped ship at the beginning of the year to start his own company, New Japan Pro-Wrestling, and rumors that Giant Baba was planning on doing the same soon. The JWA was scrounging together as many big names as it could for what would turn out to be its final World League tournament, pitting Japanese favorites against *gaijin* interlopers. This time, the tournament would feature the likes of tough Texans "Dirty" Dick Murdoch and "Killer" Tim Brooks, the latter sent over by The Sheik, who was himself cultivating strong relationships in

Japan. There was also Mighty Brutus, later known as Bugsy McGraw; San Antonio's Lothario "brothers," José and Salvador; Calypso Hurricane (aka Ciclón Negro); and two Canadians who'd already been making big waves in Japan, the rampaging lumberjack Jos LeDuc and Windsor, Ontario's Larry Shreve, who'd reinvented himself as "The Madman from the Sudan," Abdullah the Butcher.

Also along for the ride for this one and only time would be Maureen, who had gotten sick of having to say goodbye to Gino for weeks on end, and who wanted to actually see Japan herself for once. Leaving the kids with Chief Jay Strongbow and his wife, Mary, they'd made the trip together for a whirlwind six-week tour. Gino would often team with the other *gaijin* in some unusual pairings, such as when he, Murdoch and Abdullah took on Baba, Kintaro Oki and the young former Olympian Masa Saito. Perhaps as enticement to get him back in Japan, Monsoon was booked quite strongly in the tournament, getting wins over Oki, Saito, Umanosuke Ueda and the Great Kojika. He'd battle his old friend Baba on April 10 in Tochigi and on April 28 in Kagoshima, and the two behemoths would meet in the finals of the World League tournament on May 12, Baba coming in first place among Japanese competitors with sixteen points and Monsoon first among *gaijin* with fourteen. In the final best-of-three falls encounter in Tokyo, Monsoon would pin Baba to take the first fall, with Baba then scoring the next two straight falls to take the winning trophy.

It was the most success he'd ever experienced in Japan, and he got to do it with Maureen by his side, exposing her to the fascinating Japanese culture that he'd fallen in love with and that she'd only heard about up until now. But they'd had to spend the Easter holiday abroad as part of that tour and were eager to get back to the kids by the end of it. After finishing the tour on May 15, Gino left Japan with Maureen, and as he sometimes did after long trips abroad, he took it easy on himself, staying out of the ring for the next month and a half, aside from a June 2 match at the Garden with Tarzan Tyler and a quick squash match in Washington, DC, with the masked Black Demon[12] two weeks later.

Less than three months after getting back from Japan, the Marellas would be back on a plane again, this time for a much shorter trip. After overseeing a Madison Square Garden show on July 29 before 17,398 fans—one of the smaller monthly crowds in those days—in which Monsoon had faced George Steele and Morales had defended the title against "The Spoiler" Don Jardine in the main event,[13] Gino and Vince, along with their respective wives and possibly Willie Gilzenberg and his wife, Lillian, headed to Las Vegas for the NWA's twenty-fifth annual convention, the first since Capitol had rejoined the esteemed body. It was Gino's first chance as a stakeholder in Capitol to rub shoulders with other power brokers from across the industry, not as an employee but as a peer.

The convention that year was held at the Dunes—one of the crown jewels of the old-school Vegas strip, not to mention one of the most mobbed-up casino hotels in the whole town, funded in large part by money from the Teamsters pension fund, provided by Jimmy Hoffa. It had a spacious new convention center that was perfect for the NWA's needs and had just undergone an extensive renovation. As part of that renovation, giant chandeliers had been added to the main gambling rooms, and it was under the lights of those shiny new chandeliers that Gino would indulge in his great love—playing cards, with blackjack being his game of choice, particularly because he tended to win huge more often than he lost huge. For someone like Gino, Vegas was a wonderland that meant food, entertainment, hobnobbing with friends and colleagues and sharpening his skills at the tables. In those days, Vegas was one of the only places in the country where gambling at a level that Gino preferred could be enjoyed legally, and he jumped at the opportunity like a fish to water.

Back in New York, the crowds just kept coming, and a big part of that was the support of the loyal Latino fan base that adored Pedro Morales. In response to this support, Capitol leaned into appealing to that fan base, populating its regular roster with more Latino wrestlers than ever.

In fact, Capitol became known for having one of the more racially and ethnically diverse rosters at a time when that usually wasn't the case in many other places. There were some other territories like Detroit and Los Angeles that also boasted such diversity, and just as with Capitol in the Northeast, it was a wise strategy where diverse urban populations were to be found. Right from the start, Gino had great love and respect for the Latino wrestlers in the locker room, and that love and respect was more than reciprocated. He became known as their champion, advocate and protector, looking out for them to make sure they weren't taken advantage of and got as much work as possible at a time when the people at the top of the food chain were still far from diverse.

"We loved him," says Johnny Rodz, one of the most loyal WWWF wrestlers there ever was. "He was a good businessman, and he was fair, too. He wasn't a wise guy, or a finagler or a shyster . . . Whoever didn't get along with him had to be a real jerk." Rodz remembers spending lots of time with Gino in those days, along with guys like Pete Sanchez and Manny Soto. They could often be found at the smoky and Runyonesque McGirr's Billiard Academy on the edge of Hell's Kitchen, losing badly at one of Gino's other favorite games. A broomstick was enough to allow him to wipe the floor with most players, but he'd usually settle for a pool cue. "We'd start up a little game, a couple bucks. Before you know it, Gino started making all kinds of deals, and we'd all get involved. The losers have to be able to not only pay the money for losing, pay for the table and also take us out for steaks and eggs and cigars. That was Gino's way of finishing up the game.

"We were always together," Johnny continues. "We'd come up with stupid games to play. We forgot about the business when we were together. When he became part of the office, he was still the same, he never changed. He was with the office, but when he was with us, it didn't matter." If they were backstage or in a hotel room, they'd be playing cards, most likely acey-deucey, a favorite of Gino's, although not always a favorite of Pete Sanchez's, who Rodz recalls would sometimes owe Gino hundreds at a time. Still, despite his sometimes crabby demeanor, Pete loved Gino as much as anyone. "Pete used to make him laugh so hard because Pete used to love to see his belly go up and down . . . Gino loved him, because Gino could be in a miserable mood, but Pete would break him out of it right away."

Gino liked to live big, and if you were close to him, he liked to give big. And chief among those close to him was his family. As he continued to thrive in his role, it gave him an opportunity to show his love and appreciation with the things that money could buy. "I think, in his way, it was making up for not being there," his daughter Valerie explains. This might mean the time she asked him for a kid's fold-up record player, and he bought her a jukebox. Or the time he bought Maureen a mink coat, and when she felt inside the pockets, there were plane tickets to Italy. "She'd say, 'I can't take this.' And he'd say, 'Absolutely you can take this!' . . . That was just his way. You had to be really careful what you asked for at Christmas in my house!"

Maureen herself had many such fond remembrances of those days, including one about the giant painting she had hanging above the couch in her living room for the rest of her long life. She and Gino had gone to the furniture store to get Joey a new bedroom set when she spotted the picture for sale and pointed it out. Gino played it off like he didn't want to buy it. But later, after she went out to pick up food and came back: "Joey is sitting on the couch with a big smile on his face. My husband says, 'I'll have my food in the den.' I walk in, that picture is hanging on the wall! And to this day, I don't know how he did it. But he was like that. You'd never know. Christmastime, oh my God! Ten presents each. It took all afternoon. He'd be up at six in the morning getting the fireplace on, playing the music, getting everybody up for breakfast, half asleep. That was him."

They shared a special bond in a business typically known for its ravaging effect on marriages and family units. The Marellas seemed immune from those ravages, and Gino and Maureen enjoyed a marriage built on implicit trust: "My husband used to say to me, the only ones you got to worry about are me and you. So don't ask me anything about the business. And I never did. I said OK. When the phone rang, and he was in his office, I closed the door. I didn't wanna know nothing." Maureen was grateful for Gino getting his ownership stake as it meant they'd never have to uproot the family and go territory to territory, as so many other wrestlers' families did. Perhaps this was part of why they always seemed so much more grounded than most. The closeness of Gino and Maureen stood out as an inspirational anomaly. While most of the other boys looked at carousing with women as just another benefit of life on the road, in all the stories you may hear from anyone who knew him, worked with him or traveled with him, you will never hear a story of Gino being unfaithful to Maureen. And that's about as rare as it gets in the wrestling business. "I had one wife say to me, I hear you and Gino are the only ones with a good marriage in this business. I didn't know what to say to her! Because I knew her husband, and I knew what was going on with her marriage, but I didn't want to get into that."

Even still, Gino being away so often brought its share of hardships. Missed communions, missed holidays (although Gino always refused to work Christmas), and sometimes Sharon, Joey and Valerie were just too young to understand why their dad was in Japan or Australia—not to mention the confused look on teachers' faces, who would sometimes assume that their parents were just divorced. But for every missed moment, there were moments that were made—barbecues and parties at the house, wrestlers and other friends stopping by. They always wanted to be near Gino.

■

On the promotional front, the summer of 1972 saw McMahon and company putting plans in place for the most ambitious event the company had ever promoted. It was to be held outdoors in the Flushing section of Queens at Shea Stadium, home of the New York Mets. In order to draw a suitable crowd to the baseball stadium, a main event unlike any other would have to be put together, and McMahon had just the idea, something he hadn't tried in years—pitting two overwhelming fan favorites against each other. Since dropping the world title the year before, Bruno Sammartino had been largely absent, wrestling in the Capitol circuit only sporadically while he took much-needed time off and also toured in places like California, Japan, Detroit, Cleveland and his own Pittsburgh promotion. But McMahon enticed him back in the summer, reintroducing him to WWWF fans in order to set up his planned main event for the Shea super-card in which Sammartino would challenge Pedro Morales for the championship.

In the semi-main event, Monsoon was scheduled to take on Ernie Ladd in a battle of the giants. In the weeks leading up, he would stay sharp by battling a newcomer to the territory, a six-foot-ten green rookie just a few months in the business, whom McMahon, with his proclivity for Irish names, would bill as Chuck O'Connor but who would later be known as Big John Studd. He'd also take aim at the newest heel world tag team champions, the Grand Wizard's pairing of Prof. Toru Tanaka and yet another Japanese/Hawaiian, Mr. Fuji, who had taken the title from Strongbow and Sonny King on Fuji's first day in the territory. One of the several young babyface partners Monsoon took on in his matches against Fuji and Tanaka would be Jack Brisco, a promising former NCAA Division I national champion that Florida promoter Eddie Graham was sending around the country for seasoning in preparation for a run with the NWA world heavyweight title.[14]

Fuji and Tanaka were also used to build the Bruno/Pedro match, as the two babyfaces came to blows thanks to some carefully orchestrated miscommunication during a TV match in August in which they'd been paired up to challenge the tag team champions. Unfortunately, when it came time for the big show, McMahon got stuck with a chilly, drizzly day that probably kept Shea Stadium from being as full as he'd hoped. Still, with 22,508 fans showing up and paying $140,923 in ticket sales, it was the largest crowd and attendance gate in company history up to that point. Monsoon wrestled Ladd to a twenty-minute draw and got the nod via the referee's decision. In the main event, Morales and Sammartino would clash for more than sixty-five minutes before the curfew brought the match to an end, the champion keeping his belt and the two men embracing in the end. Nevertheless, it became something of an unplanned war between the Puerto Rican fans and the Italian-American fans, with the

Puerto Ricans winning out. It was the only time that Bruno Sammartino would ever be booed in a WWWF ring, and an alarmed McMahon would never again match up two top babyface attractions.

Ironically, the WWWF would beat the Shea Stadium attendance figure just three months later at Madison Square Garden for a December 18 mega-show that saw stars converge from throughout the wrestling firmament. Ray Stevens, one half of the AWA world tag team champions with Nick Bockwinkel, came to challenge Morales. Mil Máscaras made his Garden debut, flouting the New York ban on masked wrestlers. Dory Funk Sr. came up from Amarillo with his young son Terry. The Great Goliath, one half of Mike LeBell's Americas tag team champions with Black Gordman, made an appearance. And while Monsoon made only a quick mid-card appearance against Chuck O'Connor that night, his role backstage was much more important, manning his position vigilantly and making sure everything came off smoothly. That night, 22,906 fans packed the building—breaking the all-time attendance record for wrestling in the ninety-three-year history of Madison Square Garden.

Going into 1973, the WWWF picked up another important chunk of territory, spreading north to the New York state capital of Albany. Pedro Martinez had been running that city since the 1950s, but his company, by that point having broken away from the NWA and doing business as the National Wrestling Federation (NWF), was losing ground (and money) and would be out of business by the following year. Albany would remain a regular stop on the Capitol circuit from then on, adding even more miles to the demanding schedule of one of the largest territories in the industry. More than ever, someone like Gino was needed to be the eyes and ears of the company in the locker rooms, to make the towns and run the shows.

■

Someone who remembers him very well in that capacity is Davey O'Hannon, who had gone from fearing Gorilla Monsoon as a kid to thanking him for helping him break into the business as a wrestler himself by the age of twenty-one. The Irish-Italian O'Hannon had taken advice from Gino to wrestle in school, then get his feet wet in territories like Bob Geigel's Central States before bringing him to Capitol's Philadelphia TV by '73. O'Hannon can still recall with awe Gino's presence in the locker room and the commanding way that he made sure everyone knew who was in charge: "He was never sitting around. TV is never a dull moment. So he had to stay on top of things. But in a spot show, once the first match got in the ring, everybody had their instructions. You had your time, and you knew what had to be done. He would sit down and play cards or play cribbage. But he was on top of things all the time."

Davey remembers one particular time at Philadelphia TV when Gino, exasperated at wrestlers showing up late to shows around the territory, gathered everyone in the back for an impromptu meeting. "I'm not gonna get an ulcer worrying about who's showing up," he warned, standing in the midst of the crowd of wrestlers. "You guys better start being here in plenty of time—an hour early before the show." Standing behind him, having sufficiently sipped from a 7Up can that most certainly did not contain 7Up, was Lou Albano, mimicking him like a precocious schoolkid—until Gino spotted him in the reflection of his glasses. "Now keep in mind how big Gino was. He had a wingspan like a 747. He swings his arm back, and he tried to chop Lou in the head. Luckily, the Captain stepped out of the way. That hand of Gino's, which was like a baseball glove, you could hear it go by Lou's head—whoosh! I said, Lou, maybe you ought to go sit somewhere else for a little while, until he cools off at least."

Another newcomer to the territory that Gino would help to feel welcome, as well as start tag teaming with, was Tony Garea, a handsome twenty-six-year-old New Zealander who had been sent up from Florida by Eddie Graham. Tony had been in consideration at one point for a run with the NWA world title and had been wrestling outside his home country for just about a year by the time he came under Gino's care. "When I first went there, he invited me to his house," Tony recalls. "It was nice for me because I'd been away from my family. So it was good to sit down and have a home-cooked meal." And that meal was just as likely to be cooked by Maureen as it was by Gino himself, who was known for his lasagna.

But no newcomer could overshadow, either figuratively or literally, the soft-spoken, charismatic Frenchman who first set his size-24 boots in a WWWF ring in the spring of that year. Gino had prided himself on being the company's resident giant for years, but he would have to concede that title to André Rousimoff, who weighed close to four hundred pounds in those days and stood about seven feet tall, although promoters, in their typical zeal, would add about four or five inches. After five years wrestling in Europe and Japan, André had first been brought to North America by Montreal promoters Maurice and Paul Vachon in 1971, but it would be Capitol Wrestling that would eventually nail him down to an agreement whereby Vince McMahon would become his exclusive booking agent, sending him all around the territories as a touring attraction, similar to the NWA world champion (and making just as much if not more money). André the Giant would make his home in the WWWF for nearly two decades, and in those early days, it was only natural that he would be paired up on several occasions with Gorilla Monsoon—the first of these occasions being a May 14, 1973, six-man tag at the Boston Garden pitting the two mammoths with Chief Jay Strongbow against the dastardly trio of Mr. Fuji, Prof. Toru Tanaka and "Moondog" Lonnie Mayne.

■

Monsoon, along with Morales, Strongbow and André, was among the WWWF's most popular babyfaces, but when Gino got a call at the Capitol office from Jeff Walton out in California because Mike LeBell was looking to book him at the Olympic Auditorium, it was a chance to return, however briefly, to his rule-breaking ways. After all, the fans in Los Angeles hadn't seen Gorilla Monsoon in seven years and weren't aware of the change of heart he'd experienced back east. Also, since Monsoon last wrestled for LeBell's outfit, the former WWA had rejoined the NWA, and the former WWA world championship had become the NWA Americas heavyweight title. It was then in the possession of Victor

Rivera, who had transitioned to the West Coast full time, although he still made regular appearances at Madison Square Garden. It was Rivera that LeBell wanted to match against Monsoon, which resulted in two matches at the Olympic in the last week of June: one a squash handicap match for television against Héctor Lamas and Salvador Lothario to help re-establish the fearsome Gorilla, and the next being a shot at Rivera's Americas heavyweight crown in the main event.[15]

That was a big week for Gino, as he'd fly back into New York the next day (along with Victor Rivera[16]) just in time to make the June 30, 1973, show at the Garden, the very first to be televised on the fledgling cable channel HBO. This was a big deal as it was the first time in that territorial era that any regional company had gotten its show broadcast nationwide via the burgeoning new cable TV technology that would one day revolutionize the industry.[17] Again keeping himself free to run traffic backstage, Gino gave himself an easy night between the ropes, chopping a flailing and bleeding Lou Albano out of his boots and chasing him from the ring in under four minutes. There would be more blood in the main event that night as Morales defended his crown against George Steele. The HBO deal was a major one and made instant waves throughout the industry. It also showed that people were sitting up and taking notice of the crowds in the world's most famous arena, which consistently hovered around the twenty-one thousand mark on a monthly basis.

The new HBO partnership was a hot topic of discussion later that summer, when Vince, Gino and Willie returned to Vegas for the annual NWA convention—this time held at the swanky Flamingo Hilton, one of the oldest casinos on the strip, founded by Bugsy Siegel himself, the infamous gangster typically credited in Vegas folklore with building the town up from a desert stopover into a gleaming, teeming, high-rolling destination. That week, Connie Stevens, Charlie Callas and the Mills Brothers played the Flamingo lounge while the territorial wrestling kingpins conducted business, re-electing Sam Muchnick as president for the twentieth time and appointing as secretary none other than Jim Barnett, who had found his way back from Australia and was now running Georgia.

The other promoters were wary of McMahon's growing power and the consolidation of the entire Northeast under his thumb. But Gino found himself in a very well-placed position as Vince's right-hand man at a time when the company was truly running on all cylinders. The successes of the '60s seemed to almost pale in comparison to the prosperity that the '70s had brought. And this was just the beginning, as the years to immediately follow would be even more profitable than ever. Before long, McMahon would even manage to cajole Sammartino to come back and retake his crown, propelling the company to heights that would arguably exceed what he'd accomplished before. And the legend of Gorilla Monsoon had grown to such proportions that Gino didn't really need to be in the ring as often as he used to be. He had a piece of the action now—a piece he never imagined he'd ever lose.

CHAPTER 9

THE BOY, THE BOXER, THE BRUISER AND THE BLEEDER

"Ali was trying to get publicity for an upcoming gimmick fight for a fortune against a Japanese wrestler, and he apparently wanted to use me as a warm-up."

The World Wide Wrestling Federation of the mid- to late 1970s was a thing of wonder and the stuff of legend to those who remember it. Capitol Wrestling was a territory operating at the height of its powers, at a time when wrestling territories still mattered. New York was where everyone wanted to be, and if they didn't want you, you made excuses about why you didn't really want to go there anyway. If the '60s was the period when the company worked to establish itself and consolidate its control over the Northeast, then this was the period in which the rewards were reaped, bringing in even bigger crowds and even more money than ever before. The faltering steps of the past were just that, in the past. The Garden would never go dark again. As far as the business of professional wrestling went, Capitol was the crown jewel, and they knew that everywhere from Toronto to Tokyo.

For Gino Marella, the man who owned 25 percent of that glorious operation, it was a great time to be in on the action. His time in the ring was clearly winding down as he approached middle age, and for a variety of reasons, but that didn't matter. He'd already proven himself there. This was a time when he'd prove himself at so much more, continuing to be the rock that anchored Capitol's weekly television, and also acting as a goodwill ambassador, a friendly giant who could represent the business to those outside of it, and who always knew just what to say to protect the industry he loved that had been so good to him. As Nixon turned to Ford and Ford to Carter, as Morales turned to Sammartino and Sammartino to Backlund, Monsoon remained a constant, helping to pull the strings and grease the wheels that ran it all.

But the ring wasn't quite done with him yet. In fact, he'd extend his dealings to the Caribbean, where a fortuitous arrangement in Puerto Rico would keep him on active duty and bring in another healthy revenue stream—not to mention bring into his orbit an ambitious young kid with whom he'd develop a life-altering bond so strong that people would come to assume they were father and son. Although he continued to be the guy everyone got along with, he'd manage to cross paths with one of the major exceptions to that rule—a wild renegade just getting started on his own rough road to immortality. And then there would be the time he'd find himself standing across the ring from the most celebrated athlete of the twentieth century. By the end of the decade, his in-ring career would come to a bloody but welcome conclusion in the same building where Rocky Balboa fought Apollo Creed. And all the while, the promoter's son was going from a glorified errand boy and talking head to a man who would start dreaming of one day pulling the rug out from under everybody.

■

Despite all the success he'd been experiencing since he'd entered the pro wrestling ranks, Gino never forgot where he came from, and at the end of September 1973, he traveled back home to upstate New York. Not just to visit his parents and sisters in Rochester, which he did often, but this time to accept induction into the Ithaca College Sports Hall of Fame. He'd never forgotten Ithaca, returning several times to visit the campus, maintaining membership in the booster club and, of course, following the fortunes of the wrestling team, once even contributing $5,000 for their new mat. And Ithaca had never forgotten Tiny and his contributions to that dominant late-'50s team. Now, fifteen years later, Marella returned to proudly accept the accolade at the school's fifth annual induction banquet. It meant a lot to him—a glowing reminder of his very real accomplishments as a very real wrestler.

Meanwhile, back in the more showbiz-oriented world of the pro ranks, as a right-hand man and vice president of the Capitol Wrestling Corporation, Gino was more valuable to Vincent J. McMahon than ever before. This was reflected in the fact that the promoter was becoming far less willing to lend him out to other territories when requested. In fact, the last time Gorilla Monsoon would be sent out to work any other North American territory came in the fall of 1973, when he flew out to Los Angeles to bail out Mike LeBell, who was in a bit of a bind thanks to a business deal gone south with Johnny Valentine. According to most sources, LeBell had promised to make Valentine—who possessed a keen wrestling mind as ever there was—his new booker, granting him the much-coveted position long shared by Charlie Moto and Jules Strongbow, both retiring after decades of loyal service. The problem was, as Valentine would later tell it, LeBell changed his mind, wanting to use Valentine only as a wrestler. And so the already volatile and moody Valentine promptly walked out of the company just as quickly as he'd walked in, taking another offer to work for the Crockett family in the Carolinas.[1]

Unfortunately, Valentine had also been advertised for a big main event at the Olympic Auditorium against Americas champion John Tolos, then in the midst of a short-lived run as a top babyface. "He walked out on us," remembers Jeff Walton, LeBell's assistant at the time. "And Mike says, 'I'll talk to Vince Sr., and I'll get back to you real quick.' So Mike gets on the phone. Then he calls me and he says, 'I talked to

Vince, and Vince said, don't worry about it. He's gonna send Gorilla Monsoon. And that's gonna be our main event for Friday night.'" So Gino came out to the coast for a week or so to help fix things. First, in grand wrestling tradition, it was announced to fans in California that the fearsome Gorilla Monsoon had crippled Johnny Valentine and sent him home and would be taking his place against Tolos. On Halloween night at the Olympic TV tapings, Monsoon crushed two unfortunate jobbers in a handicap match to set the stage, and two days later in the same building, he faced off with the Americas champ in the main event.

The finish of the match had Monsoon stunning Tolos with his patented giant swing, then going for his Manchurian splash finisher, but bumping the ref coming off the ropes, allowing Tolos time to roll out of the way and send Monsoon crashing down to an empty canvas. Conveniently, the still-prone referee didn't see Tolos blast Monsoon with a chair but came to just in time to count the pinfall, keeping the belt around the waist of Tolos.[2] The big show had been saved; Monsoon had helped the LeBell office deliver a memorable main event and was back on a plane to New York, never to wrestle in California again.

■

By the following weekend, he'd be back working spot shows on the Jersey Shore. He'd also continue working with some of the younger talent coming into the Capitol territory, including a beefy, mustachioed rookie named Mike McCord, then in the midst of a two-year mid-card run with the WWWF. At the Memorial Auditorium in Worcester, Massachusetts, Monsoon would get a disqualification win over McCord—who just a few years later would achieve much greater fame down south as Austin Idol, the Universal Heartthrob. It was all in a day's work for Gino, even though his services in the ring were required less and less, as could be evidenced by the fact that he only worked in a backstage capacity at all three autumn 1973 shows at Madison Square Garden, the arena where fans expected him as a regular fixture in either the main event or upper mid-card by that point.

Baby Gorilla: An infant Robert Marella (right), with his older brother Lenard Jr. (aka Sonny), likely late 1937.

Robert as a youngster in the 1940s, before his dramatic growth spurt kicked in.

Late 1940s: Robert (right) quickly catching up to Sonny, who wouldn't get much taller than he is here.

Coach Roger Bunce (bottom left) with the Jefferson High School wrestling team, 1952–1953 season. Tenth grader Robert Marella is conspicuous in the upper right-hand corner.

Star heavyweight for the Ithaca Bombers, undefeated junior Robert Marella in 1958 with the first of two 4-I Conference championships.

Robert with stepmother Connie and father Lenard, college graduation, 1959.

The AAU wrestling squad that made an ill-fated tour of Europe and the Middle East in the early summer of '59. (Robert pictured second in the back row.)

Robert (left) comes to grips with Russian heavyweight Savkuz Dzarasov on his way to a crushing defeat before a crowd of thousands in Moscow for the first meet of the tour.

Rookie pro wrestler Bob Marella, as he looked when he debuted in Rochester for promoter Pedro Martinez in 1960.

Spring 1963: On tour together in Japan, Killer Kowalski takes his new friend Gino Marella shopping to pick out a Rolex watch, a major milestone in a young wrestler's career.

The formidable duo of Marella and Kowalski double-team legendary wrestler-promoter Rikidozan during the same tour.

Jersey Journal—October 3, 1963: Hyping up the first meeting of Gorilla Monsoon and WWWF world champion Bruno Sammartino, at Jersey City's Roosevelt Stadium. A copy of this cartoon once hung in Gino's home.

May 11, 1964: Monsoon and Sammartino do battle in their third of seven main events at the old Madison Square Garden, a seventy-minute curfew draw that both men called their greatest match.

Gorilla Monsoon and Cowboy Bill Watts, WWWF United States tag team champions in mid-1965.

Another Territory, Another Tag Team Title: With Crazy Luke Graham and manager Wild Red Berry in Southern California's WWA, autumn 1965.

Honeymooners: The newlywed Gino Marella and bride Maureen, August 1966. Wrestling's happiest couple.

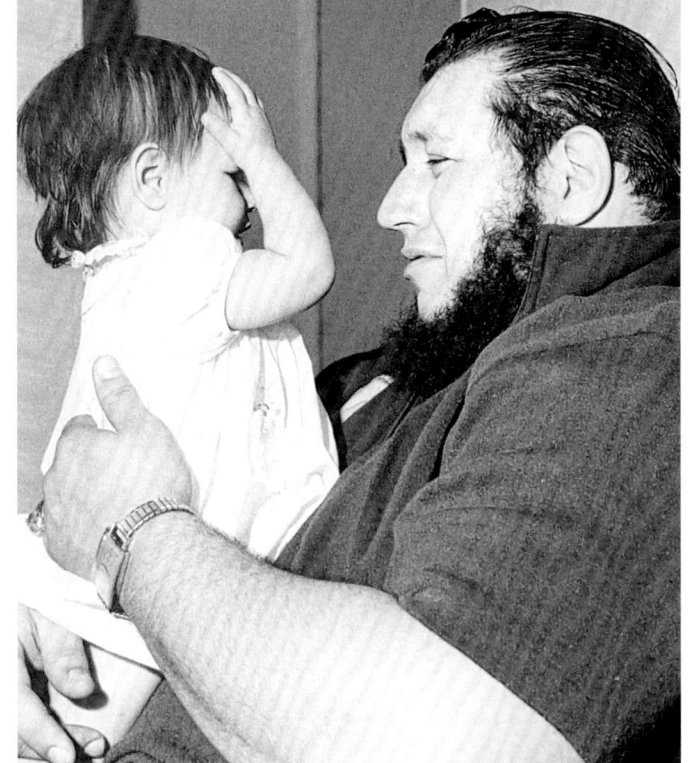

Cutie and the Beast: Baby Valerie and her dad.

A locker room card game—a regular occurrence in those days—captured with perfect timing.

Gino finds a pool hall while on tour in Japan.

WWWF President Willie Gilzenberg attempts to maintain order in this publicity shot from Monsoon and Sammartino's return program in 1967.

At home with King's Ransom, the family's rambunctious Great Pyrenees.

With Sharon and Joey in California, 1966.

Cutting up a massive steak hot off the grill at his Willingboro home, with Maureen and Valerie. From the infamous photo shoot for the October 1967 issue of *The Wrestler*.

Wild Red Berry checks on his bloodied charge. In addition to looking out for Gino as a "manager," Berry also became a family friend.

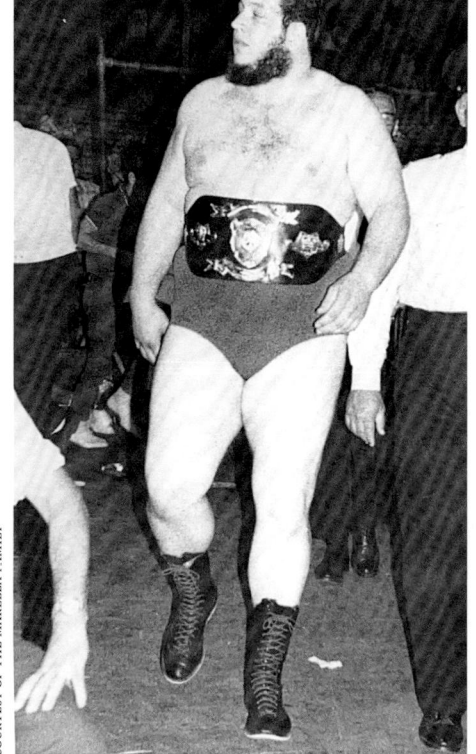

As IWA world champion for Jim Barnett's World Championship Wrestling in Australia, February or March 1968. The only world title Gino would ever hold.

Shaking hands with Shohei "Giant" Baba. Likely from Gino's autumn 1966 Japanese tour for the struggling JWA.

The *gaijin* crew arrive at Tokyo's Haneda Airport for a press conference ahead of the JWA's 1969 World League Tournament. Left to right: Bobby Duncum, Pepper Gomez, Chris Markoff, Bobo Brazil, Gino, Los Medicos, Tom Andrews.

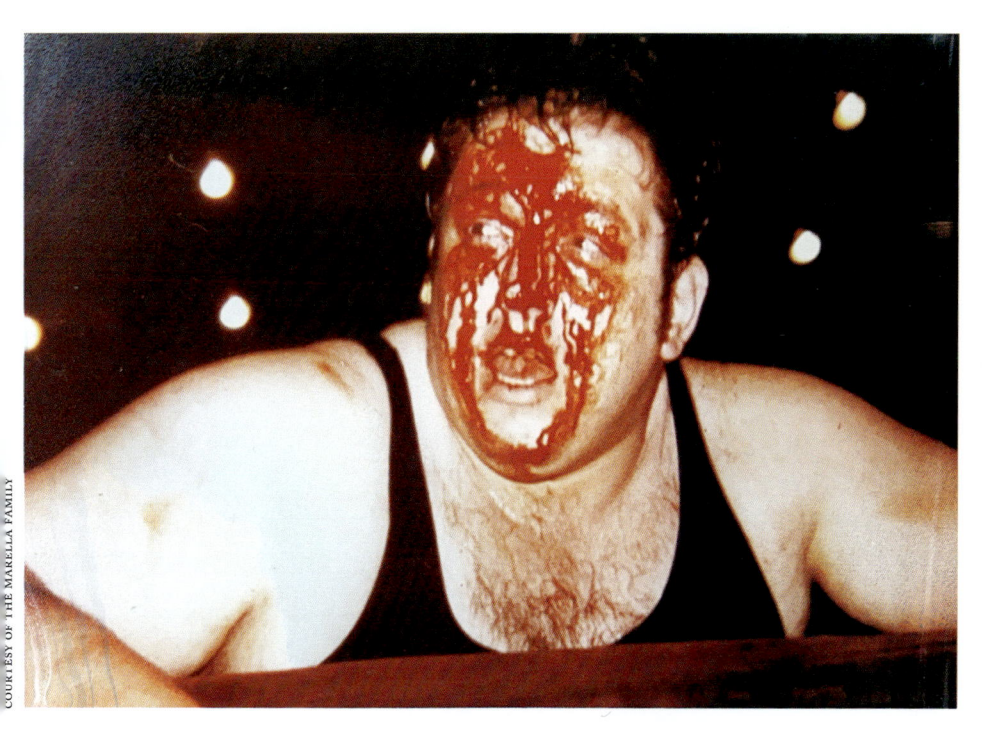

Bleeding profusely in Madison Square Garden, not long after his 1969 babyface turn, in either 1970 or 1971 judging by the iconic red velvet ring rope.

With referee Dick Woehrle and longtime LA Dodgers manager—and fellow Italian-American icon—Tommy Lasorda at a charity function.

Dancing with stepmom Connie at the wedding of one of his sisters.

Joey's confirmation, 1976.

The last of those three shows, on December 10, would be a very special one and another turning point for the company. After nearly three years with Pedro Morales on top as WWWF heavyweight champion, Vince McMahon had decided to halt the experiment. Business was hot, but he felt it could be even hotter, and to get there, he wanted to put that belt back on the man from whom he'd never really wanted to take it away in the first place. Since that fateful day in January 1971 when he'd eased the crown off his head, Bruno Sammartino had been surprisingly absent from Capitol Wrestling, focusing more on the Pittsburgh territory he owned, as well as touring other areas. In fact, during Morales's time on top, Bruno had only nineteen known matches in a WWWF ring—just six of them in his home turf of the Garden. By the end of 1973, he hadn't been seen by WWWF fans for close to a year. Just as he had ten years earlier, Vince McMahon felt he needed him once again.

Also just like last time, Bruno felt he had a little leverage and used it to get the kind of deal he wanted. If McMahon wanted him back in the driver's seat, he would have to grant him a more reduced schedule compared to last time. This time, there would be no more VFW halls, high school gymnasiums or rec centers; he would make appearances only at Capitol's major arenas (or "clubs" as he called them) throughout the circuit, effectively cutting his schedule almost in half, from roughly five to seven appearances per week to roughly two to four—giving him more time at home and an easier load to carry for his nearly middle-aged body, finely tuned though it was. The result would be a period for the company and for Bruno personally that would prove to be even more lucrative than his original celebrated championship reign.

Monsoon was there with Morales on December 1, 1973, the night the trigger was pulled before 5,412 fans at the Philadelphia Arena—the company had learned its lesson from the last time a popular babyface was beaten for the title and a near-riot ensued outside the Garden, and thus it was moved this time to a little more out-of-the-way location. No one saw it coming—even the opponent, Stan Stasiak, was someone Morales had beaten before. Similar to the manner in which he had won the title but in reverse, the finish occurred thanks to a near "double-pin," with both men's shoulders down on the mat, but Stasiak getting his shoulder up just before the referee's count of three, gaining him the WWWF heavyweight championship. Like a thief in the night, Stasiak left the ring, and Monsoon carefully escorted his charge out of the building. Just as with Koloff in '71, the title change wasn't even announced to the live crowd. And just nine days later at Madison Square Garden, twenty-two thousand fans got to celebrate wildly in the aisles and go home happy, having seen Bruno Sammartino trounce Stasiak, becoming the first man to ever regain the WWWF title, triumphantly returning to the spot that no one had ever wanted him to relinquish except Sammartino himself.

Pedro Morales remained in the Northeast for over a year afterward before returning to California, and during that year, he continued to be a hot attraction, usually the semi-main event at the Garden as Gorilla Monsoon used to be. As for Gorilla, he continued to tangle with the heels who were either on their way up or on their way down. One of these was the former Bepo Mongol, who had been repackaged as the ruthless Soviet Nikolai Volkoff—a source of endless amusement to real-life Soviet-hating Croat Josip Peruzović. Monsoon dropped a match at the Garden in January 1974 to Volkoff, who was also notable for the manager he'd been paired with at the time: "Classy" Freddie Blassie, whose wrestling career on the West Coast had been cut short, not just by his own busted-up knees and hips but by the California State Athletic Commission's regulations prohibiting wrestlers from renewing their licenses past the age of fifty-five. Vince had always loved Freddie and offered him a full-time spot as a manager in the WWWF, completing an unholy triumvirate of malevolent mouthpieces that also included Capt. Louis Albano and "Grand Wizard" Ernie Roth and would run roughshod in the Northeast for the next decade.

Other Monsoon opponents included the quickly deposed former champion Stasiak, whom he beat all around the horn through the winter. There was also fellow giant Don Leo Jonathan, whom he battled not just at the Garden but also at the very first wrestling card held at a brand-new arena just seven miles outside Queens in Uniondale, Long Island—the

Nassau Veterans Memorial Coliseum, which quickly became the New York metropolitan area's second-tier Capitol Wrestling venue.

■

Not only was Gino slowing down his bookings at home, but even his bookings abroad were slowing—specifically, his trips to Japan. Although he loved his visits there, after the last trip, when he'd finally taken Maureen with him, the pull of domestic life became stronger than ever. The kids were getting older and hated seeing their dad gone for long stretches—but with offers of $5,000 per week, it was tough to pass up. Under gentle pressure from his family, Gino decided that his tour in the late spring of 1974 would be his last. It would also be his shortest at just three weeks, as opposed to the usual six. When the choice was between family and business, Gino always chose the former.

By that point, the Japanese Wrestling Association was no more. Shohei "Giant" Baba—who had stayed on until the bitter end while his rival Antonio Inoki had left to form New Japan Pro-Wrestling—had finally struck out on his own and founded All Japan Pro Wrestling. In those early days, many foreign wrestlers like Monsoon remained loyal to Baba, thanks to their previous working relationship with him in the JWA and with Rikidozan before him. This is why All Japan quickly became much more known for its *gaijin* attractions than New Japan was. To further capitalize on the American connection, Baba and All Japan were presenting a tour called the Madison Square Garden Series,[3] featuring regular MSG talent like Monsoon, Morales, Mr. Fuji and Johnny Rodz as well as Spiros Arion, who flew in from Australia; Moose Morowski of the AWA; Texas-based luchador El Tapia; and a fresh-faced newcomer from Eddie Graham's Florida office, twenty-four-year-old Kevin Sullivan.

This final Japanese tour was not quite as dominant as his last couple. Out of sixteen matches, he only won five. The most notable occurrences would be the two tag team matches in which he found himself on the opposite side of the ring from Dick "The Destroyer" Beyer, marking the only two occasions in which he would ever face the most successful and iconic of all *gaijin* superstars. The rigors of Japanese wrestling also seemed to be taking a toll on him, and he can be seen visibly struggling in some of his appearances on this tour, most notably his final Japanese appearance, a "judo jacket match" against former world judo champion and Olympic gold medalist Anton Geesink. By this point, he had gone well past four hundred pounds, famously getting up as high as 440, and it showed. Even at his massive size and height, that was a lot of weight to be carrying around, especially by age thirty-seven. Gino loved living life. He ate well and often. He had a heavy smoking habit. And by this point, he had pretty much stopped gym training completely. None of this was helping. He began to notice that he was sweating more profusely than ever and was thirsty all the time. It was an issue he'd look into not long after returning to the States that summer.

When Gino returned to America in late June, he brought Giant Baba with him. The result was their final in-ring encounter, which took place at Madison Square Garden on June 24 and was won by Baba via count-out.[4] It would be Baba's final appearance at the Garden as well, as Capitol Wrestling would end its relationship with All Japan and strike up a decade-long partnership with Inoki and New Japan Pro-Wrestling the following year, against the protests of Baba loyalists such as Gino and of Bruno, who continued to go work for Baba because he was never one to allow the McMahons to dictate such things to him anyway.

■

Although Gino was never one for doctors at all, he did finally get himself checked out, only to discover what couldn't have been much of a surprise: Type 2 diabetes. "He knew something was wrong," remembers Maureen. He hadn't been thrilled with his weight gain in recent years, and this gave him some more motivation to get it back down. Treatment originally consisted of oral medication to help balance his blood sugar, with, of course, the strong recommendation to avoid rich foods and, one would imagine, to cut out smoking. The chances of either happening to any large degree were, as Gorilla himself might have said, highly unlikely. "We would occasionally find Hostess wrappers and things like that in the car," remembers Valerie. Food options on the road were notoriously limited, plus he had a sweet tooth. But he wanted to be healthier, and he would succeed in getting himself back down to four hundred and even well below in future years. But he'd be damned if he wasn't going to enjoy a good steak when he could, or a cigar.

Unlike so many of his compatriots, he wasn't much of a drinker, so perhaps he felt he'd earned the right to the other vices. Gino didn't like to deprive himself. Davey O'Hannon remembers a particular occasion, after coming back from playing racquetball with Gino and his great friend, referee Dick Woehrle, when they all went back to Willingboro, where Gino made sandwiches and then offered dessert. The dessert consisted of two half gallons of ice cream, each cut in halves, with an entire row of Oreo cookies crumbled on top of each. "Now I love ice cream," explains O'Hannon. "And back then I didn't care what I ate. I was working every night so it didn't matter. Or I didn't know any better. And he crushes the Oreos and I said, 'Is somebody else coming?' 'No, no this is for us.' He said, 'Do you want chocolate syrup on top?' 'Oh, you might as well, how can we go more wrong than this?'"

One constructive thing that did come out of the diagnosis right away is that Gino began to get involved with what would become his charity of choice: the Juvenile Diabetes Foundation. He knew what he was dealing with, and the thought of something like that happening to children would certainly give anyone pause, especially someone with such a fondness for kids. He became heavily involved in raising money for the cause, with some of the proceeds of the shows he promoted going toward it, including the big annual cards at JFK High School. Over the years, he'd raise money for cancer research, domestic and child abuse victims, children's burn centers and other causes. There were also his fondly remembered summer shows in the New Jersey resort town of Wildwood, which kicked off in the summer of 1974. On the second of those shows, the ring announcer was a skinny, nervous twenty-one-year-old from nearby Seaside Park, Gary Michael Cappetta—a wide-eyed wrestling fan who'd first encountered Gorilla Monsoon when he'd briefly interviewed him for a gig he'd gotten with *The Ring Wrestling* magazine.

An aspiring school teacher at the time, Cappetta had no idea that his summer job was going to lead to a ten-year mentorship with a man who would earn his undying respect, and whom he would always cite as the person who got him started on a career as one of the most recognized ring announcers of all time. In fact, at first, Gary didn't even know Gino was the man in charge. "Willie Gilzenberg was the frontman, and as far as I knew, he was the promoter," Gary recalls. "And Monsoon was simply a wrestler. But at the end of the summer, when Monsoon called me and asked me if I would start working for him, announcing for him, that's when I came to find out that he was the promoter." Cappetta was not allowed in the locker room, but Gino had been watching and listening from behind the curtain and identified someone who'd be a perfect fit for his shows.

Like many others do, Cappetta remembers Wildwood as a family affair. Maureen and Sharon would sell tickets all week on the boardwalk in front of the convention center, right off the beach. In later years, Joey and Valerie would help out as well, and they had a vacation home down the shore where they'd spend much of those summer days. On the day of the show, it wouldn't be all that unusual for Gino himself to be standing by the door, selling tickets—five dollars for bleacher seats, seven for ringside. "Someone with an ego, they couldn't do that," Gary says. "They would never be seen doing that. That wasn't him. People would come up and he would talk to them." And he would do more than talk, as he himself explained once to a reporter for the *Press of Atlantic City*: "It's a family deal. We have entire families come here. If I see a guy come in here with his wife and six kids, I'll give him a break. I won't charge him the full price."[5]

Everyone in the inner circle had their piece of the territory in those days, and Gino was comfortably settled in his. Up in Boston, meanwhile, there had been a shakeup when promoter Abe Ford, unhappy with his relationship with the Capitol office, started making overtures to other promotions in an attempt to bring in different talent. One of these promotions was Grand Prix Wrestling up in Montreal, run by brothers Maurice "Mad Dog" Vachon and Paul "Butcher" Vachon. With their territory on the decline, the Vachons saw a greater advantage in getting on Vince McMahon's good side than in working with Ford, so they snitched out Ford to McMahon, resulting in Ford's prompt removal as the WWWF's Boston promoter.[6] In his place, McMahon installed Ernie Roth and partner Bobby Harmon and also sent his son Vince Jr. to help out and learn more of the promotional ropes. Still not completely on his feet despite his father's help, the younger Vince was making every effort to follow in the family's footsteps. Angelo Savoldi, who ran most of New England for Vince the elder, was instructed to look out for him: "Once a week, Vince would call and say to my father, when you're in Boston, go over and give Vinny some money," remembers Angelo's son Mario.

The territory continued to expand, thrive and strengthen its hold, running occasional spot shows as far south as West Virginia. The old Pittsburgh territory, once a satellite promotion to Capitol, became a fully absorbed part of the WWWF territory. There were new buildings to run, including the twenty-thousand-seat Capital Centre in Landover, Maryland, which brought Capitol Wrestling back to the actual U.S. Capitol region for the first time in three years. There was also the Philadelphia Spectrum, another twenty-thousand-seater that represented a major step up from the old Philadelphia Arena and had been open for seven years before the WWWF finally ran it for the first time in August 1974. It would quickly rise in prominence to rival the Boston Garden as the WWWF's number-two building and would become especially important to Gino, as it stood just across the Delaware River, half an hour from Willingboro. He wouldn't actually wrestle at the Spectrum for almost a year after the WWWF started running the building, a testament to how involved he was in running things backstage and also to how much his health was contributing to an ever-decreasing in-ring schedule.

By August, the same month the Spectrum hosted its first WWWF card, headlined by Sammartino defending against Killer Kowalski, Monsoon was only wrestling a handful of matches per month, just a fraction of what he'd been doing at his peak back in the '60s. And it would pretty much stay that way for the remaining years of his wrestling career, which quickly appeared to be coming to an early end, especially by professional wrestling standards. And yet what fans saw on TV and in the arenas in those days was but the tiniest tip of the iceberg of what Gino's work entailed, and the less he appeared between the ropes, the busier he actually became. In the years to come, he would become more of a "special attraction"—which suited him just fine. He'd paid his dues and then some.

For young Valerie, it was also a time when she started to fully comprehend just what her father did for a living. "I was probably in second grade before I realized what was happening, what my family was," she recalls. "We came back from a Christmas break at school . . . we're going around the classroom, and everybody's telling one big thing and one little thing they got for Christmas. I started to realize that all their big things were my little things . . . When I went home, I said something to my mom, and she kinda laughed and said, 'Well, you know, Daddy's a little different than the other daddies.'" But despite the privileges and luxuries that came from being Gorilla Monsoon's child, there were also, of course, the downsides that most children of pro wrestlers have had to deal with: "I would go over to a friend's house, and they would say, we gotta clean up, my dad will be home in five minutes. And I would say, how do you know what time he's coming home? They'd say, my dad comes home every night at six p.m., and I'm like, from where?? From his office! That blew my mind. And they'd be like, when does your dad come home, and I'm like . . . Sunday?" It was the price of success, but it was true that Gino always did his best to make sure that Sundays were family days.

Valerie recalls how everyone's birthdays and other special events would be saved for Sundays to make sure the family could all be together. Barbecues in the yard would be a neighborhood event, with "local celebrity" Gorilla Monsoon manning the grill. On Christmas, the house was open to all. After a long stretch away from home, he was never too tired for his family, packing the kids and whichever of their friends they could fit in the car and heading up to the newly opened Great Adventure amusement park in Jackson Township: "A couple would say they couldn't afford it. And when I told him, he said, 'No, I didn't ask who could *afford* to go to Great Adventure—we're just going to Great Adventure.'" And so they'd jump in the car—and what a car, as Gino liked to trade in for a new one each year: Fleetwoods, Coupe de Villes, Eldorados, with a custom-made hood ornament, dipped in gold or silver to match the trim. And when he pushed the seat all the way back to get his mammoth frame behind the wheel, woe to anyone stuck in the driver's side backseat.

One of Valerie's friends in those days was her classmate Mike Canzano, who had just moved with his mom from Bayonne to Willingboro, in the Twin Hills section, not far from the Country Club section where the Marellas resided. Mike got to know the Marellas quite well in the ensuing years, which would eventually lead to a job on Gino's ring crew and later a shot at being a referee. By that time, he had taken on his stepfather's last name and become Mike Chioda.

■

But despite a reduced schedule, Gino was still on the road almost as often as ever, making the towns and performing other important office duties. Bruno was on top as the champion, and Gino liked to ride with him as much as possible, often picking him up from the airport in Hartford, Connecticut, and taking him to Boston, or making trips down to Baltimore and Washington, sometimes going out of his way just to make sure they could ride together. Dominic DeNucci might be in the car as well, or the Savoldis. "Bruno and Gino were like brothers," Mario remembers. "Whenever they could go together, they were together. They had that beyond-work friendship. And I don't speak Italian, so if I had my dad and Bruno, with Gino or Dominic in the car, I could say I drove by myself because I couldn't understand a word anybody was saying in the car."

One infamous road story from these rides, which Mario Savoldi witnessed firsthand, involved a gag planned out with veteran midget wrestler Sky Low Low on the Connecticut Turnpike on the way back from Boston. As they approached a toll booth, Gino asked Mario to pull over, and to everyone's confusion, he got out and gingerly placed the three-foot-six, eighty-five-pound French Canadian in the trunk. Gino then instructed Mario to drive just past the toll booth, stop the car and then pop the trunk. As the flustered toll clerk came out of the booth to demand the toll, out jumped Sky Low Low from the trunk to run over and plunk a quarter in the clerk's hand, then promptly hopped back in the trunk and shut the door as the car full of wrestlers continued on its way, with Gino laughing till his belly shook.

Gorilla Monsoon might still occasionally be called upon to headline Madison Square Garden, as he did on February 17, 1975, when he and Chief Jay Strongbow battled the WWWF world tag team champions, the team of Jimmy and Johnny Valiant, who had taken the area by storm after arriving the previous summer. After his earlier singles run in the WWWF, Gino's former tenant Jimmy Valiant had traveled to Dick the Bruiser's WWA in Indianapolis, where he'd been teamed up with the young wrestler who had previously wrestled as John L. Sullivan after knocking on Bruno Sammartino's door one day in Pittsburgh and asking how to break into the business. Now the Valiant Brothers were one of the hottest acts in the industry, having gotten the tag team title their first night in the company and recently headlined the Garden against Sammartino and Strongbow in two blood-soaked main events. The February match against Monsoon and Strongbow was notably the first time the WWWF's Garden show would be simulcast on a giant screen at the Felt Forum theater that sat right below the arena and held another four to five thousand people.

With box-office walk-up business on the day of the show still very common at that time, this allowed for an overflow of last-minute patrons, resulting in bigger crowds and bigger receipts than the company had ever seen before at its home arena. An astounding twenty-five thousand fans filled both rooms that night—a new record that would be swept aside the following month when twenty-six thousand turned up on St. Patrick's Day to witness a blistering Texas death match between Sammartino and the man whose betrayal of the champ had drawn the ire of fans everywhere, the formerly beloved Spiros Arion.[7] At the end of the year, a December show featuring Madison Square Garden's first steel cage match—between Bruno Sammartino and the man who once defeated him for the world title, Ivan Koloff—drew 26,350 fans, making it to this day the largest crowd in a century and a half of wrestling at the Garden. And those kinds of numbers would become common going forward, with the mid-'70s to early '80s becoming the hottest attendance period ever seen for wrestling in the historic building.

Gorilla also battled the Valiants throughout the circuit with other partners like Morales and Larry Zbyszko, another young protégé of Sammartino's, and a young lower-card wrestler from San Lorenzo, Puerto Rico—José González, who would become one of his closest friends among the many Latino wrestlers with whom he spent his time.

■

In later years, González would become involved, through Gino, in a venture that would also extend the wrestling career of Gorilla Monsoon by a few years, not to mention the size of his income. In 1974, while the Capitol Wrestling Corporation was lighting up the Northeast, a brand-new company very similarly called Capitol Sports Promotions was taking shape all the way down in Puerto Rico. And the reason for the similarity of the name may have had something to do with the fact that the company's founder, Carlos Colón, had spent significant time as an enhancement wrestler in the Northeast early in his career and, as did many Puerto Ricans at the time, had a strong connection to New York City.

Located a two-and-a-half-hour plane ride from Miami, Puerto Rico had been run in years past by Florida promoter Cowboy Luttrall and his protégé Eddie Graham, who had eventually taken over the territory from him fully in 1970. It had been quiet for a couple of years, but the Florida office was involved in making the deal to give Puerto Rico over to Colón and his new business partner and fellow wrestler, the Croatian-born Victor Jovica. Furthermore, due to the strong Florida connection to the WWWF, it's likely that Vince and Gino were involved in these dealings to a certain degree from the very beginning, or at least were very much aware of them.[8] After all, Vince now resided near Fort Lauderdale and had been close with Eddie for years. Gino had spent time in Florida as well, visiting Gilzenberg, and had been very close with Colón and other Puerto Rican wrestlers for years—it was definitely a development that was on his radar for quite a while.

On January 6, 1974, Capitol Sports Promotions (later known as the World Wrestling Council), under the ownership of Colón, Jovica and Jovica's brother, presented its debut show at the Mario Morales Coliseum in the San Juan suburb of Guaynabo. The appetite for wrestling in Puerto Rico was rabid, and growth was quick. A year later, the company was putting eighteen thousand fans in the Juan Loubriel soccer stadium in Bayamón to see the god of lucha libre himself, El Santo, team up with Colón, who had quickly transformed himself from a mid- and under-card wrestler banking on a passing resemblance to Harry Belafonte, into the center of his new promotion and a legend in the making in his own right. The company was making waves, and money, right away.

Although much of the history of pro wrestling in the Caribbean is murky and difficult to research, there appears to have been a relationship between CSP and the WWWF from the very start. Hugo Savinovich, an Ecuadorian of Croatian descent who had been getting into trouble with street gangs in the Bronx as a teenager in the 1970s before the wrestling business saved him from jail or worse, remembers shows on the island of Curaçao that were co-promotions between the Puerto Rico and New York offices, featuring talent from both. The Puerto Rican wrestling circuit included many other shows throughout the Caribbean in places like Barbados, St. Thomas, St. Croix, the Virgin Islands, Anguilla, Trinidad and Tobago, and even as far south as Panama. Although the earliest records of Gorilla Monsoon wrestling in Puerto Rico date back to 1977, it's believed he was already going down there even earlier. A place like that was not a difficult sell for Gino—like California and Hawaii, it had beautiful weather and beaches, and like Las Vegas, it had casinos aplenty, which drew Gino like a great big bee to honey. Headliners there could earn thousands of dollars per week wrestling, which Gino usually had no problem parlaying into even more at the blackjack tables.

It was a no-brainer that he would want to get involved. It's believed that sometime in 1975, most likely when Jovica's brother was looking to get out, Gino offered to buy his 10 percent interest in the promotion. And Gino was a powerful ally to have, with his connections to the hottest promotion in the business up north and the ability to facilitate talent exchanges, funneling superstar talent from the mainland into the island, as well as bringing up more Latino wrestlers and giving them opportunities on the big stage in the Northeast. And naturally, his value would also be as a draw since many Puerto Rican fans were aware of his years on top in New York. Although he'd been intent on winding down his wrestling career, and he most certainly still was, it was also hard to pass up that kind of money. And just like that, Gino now had a piece of two different white-hot wrestling territories.

By all accounts, Gino's closeness with Latino wrestlers came at least in part from a genuine desire to help them, to give them opportunities he felt they were being unfairly denied. "There was a lot of discrimination in the business," explains Savinovich. "But Gino was so different. He loved people. He didn't see color or nationality. Or whether you were doing the first match, or you were Bruno Sammartino. And he had been very pissed off about the treatment the Latino talents were getting [in the WWWF]." This would also explain Gino's close involvement in the ascension of Pedro Morales as champion up north. Besides his magnanimity, it was also just plain common sense and good for business: "He had a bigger mind . . . He knew [what] customers were selling out the Garden, Boston Garden, Philadelphia . . . They were [catering to] the Italian-American crowd with Bruno Sammartino. But he thought that [for example] the Jewish audience were not really catered to, and especially Latinos. It wasn't good on a human basis but also as a business. He knew back then what we know now."

From the very beginning, Gino was treated with great respect and admiration when he would go down to Puerto Rico—by the promoters, by the boys, by the fans and most definitely by the casinos. Puerto Rico was one of those places where pro wrestling was a religion, and the stars were truly celebrities. People saw this giant of a man, this star from New York, coming in to help support and elevate wrestling and help the company grow, and he was treated accordingly. He also treated everyone else with respect and so won the hearts of everyone wherever he went.

Situated in the heart of the bustling tourist district of San Juan on the northern coast, within walking distance of the blue-green waters of Condado Lagoon and the gorgeous white sands of Condado Beach, stood the Hotel Tanama, a boxy, seven-floor gray-and-orange structure of concrete where wrestlers working the Puerto Rico territory would often stay. The place was managed by a woman who was struggling to raise her teenaged son alone, both living in the hotel after her husband, the boy's stepfather, had committed suicide. The boy was Victor Quiñones, and Gino would get to know him quite well during his visits to the island. He would help Gino and the other wrestlers with their bags and, because he had a good command of both Spanish and English, would facilitate communication. As he got a little older, he would even drive them around the island when needed. But it was clear that his life was far from ideal—unable to read or write, with no education to speak of, and deprived of a father figure.

"Gino had some connection there," remembers Davey O'Hannon, who was one of the WWWF wrestlers who'd get booked down there thanks to him. "He might have even set it up so we got a rate . . . Sometimes guys didn't even know Gino took care of the rate. That's how Victor got the connection with Gino, seeing all the wrestlers hanging around." And the more Gino went down there, the more he grew to like this scrappy kid who seemed to really be on the ball but was clearly leading a rough life and deserved better, in his estimation. Their bond grew strong as time went on, to the point that Victor began to view Gino as the father figure he never had.

They became so close, in fact, that this relationship would eventually inspire one of the most persistent urban legends in all of pro wrestling, as many would go on to assume that Victor actually was Gino's secret son. But that assumption, widespread though it may have been, was also false and requires a brief pause in the narrative here to properly address. Although they loved each other like a father and son, Robert Marella was not the biological father of Victor Quiñones. For one thing, the unspoken (and sometimes spoken) thinking behind the assumption is that Gino had been messing around while wrestling down in Puerto Rico early in his career and that Victor had been the unintended result. However, this sordid assumption is based on a very obvious fallacy: When Victor Quiñones was born in San Juan on June 30, 1959, Bob Marella wasn't even in the business yet. In fact, at the time Victor's mother was pregnant, Marella was in his senior year at Ithaca College.

The fact is, Gino first met Victor (and Victor's mother) on those early Puerto Rico tours in the mid-1970s. And the boring truth: Gino was simply a generous person with a soft spot for underprivileged kids. Certainly, the rumors that began to spread were only further fueled in later years when Gino would take Victor to live with him and his family in New Jersey. Victor was also occasionally known to privately describe Gino as a "father" of sorts to him, or more often as a "godfather." But these terms of endearment were only ever meant as just that and were not to be taken literally, although they would be later on. As time went on, the rumors would take on a life of their own, and to be honest, one of the main reasons for this was that the parties involved, whether it be Victor, Gino or Gino's family, didn't consider them to be worthy of addressing or refuting. The fact is that Gino did come to love Victor like a figurative son, and Gino's family also came to love him as one of their own.

To this day, perhaps the most commonly referenced source for the belief that Victor was Gino's literal son would be Gino's 1999 obituary in the *New York Times*, which actually listed Victor amongst Gino's surviving children. More than anything, it only goes to show how pervasive the rumor was and how literally many took the symbolic father-son relationship they shared. Obituaries for pro wrestlers were quite a rarity in the mainstream press in those days, and when they did run, they were notorious for their sloppy reporting and inaccuracies; this was nothing more than a detail that was never properly fact-checked, reported by a stringer who probably thought he had an "inside track" that he didn't have. And again, perhaps because they considered Victor part of their family, or because they simply didn't care to address it, Maureen, Valerie, Sharon and the rest of Gino's family never bothered to publicly correct the mistake. They may not have considered it important, even if it did reinforce one of the more salacious stories about the life of Gorilla Monsoon, the debunking of which is long overdue.

■

Meanwhile, back in the States, Gino had cut back his wrestling schedule, but Gino also loved the spotlight, loved to be seen by the fans and also loved the paydays involved. So what he started doing more often was acting as a special guest enforcer referee for big matches, which would be a role fans would become very accustomed to seeing him take on during the mid- to late 1970s. The start of this phenomenon took place at the Spectrum on November 16, 1974, when he stepped in to referee the explosive rematch in which Sammartino and Strongbow took on the Valiants. He would do it again when Tony Garea and Dean Ho challenged the Valiants on April 21, 1975, at Nassau Coliseum, and in his hometown of Rochester on April 15, when Cowboy Bobby Duncum took on newcomer Ivan Putski, a burly Polish-American from Texas doing a simple-minded-immigrant gimmick, who would quickly become one of Gino's least favorite performers. Gino refereed Texas death matches between Sammartino and Bobby Duncum on April 12 in Boston and June 12 in New Haven, plus the November 12 Sammartino/Koloff match at Madison Square Garden that led directly to their historic steel cage main event the following month.

Not only was it a great idea to have Gorilla as the no-nonsense, imposing referee who would be there to maintain order, but another strategy at work was that sometimes the outcome of these matches would result in future matches for Gorilla himself, particularly when the heels would take exception to his tough officiating. It was another tried-and-true recipe to keep Monsoon involved in the mix.

On the promotional side of things, Gino and the rest of the inner circle were called upon to help bolster the company amid what was shaping up to be the first real wrestling war in New York in over a decade. The last one, in the early '60s, had taken place when Antonino Rocca jumped ship and got hooked up with Big Jim Crockett, running shows right across the East River in Sunnyside, Queens. But this was something different. This time, sports television mogul Eddie Einhorn, who had helped put college basketball on the map as a major television attraction and set the stage for what later became known as March Madness, now wanted to do the same thing with pro wrestling. Having a fascination with the business since his days selling popcorn and soda for Chicago promoter Fred Kohler in his youth, Einhorn recruited Pedro Martinez—the Buffalo-Cleveland promoter whose National Wrestling Federation had just gone belly up—to form what they called the International Wrestling Association, a Cleveland-based outfit that was going to make a play to become the first truly national wrestling promotion.

In early 1975, Einhorn and Martinez started recruiting big-name talent for the IWA, including former WWWF standouts like Ivan Koloff and Victor Rivera, who left Capitol flat despite being in the midst of a run as WWWF world tag team champions with Dominic DeNucci. They brought on board none other than Mil Máscaras, who had been a major attraction at the Garden, to be their world champion. Things started to get serious when they even got a time slot on the nationally syndicated WWOR Channel 9, the former home of the WWWF, while McMahon and company were still confined to UHF Channel 47. Striking directly into the heart of Capitol Wrestling territory, the IWA ran three major events over the summer of '75 at New Jersey's Roosevelt Stadium, the very place where Gorilla Monsoon had made his name battling Bruno Sammartino a dozen years earlier—and drew as many as fourteen thousand for the first one, featuring Mascaras defending his new title against former WWWF world champion Koloff.

Capitol was taking a hit, and in order to fight the war, it was time to circle the wagons. Gino and Vince's other partner, Phil Zacko, were called upon to infuse the company with a little more liquid cash to help things along. So were Willie Gilzenberg, Angelo Savoldi and even Arnold Skaaland, one of McMahon's most loyal wrestlers who was almost strictly making appearances as Bruno Sammartino's manager by this point. Savoldi was even offered a piece of the company but only asked for his loan to be paid back, forgoing interest as well. In exchange for his loyalty in a time of need, Angelo and his son Mario were given most of New England to run for themselves, with a particular focus on Maine, which had previously been the domain of Vince McMahon's son Vinny, who had already started attempting to move on to bigger things.

Fortunately for Vince, Gino and company, Einhorn just didn't have the stomach to really go to war in the cutthroat world of professional wrestling, which made backroom network television dealings look like preschool. By the end of the year, he had already lost his nerve, handing over the IWA to Pedro Martinez and his son and withdrawing to the safer world of so-called legitimate sports. Not only that, but when the smoke had cleared, the Capitol Wrestling Corporation had even gotten its hands on the IWA's coveted WWOR Channel 9 time slots, which helped them get seen on cable outlets throughout the country. The (W)WWF would remain a fixture on WWOR for over a decade thereafter. Martinez would reign in the IWA's ambitions, hightailing it to the Mid-Atlantic region, where he'd eventually be run out of business by the Crocketts.

■

As always, Gino's loyalty was unquestioned. And that loyalty and generosity were not just for his partners but also extended to all those he called friends. Davey O'Hannon recalls a time back in 1976 when Gino, concerned that the brand-new Cadillac Coupe de Ville Davey had bought wasn't flashy enough, pulled off the hood ornament with his bare hand, then took Davey down to his own personal guy and dropped a few hundred bucks to equip the vehicle with a more suitably pimped-out ornament. Or the time he had 250 eight-by-tens made up for Davey, then refused to allow him to pay him back, which was a common occurrence: "When you were with Gino, don't even try to put your hand in your pocket . . . I reached into my bag, and I took out the money. He takes out a half dollar, which he always had. And he says call it in the air, double or nothing. Gino would bet you the sun wasn't going to come up tomorrow. So he flips it, looks at it and says, 'You win.' And hands me the pictures [for free]. I said, 'Hold it. How do I know I won?' He said, 'Because I told you.' He wouldn't take the money from me." Gino prevented Davey, or any of his friends, from paying at restaurants. Davey even recalls a time or two when he tried to secretly pay the waitress without letting Gino know, and Gino would refuse to leave until the bill had been charged to him instead.

Gino continued to be generous in the ring as well, such as in the early months of 1976, when he was called upon to help get over an important new heel who had just arrived in the Northeast thanks to the healthy talent exchange between Vince McMahon and Eddie Graham. Eldridge Wayne Coleman was the kind of character only pro wrestling could've produced: a combination bodybuilder and revivalist preacher from Phoenix who had rechristened himself Superstar Billy Graham, partly as a tribute to the iconic evangelist and partly due to his association with the Graham wrestling family while getting his first big break in California. With a god-like body chiseled out of granite, he stood out among the somewhat smooth and beefy performers fans were used to seeing in those days, and his undeniable color and charisma had helped make him a star in both California and the AWA before he first arrived in the WWWF at the tail end of 1975.

Needless to say, McMahon envisioned the Superstar as the newest and most lethal threat to Sammartino's title, and to get him ready for a run around the circuit with the champ, he needed some big wins over important opponents. One of these would be Gorilla Monsoon, who did the job for Graham in Providence, in Nassau Coliseum and twice in Philadelphia, while the Sammartino/Graham feud began to heat up. He also teamed with Sammartino in Boston in a dream match against the evil alliance of Graham and Ivan Koloff. Koloff, of course, had been the guy to take the title off Bruno the first time. And Graham would be the one to do it the second time—only not yet. Not during this run. For now, Gino was happy to help get over Graham, which would prove very important to the company over the next couple of years.

■

Gino seemed to get along with just about everyone, and stories of anyone having any issue with him are virtually nonexistent—but not completely. One glaring and infamous exception would be the man who was first sent up to the World Wide Wrestling Federation by Eddie Graham in April 1976. A product of that bastion of future wrestling talent, the West Texas State football squad, Frank Goodish had tried his hand at sports writing before putting his six-foot-four, 250-pound frame to better use as a pro wrestler in his late twenties. He was only a couple of years in the business when he found himself at the Holland Hotel, where Vince McMahon, again showing his penchant for Irish names, christened him Bruiser Brody, debuting him at the April 20 TV tapings and starting him on what he'd hoped would be a big-money program with Bruno Sammartino.

That program would happen, but not before Goodish had made some major waves in the organization, and not in a good way. Maybe it was because he'd entered the business relatively late; maybe it was due to his higher education, similar to Gino himself; maybe he simply knew his own worth more than most wrestlers. But Frank was building a reputation as someone difficult to work with, both inside the ring and outside it. He stood up for himself, almost to a fault, in a business where talent was expected to go with the flow. He could also be rough in the ring if he knew he could get away with it, which wasn't always appreciated. Bruiser Brody would go on to become a legend in the business, particularly in the years after he left the WWWF. But his difficult reputation would gain major momentum during his time there, and partly at the expense of Gino.

While that situation was still brewing, and while Brody was still piling up TV squash match wins, Gorilla Monsoon had an important part to play in a major promotional event that would see power brokers from across the global wrestling landscape do something very rare, and that was collaborate. It was something intended to raise the profile of the entire business and would be spearheaded by Vince McMahon—and not just the father but the son as well. It involved Antonio Inoki, whose New Japan Pro-Wrestling had just entered into a co-promotional partnership with the Capitol Wrestling Corporation and perhaps the most famous human being on the planet: the undisputed heavyweight boxing champion of the world, Muhammad Ali.

In his early days as plain old Cassius Clay growing up in Louisville, Kentucky, Ali had been a huge wrestling fan, and the theatrical antics of wrestling famously informed his histrionic and brash public persona.[9] Perhaps this is why he was open to the offer proposed to him by Inoki and his financial backers in Japan for a boxer vs. wrestler encounter that would supposedly prove, once and for all, which was the superior fighting art. Plus, the $6 million they put on the table certainly didn't hurt. Ali went to his flabbergasted promoter Bob Arum to make the deal, and Arum turned for help to the thirty-year-old Vince McMahon Jr. The younger Vince had been struggling to get out from under his father's shadow, engaging in some failed real estate dealings before his dad had sent him to Arum for guidance. The result had been the Evel Knievel Snake River Canyon Jump, an ill-conceived closed-circuit television debacle that had lost a quarter of a million dollars.

Failure though it was, the Snake River Canyon Jump had forged a partnership that brought Arum and McMahon together again. The two of them went with the Muhammad Ali idea to Vince Sr., who envisioned it as an event that could be brought to fans all across North America and even around the world through cooperation among the different wrestling territories. Although the actual fight would be taking place at Budokan in

Tokyo, the closed-circuit broadcast could be paired up with live wrestling cards at special venues all across the country. For example, it was the perfect opportunity for McMahon to bring his show back to Shea Stadium. Other promoters in other areas would do similarly. And they would all come together to promote it. Gene LeBell, brother of Los Angeles promoter Mike LeBell, was tapped to be the referee. Vince enlisted the fast-talking Fred Blassie to make appearances as Ali's "manager" for the match. With Ali's farm in rural Michigan a stone's throw from Detroit, Motor City promoter and wrestler Eddie "The Sheik" Farhat would publicly "train" Ali to tangle with Inoki.

But there was another important piece of the puzzle. Leading up to the big date on June 26, it was decided that Ali should step in the ring with a wrestler to give a teaser to fans of what might happen when a boxer met a wrestler between the ropes. And that job would fall to Gino. Not only was Gino an obvious choice due to his loyalty to the promotion and the fact that he was a stakeholder, but the reality was most observers and experts didn't give a pro wrestler half a chance against any pro boxer, let alone against "The Greatest." So the idea was to put Ali in there with someone fearsome who could manhandle him convincingly and put serious doubt in fans' minds that Ali could beat Inoki. In that role, Gorilla Monsoon would do nicely. As for Monsoon himself, he had major misgivings about the whole thing, as he wasn't a fan of mixing boxers and wrestlers, or more particularly, of putting any wrestlers in a situation with outside parties who could not completely be trusted. And although he'd turn out to be right, he stepped up and did what was asked of him.

The date was Tuesday, June 1, 1976. The location was the Philadelphia Arena, where the taping for the next three episodes of *Championship Wrestling* was underway. By that time, Gorilla Monsoon very rarely wrestled on television—in fact, although he was booking and running the shows from the back, he hadn't actually stepped in the ring at a TV taping in about eight months. But there he was, in the second match, taking on the unfortunate Baron Mikel Scicluna. His official opponent wasn't important; he'd handle him with ease in seconds. What was important was that, introduced before the match, seated in the front row in a gray suit, looking suitably amused, was Muhammad Ali himself.

Getting the champ there wasn't all that difficult; it turned out his clandestine training camp / personal retreat was located just seventy-five miles outside of Philly in the rural borough of Deer Lake, Pennsylvania. Mario Savoldi, working that night as one of the referees, remembers the discussions that took place earlier in the day between Muhammad and Gino, who still wanted to protect his profession and make sure he wasn't going to be made a fool of: "They were talking in the dressing room about how they were going to get in the ring, and Gino said to him, 'We can do whatever. But if you're going to punch me, just don't punch me in the face, because I got bad vision to start with.'" An apprehensive Ali then laid out certain liberties he wanted to make sure Gorilla wasn't going to take. "Gino said, 'Don't worry about it. I'll protect you. And if we fall, I'll fall first, you'll fall on me. Then I'll cover you. You won't get hurt.'"

But that's not exactly how it played out. About a minute into his actual match, Gorilla chopped the Baron over the top rope and to the outside, at which point Ali got to his feet and pointed at Monsoon—the classic challenge pose that the champ was known for worldwide. Then, as a game Monsoon holds the ropes open, Ali proceeds to strip down to his waist, while commentator Vince Jr. shouts, "Muhammad Ali is gonna commit suicide here!" After getting in the ring, Ali kicks off his shoes as referee Dick Woehrle checks with him, and Monsoon motions to his head as if to say the champ is crazy. What follows is just a brief moment in time, but a moment that nonetheless is still remembered half a century later. Ali circles Monsoon, throws a few jabs that Monsoon effortlessly bats away, despite the fact that a couple seem to get perilously close to connecting. But Muhammad seems unsure of what exactly to do with the four-hundred-pound giant, who stands before him with his hands defiantly on his hips.

That's when Ali starts jawing at Monsoon and points at him again, extending his arm just enough for the big man to snatch it, put him up on his shoulders in a fireman's carry and, to the delight of the crowd, whirl him around in an airplane spin that seems to go on forever, before gingerly dumping him on the mat. One of Ali's handlers, who may or not have been smartened up to the proceedings, hits the ring, backs up Monsoon and checks on the fallen Louisville Lip, helping him back to his feet and out of the ring, whisking him away through the crowd as Gorilla Monsoon stands triumphant.

At ringside after the match with Vince McMahon, an unimpressed Monsoon delivered his glib and dismissive assessment of what just happened: "This guy may be a great boxer, but he don't belong inside that squared circle with a wrestler. That was proven, and that's for sure! This guy is nothing. This guy doesn't know a wristlock from a wristwatch; how can he get in there with a wrestler? All he knows is to throw a few lousy jabs—that's not gonna stop a wrestler. He was at my mercy. I could've done anything . . . Great boxer, terrible as a wrestler." Ironically, according to Savoldi, Gino's attitude may not have entirely been a put-on, as one of Ali's punches may just have gotten a little too close for comfort: "Oh, he was annoyed. You should have heard him in the dressing room. 'You motherfucker!' He was the gentle giant. But boy, if you pissed him off, leave town."

Regardless of the particulars, the incident had its intended effect. One of the photographers snapping furiously during the whole thing, legendary wrestling lensman George Napolitano of Dyker Heights, Brooklyn, headed directly afterward to the United Press International offices in Manhattan, where he had the photos developed, and UPI got them to outlets all over the country. The next day, images of Gorilla Monsoon facing off with Muhammad Ali graced multiple newspapers, including the coveted back cover of the *Daily News* in New York. That single confrontation, barely a minute in length, would get more press and mainstream attention than anything else Gorilla Monsoon would ever do in his whole storied in-ring career, and understandably so.

Monsoon had succeeded in making Ali look vulnerable—perhaps a little too vulnerable. Nine days later, Ali, McMahon and Blassie headed into AWA territory—Chicago's International Amphitheatre, to be exact, where Ali would take on AWA wrestler Buddy Wolfe, with AWA promoter Verne Gagne as the referee and Dick the Bruiser as Wolfe's cornerman. Presented as much more of a "formal" boxer vs. wrestler exhibition, with Ali in full boxing gear, the match showed the champ in charge and much more competitive than he'd been against Monsoon. The bout would be shown two days later on ABC's *Wide World of Sports*, narrated by an exasperated Howard Cosell, who made no effort to conceal his contempt for the entire ordeal.

The truth was, Cosell's attitude was pretty much the norm as far as the "legitimate" sporting world was concerned and as far as most of mainstream America was concerned. And unfortunately, the match itself between Ali and Inoki, when it finally happened, did nothing but reinforce everyone's skepticism. Widely panned as a black eye on the sport of boxing (and even on the business of wrestling, when it came down to it), it was a fifteen-round slog in which Inoki, in survival mode, remained on his back on the mat, repeatedly kicking an increasingly frustrated Ali in the legs until they were bleeding. What was supposed to be a worked match that would see Ali pinned in a fluke to set up a possible rematch instead turned into an awkward shoot when the champion refused to go along with the plan at the last minute.

■

But the whole mess that went down in Budokan had little to do with Monsoon, who had done his part and was nowhere near Tokyo that night. Instead, Gino was at Shea Stadium in Flushing, Queens, where the match was being shown on closed-circuit television before a crowd of more than thirty-two thousand—the largest ever assembled for a Capitol Wrestling / WWWF event up to that point. Co-headlining the live portion of the event that night was Bruno Sammartino defending the WWWF heavyweight crown against Stan Hansen, the bad man from Borger, Texas, who had accidentally broken Bruno's neck during a match at Madison Square Garden just two months earlier. The injury made for the perfect grudge rematch, and Vince McMahon the elder—concerned that Inoki wasn't a big enough name to draw fans to Shea—cajoled Sammartino, barely out of the hospital, to return to the ring early and bail out the company once again.

Gino would take part that night in the other co-main event, only not as a wrestler. Instead, he'd be in the corner of André the Giant as he took on "The Bayonne Bleeder" Chuck Wepner in another wrestler vs. boxer encounter. Wepner had nearly gone the distance with Ali himself the year before[10] and was the tallest boxer they could find at six foot five, yet was still dwarfed by the Giant that night. Much like the other boxer/wrestler match happening that day on the other side of the world, the backroom dealings to put together André/Wepner were a mess, and neither side knew quite what to expect or what to make of the other when they finally found themselves across the ring from each other. But one thing that the Capitol organization knew was that Gino was the man they needed to have in there to protect their French golden goose from being embarrassed or double-crossed. Almost as hulking a figure as the Giant himself, dressed head-to-toe in black and with dark sunglasses, Gino cut an imposing figure that few would want to cross—and yet that night would be one of the few times anyone did.

From the opening bell of round one, it was clear that Wepner had no idea what to do with André. His punches, even the ones that look pretty stiff, can't seem to do much damage. It's also obvious that André can take him off his feet anytime he wants and is essentially toying with him. In the second round, the Giant falls on Wepner and appears to have him pinned, but Wepner's foot is draped over the bottom rope, preventing the count. Monsoon attempts to throw the fighter's foot off the rope, resulting in Wepner and his corner becoming legitimately furious. Choreographed though the bout may have intended to be, this is where things started to get very real. Outmatched, desperate and looking to go into business for themselves, Wepner's cornermen instruct their man before the third round, telling him to grab the Giant in a headlock and jab a thumb in his eye. The problem is that André and Monsoon catch wind of the instructions and are prepared for the cheap shot. And so, when Wepner immediately tries to do just that, the Giant begins to lash out in anger, eventually hoisting up the Bleeder and tossing him right over the ropes and onto the grass.

As soon as Wepner tumbles to the ground, referee John Stanley—the same man who'd officiated Monsoon's career-making 1963 Jersey City match with Sammartino—begins to lay in the count. Wepner's cornermen, led by Al Braverman and Paddy Flood, immediately rush around the ring and grab the fallen fighter, attempting to get him back in the ring to beat the count. An incensed Monsoon comes barreling around the other side to meet them, shouting, "You can't do that!" as he neutralizes the situation, preventing their assistance and making sure that Wepner takes the ten-count. Wepner and Braverman would, in later years, insist that Monsoon had placed his size-14 triple-wide boot on Wepner's chest to make sure he wasn't going anywhere. Monsoon then made a move to go after Braverman, allowing Wepner to finally get back in the ring, albeit too late. Gino, meanwhile, seeing red through his tinted black glasses, takes Braverman off to the side, just out of view of the hard camera pointed at the ringside area, takes one of Braverman's fingers inside his mitt of a hand and snaps it like a pretzel. For trying to make the company and its top attraction look bad, he got off easy.

But while Gino is occupied, things are coming unglued inside the ring. Wepner's array of indignant cornermen rush through the ropes and start going after André, a futile effort if ever there was one. That's when, from out of nowhere, Gorilla Monsoon hits the ring, living up to both his first and last name as he wades through the handlers, tossing them aside like dolls. Wepner, meanwhile, coming to the aid of his corner, begins whaling on André himself, causing Gino to abruptly stop hurling human beings around the ring in order to get between the two fighters, perhaps the only man in the building who could hold back the Giant. The whole publicity stunt had come completely off the rails, confirming Gino's concerns about doing boxer/wrestler matches in the first place.

■

Although Bruiser Brody had been in the territory a couple of months by that point, he missed the whole Muhammad Ali affair and was not able to take part in the Shea Stadium card, because he had taken a little detour for most of June in order to work some dates in the Amarillo-based West Texas territory run by the Funk brothers, Terry and Dory Jr. It was an odd move, with the company getting ready to match him up with Sammartino, and McMahon made sure that Brody made it to the Philadelphia television tapings in the middle of his Texas run, intent on keeping his wild-eyed visage in front of the fickle TV viewership. Forming the booking brain trust, McMahon, Monsoon and Sammartino himself had Brody earmarked for two main events for the championship at Madison Square Garden in September and October. Beyond that, they intended to bring the match to Nassau Coliseum, Boston Garden, Baltimore Arena, Pittsburgh Civic Arena and the Cap Centre through the winter, finishing up in Gino's backyard at the Philadelphia Spectrum in February.

Along the way, Brody was being built up, partly by being paired up with Stan Hansen in a formidable tag team duo, but also by being given strong wins over lower-card and enhancement talent like Johnny Rivera, Man Mountain Mike, S.D. Jones, Manny Soto and twenty-seven-year-old Kevin Sullivan, who was in the midst of a fourteen-month run in the WWWF. But the one he seemed to be having more than a little trouble with was José González, who also happened to be one of Gino's dearest friends in the locker room.

The first time that Brody and González met in the ring was at the Nassau Coliseum on July 24, 1976. Naturally, González's job was to put Brody over strong, as Brody was on a collision course with Bruno for the title. A tried-and-true formula, but one that these two men seemed to have trouble following. For one thing, Brody had a reputation for sometimes being a bully in the ring if he could get away with it. And González wasn't without blame either, as his machismo seemed to invite Brody's rougher tendencies. "Brody was roughing up González," explains Davey O'Hannon. "Because González was a prima donna in the ring. If you were a heel, you had to *make* him sell. That's what it was like in Puerto Rico. It's like a cultural thing. They're in front of their people, so they don't sell. Well, that's how González was. In the ring, you'd get in his ear and say, 'Hey, we could do this the hard way, or we could do this the easy way.'" Unfortunately, with Brody, González was choosing the hard way—and Brody was more than happy to oblige him.

The friction between the two men started right away and continued as they met several more times around the territory. All the while, Gino kept an eye on things from the Gorilla position. It finally came to a head on August 19 at the Memorial Auditorium in Worcester, Massachusetts. "I was there the night that the shit went down originally with Brody and González," says Kevin Sullivan, who had teamed with Ivan Putski against then–world tag team champions the Executioners in the match immediately prior. "I didn't see the match. But I was in the dressing room when they came back. González was yelling, and Brody was firing up on him like he was gonna beat the shit out of him." Sullivan recalls González going to Gino to complain, at which point Gino finally had to get involved. What happened next has often been debated. As Sullivan remembers it, Monsoon and Brody had words, but it didn't escalate. "He was saying to Brody, 'What's going on here?' and Brody would tell him, 'Hey, fuck this guy!'"

The truth was, Brody had been on the radar of Capitol's inner circle for a while by that point. This was the era of the WWWF's classic brain trust—guys like Arnie Skaaland, Lou Albano, Freddie Blassie, the Wizard and Angelo Savoldi would sit huddled around the monitor with Vince Sr., watching everything and making judgment calls on everyone who stepped into the ring. Chief among the advisors, of course, was Gino—"bigger than life," as Sullivan described him—and so when the safety valve needed to be let loose, it was Gino who stepped in to settle the issue.

But it doesn't appear that the issue between Monsoon and Brody ended there. The truth is, we may never fully know the extent and nature of what transpired between them. Stories and opinions have circulated over the years as to what actually happened, particularly whether there ever was a physical locker room altercation. "I could pretty safely say if there was a fight, I would have known about it," offers O'Hannon. "If there was one guy in the business that you didn't want to have a scrape with, Gino was it. But Frank was a pretty scrappy guy, too, and a really outspoken guy. Gino might have told him to lighten up [on González], and if I know Frank as well as I did, he might have said, 'Mind your fucking business.'" Wrestling historian Matt Farmer recalls being told by St. Louis promoter Larry Matysik, who was close with Brody, that the incident was more of a screaming match than any kind of physical fight and that the details have been exaggerated over the years.

However, one particular story, related on a 2019 episode of the *Stick to Wrestling* podcast, gives what's claimed to be an eyewitness account of a whole lot more than that happening six days after the Worcester incident in the Hamburg Field House at the conclusion of a marathon taping of *All-Star Wrestling*. The picture—painted by longtime fan Craig Fair, a frequent attendee at the WWWF's Hamburg TV tapings in those days—is one of a renegade wrestler who was clearly on the wrong side of management. Fair recounted how Brody was wrestling Chief Jay Strongbow in the main event, a dark match put on for the live crowd only after the TV cameras were turned off. Typically, announcer Vince McMahon Jr. would be gone by that point, but Fair remembers him remaining seated at the announce table to watch the match, which turned into a wild outside-the-ring brawl that resulted in a double count-out.

With a near-riot ensuing, and local police getting involved, Monsoon allegedly came out of the locker room and tapped Brody on the back with his notebook, indicating that the match was over and it was time to get back to the locker room. Brody appeared to comply, with Monsoon following behind him, but then Fair remembers him turning around and punching Gino square in the face, breaking his glasses. Monsoon then came after Brody, chasing him back through the locker room door, which slammed shut, obscuring all view of whatever may have happened next. Assuming this to be an accurate description of what happened, it would be hard to imagine that the fight ended with just that one punch. It would also make sense for it to have happened so soon after Worcester since it's easy to imagine that tempers were running high.

Clearly, WWWF management had an issue on its hands, especially with the plans they had for Brody. But in the end, professionalism won out. The philosophy of the Capitol office, and in most of the industry, was never to leave money on the table. And there was money to be made with Brody and Sammartino. They had committed resources to getting Brody over, and they were going to follow through. But once the money was made, it would be a different story. González continued to work with him, with more squash matches in Albany, New Haven, Boston and Kingston, New York. To his credit, Gino himself would work with Brody after all this in six known matches taking place between September 1976 and January 1977, with Brody going over in at least four and two draws. And the Sammartino program happened as planned. Although neither was a sellout, the two Garden main events alone brought in a combined thirty-eight thousand fans.

But after that last decisive loss to Bruno at the Spectrum in February, after all the money had been wrung from the program, Frank Goodish was promptly sent packing from the WWWF, taking his new ring name with him back to Texas and turning that name into one of the most revered in the history of the wrestling business. But he would never set foot in a McMahon-owned ring ever again. To the old man, and certainly to Gino, for a virtual rookie to come into the most high-profile promotion in the country, get slotted into a top spot with the biggest draw in the business and then cause that kind of trouble was the ultimate sign of ingratitude. To Frank, it was just standing up for himself. But to McMahon, it was a surefire way to ensure you never got hired again.

When it comes to breaking down what little we know of the dealings between Gorilla Monsoon and Bruiser Brody, what it essentially comes down to is a clash of personalities. By all accounts, Gino was someone whom everyone in the business liked and got along with. He was also someone who valued company loyalty and was very serious about the way he did business. Ironically, Frank was also someone very serious about his business and about the money he made in it. But the approach both men took to the business could not have been more different. Brody was a true renegade at a time when the business still allowed you to be one, so long as you drew money, which he always did. He had his friends, but he was not always the most popular person among promoters, or even among the boys. He looked out for himself and put his own needs first, which was understandable—after all, that's what all the promoters did, wasn't it? But sometimes that would make him enemies in the business. Perhaps it made an enemy of Gino, who believed in doing what was best for the business as a whole, not just the individual. And it definitely made an enemy out of the target of all those in-ring humiliations, José González—although no one, including Gino, could've ever envisioned how far he'd take it.

CHAPTER 10

THE ONLY WRESTLER TO RETIRE FOR GOOD

> "I've been knocked around in the squared circle for twenty-one years, and I can honestly say I don't enjoy it anymore. There comes a time when a man has to know his limitations, and I think I'm intelligent enough to know mine."

In the wake of the Ali promotion, and also judging by his presence during the alleged Monsoon/Brody scuffle in Hamburg, the younger Vince McMahon—still "Vinny" to his father's friends—was becoming more of a presence behind the scenes, exerting his influence and always pushing for more. And although they would grow to respect each other in later years, in those days, they were very much rivals. Gino, after all, was the boss's right-hand man and handpicked successor—which would make the boss's son one to keep an eye on. As McMahon himself would state in the 2024 Netflix docuseries *Mr. McMahon*, "When I joined the company, Gorilla Monsoon was the heir apparent. And I could feel the tension right away. Gorilla Monsoon thinks I'm competition. And boy, was he right."

"There was always a Team Monsoon and a Team Vinny McMahon," remembers Gary Cappetta, who by the bicentennial summer of '76 had been plucked out of the Wildwood shows by Gino and made into his permanent ring announcer, first on *Championship Wrestling* and later on *All-Star Wrestling*. Gino would also use him on most of the house shows that he personally promoted throughout Jersey, Pennsylvania and Delaware, with the idea being that fans would consider those shows important since they featured the same announcer they saw each week on TV. Vinny preferred Howard Finkel, a fervent wrestling fan from Newark who'd started out as an usher at the New Haven Coliseum and wound up as the permanent ring announcer at Madison Square Garden by the start of 1977.

Even to this day, it's for his kindness that Gary remembers Gino best. It's what he remembers Maureen for as well: "She was an angel. I don't mean to cast any aspersions on the other wives. But they were . . . you knew they had money. You know what I'm saying? You felt less than them when you were around them. And Maureen was like a regular person." Gary tells a particular story that illustrates this well, of a rare opportunity one rainy night to ride with Gino after one of the Garden shows over to Jimmy Weston's, where McMahon and his associates would congregate. Once there, Gino was quickly called away by Vince to talk business, leaving Gary to fend for himself. Not having anyone to talk to, and being just about the lowest person on the totem pole there, he surveyed all the big shots and their wives sitting at the table, too intimidated to approach anyone, until Maureen warmly called him over and made him feel instantly welcome and comfortable. Gary would also receive regular invitations to the Marella home and remembers how Gino's parents would come down from Rochester a few times a year and stay for a week or so: "His dad was very soft-spoken. But you could see he was filled with pride about his son."

■

This kind of domestic family bliss was also what played out in the press, as heading into the late 1970s, Gino leaned more than ever into his role as goodwill ambassador and the public-relations face of the company. He and his family would often be the subject of in-depth newspaper features around this time, as Gino wooed reporters and dutifully defended the honor of his business. Vince appreciated having him play this part since it subverted expectations and stereotypes: Here was this gigantic bruiser of a man with a name that played into exactly what outsiders expected of the rasslin' business, and then when he opened his mouth, he was a well-spoken, educated and erudite individual, living a completely well-adjusted suburban American life—"the epitome of middle-class respectability," as he was once described.[1] It was an endless source of amusement to reporters whose instinct to disparage and ridicule the business was routinely disarmed and neutralized by this charismatic man, who then turned them into goodwill ambassadors for the business as well, whether they realized it or not.

Whether it was gently guiding them through his den filled with memorabilia of his career; inviting them into his kitchen, where he'd be working on his prize lasagna; stepping outside to play ball with Joey and stack firewood out front of the house on his quiet, idyllic Willingboro street; or showing off the motorcycle he'd bought himself for his fortieth birthday, the once fearsome Manchurian monster now presented the picture of normalcy to reporters who couldn't help but be charmed. He regaled them with colorful stories of his career and also worked hard to dispel suspicions about what he did for a living. As was expected in those days, he played the kayfabe card to the max, and going through so many of these interviews and profiles, it becomes clear that he had an arsenal of anecdotes, explanations and rationalizations at the ready for any non-believers who sought to cast doubt on the legitimacy of what he and his colleagues did between the ropes. As many wrestlers would do, he'd catalog his laundry list of injuries, inviting anyone who called what he did "fake" to pay his medical bills. Although he'd admit to sometimes "prolonging" a match to provide greater entertainment value, he'd also solemnly declare that he'd never been asked to "take a dive" in the ring and didn't know anyone else who had been. He would admit to pro wrestling's innate violence but stress that people responded to it because it was a "good tension reliever"—after all, as he would often explain, "It's a proven fact that we're all sadistic by nature . . . If the circus was coming, and you could advertise that that night someone would fall from the high wire, you wouldn't be able to buy a ticket." His way with words, and the frankness with which he could somehow manage to sell the illusions of his business, was irresistible. And in this sense, he did his job well.

And yet this is not to say that his home life wasn't as blissful as it appeared in the papers, because it was. It was no mere façade created for reporters. And as Valerie grew older and more aware, she began to appreciate the more unusual aspects of this life that her father had created for all of them. The parties at the house, such as the ones after the annual JFK High School show, remain vivid memories, filled with unforgettable people like André the Giant, Ivan Putski and Mr. Fuji, who would pack their home and yard: "What I couldn't understand was how these guys were beating the shit out of each other, and then they were at my house having a big party. My dad would say, 'You know how you can have a big argument with your friends, but you're still friends? It's the same thing.'" There would be midget wrestlers playing pool while standing on the pool table. André, the only person who could make her dad look small, sitting at the kitchen counter, eating an entire sandwich in one bite as she tried her best, at her father's request, not to stare at him.[2] Fuji playing his notorious pranks, such as sneaking inside while everyone was swimming, and turning the thermostat up to ninety, which wouldn't be discovered until it was time to go to bed. It was almost literally like the circus coming to town.

■

Although he'd almost certainly been down to Puerto Rico before, the earliest known record of Gorilla Monsoon wrestling there is a match on February 26, 1977, in Caguas, against Abdul Zaatar (Nicaraguan wrestler Ricky Sánchez doing an Arabian sheik gimmick). He'd be back again in early April, this time teaming with Hercules Ayala to challenge for the North American tag team title. With a 10 percent ownership stake, he would try to show his face whenever possible, and when in the ring, he would revert to his evil, rule-breaking ways—a far cry from the genial giant fans had grown to love back home. It was all about drawing heat—but in Puerto Rico, sometimes that could be a dangerous proposition. Davey O'Hannon remembers a Sunday show way out in the country in Mayagüez, on the other side of the island from San Juan, when he, Gino and Larry Sharpe got their car turned upside-down by irate fans in the parking lot. When Gino stuck his head out of the dressing room back door to check it out, someone dropped a piece of a cinderblock on his head from the roof, where he'd been apparently lying in wait. "He was half-knocked out in the doorway," Davey remembers. "I said, 'Larry, help him up!' and Larry says, 'How the hell are we going to pick him up and get him back in here?'" His head split open, Gino had to be rushed to the hospital for staples to close the wound, and then he, Davey and Larry had to secure another car to get them back to the safety of San Juan and the Tanama. It was a rough reminder for Gino of what it meant to be a heel, especially in a place where they took wrestling very, very seriously.

Mario Savoldi also remembers learning this lesson the hard way when Gino invited him down to Puerto Rico to referee one of his matches with Carlos Colón. What Gino didn't tell Mario was that he and Carlos had planned out a screwjob finish that would give the match to Gino—and result in an extremely angry crowd. The heat would all be on the referee, which is why Gino wanted someone in there that he knew and trusted. Mario remembers having to be hustled away from the ring by guards after the match, with a garbage can over his head to protect him from the hail of trash and dangerous objects being hurled from the stands.

■

Meanwhile, back on the mainland, the landscape of the WWWF was shifting once again. On April 25 at the Garden, Monsoon defeated Nikolai Volkoff on the way down the card after challenging Sammartino a couple of years earlier. As for the champ, he'd defend his title that night against the insidious Baron Von Raschke, who had been plain old

Jim Raschke, amateur standout for the University of Nebraska-Lincoln, before taking on his pseudo-Nazi persona. None of the 17,111 fans on hand realized it, but it would be the last time Bruno Sammartino would ever defend the WWWF championship at Madison Square Garden. What they also didn't know was that on that very same card, trouncing Executioner #2 (the future Big John Studd) with relative ease, was the man who would eventually replace Bruno as the company's beloved long-term titleholder and standard-bearer, the ginger-haired All-American boy from Princeton, Minnesota, Bob Backlund. But that replacement wouldn't be an immediate one. Along the way, there was a major Technicolor detour to be taken first.

The bottom line was that after carrying the company on his back for most of the past fourteen years, and after having to be cajoled back once before, Bruno was tired. Very tired. And not even the reduced schedule and percentage of the gate granted to him to lure him back in 1973 were enough anymore. Despite Bruno continuing to be the company's most reliable draw even after all this time, Vince McMahon was forced to relent and grant his workhorse a second—and what would be his final—reprieve. Just five days after his defense against Raschke at the Garden, in the Baltimore Arena on the other side of the territory, about as far from those rowdy New York fans as you could get, Superstar Billy Graham got the nod, taking the belt off Sammartino for good.

The colorful, preening Graham, with the Grand Wizard by his side, was a very different kind of WWWF world champion. With his counter-culture sensibility and bombastic promo style, he somehow perfectly represented the culture of his era. He also happened to be a heel, which led everyone to assume, just as with Koloff and Stasiak, that his title reign would be an exceedingly short one, leading to the next top babyface coming in and saving the day. And while this would eventually happen, it was a lot further off than fans thought. Perhaps that was why you could feel the palpable energy in the crowd at the following month's Garden card, where none other than Gorilla Monsoon would be lined up for Graham's first title defense at the world's most famous arena. Given what they'd seen before with Morales in '71 and Sammartino in '73, it's a safe bet that many on hand assumed that Gorilla was about to finally get his run with the gold.

That especially seemed to be the case just a minute and a half into the match, when Monsoon felled Graham with a knife-edge chop, then caught him in his patented giant swing, followed by the Manchurian splash finisher. The crowd seemed on the verge of an explosion as referee John Stanley counted the pinfall attempt, only to stop short when he realized Graham's feet were through the ropes, taking the wind out of everyone's sails. From there, it was just a matter of time before, just six minutes later, Graham came crashing down on Monsoon with a kneedrop from the top turnbuckle, ironically logging the pin despite the fact that Gorilla's leg was under the ropes this time. It had been Monsoon's first title shot at the Garden in a decade and the only one he'd ever get in the new building.

It was becoming evident that things were going to be a little different this time, and indeed they were. The Superstar would be granted nearly ten months with the title, by far the longest any heel had ever held it in the hero-centric WWWF, and in fact, it would not be equaled for another forty years.[3] But it was all part of the plan, as McMahon and his booker, the very man who'd lost to Graham in his first Garden title defense, had already promised that Bob Backlund would be getting the gold from the Superstar on the February 20, 1978, Madison Square Garden show. The deal was already made and set in stone from the moment Graham got the belt. And although the Superstar would hold out hope he could change their minds during those intervening months, he would be mistaken. In the meantime, the next ten months would be quite a rollercoaster ride for the rather traditional, conservative Capitol Wrestling territory, guided by the feathered boas, tie-dyes and twenty-two-inch pythons of Superstar Billy Graham. During that reign, many babyfaces would finally get their crack at the crown, as Monsoon had at the Garden and would again two more times—once on December 15 at one of Gorilla's own spot shows at Midland, Pennsylvania's Lincoln High School, which was most likely something of a dress rehearsal for the one that happened eleven days later for the Christmas week show at the Nassau Coliseum.

Just three weeks after his match with Graham at the Garden, Gino had the chance to wrestle once again for Frank Tunney, the Toronto promoter who had helped to give him his first big break all those years ago. The Capitol office was once again forging a promotional alliance with Tunney's Maple Leaf Wrestling outfit, thanks in part to Tunney's crumbling relationship with his current promotional partner and booker, The Sheik. After years of booking himself on top and running over all the babyfaces, Sheik had burnt out the Toronto fan base, just as he'd been busy doing in his home territory of Detroit. The last straw was two major events that Tunney had planned for Toronto's Canadian National Exhibition Stadium, which fell apart thanks to talent no-shows and other decisions that Tunney pinned on The Sheik. For one of these, on June 5, McMahon tried to help out Tunney by sending in Gorilla Monsoon, along with Chief Jay Strongbow and 264 pounds of attitude and raw power by the name of Ken Patera, a U.S. weightlifting champion and former Olympian who would one day have a crucial role to play in Monsoon's wrestling career.

Monsoon did the honors for Patera in the semi-main event that day before a disappointing crowd. By the end of the summer, Tunney would push The Sheik out of Toronto and begin a full-on promotional partnership with the WWWF, as well as work with other offices like Verne Gagne's AWA and the Carolinas-based Jim Crockett Promotions. It was the start of a fruitful period of inter-promotional cooperation in Toronto that would lead to some of the most stacked all-star cards ever seen. It would also allow Gino to reconnect with some of his old friends up north, such as Ilio DiPaolo and his son Dennis, as well as Tony Parisi. With Bruno and Dominic DeNucci along for the ride, too, many of these reunions took place at DiPaolo's celebrated Italian restaurant in the greater Buffalo area, across Lake Ontario—Dennis called it "The Italian Connection." It was an unexpected surprise for Gino to get to work Toronto again several times in the final years of his in-ring career.

■

The summer of 1977—that same summer when *Star Wars* ruled the box office, and Billy Martin's New York Yankees ruled baseball, while the Son of Sam stalked the streets of a boiling-hot New York City—was a period of great activity for Gino. In addition to expanding his activities in Toronto, he'd been looking to break into a whole new business in Atlantic City, right on the coast of his home state of New Jersey. He'd been going to wrestle there for years, but now the state was in the process of legalizing gambling within the city limits in what was intended to be a tax bonanza that would effectively turn Atlantic City into the East Coast's answer to Las Vegas, one of Gino's favorite places on Earth. Gino loved being in and around casinos more than anything and saw an opportunity to get in on this action in a manner in which he was uniquely qualified. His plan was to put together a private security agency, made up of himself and some willing recruits from within the ranks of pro wrestling, that would offer its services to the brand-new establishments that would soon be going up on the waterfront.

Dressed in a pinstripe suit with a dark button-up shirt, sporting his tinted shades with his hair slicked back, Gino turned heads when he showed up for the state assembly meeting in Trenton, where the final decisions regarding gambling in the state of New Jersey were being made in a public forum. Naturally, the press gravitated to him. "I have experience in crowd control, and I know how to deal with the public," he told reporters, adding that if he spotted any trouble being made in the casino, he'd "try to verbally give people a negative attitude toward starting a problem."[4]

The legalization of gambling would go through, and Atlantic City would soon become an oasis for gamblers on the East Coast who didn't necessarily want to get on a plane to Nevada. The proposed security agency never materialized, but Gino would certainly enjoy the gambling facilities in the years to come, taking full advantage of having such a place so close to home and making regular getaways there with Maureen. And even though his security concept fell through, Gino would find another way to get in on the action, as by 1979, he would start running summer wrestling shows on Atlantic City's famous Steel Pier, taking full advantage of the increased business that the casinos were bringing in. He would even personally work out a deal with PRISM, a new local premium cable TV outlet, to air the shows on its systems throughout Pennsylvania and New Jersey, just as he had already done for the cards at the Philadelphia Spectrum.[5] Some of those televised cards from the Steel Pier would also feature Monsoon in a role that was entirely new to him, but would eventually define the later phase of his career in the industry, that of TV play-by-play commentator.

■

Gino's presence in Puerto Rico was also expanding in that summer of '77, and he spent a significant portion of July down there, culminating in a show in San Juan on July 30, in which he defeated Hartford Love to win the North American championship, the top title in the territory at the time. It was the first title he'd held in nearly a decade, and in fact, he would hold it for nine months, making it the longest championship run of his entire wrestling career. In addition to reigning as the promotion's top champion and most hated villain, he was also bringing in top talent like Nikolai Volkoff and Ernie Ladd to come and wrestle in Puerto Rico, quickly helping to turn it into one of the hottest promotions in the world.

Immediately after getting back from Puerto Rico, Monsoon refereed a memorable main event at Madison Square Garden, the final blow-off of the feud between Superstar Billy Graham and the man he'd dethroned for the title, Bruno Sammartino. What the bout is best remembered for is the moment when a disgusted Graham tries to wave off the match, staggering back to the locker room, only to have Gorilla Monsoon, in a referee's white shirt and bow tie, chase down the champion and carry him back to the ring on his shoulders, unceremoniously tossing him back in so Bruno could beat on him some more. "The pop that Gorilla Monsoon got when he brought Superstar Billy Graham back was unforgettably loud," remembered wrestling historian Evan Ginzburg, who was there that night. "Like a primeval roar of pure bloodlust. It was beautiful."[6] The match would end with a double disqualification, but the sight of a bloody and battered Superstar still managed to send the fans home happy.

From there, it was off to Nevada for the NWA convention, this time being held at the massive Las Vegas Hilton, where Elvis Presley had concluded his seven-year residency just eight months before. There had been talk of him coming back that summer, but any hopes that the NWA promoters had of getting to see "The King" were dashed less than a week after the end of the convention, when he was found dead in his master suite at Graceland in Memphis. By this point, Eddie Graham had been voted in as president of the NWA, which boded well for Capitol thanks to Vince's close relationship with Eddie.

In fact, this partnership led to a truly historic event, namely the first time that a WWWF world champion had ever faced off with the NWA world champion, in what was ostensibly advertised as a "title unification match"—despite neither side having any intention of sharing a single champion. But still, they could reap the rewards of the interest that would come from staging such a match, which would've been unthinkable back when Capitol Wrestling had seceded from the NWA some fifteen years earlier. Still and all, even with strong working relationships and friendships between promoters, this was a business—and when it came to a situation like this, you could never be too careful to avoid a double-cross. After all, McMahon breaking away from the Alliance in 1963 had not exactly been a harmonious divorce, and who knows if anyone might still have been harboring any long-standing grudges. A time limit draw finish had been agreed upon, but just in case anyone decided to go into business for themselves and walk away with both titles, there had to be people in there who could be trusted. Vince McMahon sent Gino down for that purpose, to be one of two officials refereeing the match. The representative for the other side would be Don Curtis, one of Eddie Graham's veteran wrestlers and front office employees, whom McMahon also liked because Curtis had teamed extensively with Mark Lewin as a classic white-meat babyface tag team for him up in New York back in the late 1950s.

It would be called the Super Bowl of Wrestling, and one of the reasons that McMahon might have been on alert was that the man in possession of the NWA world heavyweight championship, who'd be opposing Graham, was Harley Race, a tough-as-nails barroom brawler from Missouri. Although the hard-drinking, chain-smoking Race was the visual opposite of the perfectly toned and tanned Superstar, there was little doubt in anyone's mind that if this degenerated into a real fight, it would be Race walking out as the undisputed champion. To prevent any chance of that happening, Gino was there to oversee the proceedings, alternating referee duties with Curtis throughout the match and watching like a hawk even when he was outside the ring. Much like at Shea Stadium in '72, intermittent rain undoubtedly kept some people away, as the crowd was only twelve thousand—decidedly small, especially for such a large venue. There was also the problem, inherent in the territory system in those days, that fans mainly only cared about what went on in their own backyard. The WWWF world title didn't mean a hell of a lot there, especially without Sammartino holding it. Fans in Florida were much more conditioned to recognize the NWA world title as important. Meanwhile, the WWWF's most rabid fans were a thousand miles away—and even if they had been there, they had been conditioned to largely ignore the importance of the NWA world title anyway.

With both combatants slipping and sliding on the wet mat, it was difficult to put on an effective match. Tied at one fall apiece, the match ended with Graham trapped in Race's sleeper hold, Curtis in the ring checking on the WWWF champion, while Monsoon watched intently from outside. As Graham's shoulders touch the mat, Curtis slaps the canvas for a count of one but is stopped from continuing the count by the expiration of the time limit. A focused Monsoon, determined to make sure that the NWA had no last-minute plan to snatch the WWWF title, immediately yells, "Time!" then looks at Curtis and makes a hand gesture indicating the match was over. Both men would keep their titles, and Gino and the Superstar—along with Ken Patera, who had also come down for the show—would be back on a plane to New York, where they'd all be present for a Nassau Coliseum show just two days later.

THE ONLY WRESTLER TO RETIRE FOR GOOD

■

By this point, the controlling partners of the Capitol Wrestling Corporation had grown by one member. That's because, back in early October of 1977, Vince McMahon, Gino Marella and Phil Zacko had decided to cut in Arnold Skaaland, a trustworthy and loyal soldier to the organization since its very beginnings back in the 1950s. Arnie had more or less finished up his wrestling career by that point and would soon be enlisted as Bob Backlund's manager, just as he had been all those years for Bruno. In addition to running regular shows at the Westchester County Center, not to mention spot shows throughout the region, Arnie also was entrusted with keeping track of the receipts at the Garden and other venues, so it was important to keep him close. He had been generous in the past by lending money to the corporation when needed, and now his generosity would be rewarded when both Marella and Zacko sold him one-fifth of their own shares in the organization. From that point on, the breakdown would be 50 percent to McMahon, 20 percent each to Marella and Zacko and now 10 percent to Skaaland.[7]

At the side of Bob Backlund, Arnie was about to return to a very high-profile position as the manager of the WWWF world champion, a position which brought real responsibilities as the champion's handler and travel companion on the road—a role he was also filling for André the Giant. That February 20 Madison Square Garden date loomed, and Graham was desperate to convince management that it was a bad idea to take the title off him while he was on such a roll—which, in fairness, he was. Business had been hot with Graham on top, but McMahon took the promise he'd made to Backlund very seriously and intended to keep it. Pivoting from the ethnic appeal of past champs like Sammartino and Morales, McMahon wanted a squeaky-clean collegiate-style All-American champion, similar to the direction the NWA had gone with world champions like Dory Funk Jr. and Jack Brisco. It could be argued that his views were a bit antiquated, as he simply didn't see someone like Graham—a wrestler who personified the future of the business more than anyone—as a star to build his company around.

But Graham would not go gently into that good night. Two days before the scheduled title switch, he was booked for one last title defense against Sammartino at the Spectrum inside a steel cage. As Bruno would later recall, the Superstar begged him to go off script and beat him for the belt that night. Graham just didn't think Backlund made sense from a business standpoint and would rather Bruno get the belt back—plus that had the potential for more rematches around the horn with a proven drawing card, as opposed to an unproven newcomer. Needless to say, the Living Legend wanted no part of it, and so things went as planned that night.

Of note, however, is that the match, broadcast on PRISM, features the first-ever known instance of Gorilla Monsoon doing television commentary. Set to team up later in the night with Chief Jay Strongbow to challenge WWWF world tag team champions Fuji and Tanaka, Monsoon sat in as a guest analyst for the match, joining announcer Vince McMahon Jr. and his regular partner Dick Graham, a local radio host and somewhat awkward broadcaster employed by PRISM. And although he only called that one match, Monsoon distinguished himself by showing great enthusiasm as he called the exciting finish, which saw Sammartino "accidentally" kick the champion through the cage door, giving him the sketchy victory. Already, even in this very first example, you can hear the energy, earnestness and articulate diction that would later come to be Gorilla Monsoon's stock-in-trade. Clearly, the younger McMahon was impressed with what he heard that night.

Two days later, in front of a sold-out Madison Square Garden crowd, a bitter Superstar Billy Graham did as he was asked, and Bob Backlund emerged triumphant with the championship he would proudly hold for the next six years. It was a new era for the World Wide Wrestling Federation. Graham had not made it easy for management and did little to hide his disdain. Some have even said that the whole experience left a bad taste in the mouth of McMahon, Marella and the rest of Capitol management and earned Graham that one descriptor no wrestler wants attached to their name: "difficult."

THE ONLY WRESTLER TO RETIRE FOR GOOD

By this point, Gino was regularly alternating between the Northeast and Puerto Rico, especially due to the fact that he remained the reigning North American champion. His status as Puerto Rico's most hated heel was cemented thanks to an angle shot at El Zipperle, a delightfully gaudy Spanish/Bavarian-themed restaurant in San Juan, where Carlos Colón was being presented with an award for Fighter of the Year. Amidst the colorful mosaics and handcrafted stained-glass windows, Gorilla Monsoon cut an imposing figure as he crashed the festivities and smashed the coveted award trophy over Colón's head, igniting a blood feud that raged across the territory in the winter of 1978, with bloody grudge matches in Caguas, at Roberto Clemente Coliseum in San Juan and even on the island of St. Thomas, a forty-five-minute puddle-jump east across the Caribbean.

Yet surprisingly, and perhaps owing to the amount of respect Carlos had for Gino, Gorilla Monsoon survived the blood feud with the King of Puerto Rican Wrestling with his title intact. The man who would finally end his reign of terror and take the North American title off him would be the man who had been his greatest opponent and in-ring rival, the man no one ever imagined he'd be wrestling ever again. It would be the revival of a feud that had raged through the WWWF of a previous generation, and one which no fan on the mainland had any idea was being waged once again. And most aren't even aware of it outside of Puerto Rico to this day.

After dropping the world title to Superstar Billy Graham, Bruno Sammartino had been more or less in a state of semi-retirement, taking on one or two matches a month as a "special attraction." Owing to his closeness to Gino, he would consent to becoming the greatest talent acquisition Gino would ever make for Colón and Jovica, as he and Gino would wage the final battles of their iconic rivalry in Puerto Rico. It was a series of at least seven known matches that began March 24, 1978, in Hiram Bithorn Stadium in San Juan, where the first match ended when the referee deemed Monsoon too bloody to continue, giving Sammartino the win but not the title. They would rematch on April 15 in a no-disqualification match in Juan Ramón Loubriel Stadium in Bayomón, and then finally, three weeks later in the same building, Sammartino defeated Monsoon to win the North American championship, the last title of Bruno's illustrious career. He'd beat Monsoon as well in two rematches later that month in Bayomón and San Juan.

The stage was set for what would be the last scores of matches between Gorilla Monsoon and Bruno Sammartino, which took place July 22, 1978, at Roberto Clemente Coliseum. It was the final chapter of a rivalry that had begun fifteen years earlier on that chilly autumn evening in Roosevelt Stadium, New Jersey. They were wrestling's young lions back in the day, and now here they were, 1,500 miles away, on a warm and humid summer night in San Juan, two of the most famous pro wrestlers who had ever lived, locking up just one more time before thirteen thousand appreciative fans.

It was a chain match, which was deliberately booked because this would also be the one and only time, outside of disqualifications, count-outs and disputed finishes, that Gorilla Monsoon would ever definitely defeat Bruno Sammartino in over one hundred singles matches between the two. Like the steel cage match, the chain match was a way to have one wrestler defeat another wrestler without a pinfall or submission required. Specifically, both combatants would be chained to each other by the wrist, and the winner would be the one who could tag all four corner turnbuckles in succession, while dragging his opponent behind him. By winning the match, Monsoon was able to walk out of the ring once again as the North American champion, ending Sammartino's four-month run in Puerto Rico, while also allowing Bruno to save face by not having to take a pinfall, which was something he almost never did anyway. Barring count-outs and disqualifications, it would be the last time that Bruno Sammartino would ever lose a one-on-one match. After all those years and all those matches, Gino had at least earned that honor. It would also mark the last title win of Gino's own career.

Gino must've been getting a taste for working heel again, because Puerto Rico wasn't the only place he did it at the time. Up in Toronto at the Maple Leaf Gardens, where Vince McMahon was regularly sending talent once every month or two, a mini-program was planned involving Gorilla Monsoon just for the Toronto faithful. On June 25, Monsoon turned on André the Giant, his tag team partner for the night, in a match against the vaunted team of Pat Patterson and Ray Stevens.[8] When Monsoon returned to the Maple Leaf Gardens in July and August, he was met with the disdain of the fans, just as expected, and easily dispatched his opponents, Nick DeCarlo and one of his best friends, Dominic DeNucci. It was all building toward the September 10 show, where Gorilla Monsoon actually challenged Bob Backlund for the WWWF world title in the main event. Gino had been working hard to help get Backlund over strong, which typically had involved tag teaming with him; but on this night, he did the honors for Backlund, looking at the lights after a tough twenty minutes of battle that made Backlund look like a world-beater. It would be Monsoon's last appearance at the Maple Leaf Gardens. It would also be the final time that he would ever get a shot at the world title in his career.

■

Now in his forties, the in-ring portion of Gino's career may have been winding down, but he still did his part to protect the business he loved as well as he could. He certainly was more than capable of lighting someone up in the ring when called upon to do so, which Davey O'Hannon remembers happened one night at one of Gino's spot shows at Upsala College in East Orange, New Jersey, in June of '78. In those days, it wasn't unusual for some joker tough guy who thought he could handle himself, with no proper training, to drop by the locker room ostensibly looking for work but really looking to humiliate one of the "fake wrestlers." That was the case when a big guy in a mask showed up at Upsala and set foot in the locker room while Gino was busy taking Arnie Skaaland's lunch at cards as usual and asked to be booked. "So Gino says, 'You know how to wrestle?' He says, 'Yeah, especially that crap that you guys are doing.' So Gino says, 'Well, you know what? Why don't we have a little tryout? Maybe you can make some money here.' So this nitwit says okay. They went out to the ring. I think it might have taken about thirty seconds before this guy was crying. And I mean crying. Gino was about to remove his shoulder from his body. And of course, we all went out to watch. You don't want to miss a good show like this." With Gino around, when it came down to disrespect for the business, all bets were off, and there was a real good chance it could get you hurt—and that even went for someone who was in the business but didn't take it seriously enough. Not severely injured, but just enough that you'd never dare to try it again.

And just as much of an imperious presence as Gino could be in the ring, he was even more so while manning the so-called Gorilla position. Ken Patera, who became quite close with Gino in those days, describes with typically vivid detail and vocabulary just what that entailed: "He watched them all and made sure nobody fucked up or was out there loafing. That really pissed him off, somebody not putting 100 percent into the match. He didn't have to worry about that with Bruno, me and Backlund. We were like buzzsaws, always moving, always giving the fans their money's worth." Patera's viewpoint isn't hard to understand. After all, Gino was a literal stakeholder. These shows were his livelihood, and he wasn't about to book the talent only to have someone drag everything down with unprofessionalism. He also adhered to a very strict schedule. "He let everybody know about it in the locker room," Patera says. "The locker room is where everything got done."

Gino was typically a constructive critic, and no one has ever accused him of being in any way abusive in his role; however, his patience would run thin when he felt someone was phoning it in or holding up the show in any other way. He already didn't have much love or use for Ivan Putski, and Patera confirms that the posing, muscle-bound Putski was an example of someone who could get on Gino's bad side: "Ivan was a good performer, but sometimes he'd go out there and just give a double bicep flex, and people would all holler and hoot, and then he wouldn't initiate anything. So, if I was wrestling Ivan, I'd be all over him if he was doing that stuff. You've got to keep moving." It all came down to Gino taking his work and his business seriously and expecting everyone around him to do the same.

Before the end of 1978, the time-tested Capitol Wrestling Corporation trust would be reduced by one, with the tragic loss of Willie Gilzenberg at the age of seventy-seven. Willie had been struggling with health issues for years, dating back to a stroke he'd suffered back in the '60s. During the annual trip to Vegas for the NWA convention, it was noted that he did not look or seem well, and that's because he was dealing with undiagnosed cancer. Yet his unflagging dedication to the business caused him to press on. Instead of going home to Florida, he and his wife, Lillian, went from Vegas to New York. On the evening of September 25, he was getting ready to leave his Newark office to make his customary trek over to Madison Square Garden, something he'd done hundreds of times in his career, when he took seriously ill and was rushed to the hospital, where the cancer was discovered. At the pleading of Lillian, he returned home to Miami, where he passed away on November 15. He'd been the elder statesman of Capitol's inner circle, a valuable advisor and fixer who had helped get the company established in New York, and his loss was keenly felt.

In his absence, and in a nod to Capitol's strong relationship with New Japan Pro-Wrestling, NJPW Chairman and booker Hisashi Shinma would be named the new official president of the World Wide Wrestling Federation. Although it was only a figurehead title to begin with, Shinma would have none of the influence and genuine value to the promotion that Gilzenberg had, and his position was more an honorary token to give the WWWF a truly international flavor than anything else. The days of the old guard like Mondt and Gilzenberg and even the aging Phil Zacko were fading away as younger members of the group like Marella, Skaaland and, of course, Vince McMahon Jr. were growing in power.

But the Capitol machine rolled on, and in the fall of 1978—just six days after Gilzenberg's death, in fact—the company's flagship TV program, *Championship Wrestling*, moved its regular tri-weekly tapings away from the archaic and aging Philadelphia Arena, a building they'd been running for nearly twenty years (as Toots Mondt and Ray Fabiani had done before them) further west to the working-class Pennsylvania enclave of Allentown, a steel city on the decline which happened to boast a fairground dating back to the nineteenth century. On that fairground stood the ramshackle Agricultural Hall, which would become the new home of *Championship Wrestling*.

Just as he'd done in Philadelphia, Gino would book the tapings and run the operation from his position behind the curtain. With the switch-over, Gary Cappetta, Gino's handpicked ring announcer, would be sent to Hamburg to take over announcing duties for *All-Star Wrestling*. That's because the Agricultural Hall already had its own regular ring announcer, seventy-four-year-old Joe McHugh, a retired roofing and siding salesman and former vaudeville emcee and a lifelong Allentown native. He'd been ring announcing boxing and wrestling since the '20s and had been filling that role at the Ag Hall since 1964. Just as he'd do with Cappetta in Hamburg, Gino would establish a system of signaling McHugh in those days before remote headsets to keep the show running as smoothly as possible. For the next six years, the mid-week Allentown and Hamburg tapings, typically held on back-to-back days each month, would run like clockwork.

■

However, right after the first set of Allentown tapings and spending Thanksgiving with his family as he always made sure to do, Gino was bound for Puerto Rico for a couple of weeks to take part in an important angle. He was still in possession of the North American title, and on November 25, he defended it against another major talent acquisition he'd brought in for Colón and company, his good friend André the Giant. It was the first time the two behemoths had ever faced off against each other anywhere in the world, but the one better remembered today is the rematch that took place one week later at Hiram Bithorn Stadium in San Juan—because this time, they ostensibly would not be wrestling but boxing, if what happened in the ring that night could properly be called that.[9]

A tropical storm had just soaked the island, but that wouldn't stop André and Gorilla from putting on the best show they possibly could. Former world heavyweight boxing champ Jersey Joe Walcott had been enlisted as the special referee—a relatively easy get since his mother's family was from St. Thomas. A young Hugo Savinovich played the obnoxious manager, standing at the side of Gorilla Monsoon, who entered the ring in a custom-made yellow nylon tracksuit that his own daughter Valerie would say made him look like a giant lemon. It would be a spectacle that nearly defied description. Cartoonish in the extreme, filled with wild haymakers that missed by a country mile and over-the-top selling from Monsoon that would make Yosemite Sam proud, Ali vs. Frazier it was not. What it was, however, was highly entertaining and showcased the surprising amount of skill and mobility that Gino still had despite being far removed from his prime.

"André wanted me so much to take a punch from him, and normally I would not hesitate," remembers Savinovich of that night. "But I was involved in a big angle [later that night] with Carlos Colón, and he had said whatever they do, they cannot touch you . . . And André kept saying, 'Let me get you, son of a bitch!' And Gino kept saying, 'Don't let him!' Because he knew what I was doing later." In the end, André "knocked out" Gorilla with an overhand right that sent him sprawling to the mat like something out of *Popeye*, giving André the win fifty seconds into the third round. Never wanting to pass up an opportunity to take advantage of any situation, they later brawled outside the ring, leaving Monsoon beached on a rain-soaked tarp as the Giant chased Savinovich into the dugout. If anyone needed proof of how far Gino would go to support Capitol Sports Promotions and please the Puerto Rican fans, this was it. Plus it enabled Gorilla Monsoon to make the curious claim of being the only man to ever wrestle Muhammad Ali and box André the Giant.

Gino was spending a lot of time in Puerto Rico and at the Tanama and was closer to young Victor Quiñones than ever. At heart, Gino was a giving man and sensitive to the plight of a young person who appeared to be somewhat lost. Within a year or more, Victor was beginning to look at Gino as the father he never had and would describe him as such to others. "There was so much honesty in Victor's heart that the moment you met him, you just knew that he was a guy that loved people, but he was hungry for love," explains Savinovich, who was there to watch that bond grow. "I think his relationship with his mom was good. But he never had that father relationship, and I think the moment that he met Gino and Gino met him, there was that connection, and Gino became that father figure." Hugo and others would also describe it as a mutual respect and a true love. "If you were to talk to Victor," says Mario Savoldi, "And you asked him, who's your father? It was Monsoon."

What must have made life for Victor even tougher growing up in the '60s and '70s in the hyper-macho Latino culture of Puerto Rico was the fact that he happened to be gay. But ironically, even though the professional wrestling industry was another hyper-macho world, being akin to the circus or other subversive subcultures, it could be surprisingly welcoming in those days to people of all stripes, including those with alternative lifestyles. In a business that was typically looked down upon and ridiculed by mainstream society, there wasn't much room for casting stones. In other words, being a gay man in the wrestling business was a much more tolerant place to be than most other places in American life. It's not clear at what point Gino became aware of Victor's homosexuality, but he did become aware of it, and it bothered him not one bit. If anything, it was one more reason Victor needed protection. Gino wanted to help him have a good life and possibly an education. At the time, Victor could neither read nor write, and although the details of his education are not known, in later years, he was not only known to read and write in English and Spanish but was fairly fluent in Japanese as well.

By this point, either in 1978 or 1979, with the blessing of Victor's mother, Gino invited Victor to come live with him and his family in New Jersey. He wasn't really doing much to challenge himself for Colón's promotion, and now that he'd reached adulthood, Gino felt he could actually be of use in certain capacities for the WWWF and make some decent money doing it. At the time, Gino was still running all his towns with his own ring, truck and a ring crew he employed. His own son, Joey, was still in high school and a little too young, but Victor was the perfect age to really start learning about the business, and Gino intended to give him that opportunity. Victor jumped at the chance to get out of Puerto Rico and also had some family in the New York area that he'd be able to visit. Maureen and the kids had already gotten to know Victor quite a bit from visits to Puerto Rico with Gino.

"He was like another son to us," Maureen remembers of the young man who came to be part of their family. "He was fun. And he was definitely a part of our family," agrees Valerie. "They couldn't have been more opposite, but for whatever reason, my dad took a liking to him. Whether he felt bad because he was this poor kid carrying guys' suitcases, I don't know. But he brought him home." For his part, Victor fell in love with the Marella family and the way they all accepted him. "Victor would do anything for you if he loved you, and he loved Gino and his family," adds Hugo. "Everybody understood that, especially Joey. Victor was like a real brother to him . . . It was no longer a Puerto Rican guy with an Italian-American family. It was just a family. It was just beautiful. Gino just was that father that Victor needed."

One day, Victor just popped up on the ring crew, driving the truck and hauling the ring. Over time, he even started learning a little bit about being between the ropes as well. Once he'd learned how to bump a little bit, he might even be asked from time to time to work an opening match, which he'd do under a mask as "Mr. X" or some other similarly anonymous moniker. Gino also asked Mario Savoldi to work with Victor to help him learn to be a referee, which Gino regarded as a path in the business with far more stability and longevity than being a wrestler. For this, he'd be sent up to New England, particularly Maine, to work with Mario and the ring crew on that end of the territory as well. It was a ground-floor introduction to the most elite organization in the business.

Gino was able to set Victor up with the Savoldis thanks to an ongoing relationship of cooperation with Mario and Angelo that continued even when the Savoldis began to spread their wings to book and scout talent in far-off territories. Thanks to working arrangements Vince Sr. had with Houston wrestling kingpin and transplanted Brooklyn native Paul Boesch, as well as Blackjack Mulligan and Dick Murdoch, who had purchased the Amarillo territory from the Funk brothers, the Savoldis would bring back promising talent from Texas like Tito Santana and Ted DiBiase, and in exchange, they'd work to bring Capitol talent into the Lone Star State, courtesy of Gino. Mario remembers the time he hit the motherlode in February 1980, when Gino brokered a deal with the Savoldis to actually bring in Bruno Sammartino for appearances in Houston and Amarillo.[10] In gratitude, Mario sent Gino two cases of the finest Scotch, amaretto and sambuca via UPS. The problem was, he didn't realize it was illegal to send liquor through the mail that way until he received a concerned phone call from Gino informing him that the FBI had arrived at his home in New Jersey. When Gino called back about an hour later, Mario tried to apologize, but Gino was laughing. After a while, he and the FBI agents sat down, had a few drinks, and everything was fine.

Victor being gay was known within the family, but not something that was really discussed. Around others in the business, it was not something he was yet comfortable being open about, although some, like Gary Cappetta, did know. "Being gay then was very different from being gay now," Gary explains. "I can remember him saying suggestive kinds of things. But never coming out. We never spoke frankly." Although Gino may have come from a rather traditional and culturally conservative background as the son of immigrants, he was also a well-educated man of the world, and the business itself had opened his mind up even further. "How traditional was he really?" remarks Valerie. "Pat Patterson and his boyfriend [Louie Dondero] came over to our house all the time. Louie would come over and make his 'Louie spaghetti' all the time for us."

Valerie has fond memories of the few years that Victor spent living with them in Willingboro. One story that communicates how friendly and comfortable they were with each other has to do with Gino one day ribbing Victor by bringing home an accordion and convincing him that he wanted him to play it for the fans at shows, between matches, with Victor earnestly insisting he didn't know how. Gino stayed with the bit for several more minutes, insisting that Victor learn some songs. "He said, 'You set up the ring, sell the pictures, then come out and play the accordion.' . . . My mom started cracking up, and we all just lost it. He was very gullible."

While Victor was settling in up north, Gino continued to travel to Puerto Rico on a regular basis. His in-ring wars with his great friend and business partner Carlos Colón raged on in 1979 until, on March 3, he finally lost the North American title to Colón, ending his last championship reign as a professional wrestler. He'd finally turn himself babyface in Puerto Rico after an angle in which he and his old Japan running buddy Abdullah the Butcher had a violent falling-out during a match against Terry and Dory Funk. Gorilla and Abdullah would then feud over Abdullah's Puerto Rican championship, including a match on June 9 that set a new attendance record at Loubriel Stadium, topping twenty thousand fans. Ten months later, he would even have at least one known match against the Dominican Republic's most celebrated wrestling hero, Jack Veneno. Colón's promotion was starting to run occasional shows as far across the Caribbean as Barbados, and that's where the match took place on April 17, 1980, thanks to a working agreement with Veneno's promotion, Lucha Libre Internacional.

■

Back home, Vincent Kennedy McMahon, aka Vinny, was growing in influence. The Ali-Inoki promotion had given him more strokes within the company, and it has even been reported that he was the person largely responsible for pushing the Capitol Wrestling Corporation to shorten the name of its fictional governing body to simply the World Wrestling Federation or WWF, believing it to be more marketable as a brand name. The change officially went into effect in mid-1979 and would remain that way going forward. Vinny was all about marketing and had new ideas he was always looking to implement. He even had an eye toward forming his own independent promotional company. In the summer of 1979, he purchased the Cape Cod Coliseum in South Yarmouth, Massachusetts, getting into the business of promoting hockey, rock concerts and other events, and even relocating his family there, including Linda, nine-year-old Shane and their three-year-old daughter, Stephanie. From their new home base in the Coliseum, Vince and Linda formed the core of a company that he would officially incorporate the following year as Titan Sports.

Gino, meanwhile, as his in-ring duties lessened, focused on his backstage duties, and most importantly, on his family. Joey was shaping into a hell of a baseball player, particularly good on the mound, and played both in the Willingboro softball league and at Willingboro High School. Baseball was the most important thing to him, which could also be a problem, as he began to slack off a bit at school and struggle with discipline. Thinking it would do him good, Gino and Maureen decided to try and enroll him in Holy Cross, the much tougher Catholic high school in nearby Delran Township, which Joey's friend Tony Chimel already attended. In fact, Chimel remembers a conversation he had with the principal, Rev. Joseph LaForge, who recalled meeting with Gino to discuss Joey's enrollment. When LaForge informed Gino that the tuition was $700 per year, Gino reached into his pocket, pulled out a giant wad of bills wrapped in a rubber band, peeled off $700 in cash, and handed it to the good reverend right then and there. Mike Chioda, whose sisters went to Holy Cross, even remembers hearing that Gino wound up donating about ten grand to the school: "I tried to get in, and I couldn't. My father tried to grease their palms, too. It didn't work."

But with Gino, it did. And the story is far from difficult to believe, as it falls in line with what so many remember even all these years later about him, namely, the gigantic bankrolls that he carried with him at all times. It would not be uncommon for Gino to have upwards of $5,000 to $10,000 in walking-around money rolled up in his pockets in two rolls—one in small bills for everyday expenses and the other in hundreds for whatever else might come up. When asked why he would do this, his response was a simple one: "What if I want to buy something?" The other reason he carried all that money with him was just as simple: Because he could. After all, who was going to take it from him?

Valerie once discovered this firsthand while on laundry duty at home. The house rule was that whatever anyone left in their pockets became the property of whoever was doing the laundry. It was intended to teach Joey a lesson, but Gino never imagined that he'd be the one impacted by it. Until the day Valerie was unloading the laundry and discovered that the entire side walls of the washing machine were coated in cash, which had apparently been left in a pair of her dad's tracksuit pants. She laid all the bills out in the kitchen to dry, covering almost every inch of the eight-foot butcher block table. The grand total: $8,240. When her dad got home, she ran to the door and reminded him of the "finders keepers" rule before he made it to the kitchen. He laughed as he finally walked into the kitchen and saw the table. The house rule was waived that day, but Gino let her keep a $100 finder's fee.

The best part was, he hadn't even realized it was missing.

With more time on his hands, Gino even used his connections in the Philadelphia media and sports worlds to land a weekly column, "In This Corner," which ran in the now-defunct *Philadelphia Journal* starting with the July 25, 1979, edition. Always keen to use his public platform to defend the honor of his business, his very first column was suitably titled, "Pro wrestling is not phony." Over the years, the column would give him a chance to speak directly to his fans on a variety of topics about his own career and his industry, and it was something he dearly loved doing, collecting every clipping into a scrapbook that is still in the family's possession.

■

But that doesn't mean that Gino was entirely done with stepping inside the ropes. In his final year as a somewhat full-time performer, his presence was still felt, including in the fall of '79, when he got involved in what was then just about the hottest angle in the company, pitting Chief Jay Strongbow against the man who had ostensibly "broken" his leg, WWF newcomer Greg "The Hammer" Valentine—the son of Gino's old colleague, Johnny Valentine. When the angle had taken place on WWF television, fans had gotten a rare chance to see Gino in his backstage capacity as he ran out from the back in his street clothes to assist the fallen Strongbow.[11] This was meant to indicate to the fans that this was indeed serious and perhaps "not part of the show." It was, of course, but it was the kind of "worked shoot" angle that was tantalizing to a certain segment of the more informed fan base even back then.

Monsoon teamed with Strongbow to take on the Hammer and his manager, Capt. Lou Albano, at the Broome County Arena in Binghamton, New York. He also teamed with Strongbow in the Cap Centre to challenge for the world tag team title against Johnny Valiant and his new "brother" Jerry. The final tag team champions he'd go up against would be a team new to the territory, but who'd been wreaking havoc just about everywhere else: Afa and Sika, the Wild Samoans.[12] He'd face them throughout the territory, teamed up with the likes of Dominic DeNucci, Rene Goulet, Ivan Putski, Tito Santana (then the company's newest babyface) as well as Pat Patterson, who had just arrived in the territory full time the previous summer.

In a hint toward his future role in the company, Gino actually got behind the microphone for a special event on April 12, 1980, at the Cap Centre. A relatively new cable TV channel called USA Network—which was affiliated with the MSG Network in New York that had taken over airing Madison Square Garden cards from HBO—was starved for programming and had begun simulcasting house shows from the Garden, as well as the Spectrum shows from PRISM. Now, USA Network had worked out a deal to have exclusive rights to broadcast Cap Centre shows on its fledgling platform, and based on his previous work on the Atlantic City Steel Pier shows, Gorilla Monsoon was chosen to be the ringside commentator for the very first Cap Centre broadcast on USA. It would turn out to be just the very beginning of a relationship between the WWF/E and USA Network that has spanned nearly half a century and continues to this day.

Meanwhile, one of the most important in-ring roles Gorilla Monsoon still had to play in those final months was helping to get over one of the industry's hottest new prospects, who'd just fallen into Vince McMahon's lap. Terry Bollea was a twenty-six-year-old bodybuilder and bass player from Tampa, Florida, with barely six months' experience as a full-time pro wrestler when Jim Barnett had sent him up to McMahon from Georgia in November 1979. He was just about as tall as Monsoon but with a perfectly honed and tanned, granite three-hundred-pound physique and bleached-blond hair. He was also green as grass, but they'd work on that. In addition to Georgia Championship Wrestling, he'd been bouncing around Memphis and the Alabama territory under the names Terry Boulder and Sterling Golden. Just as the old man had done when he turned Gino Marella into Gorilla Monsoon some sixteen years earlier, Vince Sr. took one look at Bollea and gifted him with a new name that would eventually make him millions: Hulk Hogan. McMahon and his son (especially his son) saw great potential in Bollea and had big plans for him. They paired him up with Blassie as his manager and were considering him for big matches against Bob Backlund for the title, but perhaps even bigger than that, they wanted to program him against André the Giant in what was sure to be a big-money match, eyeing another big date the company had coming up at Shea Stadium toward the end of the summer of 1980.

They had a few months to get him ready and, in typical fashion, began feeding him ham-and-eggers to squash on a weekly basis. But the rookie also needed real opposition to beat in order to get over as the powerhouse steamroller the office needed him to be. It had to be people the fans respected, and one of the most important of them turned out to be Gorilla Monsoon. In a later time, in his celebrated role as WWF play-by-play commentator, when Hulk Hogan was the golden goose with the company on his back, Gino would do everything in his power to get him over like a million bucks, and in a very different way, he did the same thing for Hogan as a monster heel back in 1980. They would face off on five occasions in the months leading up to Hogan's match against André at what was being called the *Showdown at Shea*. Naturally, Monsoon lost every one in convincing fashion. The first took place on January 18 at the Cap Centre and was fairly competitive. On April 19, Hogan squashed Monsoon in under a minute at the Providence Civic Center. On May 9, they clashed at the Glens Falls Civic Center in upstate New York.

Their most high-profile encounter happened on June 16, when they brought the match to Madison Square Garden. Hogan scored the win again that night after Monsoon missed with his Manchurian splash. In stark contrast to the roaring ovations Hulk would receive there in a later generation, the more than twenty thousand faithful on hand that night were not pleased—and a bunch of them let him know after the matches, when they accosted Hogan's car as he was trying to leave the arena parking lot and tried to turn it over. Perhaps those angry folks would've been even more dejected if they had known that that would be Gorilla Monsoon's final match at Madison Square Garden as a full-time wrestler. Leading up to Shea Stadium that summer, there would be one more quick loss to Hogan on July 12 at the Boston Garden.

Gino had done his job, both literally and figuratively, and from an esteemed veteran star like him, it truly was a gift to the young rookie. Hogan was on a roll and taken very seriously as a dangerous threat when he finally stepped in the ring against André the Giant for the first time inside a WWF ring on August 9, in the semi-main event at *Showdown at Shea* before 36,295 fans—a new all-time attendance record for the Capitol Wrestling Corporation and the largest show ever promoted by Vince McMahon Sr. Hogan would suffer his first WWF loss that night, of course, as he was intended to.[13] He and André would then take the match around the WWF circuit, squaring off eleven more times at most of the major venues through the rest of the year. And although Hogan would only stick around for another few months during that original run, he was destined for much greater things in that company in just a few short years.

■

All things must come to an end, and so there was one more big job for Gino to do.

After Gino had helped get Hulk over and as the *Showdown at Shea* was in the works, Gino began at last to give serious consideration his body's demands, hanging up his size-14 triple-wide boots for good. Although only forty-three years of age, not terribly over the hill at all by pro wrestling standards even then, Gino's weight and diabetes issues were wearing on him. He genuinely enjoyed working in the ring and certainly didn't mind the extra money it brought in, but he also didn't need to do it and hadn't needed to do it for quite some time. He'd been fortunate enough to be afforded an enviable position in the wrestling industry, and it was time to lean into that. In other words, he was at a point in his life and career when he wanted to focus strictly on promoting, booking and his other front office responsibilities without having to also worry about stepping in the ring three or four times a week on top of it. For the past few years, his main role had been to put over younger talent anyway, and he'd filled that role well. But now it was time to hand it off to younger men.

For the most part, it would not be something officially acknowledged on WWF television. To the average fan watching at home, Gorilla just seemed to quietly fade away without much fanfare. But in typical fashion, Gino had wanted to use his planned retirement in a constructive way for the business; in other words, to help get someone over. At least for his beloved Philadelphia fans at the Spectrum, where his influence was arguably strongest. And when it came time to choose who would put Gorilla Monsoon out to pasture, he picked the man who happened to be the WWF's hottest heel at the moment, someone Gino felt comfortable with: Ken Patera.

The decision wasn't that difficult. In addition to being programmed against WWF world champion Bob Backlund and being someone who had to be kept as strong as possible, Patera was also one of Gino's best friends in the locker room and away from it—the only one swift enough to spot Gino dealing from the bottom of the deck when they played cribbage and the only one brave enough to call bullshit when he did. On many occasions, he had been afforded the privilege of being a guest of the Marellas and enjoyed Maureen and Gino's delicious Italian dinners. And it was on one of those occasions that Gino took him aside and sprung the idea on him to shoot an angle that would be just for the Philadelphia fans (and PRISM viewers) and would bring an end to Gorilla Monsoon's wrestling career in the WWF.

The angle was put in motion on the July 26 Spectrum show, in which Backlund was defending the world title against Patera in the main event, with Monsoon as the special referee. The match was billed as title vs. title since Patera was in possession of the Intercontinental championship at the time, a secondary singles title that the WWF had introduced the previous year. During the match, Backlund dumped Patera to the outside of the ring, leading the enraged Olympic strongman to grab the announcer's microphone stand and bring it back into the ring with him. When Gorilla attempted to admonish him as he stepped through the ropes, Patera brought the microphone stand down over Gorilla's head. As soon as Monsoon got back to his feet, he called for the bell, disqualifying Patera and giving the match to Backlund. The match was over, but instead of Backlund, it was now Monsoon who was in Patera's cross-hairs. As Backlund exulted with the championship belt, an enraged Monsoon grabbed it right from his hands and took a swing at Patera with it. The two then briefly squared off, with Monsoon getting the better of it as Patera skulked from the ring. The stage was set.

It was declared that to settle the grudge, Ken Patera and Gorilla Monsoon would meet in the ring in the main event at the following month's Spectrum show on August 23. Patera's Intercontinental title would be on the line, but to sweeten the pot, Monsoon declared publicly on localized TV promos and in his newspaper column that if Patera defeated him, he would retire from wrestling. In his column the week leading up to the big match, Gino tipped his hand just a bit, seeming to indicate with some especially candid comments that he'd probably be calling it quits whether he won the match or not. It was an unusual bit of reality from the usually guarded veteran, but he was likely preparing his fans emotionally for what was to come.

Finally the day arrived, and Gorilla Monsoon stood across the ring from Ken Patera before a Philadelphia Spectrum crowd bursting at the seams with fans who had come to witness it. For nearly twelve minutes, the two mountains of humanity fought hammer and tong, as Monsoon gave everything he had to give the fans their money's worth one last time. The finish they had worked out would give Patera the win but leave

Monsoon with the ability to walk out of the ring with his head—though bloody as all hell—held high. When Patera's vaunted full nelson, his surefire finishing hold, failed to elicit a submission, he would resort to a hidden foreign object (purported to be brass knuckles), blasting Gorilla when the referee wasn't looking and putting the big man's shoulders down to the mat for the three-count.

All these years later, Patera remembers it well: "He's fucking bleeding like a pig. And, I mean, he really did a job . . . Every time his heart beat, a big fucking gusher would come out of his forehead. I'm thinking to myself, that's the best blade job I've ever seen!" It was one of those moments that wrestlers often dread, when the heat from the crowd, the goal of any wrestler worth his salt, reaches a boiling point beyond control and becomes something undesirable—when safety becomes an issue. Philadelphia fans on their best day were out for blood; seeing so much of it, and coming from one of their most beloved heroes, was too much to bear. As both wrestlers attempted to leave the ring and get back to the refuge of the locker room, a near riot broke out, with Philadelphia police throwing people off Patera as he fled. And as they emerged back through the curtain—a few minutes apart to protect kayfabe—Patera remembers his future wife horrified at the sight of his opponent, blood still pumping from his head. "She comes over to me, looks at Monsoon and looks at me. 'How could you have done that? That poor man!' Oh, she was so pissed off. I say, 'I'll explain to you later.' Because I had never smartened her up."

The wound on Gino's head would heal; they always did. It was one last blood sacrifice on the altar of the business. The angle had been executed to perfection. There was some doubt among fans as to whether he would honor the stipulation, considering the dubious method of Patera's victory. But Gino put those doubts to rest in his next column, entitled, "My career is over," in which he confirmed that he had decided to go through with it:

> Patera getting the victory over me in this manner was not necessarily what makes me hang it up. Rather, what happened during the match is what made my mind up for me.

> From the opening bell, and for the next ten minutes, I used everything in my arsenal trying to dethrone Patera. Although hurt and stunned, Patera somehow managed to weather the storm. There isn't anything else I know of that I might have tried. So I figure I don't have in my attack anymore what it takes to beat a man of the ability of a Ken Patera.

Shrouded in kayfabe though it may have been, there was a kernel of real truth in Gino's remarks. He was no longer that kid out of Ithaca doing cartwheels nor that tireless Manchurian beast, and he knew it. Better to go out while he still had a little bit left in the tank, rather than wait till he was completely out of gas, coasting on the goodwill of adoring fans to get to that next paycheck. He left readers with these closing remarks, summing up a Hall of Fame career as only he could: "Only time will tell how much I will miss the action and excitement of the squared circle. I take with me some lovely memories and horrible nightmares. I hope I have, over the past twenty-one years, brought some joy and entertainment to wrestling fans. I leave the ring with no regrets." For years after, during his career as a WWF television broadcaster, when calling a Ken Patera match, Gorilla would almost never fail to mention that he was the man who had retired him, never missing a chance to put him over.

The retirement was official. Perhaps owing to the fact that the retirement angle may have been somewhat of a last-minute decision, Gorilla Monsoon had been advertised for four more matches over the next few weeks, and he would honor those commitments before packing it in. On August 26 in Allentown, he teamed with Rene Goulet against Afa the Wild Samoan and his manager, Lou Albano; on August 30, he took part in a battle royal in Springfield, Massachusetts; on September 12, he did one more decisive job for Ken Patera at the Pittsburgh Civic Arena for good measure; and finally, on September 20, back at the Springfield Civic Center, he dropped one more match to Hulk Hogan in four minutes and twenty-two seconds.

On his way back to New Jersey the next day, Gino tossed his entire wrestling gear bag out the car window and off the George Washington

Bridge, sending it to the bottom of the Hudson River, where it presumably still lies.[14]

When the WWF came back to the Spectrum on October 11, Gorilla Monsoon was honored with a special retirement ceremony held between the second and third match on the card. As he stood in the ring, it was a transformed Gorilla Monsoon that fans would later come to know well—wearing a suit and tie with tinted glasses, his once-wild hair coiffed into a perm. He was presented with a trophy from local sports radio station 94-WIP and awarded a citation from his good friend and neighbor, Burlington County assemblywoman Barbara Kalik, in honor of his charity work for orphans and other underprivileged children. Finally, the microphone was handed to a humbled Gino, far from his typically verbose self. "I'm at a loss for words," he said as he choked up. "Whatever success I've had in my career, I owe to you fans."

CHAPTER 11
VINNY MAKES HIS MOVE

"It certainly is an asset to be associated with an organization that can produce this kind of programming, and it's a great testament to you, Vinny, personally."

One of life's truer aphorisms states that history is written by the winners. And that is most certainly true in the realm of professional wrestling. So it stands to reason that when it comes to the most powerful professional wrestling company in the world, the one that conquered the entire industry, the company that controls the narrative, this would be truest of all. WWE is fond of telling and retelling its origin stories to the point that fact becomes legend, and legend becomes myth. The mythologized version is the easy version; the safe version. But real life is messy. It's complicated and nuanced. And even in something as fanciful and mercurial as wrestling, it's important to dig down into reality and to separate the fact from the fiction.

The reality is that we will never fully know all the ins and outs of what happened in the Capitol Wrestling Corporation's luxury suite at the Warwick Hotel in Manhattan on the afternoon of Saturday, June 5, 1982.

Of the six people in the room at the time, only two are still living, and they won't be providing clarification any time soon. But one thing has become fairly certain: It was not the warm, glowing, peaceful transition of power we've often been led to believe. The picture that the WWE storytelling machine has sometimes weaved over the years, the benevolent figures of Vince Senior, Gorilla Monsoon, Phil Zacko and Arnold Skaaland handing the keys to the kingdom to Vincent Kennedy McMahon and Linda McMahon, is a simplification that obscures just how contentious it actually was. Especially in the case of the last holdout, the man who was most opposed to the deal going through, Bob "Gino" Marella.

The last thing Gino ever expected was that he would one day have to give up his ownership stake in the company he'd helped build into the most successful in the business. It was something he'd worked hard for and something he fully intended to go to his grave with, passing the shares—and the income that came along with them—to his children when the time came. And he certainly didn't foresee being bought out by the guy he would always insist on calling "Vinny" to his dying day, despite the fact (or perhaps because of the fact) Junior hated being called that. The truth was, the old guard, Senior included, had never really looked at Vinny as a serious peer, or someone with the wherewithal to one day run the operation. He was the promoter's kid, and typically in the industry, such a position aroused immediate suspicion and skepticism from the boys to begin with. Vinny had been no different. He was only eight years younger than Gino, but in terms of perception, it might as well have been twenty.

In the end, Gino along with Senior's other partners would find out that they didn't really have a choice. Not in any practical sense anyway. With the partnership and assistance of his more business-savvy wife, Vinny McMahon Jr. had been planning something beyond what any of the old-timers, both in his own company and in any of the other ones, would ever see coming. Nothing short of a carefully plotted coup, the plan required the complete and total takeover of the Capitol Wrestling Corporation. There would be no partners. Vinny wanted it all. And then, he wanted the rest of the business, too. As he was fond of saying in later years, if his father had known what he had in mind, he would never have sold to him in the first place. But even if any of them had known, they most certainly wouldn't have had the confidence that he could pull it off.

Disgruntled and dejected though he may have been, of all the partners, Gino was also the smartest. If he was going to allow this sale to go through, he was also going to make sure that he got himself a deal that would ensure he was well taken care of. If he was losing his points in the company, he was going to make damn sure that he would be compensated in a manner to make it worthwhile and that he would continue to be a crucial part of the company. He took a gamble, as he was wont to do, that the whole crazy operation would work—and in doing so, he wound up in the best possible scenario for himself under the circumstances. He would not be cast aside like a relic, as Vinny would eventually do to so many in the industry on whom he'd set his sights. And in the end, the two men, who certainly had had no special affection for each other in the early years, would develop a kind of respect and a professional bond that would be the closest thing to friendship of which the younger Vince McMahon seemed capable.

But with or without the respect or the friendship, it was happening. All previous relationships, agreements, industry norms and recognized boundaries would be null and void. Vinny was coming for everything. And Gino knew that he could either be in or in the way. In the end, he chose the former, the wisdom of which is difficult to dispute.

■

Ironically, one of the main reasons Gino chose to hang up his boots in the summer of 1980 was to focus more on his behind-the-scenes responsibilities as part owner of Capitol Wrestling, producing television and working with talent on matches and finishes, without the distractions of having to put his own body on the line. In many interviews and discussions in later years, he would say that there were just too many young guys out there who wanted to beat on his old body—perhaps an unexpected thing for a wrestler in his forties to say, but the ring wars had taken their toll on him. That, combined with his weight, he could focus more on getting under control now that he wasn't wrestling anymore. He stayed active and was an avid racquetball player with family and friends. In the years immediately after retirement, he'd get himself down as low as 350 pounds, the lightest he'd been since his amateur wrestling days, yet still imposing on his six-foot-six frame.

To the wrestlers he worked with in the locker room, he was a treasure trove of wisdom and useful advice. Tony Garea, who would eventually follow in Gino's footsteps as a long-tenured road agent but was then still an active performer, sums up Gino's approach perfectly: "He would say, just go in there and do what you think is right. And if it's not right, we'll correct you. If you made a mistake, he'd say, 'Don't get upset about it. You learned something today. I could have told you for a month not to do this. And you wouldn't know why. And now you've done it, and you realize it was wrong. So, you learned something tonight.'" His main advantage over Vince McMahon Sr., and why McMahon had installed him where he was, was that he was one of the boys, too. He had come into the business just like them and understood that any day could be the last day of your career. Plus, he'd achieved in the ring for the company at the very highest level, which caused the boys to always respect him. He wasn't just speaking hypothetically. He was speaking from experience.

He'd earned his place in the business. He'd earned his retirement. It was time to focus more on enjoying the money he'd made, enjoying his life and enjoying his family. Getaways to Atlantic City with Maureen became more common than ever—and for the kids, who were now in their teens and early twenties, that also meant the Marella home became the place to party on weekends when mom and dad were away, always making sure to clean up before they got back, of course. Included in that group with the kids was Victor, who became closer to Gino than ever and continued to be treated like one of the family.[1]

And yet even then, there was a brazenness to Victor that was starting to come out, or perhaps was always there: the streetwise kid from San Juan who had grown up with little in the way of parental guidance or regulation. If anything, the freedom and privilege afforded by life with the Marellas seemed to be enabling it even more. "He had no shame at all," recalls Valerie when discussing those house party days. While she and her friends were fine with just getting drunk, she remembers Victor's fondness for "whippets," pressurized steel cannisters of the kind used for whipped cream dispensers, only filled with nitrous oxide ("laughing gas") that could be used as an inhalant. "He always had them somewhere, and he was always trying to get people to do them . . . We'd say, 'Get away from me with that.'" Victor was also gaining a reputation for making unwanted advances that made some of Valerie's male friends uncomfortable. "They would say, 'Don't leave me alone with him. You're gonna be here all night, right?'"

Among those present at a lot of those parties was Tony Chimel, by now a regular member of the ring crew with Victor for the shows Gino promoted. And just a little bit later, Valerie's friend Mike Chioda came along. During his high school years, Mike worked summers and weekends with Gino and Victor's crew—between setting up the ring, selling programs and other odds and ends, many nights he'd come home with as much as $500 in cash. He was doing so well, in fact, that he started to attract a little understandable parental suspicion. By the time he was seventeen, he was buying cars and expensive stereo equipment and had even put a water bed in his room. Finally, he came home one night to find that his mother had laid out about $7,000 in cash on the water bed, which she'd found in the back of his sock drawer. "She was like, 'What the fuck is this?' My dad was like, 'Where the fuck are you getting all this money?' He went and called Gino, to see if I was really making that much money working with him, because he couldn't believe I was making all that fucking money from wrestling." But he was. For a kid willing to hustle, it was what you could make working for Gino in those days. And once his parents were convinced he wasn't selling drugs, he was allowed to continue.

∎

Gino had genuinely meant it when he had walked away from the ring in 1980, and there was never to be a comeback. However, ironically, it would be just a couple months after his official retirement that he almost got pressed into playing a fictionalized version of himself in a movie—a layer of illusion on top of illusion that could only happen in the wrestling business. It was all thanks to a chance encounter at Los Angeles International Airport near the holidays. The Marellas were headed home from a family vacation, but unbeknownst to them, an even bigger celebrity was also preparing to board the same plane. Gino had drawn some attention to himself in the terminal and soon found himself surrounded by eager fans. As he attempted to interact with them all as graciously as possible, suddenly a voice familiar to any movie fan rang out over the din of the throng:

"Gorilla Monsoon!"

The crowd parted to reveal Sylvester Stallone, trailed by his own mob of fans but still nothing more than a fan himself in the presence of Gino. As it turned out, Stallone was a huge wrestling nut, and the two struck up a conversation. Sly was in preproduction for *Rocky III* and was headed to Philly to talk with city officials about his plan to donate to the city the giant Rocky statue he had just had commissioned, which was to be used during imminent location filming. As he and Gino sat in first class together on the way to the East Coast, Sly mentioned to Gino that he had a scene planned for the new movie in which Rocky would face off against a professional wrestler and asked Gino to come try out for the part.

Gino was hesitant, but partly at the urging of Valerie, a starstruck Stallone fan of epic proportions, he would later wind up going through with the audition and screen test. There were a variety of reasons why it didn't pan out. One was that, at this stage of his life and career, Gino lacked the confidence to pull off what was required of him, later insisting to Valerie that he just wasn't an actor—despite his daughter's not-incorrect assertion that that was largely what he'd been for the past twenty years anyway. The other reason appears to have been a shift in direction for the part, away from a burly, old-school bruiser heel that Gino no doubt would've played to a younger, more buff and muscular type. In the end, of course, the part would wind up going to Hulk Hogan, who, after finishing up his first WWF run in the spring of 1981, headed out to California to take on Rocky Balboa and secure his own eventual wrestling immortality.

■

But in addition to the movie role that almost happened, there would also be a handful of actual one-offs in the ring in the early 1980s: special occasions when necessity called on Gino to dust off the jacket and boots and step out from behind the curtain. He didn't romanticize these moments; they didn't lead to an inevitable "one last run" as was common with so many of his colleagues. Rather than relish them, he viewed them as part of his duty to the office. The first of these took place on May 4, 1981, before a sellout crowd at Madison Square Garden and would prove to be the very last time Gorilla Monsoon ever wrestled at the arena that was just as much his home as it had been Bruno's.[2]

He had been called back into active duty thanks to a freak accident suffered by the WWF's other resident gargantuan. Although André the Giant's broken ankle had been blamed on the fearsome Killer Khan, the reality was that the Giant, growing increasingly unsteady and unwieldy as he got older, had sustained the freak injury while trying to get out of bed one morning. In any event, Gino was conscripted to take his place beside Tony Garea and Rick Martel as they took on Moondog Rex and his manager Capt. Lou Albano, along with Stan Hansen, also making his final appearance at the Garden. Monsoon had even been granted the honor of scoring the second and deciding fall in the best-of-three affair, squashing Rex with his famous Manchurian splash and taking one last bow before the New York faithful who had buoyed him to greatness.

Following the example being set by his greatest in-ring rival, Gorilla Monsoon, Bruno Sammartino had made the decision to officially call it quits once and for all. He'd been winding down for a couple of years ever since losing the title to Superstar Billy Graham, and had just drawn the biggest house in company history to Shea Stadium to see him settle his blood feud with his former protégé Larry Zbyszko, proving that he still had it even after all these years. He probably could've kept on going, but like Gino, he didn't want to wait until his body had totally failed him, and wanted to go out while still on top. A new arena had just gone up in Gino's territory, named after New Jersey governor Brendan Byrne, no stranger to Gino, as he was the same man responsible for opening up Atlantic City to the casinos. Together with Giants Stadium, it was part of the new Meadlowlands Sports Complex and intended as the home of the New Jersey Nets basketball team, as well as the future New Jersey Devils hockey team, which Byrne was in the process of luring from Colorado. But just twenty-six days before the Nets officially moved in, thanks to a deal worked out with the Capitol Wrestling Corporation, it would be the site of Bruno Sammartino's retirement match, as he took on another longtime rival, George "The Animal" Steele, whom he trounced in under seven minutes.

The truth was, the relationship between Bruno and the McMahons had been just as strained as ever, with the former champion always more than a little suspicious that he was being taken advantage of, or not paid what he was owed. In fact, the last straw turned out to be the big retirement show itself, which became a bone of contention when both sides disputed what the correct payout should be. It was a fittingly bitter and chaotic end (at least for the moment) to a dysfunctional yet mutually profitable business relationship, as Bruno walked away not just from the ring but from the entire organization and would begin setting a lawsuit into motion. Whatever the reason, Bruno had never been able to coexist with the front office the way his great friend Gino could. Although Gino had his strong personal views, he was never one to rock the boat and found great personal success by working with the office, while Bruno was successful enough that he never needed to work well with them in order to make everyone, including himself, very, very rich. This new rift was the latest example of the vast difference in the way the two men dealt with authority. There would be more to come.

Still, despite their difference in business philosophy and temperament, Bruno and Gino would remain friends and in regular contact, although whether the office knew about it or not is unclear. Loyalty was important to Gino, but he no doubt understood Bruno's reasons to do what he did. However, he wasn't always as forgiving of those who crossed the office, or who made life difficult in general for himself and the other partners. This could have been the reason for one of the strangest incidents of his career, which remains largely unexplained to this day. In the November 4, 1981, edition of his *Philadelphia Journal* column, Monsoon infamously reported that Superstar Billy Graham had died of cancer, setting off one of wrestling's most persistent urban legends of the time. The reality was that Graham, in a state of frustration, anger and deep depression after being stripped of the WWWF world title, had departed the territory at the end of 1978 and had been keeping a relatively low profile in the business. At the time of the column, he had only had one match in the previous year and a half and had more or less gone into seclusion at home in Phoenix. But he was very much alive; and it's even possible, and honestly quite likely, that Gino knew this.

But whether he knew it or not, what made the whole thing even stranger was that he never retracted the statement publicly, even when it was made clear he was wrong. "A few of us said to him, 'You know what, he's looking pretty good to me, for a dead guy,'" Davey O'Hannon recalls. So what could possibly have been the reason for this? In a 2000 interview with *Slam Wrestling*, Graham indicated that the rumor of his death had been started as a joke by his dear friend and epic in-ring rival, Dusty Rhodes—the kind of twistedly humorous rib very common in the business at the time. It would've been very easy for such a rumor to reach Gino's ears—in fact, Dusty had come into New York for a shot at the Garden just a couple of weeks before Gino wrote the column, so it's conceivable he'd even repeated it to Gino directly. If so, was Dusty working him in order to help further the rib? Or was Gino a willing co-conspirator in helping to spread the phony story?

It is likely we will never really know, as no one has ever come forward with any inside knowledge and probably never will. Whatever the case, the lack of a retraction is rather telling and would fit with the theory that this was something deliberate. But why? For one thing, Graham had been a notoriously difficult talent to work with during his time with Capitol, at least from the perspective of the office. He'd always been trying to change McMahon's booking to keep himself on top as champion and chafed mightily when the trigger had been pulled and the title passed to Backlund. He had become something of a pain in the ass to those in charge and likely was not on Gino's list of favorite individuals when he finally parted ways with the company on less-than-glowing terms. Could the greatly exaggerated rumor of his death have been a parting shot from Gino to the Superstar?

Graham did finally snap out of his funk to a certain degree and would return to the territory in the summer of 1982, although a shell of his former self and with a chip on his shoulder, sporting a shaved-bald head and ditching his colorful boas and tie-dye for a dour, karate-master gimmick. It certainly did him no favors, and his comeback run was a decided disaster—and at least in Philadelphia, this was partly attributed to Monsoon's unretracted column, which had led many fans to believe that Graham really was dead and that this nearly unrecognizable version was actually a different person entirely. His return to the WWF would last a mere eight months before totally fizzling out. It was while he was on his way out in March 1983, doing jobs to everyone from Jimmy Snuka to Salvatore Bellomo, that Monsoon put the icing on the cake during a live interview on Philadelphia radio, curtly dismissing Graham as a world championship contender in a manner that only further supports the theory of some kind of heat between the two that we'll never fully know about.

■

Generally speaking, things were going very well for Gino heading into 1982, both professionally and personally. In April, he got to have what surely was a supremely gratifying experience when he joined seven of his teammates from the ill-fated 1959 U.S. national wrestling team in presenting special awards to the members of the U.S. World Cup team at the finals of the National AAU Freestyle Wrestling Championships in Lincoln, Nebraska. The reason was that the team had accomplished what Marella's squad had failed to do all those years ago and defeated the Soviet Union. It was a moment well worth a five-hour plane trip and a little getaway that Gino now had the luxury of indulging in thanks to no longer having to fulfill any in-ring obligations.

But while all this was going on—the backyard barbecues by the pool, the dinners at Jimmy Weston's supper club, the vacations on the beach in Fort Lauderdale, the trips to Vegas that were 10 percent business and 90 percent pleasure—a much colder, shrewd intelligence was watching and waiting for an opportunity. He wasn't so much interested in the trappings of the good life, in the smelling of roses; his interest was much more in raw, naked power. Control. Domination. He was in many ways the living embodiment of the worst aspects and stereotypes of his generation. While his father and his father's partners sat contentedly on top of the most lucrative wrestling company in the business, perfectly happy to allow the hundreds of thousands of dollars to roll in every month, the thirty-seven-year-old Vincent Kennedy McMahon was envisioning a way to multiply that many times over, and he didn't care who or what he had to run over to do it.

Far more than simple greed or ambition, he was fueled by a burning need to make his mark and prove himself in an industry that most certainly did not take him seriously. To subvert, infiltrate and decimate the old-boys' club that ran the business—a collection of soon-to-be dinosaurs that viewed him as the ineffectual son of a man they greatly respected, who had been given much only due to his privilege. To prove himself to the father who, for the first dozen years of his life, had not even wanted to know him, and who had actively sought to keep him away from the business entirely.

The old man had never wanted Vinny to be involved and had discouraged him at every turn—but inch by inch, Vinny had worn his father down. First a ring announcer, then a TV commentator; then relegated to the furthest promotional outpost out in Maine; then Boston with Ernie Roth and Bobby Harmon; then he'd been allowed to start his own promotional company out of Cape Cod, likely with the idea that it would keep him busy and out of anyone's hair. The Muhammad Ali / Antonio Inoki promotion back in '76, which had largely been spearheaded by the younger Vince, had been a double-edged sword. It had raised his profile in the organization and given him a chance to take the lead on something important—but it also was more or less a total disaster that had made everyone involved look very bad in the public eye. The jury was out on whether Vinny was capable of much more.

But it didn't matter what the perception was, because he believed in his own vision, and so did Linda, who had become a true fifty-fifty business partner with him by this point. Titan Sports had been growing and developing since its founding in February 1980, and it's likely that Vinny had had his big plan in mind even then. The new company allowed him to be taken more seriously, to raise capital, and it was to be a means to an end—that end being the complete takeover of his father's company, the Capitol Wrestling Corporation.

It didn't hurt that his father was already looking to get out. He was approaching sixty-eight years of age, and three decades of the wheelings and dealings of the business, of putting out fires and playing politics with promoters, of placating and pacifying talent and moving them around with his mighty pencil like pieces on a chess board, had worn him down and burnt him out. There was also the issue of his health. He was in the early stages of pancreatic cancer, although it's not clear if he knew that yet. Those around him definitely didn't know it. But he was sick, and he was feeling it.

Wanting to keep Marella, Zacko and Skaaland in place, he was only interested in selling off his 50 percent share of the business. The problem was finding a buyer—this was a very valuable property, after all. There were apparently several interested parties, the most notable among them being a name from Capitol Wrestling's past: Buddy Rogers, the first WWWF world heavyweight champion, for whom McMahon still had a soft spot in his heart, in spite of all the water under the bridge. But the asking price was simply too rich for Buddy's blood, and the "Nature Boy" had to back out—although later that year, he'd be welcomed back into the fold as an on-air personality for the first time in nineteen years, a maneuver seen by some as a petty swipe at the estranged Sammartino, who could never stand him and had largely made sure he stayed away all that time.

Losing hope in getting a viable buyer, he next considered selling his half of the company to his three partners, leaving three owners instead of four. This would've been a very beneficial scenario for Gino, as assuming the portions remained the same, that would've given him 40 percent of the company, with Zacko getting 40 percent and Skaaland 20 percent. With Zacko the eldest partner at seventy-five, Gino would've likely been the leader of the triumvirate at that point—a scenario he'd likely been envisioning since he'd first bought in some thirteen years earlier. But none of them counted on Vinny.

Getting wind of the situation, the younger Vince swooped in with an offer. Naturally, he first approached his father privately. Senior was the most important one to get on board. But to his father's surprise, the offer wasn't for the 50 percent share. Vinny wasn't interested in maintaining the status quo. The vision he had in mind left no room for partners. Vinny wanted to buy everyone out and take the whole thing.

Vince Senior hesitantly entertained the notion and went to the partners with it. To say that they were skeptical would be an understatement. Here was the kid who couldn't figure out how to make money selling paper cups, whom they'd watched the old man bail out on failed venture after failed venture. And now he wanted to run their company, the most successful in the industry. Arnie, the least ambitious of the bunch, was the first to be swayed by the two McMahons. "It was Gino and Phil Zacko who were kinda like, 'We really don't want to do this,'" remembers Mario Savoldi. "It was Arnold with Vince that were really pushing it. But if anybody was not in favor of doing it, it was Gino." And with good reason. After all, he'd hit the motherlode in the business and was now being asked to give all that up for uncertainty. He was the one with the most to gain by things staying the way they were. He was set for life and had been the unofficial successor. It was going to be his. And if Vinny hadn't jumped in, that might have been happening sooner rather than later. Now he was being pressured to essentially step aside to make way for the ambitions of the son, someone with whom he had not been close at all up to that point. ("They were not fans of each other," bluntly remembers Valerie of those days.)

And so Gino became the holdout. Getting everyone on the same page became a difficult matter. But with the father now on board with his son's offer, it was really only a matter of time. It was contentious there for a while, but realistically, what would have happened had the partners stood firm and refused to be bought out? It is very likely that it would have turned into a legal situation, and their hands might've been forced. There were options in a situation like this. As 50 percent shareholder, Vince Senior could've found ways to exert pressure on the minority partners in a court of law. There was even a last-resort shell-game practice for such holdout situations, in which Senior could've dissolved the entire Capitol Wrestling Corporation, thereby leaving the partners totally out in the cold while he and his son established a new company. No one wanted that scenario. Besides, what options did Gino have? Wrestling, and in particular Capitol Wrestling, was his life and his livelihood. If he had opted to take the McMahons to court, all he'd likely have been left with was his 10 percent of Puerto Rico. And there was no way he was going back into a classroom now, not after the life he'd been leading. He was determined to find a way to make this work. If he was going to give in, he was going to make it worth his while. He didn't have too much leverage, but he had some, being the primary booker and event producer, not to mention the ring crews he controlled and the rings that he outright owned.

Tom Carlucci, a longtime former WWE employee who came to know Gino very well over more than a decade while he worked as a television director and producer, vividly recalls Gino recounting the situation to him in detail while they were spending time in Atlantic City: "He said, 'I was the last one to sell to Vince. And I took everything I could from him. Because I knew in the end, he kind of bamboozled the other guys a little bit.' But he wasn't bamboozling Gino. He said, 'Look, I want a guaranteed job for life. I want this much money. And I want to be on TV.' And Vince did everything that Gino wanted."

■

Once Gino was satisfied, Vince and Linda went to work getting some cash together, using the capital of Titan Sports in addition to some money lent by various New England banks with which they'd cultivated relationships. On the morning of June 5, 1982—along with early Titan employee Jim Troy, a rough-hewn former hockey player who'd become a confidante to Vince[3]—they boarded a puddle jumper from Cape Cod Gateway Airport with briefcases containing a down payment of $230,736 in cash,[4] one-fifth of which was intended for Gino. They made the one-hour flight to New York City, where the WWF was putting on its monthly show at Madison Square Garden that night. But that afternoon, before everyone headed over to the Garden, they would all meet at the Warwick Hotel, in the suite Toots Mondt had bequeathed to the Capitol Wrestling Corporation. It was there, in the very rooms the old Wrestling Trust had once done its business half a century earlier, that the business was about to come full circle, and an entirely different kind of wrestling trust would be born.

While Troy waited downstairs in the hotel restaurant, Vince and Linda McMahon sat down with Vince Senior, Gino Marella, Phil Zacko and Arnold Skaaland. The deal had been agreed upon, but now it was time to make it official, in black and white on paper. All told, the full asking price for all one thousand shares of the Capitol Wrestling Corporation came to $1,644,264—a rather low number that likely would've been higher if it were anyone else but the boss's son who was buying.[5] This is how it broke down: 615 of the shares were valued at $1 million total, with $822,132 going to Vince Senior alone, $71,147 each to Gino and Zacko, and $35,574 to Arnie. Perhaps as a gesture of gratitude, the remaining 385 shares were valued at $644,264 ($47.39 higher per share) and would be divided exclusively among the junior partners according to their percentages. For his points, Gino would be walking away (on paper) with a grand total of $328,852. Zacko got the same, and Arnie wound up with $164,426, with Senior getting the rest.[6] After the down payment, the remainder of the money was to paid out in four installments over the course of the next year, after which the sale would be final. However, the sellers were not fully confident that they would ever get the rest of the money, which is why they had put in a clause stating that should Titan Sports default on any of the payments, the sale would be nullified, the company would remain with the partners and they would also get to keep whatever money had already been paid up to that point.

But there was more to the deal than just money. Per the contract, the CWC was to remain a wholly owned but distinct subsidiary of Titan Sports—an agreement that Vinny would later cast aside when it no longer suited him, as he did many times. Titan Sports would acquire everything that came with Capitol Wrestling—the television contracts and existing agreements with venues throughout the Northeast, the services of all the talent who had their handshake agreements with the office and the rights to the "World Wrestling Federation" brand name they did business under, which the marketing-minded Vinny was especially keen on. Senior would stay on as chief advisor and promotional figurehead for as long as he chose.

And of course, Senior had to make sure his erstwhile partners would be taken care of going forward. The elderly Zacko had no interest in remaining with the new organization, choosing to take his money and go home to his wife, Freda, in Harrisburg, Pennsylvania, where he'd live out his eleven remaining years. Arnie would remain for the time being as the onscreen manager of the world champion, Bob Backlund, and retain his office responsibilities, in addition to taking a wider role as a road agent on many WWF shows. But for Gino, who had been the vice president of the CWC and Senior's second-in-command, it was especially important that he be protected. "He basically told Junior, as long as Monsoon's alive, he has a job," remembers Valerie. "I don't care what he does, but you find a job for him."

To start, Gino was offered a ten-year contract with the new company. As for his requested presence on television, Gino had done some ringside commentary in the past on the Steel Pier shows, as well as the initial Cap Centre show on the USA Network, but the contract now called for a regular spot at the commentary table, where his presence would be a more constant part of the show than anyone's other than Vinny himself. And in what would turn out to be the most fortuitous part of the deal considering what Vinny eventually had planned, the contract called for Gino to be paid 1.5 times the basic salary of a prelim match wrestler for every single event the company presented, whether he was there or not. This amounted in part to a no-show job that would mean the more events there were, the more money in Gino's pocket. It was all intended to keep him happy and to make up for what he was giving up.

What happened in that suite remained unknown to nearly everyone other than the people who were there. As far as all the wrestlers were aware, as far as all the other promoters in other territories were aware, nothing had changed. The old man was still in charge. And for a time, that would be largely true, as the next year would be a period of transition, during which the power had not yet fully been transferred. That night after the contract signing, everyone went to the Garden, and it was business as usual. Vince McMahon Jr. sat at the announce desk as he always did, calling the action for a card headlined by Backlund defending the title against "Superfly" Jimmy Snuka, and a bloody brawl between André the Giant and Blackjack Mulligan. But despite appearances, nothing would ever be the same. Just how much it would change was far from apparent, and was certainly unknown to the four men who signed the contracts put in front of them that day.

■

Yet despite the deal he'd worked out for himself, Gino was still far from happy. After all, he had no way of knowing if any of this was actually going to pan out. If the kid would even actually be able to run a successful company or would just drive it into the ground like everything else he'd ever put his mind to, casting many years of hard work to the wind. Although it would all work out as well as it possibly could for Gino, by all accounts, the loss of his ownership stake in the WWF was, at the time, the most crushing and disillusioning professional disappointment of his life. Gary Cappetta, who was still Gino's ring announcer and spent as much time around him professionally as anyone, remembers well the drastic change in his mentor's state of mind: "*Angry* is not the word. It was a lot more than that. It was the only time in my long relationship with him that I saw him act unprofessionally. This lasted probably for a few months, where he would come to the show, and he would be dejected. Someone would ask him a question about a finish or something, and he would bark at them, 'Oh, how the fuck would I know? I only work here, like you.' He'd yell it, loudly. And that wasn't the guy that I knew." The way that Vinny had muscled his way in had rocked Gino to his foundations and unsettled his usually even-tempered demeanor in the extreme. Before it became clear how it was all going to shake out, it was a tough pill to swallow—and even later, it's easy to imagine that he'd wish he could've held on to his piece of the pie.

Perhaps to distract himself as much as to keep a close eye on his remaining interests in Puerto Rico, Gino started to relent ever so slightly on the whole "retirement" thing and began spending more time down on the island again. Besides, the fans down there had no idea he'd retired, and the fans up north weren't going to find out about it. Just eight weeks after signing the contract of sale in New York, Gorilla Monsoon was back in the ring in San Juan for his first match in fifteen months, and his first match in Puerto Rico in longer than that, battling the mammoth Kareem Muhammad (who was really Decatur, Georgia's Ray Candy doing a Nation of Islam militant-Muslim gimmick). All told, Monsoon would wrestle a total of nine known matches in the Caribbean between the summer of 1982 and the summer of 1983. In addition to his matches with Muhammad, he would square off against the twenty-four-year-old King Tonga, a notoriously tough former sumo who was just a couple of years away from joining the WWF and eventually becoming known as Haku. Monsoon and Tonga would also form a short-lived tag team in the spring of '83, making several appearances to challenge the duo of Buddy

Landel and Terry Gibbs for the North American tag team championship in what would be the last title matches of Monsoon's career.

Hugo Savinovich remembers those final Puerto Rico matches well: "He was a very proud man, proud of what he had accomplished... And once that bell rang, he was like a little kid in the ring. It felt to me like there was a shining aura of happiness, where he just let go. He just enjoyed it and wanted to give the people the best of times."

A similarly final yet completely unheralded milestone occurred on October 18, 1982, at one of Gino's spot shows at the Plaza Arena ice skating rink in Hazlet, New Jersey. When Ivan Putski was unable to make his scheduled match against the raw-boned Swede Hanson, it was Gorilla Monsoon who stepped in to take his place, although the forty-two seconds it took him to squash the Swede is likely an indicator of how eager he was to do it. Those few moments comprised the final match Gorilla Monsoon would ever have in a WWF ring.[7]

■

Word of the in-progress sale of the company was starting to trickle out in the business, and it was also having a ripple effect within the territory itself. Among those old-guard loyalists who'd not been a part of the new deal were the Savoldis. Angelo was approaching seventy, had recently retired from his front office job and never had a real ownership stake in the company anyway. "Angelo Savoldi was nice, but sometime after the business was sold, everybody kinda split," remembers Maureen Marella. "Before, it was family; everybody used to live around where we lived. Then it was like, this one did this, this one did that..." Mario had still been with the company, doing refereeing and other jobs, but that had come to an end around the time of the sale, when he had gone to join his father in an independent promotional venture—with Vince Senior's blessing, despite the fact that they'd be working with Bruno, whose lawsuit against the Capitol Wrestling Corporation was in full swing and who had no qualms whatsoever about running a little opposition against his former employers, with the right backing.

"Bruno became involved with a group that I had friends with, that offered to start a new organization, and that's when I started International Championship Wrestling," Mario recalls. "These guys were, well, in today's words . . . they were racketeers. And they offered the funding." Sammartino would be doing announcing, with his son David getting his feet wet there as a wrestler, which Mario freely admits was an attempt by him and his dad to try and convince Bruno to eventually tag team with Mario to help get the new promotion off the ground. Other prior WWF talent like Larry Zbyszko, the Valiants and Dominic DeNucci also came over. Bruno and Angelo had kept in touch with Gino and were well aware of how unhappy he and the other Capitol partners had been with the Titan deal. This led them to wonder just *how* unhappy he really was and what he'd be willing to do about it. "Bruno thought we could pull him over," explains Mario. The Savoldis never actually went so far as to approach Gino with an offer, so we'll never know what his response might've been. But as unhappy as he was, it's still unlikely he would've budged. His unhappiness didn't trump his loyalty. In his 1983 Philadelphia radio interview, he would even deny having any knowledge of the Sammartino lawsuit whatsoever.

However, the partners continued to be disgruntled in general, and part of the reason was that, just as they'd feared, the structured payments weren't going exactly as promised. Vinny was struggling to come up with the money and keep up with the agreed-upon quarterly payoffs. In fact, the rumor was that the money he was gathering together partly came from the Capitol Wrestling Corporation's own profits, a clear sign the old man was giving his son some serious leeway that no other buyer would've enjoyed. It was borrowing from Peter to pay Paul, but this was how things were dragging along into 1983 as Gino and the others bided their time.

■

One thing that did happen, as Junior had promised, was that Gorilla Monsoon became more of a regular presence behind the commentator's microphone. Starting with the November 22, 1982, show, he made up one half of the broadcast team for the monthly Madison Square Garden events shown on the USA and MSG Network. The first four months, he would serve not as a play-by-play announcer, where he'd eventually find his groove, but as the color commentator, the more typical position for an ex-wrestler-turned-announcer in those days. Joining him on play-by-play would be the voice of the WWF, Vince himself. Not quite at the height of his powers yet, Monsoon is uncharacteristically low-key on those early broadcasts, clearly giving Vinny some room, as well as no doubt doing all he could to learn from the guy who'd been calling the action for a decade by that point, so that he could give him what he wanted. There are also times when it seems like he's half-heartedly trying to play the heel as if to give himself a way to play against Vince, a straitlaced babyface announcer at the time.

The very same month that Gorilla Monsoon debuted as the Garden's newest ringside commentator, he'd do the same thing for the Philadelphia Spectrum shows aired on PRISM. Gino had always been a very important presence at the Spectrum, but now he'd be in front of the camera as well as behind it. Monsoon was joined by Dick Graham, who'd been a fixture of the Spectrum broadcast booth since the shows had first started airing on PRISM (and who would remain there until the very end, thanks to being an employee of the network). Monsoon and Graham would remain the regular broadcast team for monthly shows at the Spectrum for the next five years, making Dick Graham Gorilla Monsoon's third-most prolific broadcast partner.

The pairing of Monsoon and McMahon at the Garden didn't last nearly as long. Vince had been calling the Garden shows by himself for years and was probably glad to hand off the responsibility, especially as he was starting to take more of a hands-on role in running those shows from the back—the very role that Gino used to play. By April 1983, Gorilla had stepped into the lead play-by-play announcer role at the Garden and would be joined by Pat Patterson, who was winding down his in-ring career and had been Vince's color guy on weekly TV for a couple of years by that point. The irony was that Patterson was someone who also seemed to be gaining influence behind the scenes and was poised to assume a similar right-hand man spot beside Vince Junior as Gino had filled alongside

Vince Senior. Junior had identified Pat as someone with a keen wrestling mind, and once the takeover was complete, he was going to play a vital role in booking angles and matches, as well as acting as a liaison to the locker room.

For the time being, he and Gorilla formed an announce team for the monthly Garden shows that, while perhaps not one of Gorilla's most memorable pairings, allowed him to stretch his wings for the first time as a regular lead commentator. Both experienced wrestlers who had performed at a very high level and commanded great respect in the business, they did enjoy some on-air chemistry and gave the impression that they knew what they were talking about and were qualified to comment on it, because they had both been there and done that. But this was still a fairly low-key and matter-of-fact Gorilla Monsoon, calling the action in a sports-like manner alongside someone who didn't exactly light up a broadcast booth and for whom English was famously a distant second language. It was clear Monsoon needed the right people to really bring out the best in him as a commentator, but that was still to come.

Right around when Gino starting calling the monthly Garden shows with Pat, he was also given the responsibility of calling the monthly USA Network shows from the Cap Centre in Landover by himself, surely a sign that the office was pleased with how he was coming into his own as an announcer. Gino had always been an erudite and well-spoken guy with a flair for genial turns of phrase, an educated person who often stood out in the locker room for that reason. Now he was getting to put that to good use—not to mention the anatomical knowledge he'd accumulated in college. Of all the guys in the back, it was easy to see, even from the start, why Monsoon would've been an easy choice to transition from wrestler to announcer.

This was still a regional WWF audience that well remembered and best knew Gorilla Monsoon from his role as a wrestler, which became evident when he participated in one last TV angle, something he really wouldn't engage in any longer once he fully transformed into his commentator incarnation. The 365-pound Big John Studd, whom Monsoon had wrestled numerous times back in the early '70s under his previous ring name of Chuck O'Connor,[8] had been going around with his manager "Classy" Freddie Blassie, offering $10,000 to anyone who could pick him up off his feet and bodyslam him—an ongoing trope in his seemingly never-ending feud with André the Giant.

On the February 19, 1983, edition of *Championship Wrestling* from Allentown, Monsoon came out from the Gorilla position and stepped into the ring to accept the bodyslam challenge, with Vince putting over his reputation on commentary, presenting him as a serious contender to take that $10,000. And after a couple of minutes of shameless stalling from Studd, Monsoon came closer than anyone else ever had, lifting Studd clear off the mat, only for the resourceful Studd to grab the top rope, causing Gorilla to lose his footing and plant Studd right on top of him. Studd then drops an elbow on a fallen Monsoon and puts the boots to him, as Blassie goes to work holding back referee Dick Woehrle, until Pedro Morales and Tony Garea hit the ring, send the heels packing and tend to the fallen Gorilla. It was all intended to build up Studd as an unstoppable force in his brewing war with André, as well as a leading contender to Bob Backlund, which it accomplished. It would also be the last time anyone would put their hands on Gorilla Monsoon for years.

■

The in-progress sale of the Capitol Wrestling Corporation to Titan Sports—and the financial struggles associated with it—came to a head in June 1983, one year after it had been initiated. June 5 had come and gone, and the final payment had not been made. It was the partners' worst fear, and there was serious consideration of exercising the emergency clause and taking the company back. There was still an optional fifteen-day grace period built into the contract, and Vince and Linda begged the old man and his cohorts to give them that time. They scrambled like hell, and on June 17, with just three days left in the grace period, they all convened once again in New York City on the day of that month's Madison Square Garden event. It was the first Garden card in eight months not to be televised, which may have been due to the chaos going on behind the scenes. In any event, the partners agreed to hold off on exercising their right to reclaim what was theirs, and Vinny was able to come up with the last installment on that fateful day, making the sale of the World Wrestling Federation complete. He would remain eternally grateful to his father, to Arnie, to Zacko and especially to the reluctant Gino for giving him the benefit of the doubt. It was a favor he'd never forget.

It was a true changing of the guard—although the World Wrestling Federation name would still be used, a whole new company was effectively taking shape in real time. Vince McMahon Sr., though still outwardly the figurehead leader of the company to those within the business and every bit the presence backstage at the Garden, stepped back to become more of a counselor and advisor to his son, who soon relocated his own corporate headquarters from Cape Cod to Greenwich, Connecticut, where he'd also relocated his family. Arnie would focus more on his duties as a lead road agent, especially since his other important role, that of manager to world champion Bob Backlund, was very soon to be phased out—as was Backlund himself, whose humble, low-key persona and Boy Scout image had absolutely no place in the new WWF that the new Vince McMahon had in mind. Arnie would be just one of several key road agents McMahon would put into place, as he took a much more hands-on approach to producing individual matches than his father ever had—eventually making this transition would be longtime WWF wrestlers such as Chief Jay Strongbow, Tony Garea and Rene Goulet. Vince kept them in the fold and kept them happy. They were the last link to the old school.

As for Gorilla, he would continue to man his position for the TV tapings and major arena events when he wasn't doing ringside commentary. But he quickly found himself a little further from the center of power than he had once been. For one thing, although his advice was always welcome and taken, he'd no longer be directly involved in booking. More and more, Vince was leaning on the expertise of Pat Patterson in much the same way as his father had relied on Gino. Additionally, to help his son get off on the right foot, Vince Senior had wanted someone reliable and proven to assist him with booking, and used his influence to bring in the services of George Scott, a former wrestler who had just finished completely rebuilding and revitalizing the Carolinas-based Jim Crockett Promotions during the mid-1970s through the start of the '80s.

There was no question that Gino was less directly plugged in than he used to be; on the bright side, that, in addition to his retirement from the ring, did give him more of a chance to relax, to spend time with family and friends, to travel more. In fact, when his old friend Shohei "Giant" Baba finally made public his marriage to Japanese actress Motoko Kawai (which had begun in secret a dozen years earlier) in 1983, Gino was able to make the trip to Hawaii to attend the wedding commemoration ceremony—and legend has it that he even sang for the happy couple.

■

Now that he was fully in control of the company, Vinny could finally set in motion the big moves he had been planning. This also involved sending a strong message about who was now in charge—and who was not. Unfortunately, one of the first people to find this out the hard way was Gary Michael Cappetta, who, for nearly a decade, had been one of the lead members of "Team Monsoon." He showed up to the August 13, 1983, Philadelphia Spectrum show just like all the rest, but the last thing he expected was to get pulled from the ring and replaced between the first and second matches. When he went backstage, Vinny abruptly informed him that his services at the Spectrum, which had always been Gino's show, were no longer required. There also, sitting quietly in the background, were Gino and Zacko. And there was nothing they could do about it. They just had to sit still and take it. "Monsoon didn't say one word," remembers Gary. "It probably was killing him . . . It was Vinny flexing his muscle and rubbing Gino's face in it. He and Zacko had had their power pulled from them, and they were silent. The relationships had changed." Gino would also be in the room nine months later at the last TV tapings in Hamburg, when Gary was fired from his post as ring announcer for *All-Star Wrestling*. He was now off TV entirely and began announcing for rival wrestling promotions. Despite this, and perhaps in a show of defiance, Gino would continue to use him for his local charity events and monthly Brendan Byrne Arena shows in Jersey for more than a full year afterward.

Of course, it was far more than mere personnel changes that Vince McMahon Jr. was interested in. His goal, as has been thoroughly detailed and covered in countless books, articles and documentaries over the past several decades, was the total expansion of the World Wrestling Federation across all territorial boundaries, from one coast of North America to the other and eventually even beyond, wiping away the mutually respected regional fiefdoms that had been in place in one form or another for half a century. His plan was coldly simple, so much so that it was astonishing that none of the other cutthroats had had the balls to pull it off before him: He would buy up television time slots in markets throughout the United States and Canada, offering deals that were too good for local affiliates to pass up, even pushing out long-running regional programs from other wrestling companies in the process. He would begin luring away the top talent from many of those promotions, assembling a kind of super-roster of major stars. And then, once fans in different regions had gotten a taste for his TV programming, with its heightened production values and top stars, the WWF would begin to come to their towns, playing at all the top local venues and eventually choking out the established promotions that wouldn't know what hit them. It was so calculated and methodical in its surgical destructiveness that one couldn't help but almost admire its bold ambition and single-minded purity—unless you were one of the gobsmacked promoters whose once-secure business was being snatched right out from under them.

Little by little, the initial shockwaves started to spread throughout the business as the other promoters and owners started to get the earliest inkling of what was being attempted. The gauntlet was thrown down at the thirty-sixth annual National Wrestling Alliance convention at the end of August at the Dunes Hotel and Casino in Las Vegas. Unlike years past, which involved Senior, Gino, the other partners and wives cavorting on the Strip, holding court and occasionally getting some work done, the old guard sat this one out. This time, it was Vinny who went, and it was all business. Unbeknownst to anyone, he'd formed a partnership with Jim Barnett, one of the most valuable members of the NWA and a man with contacts throughout both the TV and wrestling industries. For nearly a decade, Barnett had been running Georgia Championship Wrestling, a company Vinny saw as a direct threat but also one whose model he wanted to emulate since they'd been doing their own modest expansion, thanks to national cable exposure on Superstation TBS. Barnett was on the outs with GCW, having been ousted in a power play that included wrestler/promoters Jack and Jerry Brisco, as well as the rugged, terminally old-school and perpetually angry Alan Rogowski, better known as Ole Anderson.

Vinny was more than happy to swoop in and snatch up Barnett, whom he saw as extremely valuable to his plans for national expansion. Neither man was known for his subtlety, and outrage prevailed at the convention when Barnett unexpectedly resigned, effective immediately, from all his NWA positions, which included treasurer, secretary and booker for the NWA world heavyweight champion. McMahon then informed the mortified group that the WWF would also be withdrawing its membership. Heated words were exchanged, especially from the shrewd Anderson, who could clearly read the writing on the wall. As the story goes, after dropping the bomb on all of them, Vinny quietly excused himself from the room rather than face the wrath of the collective of promoters. One week later, from his home in Fort Lauderdale, Vince Senior made it official, penning a letter of resignation that he sent to NWA president Bob Geigel in Kansas City.

■

Nevertheless, in those early months, with his father looking over his shoulder, McMahon was relatively conservative and careful in his maneuvering. At first, he was mainly targeting areas where the regional promotions had dried up: places that were considered relatively "open," such as California, which had been his first move in early 1983, even before the sale had been finalized. He also moved into the Michigan/Ohio circuit that had been abandoned years earlier by The Sheik's failing promotion, and rather brazenly set his sights on venerable old St. Louis, the heart of the NWA, where Sam Muchnick had already ceded power and others were fighting over the scraps. More than the city itself, Vinny wanted to get his hands on *Wrestling at the Chase*, the St. Louis wrestling program that had been an institution on local TV for nearly a quarter century. By the end of the year, he'd have it.

Cautious though he was, he was already stoking more than enough outrage among the men who considered themselves friends and colleagues of the elder Vince McMahon, and who'd been doing business with him for decades. The old man started to receive some angry phone calls from former associates asking him to straighten the kid out, which dismayed him and certainly only added more stress on top of his private health struggles. But he wasn't really in a position to do anything about it anymore, other than to urge his son to think twice about what he was doing. And Senior certainly wasn't the only one disturbed and bothered by the aggression of the WWF's new owner. All the old-timers like Gino, Skaaland, Blassie, the Wizard, Albano and Patterson had strong relationships with many of the other promoters—despite whatever differences there had been, these were men they had known for years, had broken bread with, had even called friends in some cases. Frank Tunney in Toronto had given Gino a major break early in his career, as had Stu Hart in Calgary. Kansas City and St. Louis were places where he'd learned his trade. Eddie Graham in Florida had been a dear friend and partner to the entire Capitol crew going back to the '60s.

Mike LeBell in Los Angeles, who had entered into an ill-fated and decidedly one-sided partnership that allowed the WWF access to California, had given Gino a West Coast home away from home. Gino had kept in touch with LeBell for years. In fact, Gino was thrilled one day in late '83 to come up to the Connecticut office and find Jeff Walton, LeBell's right-hand man, who had come over to help McMahon launch WWF's own in-house magazine.[9] Seeing Jeff reminded Gino of the old days in Los Angeles.

What Vinny was doing was shaking this entire system to its foundations, and a part of Gino was greatly pained to see it threatened. "It was hard," Maureen remembers. "Everybody had their own territory. But Vince was wiping everybody out. There was a lot of tension. I don't think Vince Senior liked the idea of that. And Vince Junior never stopped. He never stopped to enjoy what he created. He never enjoyed it." Longtime Titan Sports audio engineer Larry Rosen, who worked with Gino extensively on television projects in later years, remembers his mixed feelings as well: "He was old school. He liked that there were different territories. Many of those guys were his friends. I don't think he was happy that it all got busted up. It's like Walmart taking over every convenience store. He liked when it was the neighborhood shops, and then Vince turned it into wrestling Walmart. Gorilla was from another generation."

■

Even internally, Vinny was taking a consolidated, all-or-nothing approach that meant the days of the Northeast sub-territories would be coming to an end as well. Everything was falling directly under the Titan umbrella, which in Gino's case meant that most, if not all of the local Jersey/Delaware/Pennsylvania shows would no longer be his to run. In fact, many of the smaller spot show venues were being totally phased out as the touring crew of wrestlers would be expected to do much more traveling with the company, expanding far beyond the Northeast. There would be no more JFK High School charity shows in Willingboro; the biweekly summer shows in Wildwood were cut down to one per season. Gino's wrestling rings now belonged to Vinny, as did his ring crews. "It didn't work out for him the way I think he wanted it to go," remembers Mike Chioda, whom Gino would help get onto Vince's new ring crew. "Vince wanted to take over all the territories no matter what it took, and if he had to step on you, Vince was going to step on you. That's all. He really didn't give a shit." Gino wasn't happy about any of it, but he had made the decision to stay loyal to the McMahon family, no matter who was in charge. "It was a rocky relationship," explains Tom Carlucci. "But it was respectful, because Vince knew that Gino was with the old man, and Vince respected guys that stuck with the old man, especially Gino. Vince respected the loyalty they showed."

Ironically, just as Gino was losing his ring crews, his son, Joey, was starting to get involved—even if his father wasn't thrilled with it at first. Joey was a natural athlete and a promising baseball pitcher, and Gino had wanted him to play ball. He'd even gotten him a tryout with the Cincinnati Reds. But Joey had a self-sabotaging streak, and the day before the tryout, he'd played two rounds of golf. The next day, he wound up throwing out his arm by about the third pitch. But it didn't matter, because Joey didn't really have a strong desire to be a baseball player anyway—he wanted to get into the wrestling business. "In his mind, baseball was a lot of pressure, and he had that pressure his whole life," explains his sister Valerie. Becoming a wrestler was out of the question—even if he had been big enough, which he wasn't, Gino was never going to allow it. As he saw it, there was much more longevity and stability in being a referee anyway: "I think Joey thought if he was a referee, there's no pressure. And he got to be with my dad on the road." But before he got to be a referee, Joey started out on Vince's new ring crew, Tony Chimel getting his foot in the door that way as well. Chioda would join them just a few months later.

In the midst of all the change, the one thing Gino didn't have to worry about was job security. He continued calling the action from ringside at major house shows, all of which began to fall under Vince's new, more modern approach to television production. From its early days, Titan Sports had contracted with an independent production company based in Baltimore and run by producer/director Nelson Sweglar, whose team had helped produce the WWF events that were being televised on the USA Network from the Cap Centre. Now McMahon had secured an exclusive deal for wrestling on USA, snatching up the contract that had previously belonged to Joe Blanchard's Southwest Championship Wrestling out of San Antonio. Sweglar was helping McMahon to expand his TV operations, putting together a new weekly show called

All-American Wrestling, which would reach cable-ready homes throughout the country and provide a showcase for his wrestlers—or as he called them, Superstars. Things were getting so busy that Sweglar was hired outright by Titan Sports, as Vince started putting together his own in-house TV production operation.

In his producer capacity, Sweglar had the opportunity to get to know Gino well, sitting beside him on most ringside broadcasts in those early years, making sure everything was running smoothly from a production standpoint. To a seasoned television professional like himself, who was a bit suspicious and skeptical of wrestling types, Gino was a breath of fresh air: "He had a different kind of persona from the other guys. And keep in mind, Gorilla was a college graduate . . . He was very free-form. His commentary, whether it was on camera in the studio or out ringside at an event, seemed to be very natural and not staged. It was never as if somebody had written out certain things for him or bullet points for him to cover. That was never the case. He was very much at ease on camera and doing commentary."

■

With everything changing and McMahon circling the wagons, it wasn't clear how long Gino would be able to maintain his outside affiliation with the Puerto Rican office. Carlos Colón and Victor Jovica were still NWA members, and with the battle lines being drawn, it was becoming tricky for Gino to serve two masters. Following the WWF's withdrawal from the NWA, the Puerto Rico territory had only gotten closer to the other Alliance members, even working out a deal with Jim Crockett Promotions, the company swiftly becoming the new center of the NWA and leading the opposition against Vince McMahon's ambitions. By November, Colón would be collaborating with Crockett on the first *Starrcade*, a closed-circuit spectacular designed to showcase the talent of the NWA. How did it look for a company that was essentially taking part in a show designed to run directly against the WWF to have Gino as one of its minority owners?

Gino had been continuing to make wrestling appearances in Puerto Rico on rare occasions, but heading into the fall of 1983, the relationship was clearly approaching its end, which led to Gino closing the book on his in-ring career once and for all with one final epilogue. He and the family flew down to Puerto Rico for one last show—a massive spectacular put together for the tenth anniversary of Capitol Sports Promotions, at Hiram Bithorn Stadium in San Juan on September 17, 1983. Thanks to NWA affiliations, Colón and Jovica were able to pull together a star-studded crew for the occasion: Puerto Rican legend emeritus Miguel Pérez wrestled his last singles match on that card. Gino's old friend Pete Sanchez was there, as were Johnny Rodz and José Estrada, who wrestled under masks as Los Medicos. From the WWF also came Pedro Morales to defend his North American title against former NWA world champion Ric Flair. André the Giant was there, as well as one of Vince's new acquisitions from Georgia Championship Wrestling, the musclebound Iron Sheik. The likes of Ox Baker, "Bulldog" Don Kent and Abdullah the Butcher were there, and so was King Tonga, on hand to defend his Puerto Rican title against Dory Funk Jr. From Mexico came Mil Máscaras and his brother Dos Caras. And in the main event, Colón himself would defend his Universal heavyweight strap in a title vs. title match with the current NWA world champ, Harley Race.

It was the kind of cross-promotional cooperation that was fast becoming an alien concept in Vince McMahon Jr.'s WWF, and Gorilla Monsoon got to participate in that one last time. His opponent that night was veteran luchador mid-carder Francisco Arreola Ramirez, who was on a tour of Puerto Rico as Abdullah Tamba, junior partner of Abdullah the Butcher. The match itself was not much to speak of, with Tamba scoring the pinfall on Monsoon following a senton splash in just a little over a minute. The capacity attendance that night was reported in some places as high as thirty-two thousand, which would've made it the largest crowd of Gino's entire pro wrestling career. They would also be the last people to ever see Gorilla Monsoon wrestle live. Going in, he'd told Maureen that this was really going to be it for him, and she'd remained skeptical until the moment he left the ring and headed back to the locker room, when she saw him take off his wrestling boots and toss them over the dugout.

As it turned out, he really meant it. Gorilla Monsoon would never wrestle again. And later generations would come to know him as something completely different.

Hugo Savinovich, who had managed Tamba against Monsoon that day, fondly remembers a giant pool tournament after the show, organized by Don Kent for all the boys to take part in, with a real trophy and everything. Hugo had made it to the finals against Gino and was losing to the big man when Gino missed a crucial shot, allowing Hugo to mount a comeback. Gino, who was extremely competitive when it came to pool, was so pissed off that he broke his pool cue in half like it was a toothpick. Hugo then looked over at Victor, and out of great affection for Gino—and maybe a tiny bit of fear—he made a fateful decision: "I realized how much that game meant to him . . . And I just decided that I had to put him over. My pride was not bigger than the love and respect I felt for Gino . . . He was so happy when he won. And now as I look back, I'm so happy that I did, because that moment was very special for him."

■

As much as winning, it was the camaraderie among the boys that was so important to Gino, who had never stopped being one of them. It was a reminder of earlier, simpler times, but eventually he had to return to the harsher reality of what was happening back home. Big changes were going on, and the company was right on the cusp of its big push to national expansion. Tragically, one member of the trusted inner circle who wouldn't live to see everything Vince had in store was "The Grand Wizard" Ernie Roth, who, on October 12, 1983, was found dead of a heart attack in his Fort Lauderdale home at the age of fifty-seven.[10] It was a shock to everyone, especially Vince, who had major plans for the nefarious Wizard—younger than Blassie and more reliable than Albano—to play a key role as a top manager in the expanding WWF. In just a few months, McMahon would look outside the company to replace the Grand Wizard with a man who would go on to become Gino's greatest friend and associate. But that was still to come.

All of Vinny's planning and ambition wouldn't amount to much without the right headliner to carry the whole thing and draw the attention of what he'd hoped would be the WWF's nationally expanding audience. His father had had Bruno, but Vinny wanted something entirely different—a living superhero perfect for the larger-than-life 1980s zeitgeist. A new star for a new era. As he began his process of cherry-picking his new roster from the best of the other territories, he found exactly who he wanted for the role, and it was someone whose potential he'd already recognized years before: Hulk Hogan, who was then wrestling for Verne Gagne's AWA. With the right dollar amount and the promise to strap the rocket to his back, Hogan couldn't get his bags packed for New York fast enough. In the meantime, against his father's instincts, as the WWF world title belt awaited its new owner, Vinny made sure to get it off Bob Backlund, the milquetoast collegiate grappler who represented everything he was trying to move the WWF away from.

It was Gorilla Monsoon, along with Pat Patterson, who called the action at the Garden the night of December 26, 1983, when the Iron Sheik dethroned Backlund for the title. It was Arnie Skaaland who threw in the towel with Backlund trapped in the Sheik's camel clutch submission hold, just in case Bobby had any second thoughts about doing the job. But the hated Sheik was just another transitional champion, designed to get the championship to where they really wanted it. And it was Monsoon and Patterson once again at ringside in Madison Square Garden exactly four weeks later on January 23, 1984, when Hulk Hogan made his triumphant return to New York, this time not as an arrogant heel but as a conquering hero, annihilating the Iron Sheik in five minutes to be coronated as the new WWF world heavyweight champion in front of 26,292 ecstatic fans at the Garden and Felt Forum—the second-largest crowd in the history of wrestling at MSG.

The old man made sure to be there that night, sick though he was with the pancreatic cancer quietly claiming his body. It would be his final night at the Garden, where he'd held the keys to the wrestling kingdom for two and a half decades. And as Hogan made his way from the locker room to the ring to start the match, it was the old man who graciously held the curtain open for him. It was as much an official stamp of approval as it was a resigned acceptance of the inevitable.

Monsoon took the decided lead on commentary for the match, seeming to understand very well the importance of his job. And his call of that match is every bit as iconic as the match itself, helping to usher in not just an entirely new era in the World Wrestling Federation but a new era in the business. His energy, his enthusiasm and, most importantly, his unbridled support of Hogan sell the match, the moment and the new champion. It would be a sign of things to come as, over the years, Gorilla Monsoon would contribute just as much on commentary as Vince McMahon himself in getting over Hulk Hogan and maintaining his aura, providing the narration for so many of his most indelible moments. On that fateful night, Hogan held aloft his newly won championship belt as Monsoon proclaimed in his customary fashion, "History made in Madison Square Garden, and the fans on their feet! Hulkamania is here." And it was. Going forward, it would be the literal power of Hulkamania that would propel Vince McMahon's vision and will it into reality. And ironically, Gino's voice would accompany much of it.

■

If ever there was a sign that it was time to get out of Puerto Rico, this was it. It also didn't help that the relationship had grown pretty sour, particularly when it came to payoffs. Gino was a 10 percent owner, and yet he hadn't been seeing anything—despite the fact that business was on fire. "They were cheating him, basically," explains Hugo Savinovich. "He felt like he was being disrespected, not just with the monetary situation but disrespected as a true friend of Carlos Colón. Gino was a man of his word. He thought they were family—and you don't mess with family." Gino was generous by nature, but even he had his limits. Meanwhile, Victor Quiñones had been waiting a while for an opportunity to take on a bigger role in the wrestling business, and this was just that opportunity.

VINNY MAKES HIS MOVE

Gino had already considered his shares to be partly Victor's anyway—a way of getting him set up in the business—and so in 1984, he granted Victor his wish, washing his hands of the whole thing and handing over his points officially to him, with an understanding from Colón, ill-fated though it was, that they'd be able to straighten out the money situation.

Gino's generous nature led him to save Victor from a rough childhood in Puerto Rico and take him in as one of his own. He'd shown him the ropes and helped set him up, but now it was time for Victor to strike out on his own, and he'd return to Puerto Rico with Gino's blessing in a much better situation than when he'd left. Gino would no longer be directly invested in Puerto Rico from that time forward, but he'd continue to monitor the goings-on there, and he'd continue to look out for Victor whenever he could.

■

As the pivotal year of 1984 progressed, things were changing, and fast. Dismayed by the angry phone calls from longtime colleagues, not to mention the manner in which Bob Backlund, his handpicked All-American boy, was being unceremoniously swept aside, Vince Senior continued to clash privately behind the scenes with his son over the direction of the company. It finally came to a head during a heated closed-door meeting between father and son, in which Vinny leveled with the old man: "I can't have this keep happening. You work for me now. You have to let me run the company the way I see fit. I'm gonna do this with or without you. So are you with me, or not?" To which the old man paused, considering his son's question, considering the relationships he had with so many people whose business he was now threatening.

And then responded: "You're right, Vinny. Fuck those guys."[11]

There was no stopping what was happening, but Senior had been the only person capable of at least mitigating it, and he was also the only person really holding Vinny back from the full breadth of what he wanted to do. But that was all about to be a moot point. Senior's health took a precipitous turn for the worse in early 1984, and it soon became obvious to everyone. Rather than attend to his health diligently, he'd been trying to keep it quiet by consulting only with the New York State Athletic Commission doctor who tended to the wrestlers at the Garden, and who had misdiagnosed it as a mild prostate issue. By the time it was discovered that it was indeed pancreatic cancer, it was already very far gone. He was given chemotherapy treatment, but hopes were not high. It was quickly becoming obvious that this was the end.

As he lay sick and dying at Parkway Regional Hospital in North Miami, Vince McMahon Sr. was very clear with his son that once he was gone, there were certain people to take care of indefinitely. At the top of this list was Gino, once his chief lieutenant and most trusted advisor and policeman. Reiterating the conditions he'd made when he sold the company, he included Arnold Skaaland among the protected few—but there were also others who had served him well through the years, including Freddie Blassie, Lou Albano and James Dudley, who had worked for his own father and managed the Capitol Arena back in the Washington, DC, days. Finally, on Sunday, May 27, 1984, Vincent James McMahon passed away at the age of sixty-nine.

■

Unfortunately, despite how close they'd been and how long they'd worked together, Gino was unable to attend the funeral services and sent Maureen without him. While Vinny was down in Florida paying his last respects to his father, Gino was needed to run the two consecutive days of television tapings in Allentown and Hamburg, which happened to fall on the same two days as Senior's wake, funeral and burial. The first day of tapings for *Championship Wrestling* was of particularly vital importance, representing a pivotal moment in the WWF's imminent national explosion and the culmination of a deal Vinny had been working out for weeks. On Tuesday, May 29, as Vince McMahon Sr. lay in state at Baird-Case Funeral Home in Fort Lauderdale, the Agricultural Hall in Allentown played host to none other than Cyndi Lauper, the hottest new pop sensation in the country, who was making a fateful appearance on "Piper's

Pit," the talk-show segment hosted by the WWF's new top heel, freshly snatched from Jim Crockett Promotions, "Rowdy" Roddy Piper.

Landing Lauper was a major coup, orchestrated in part by her real-life friendship with Capt. Lou Albano, and brought major mainstream attention to the WWF. It also helped to kick off what became known as the "Rock 'n' Wrestling Connection," a bona fide cultural movement which, by the summer, would bring the WWF to the epicenter of '80s pop culture, MTV. The special event, known as *The Brawl to End It All*, featured Lauper managing Wendi Richter—a female Hulk Hogan of sorts—against entrenched world women's champion the Fabulous Moolah. Once again featuring Gorilla Monsoon on lead commentary from Madison Square Garden, the special scored a 9.0 rating—the highest in the history of the immensely popular cable channel. That show went a long way toward establishing Monsoon with a national audience as one of the lead voices of the World Wrestling Federation, if not *the* lead voice. In place of Patterson that day, calling the action alongside Gino, would be another of McMahon's acquisitions from the AWA, the diminutive yet bombastic veteran announcer "Mean" Gene Okerlund, who would become yet another instantly recognizable voice of the new, national WWF.

In addition to now calling Garden shows regularly with Okerlund, by the end of the summer, Gino would sometimes be joined by the frilly and facetiously formal Lord Alfred Hayes, the proper English gentlemen who'd started out as a road agent before Vince realized what a perfect on-camera foil he could be. While Mean Gene was a bit stilted doing ringside commentary and was clearly better suited to the backstage interviewer role he filled better than anyone, Lord Alfred complemented Gorilla in an odd way. More naturally conversant and eloquent than Patterson, he was a fellow ring veteran who provided an amusing bouncing-off point for discussion, and although he was a lesser broadcast partner of Gino's, they did share a decent amount of chemistry and came off as comfortable old friends having a casual and somewhat bemused chat. Hayes was also the perfect comic relief co-host for McMahon himself on the newly launched USA Network program *Tuesday Night Titans*—a radical departure for wrestling TV that was part late night talk show and part campy variety show, with the occasional pretaped wrestling match thrown in. Gino even got to appear as one of the earliest guests, discussing his career and background with refreshing candor and ease. It was the kind of show that never would've been attempted under the old regime and naturally infuriated wrestling purists to no end.

It was also a show that no doubt Vince's traditionalist father—who had once infamously dismissed Andy Kaufman's pitch to do a wrestling angle with the WWF, sending the comedian packing to Memphis to make history with Jerry "The King" Lawler—would never have approved of. But there were a lot of things happening that the late McMahon would've possibly opposed, and now that he was gone, his son would take advantage of his newfound freedom to go further and operate more aggressively than ever before. Without the old man around, Gino, like the other members of the old guard, was falling in line. He had chosen his side in the wrestling war that was erupting. Not only that, but he'd have an important role to play at Vince's side. The younger McMahon was still an unproven commodity to most of his competitors, as unpopular as he was unrespected at that time. He would need someone like Gino—a formidable veteran and major power broker of the business who was known, liked, respected and feared by all—to back him up and lend him legitimacy. They might be willing to screw with "Junior." But they'd think twice before screwing with Gino.

■

Now, for the first time, Vince was looking at expanding into places where there were already thriving, fully operational wrestling territories—moving into direct competition with existing promotions that made up the heart and soul of the National Wrestling Alliance. As outraged as the other promoters may have been, it was certainly something most of them would have tried (and in some cases, *had* tried) if they'd had the nerve, the resources and the total disregard for the norms of the business that Vince did. From his secure base of operations in the Northeast, it only made sense to spread down the eastern seaboard entirely, and so McMahon had set his sights on creeping into the Southeast, which contained three of the strongest and most established NWA promotions: Jim Crockett Promotions in the Mid-Atlantic region, Georgia Championship Wrestling and Eddie Graham's Championship Wrestling from Florida.

More than any of them, it was GCW that he coveted, thanks to that company's prime position on SuperStation TBS out of Atlanta—a cable channel with powerful reach and an established wrestling audience. When he was denied a spot on the network by TBS mogul Ted Turner, he went to work taking over GCW itself from the inside. He already had Barnett. And the raging Ole Anderson had alienated his other partners—Jack and Jerry Brisco, along with the ancient Paul Jones, who had owned the territory since the Second World War—to the point that McMahon was able to woo them, buying up their shares and leaving Ole out in the cold as a powerless minority owner. Now McMahon owned Georgia Championship Wrestling, meaning that he'd also inherited the greatly desired 6:05 Saturday night time slot on TBS, whether Turner wanted him there or not.

Now all that remained was for Vince to actually take possession—an awkward situation, to say the least. Georgia Championship Wrestling had taped its weekly television program, ambitiously renamed *World Championship Wrestling* by that point, at the TBS Studios at 1050 Techwood Drive in midtown Atlanta. The sale had officially gone through in early July 1984, prompting Vince and Linda to fly down to Atlanta, where they would survey the studios and assess the physical assets and personnel of the company and TV program they were absorbing. They would also have to come face to face with their hostile junior partner, Ole Anderson. Anticipating the possibility of a less-than-peaceful transition of power, the McMahons brought along their insurance policy: Gino. It was a role he'd filled quite well in the past for Vince's father, and even at age forty-seven and down to a streamlined 350 pounds, he was more than capable of filling it. Ole had a volatile temper and reputation and wasn't above getting physical. But with Gino overseeing the interactions between the two parties, the hope was that Ole's desire to get his hands on Vince would be superseded by his desire to stay out of the hospital.

Vince had no interest in confrontation and was certainly willing to offer Anderson a job in the restructured organization, as he'd been doing for other rival promoters whose path he was crossing. But in the end, Ole's mouth got the better of him, as it often did. In the studio, when Vince attempted to be cordial and invite Ole over to meet Linda, the irate booker was far from cooperative.

The exact verbiage of his response as reported in wrestling lore has varied over the years, with most agreeing that it was something to the effect of, "Fuck you, Vince. And fuck your wife, too."

The fact that he'd even be willing to say those words with Gorilla Monsoon standing mere feet away speaks volumes on just how pissed off he clearly was. The precise details of what transpired next are hazy. In one of the first times the incident was detailed in public, in the 2004 book *Sex, Lies and Headlocks* by Shaun Assael and Mike Mooneyham, the scene fades to black at this point, with the reader invited to imagine Ole Anderson on the receiving end of a Gorilla Monsoon stomping. The reality is perhaps a bit more mundane. The general consensus seems to be that heated words were exchanged, but in the end, cooler heads prevailed and the two parties agreed to go their separate ways. As usual, Gino's mere presence was enough to keep things from getting too out of hand and to keep his boss in one piece. In the end, Ole handed over the keys.

Bruce Prichard, a former member of Paul Boesch's Houston Wrestling front office who later became a member of Vince's new inner circle after the WWF took over the Houston territory in 1987 and was a close friend of Gino's, discussed the incident on a 2019 episode of his podcast, *Something to Wrestle With*:

> I know how [Ole] was, and I know he was as resistant as you could possibly be and not get arrested . . . Ole was a bully, but he was a bully to guys that wouldn't stand up to him. He knew he couldn't bully Gino . . . I don't care what territory you worked, you knew who Gorilla Monsoon

was, and you knew his background. And you knew he was a guy that wouldn't take no crap off of anybody. So Ole resisted as hard as he could. But he didn't resist past that point where Gino had to take action . . . Part of that would also be Gino's own restraint, because there's some people that wouldn't let him get away with what he supposedly said to Vince and Linda. But I guess that speaks a lot about him . . . Just the idea that he's going to be there is enough.

On July 14, 1984—remembered by Georgia wrestling loyalists to this day as "Black Saturday"—Vince McMahon appeared at 6:05 p.m. on televisions tuned into TBS across the country to introduce the new *World Championship Wrestling*, featuring the Superstars of the World Wrestling Federation. The strong-arm ploy had worked. For fans and all those within the business who were watching, it was a cataclysmic event. A full-on wrestling war was in full swing, and the entire industry was on the verge of absolute chaos.

And yet ironically, conflicted though he may have been, it was also a sign to Gino that this new Vince McMahon meant business. And that the "kid" he knew as Junior might actually be able to pull this whole thing off. And if he did, then Gino would be in on the ground floor of something unprecedented in the history of the business: a truly national professional wrestling company. He may have lost his 20 percent of that company, but the more towns and the more buildings the WWF spread into, the more money he stood to make. There can be no doubt that the success of the WWF's national expansion was in Gino's best interest, and he knew it.

CHAPTER 12
PRIME TIME

> "Welcome, everyone! Gorilla Monsoon here at ringside with my colleague, Jesse 'The Body' Ventura, as the World Wrestling Federation presents the wrestling extravaganza of all time..."

The wrestling promotion that Gino had worked for at the start of the 1980s could not have been more different from the one he found himself working for by the middle of that decade. If the 1980s can rightly be termed the most tumultuous and revolutionary decade in pro wrestling history, and it can, then 1984 would have to be in the running for the most tumultuous and revolutionary single year. And that epochal change would only continue over the next few years, as Vince McMahon's dream of a World Wrestling Federation that stretched across North America became a reality, and the fake-it-till-you-make-it boasting became truth. In short, the company that Vince McMahon was pretending Titan Sports was in 1984 would, by the end of the decade, really be what it was. As Hulkamania led to *WrestleMania*, which led to national network television, which led to a crowd at the Pontiac Silverdome that made the world sit up and take notice, the WWF would quite literally become synonymous with professional wrestling. Many fans wouldn't even realize there was any other brand.

And in much the same way during that period, the hordes of new fans swarming in would get to know Gorilla Monsoon as the friendly, welcoming, avuncular voice of wrestling—the warm, fatherly or even grandfatherly figure they trusted to be the voice of reason, to guide them through the chaos and always champion the side of righteousness against the heinous hypocrisies of the bad guys. His iconic image—the frilly shirts, the color-splashed tuxedoes, the blue-tinted prescription shades—would almost completely eclipse the previous image of the four-hundred-pounder in black tights and sequined ring jacket and would most certainly eclipse the rampaging Manchurian Giant of yore. To the kids who were drawn to the WWF in droves, and to the fans from other corners of the wrestling world who had never known the WWF before, this would be the only Gorilla Monsoon they would ever know.

He'd lend his enthusiastic voice to many of the WWF's most important shows of the era, including the pay-per-view events that would soon become the bread and butter of the business, not to mention becoming a regular presence behind the microphone on weekly broadcasts as well. And while doing these, he'd be joined by the two greatest broadcast partners he'd ever have: one a brash, psychedelic wrestler forced into early retirement, who became the first WWF announcer to ever take the side of the villains; the other, a newly acquired manager with a comedian's gift of timing, would join with Gorilla to become the greatest and most unlikely comedy team professional wrestling has ever known. Along the way, he and Gino would come to love each other as the truest of friends. And along with all the money, that friendship would be the greatest thing the WWF's national expansion would give to Gino.

■

The dawn of Gorilla Monsoon's broadcast career had come at the perfect time, with the company spreading itself out and more hours of television being produced—especially with Vince McMahon focused on driving the engines of expansion behind the scenes. Vince would still place himself front and center in front of the camera as an announcer, but he needed more help now, and Monsoon led the group of those who stepped in to fill that breach. Gino was also still heavily relied on for television production, with the shows leaving their comfortable longtime homes in suburban Pennsylvania. By mid-1984, *Championship Wrestling* had left Allentown and headed to upstate New York to the much larger Mid-Hudson Civic Center in Poughkeepsie. Meanwhile, by the end of summer, *All-Star Wrestling* had left Hamburg and begun taping in different locations up in Ontario, Canada, one of the first major territories to fall under the WWF's purview. They would also take over the taping of *Maple Leaf Wrestling*, the show that aired in local Canadian markets and across the Great Lakes in select Midwestern U.S. markets.

The McMahon family had long done business with Toronto promoter Frank Tunney, who had passed away the previous year—now, with his nephew Jack in charge, a much more direct relationship between the WWF and Maple Leaf Wrestling had taken shape. In short, the WWF had taken over the Toronto office, installing Jack Tunney as the company's liaison for a crucial expansion across Canada, as well as making him the new figurehead president of the company, in the grand tradition, started by Vince's father, of obscuring from the public who was really in charge.

When the pieces really began to fall into place, they fell into place quickly, and just as it had been in Atlanta, Gino's presence and reputation continued to be crucial to pulling it off. By May, the WWF was in Virginia; North Carolina and Florida followed in June; by August, the company was running the venerable Atlanta Omni on a regular basis. Key to this southeastern expansion was another new business partner, who had come on board as part of the GCW deal, Jerry Brisco. Jerry had been brought in as a tag team with his brother Jack, but thanks to his many connections in the Carolinas, Georgia and Florida territories, was also moving into the position of regional promoter, helping to open doors with building managers and others who knew him well. He'd crossed paths with Gino in Puerto Rico and also knew him thanks to Vince Senior's close relationship with Eddie Graham, who had been a mentor to both Jerry and Jack. They all had the extra bond of having been standout amateur wrestlers, with Jack and Jerry both stars for Oklahoma State in the '60s, Jack in particular going all the way to the NCAA Division I championship at 191 pounds in 1965.

In fact, Jerry remembers teasing Gino about how close he'd come to the NCAA heavyweight title in 1959, edged out by Oklahoma State's Ted Ellis: "He got beat by an Oklahoma State Cowboy, that was always my rib on him. 'Don't mess with another Cowboy! You got beat by one; don't get beat by more!'" But Gino had great affection for the Briscos and made sure to bring Jerry under his guidance and protection, especially when another road agent and Vince advisor, Chief Jay Strongbow, seemed to not feel the same about him. Strongbow got along well with Jack but still saw Jerry as the snot-nosed younger brother. He also had a strained relationship with Jerry partly due to the fact that Jerry, a true Native American and proud member of the Chickasaw Nation who hadn't resorted to playing a caricature to achieve his in-ring success, resented Strongbow's impersonation of a Native American, always insisting on calling him by his real name, Joe Scarpa.

Things had changed. Jerry wasn't that snot-nosed kid anymore; he was an important part of the WWF's southern expansion and wanted the respect that came with the position, which Scarpa refused to give: "Strongbow always thought I was a mole down here, that I was sent by the NWA to sabotage Vince, which was the farthest thing from the truth, and Gino knew how it really was. He knew my friendship with Junior was strong." Scarpa always mistrusted Brisco around the box office, and it came to a head one night in Orlando, when Scarpa tried to step in and take credit for a big sellout at one of Brisco's buildings. Brisco complained to Vince about it, but then the word also got to Gino. And while Gino and the Chief were close, going back years together in the business, Gino wasn't above straightening him out. "Gino really read Joe the riot act over that. He took Strongbow aside and really got on him because of how he was treating me. Then Joe started treating me a little bit differently. He didn't treat me great after that. But he treated me a little bit different, because he didn't want the wrath of Gino coming down on him."

It was a classic example of how Gino was still very much needed in those early expansion years to help keep people in line, especially people who hadn't yet gotten really used to the notion of fearing and respecting the younger Vince McMahon. Strongbow was a notoriously bristly example, and he was known to sarcastically refer to Vince as "Caesar" behind his back. Truth be told, even Gino wasn't above that sort of thing, except he would do it right to Vince's face, insisting on continuing to call him "Junior," as he always had; or "Vinny"; or even, if he was in a particularly ball-busting mood, "Little Vinny." As McMahon rose in stature and lorded his power over others more over the years, this would become strictly forbidden as a general rule. But not for someone of Gino's stature. The main reason he continued to call McMahon those names was that he could. And he knew how much it annoyed him, which gave him a certain amount of mischievous joy. Some of the other old-timers would do it, too, but the main difference between Gino and the rest of them was that Gino truly never feared Vince. He grew to respect him, but never feared him.

Perhaps this was the very reason that Vince himself respected Gino so much. In any event, he continued to use him to smooth things over in many of the new places the company was going at the time. As Prichard said on his podcast:

> Gorilla a lot of times was the first guy he would send in. If there was ever a thought that this may go awry, or somebody may not want to do business, or if it could be iffy, you sent Monsoon. He was no-nonsense, he would take care of whatever situation there was, and there would never be an issue. So there was a huge trust factor there with Vince and Gorilla, in that he was very comfortable with Monsoon being . . . the face of the company out on the road. Monsoon didn't take shit from anybody . . . He just had that presence. He walks into a room; he owned the

room . . . He just commanded respect with people, and he did it in a classy way, by showing respect to people.

The sentiment is echoed by Jerry, who also recalls Gino playing that policeman role for Vince and always being at his side or a few feet behind him at all times: "I don't know if that was by design, or if it was just Gino's instinct. I kind of lean toward it being instinct." And it wasn't just a physical thing but mental as well. Everyone knew Gino was a sharp guy, including, most importantly of all, Vince. He had all that experience working for the old man and knew what he was talking about. This came in handy going into some tough territories that the WWF was trying out, whether it be someplace like Kansas City, where a gun-packing Harley Race was used to running wrestling, or even Oklahoma City, where Gino's old traveling buddy, neighbor and tag team partner Cowboy Bill Watts had carved out his own kingdom.

Brisco also recalls how Gino's instincts were valuable in keeping the talent in line so that everyone was producing exactly what the company wanted. There were a lot of new performers funneling into the promotion from all corners of the business, including places that worked very differently from the "New York style." Included in that were Jack and Jerry themselves—world-class athletes and wrestling attractions who'd competed at an elite level all over the world—but who were totally new to the WWF system during their brief run there as a tag team in late '84 and early '85. Jerry remembers one occasion at the Holiday Inn bar after Poughkeepsie TV, when Gino called them over: "He says, 'Sit down, boys. You guys got a lot of talent. Everybody knows that. I'm not saying anything nobody knows. You're getting a good push here. But your style is a southern style. The fans up here are used to a stronger style of work. You're very giving in the ring. That's good for house shows, but not for TV. You got to work the more dominant style when they're pushing you. Don't let these guys be doing false finishes on you. I wouldn't do any more than one false finish, and after that you just dominate.'" Gino was known for giving that kind of advice, but he'd also be the first one to pat someone on the back and tell them when they'd done something right.

With the wrestling war raging, lines of loyalty were being drawn. In one of the more unexpected maneuvers of the time, even Bruno Sammartino had decided that it would be a good idea to return to the company he'd left three years earlier, although it had changed quite a bit from the company he remembered—more than he realized. But the interest between the two parties was mutual. He'd tried running independently with the Savoldis and had even briefly gone to work for Ole Anderson when Ole had brought Georgia Championship Wrestling to the Pittsburgh area in a half-assed invasion. But it was clear he had been backing the wrong horses, and it was time to go home.

Vince wanted Bruno back in the fold as a way of settling the lawsuit Bruno had filed against the company regarding all that money he believed he was owed. Once Bruno returned to the company, the lawsuit went away, and the former world champion was given a spot on the broadcast team, doing ringside commentary with McMahon on *Championship Wrestling* starting with the September 11, 1984, TV taping. That very same taping would see the WWF in-ring debut of Bruno's son David, who'd been bouncing around the business for the past five years and whose inclusion on the WWF roster was part of the deal Bruno made to come back.

And although Bruno resisted it at first, Vince was also trying to persuade him to get back in the ring as well. After all, Sammartino was the WWF's greatest legend of the past, and it made sense to have him aboard during this new phase of the company, especially since he still had major regional appeal in the Northeast. McMahon had Hogan, his number-one attraction, touring the continent, but he was always interested in snatching up other top stars who could help draw houses in certain parts of the wrestling landscape—Bruno could certainly still fill that role in many of the towns that had cheered him on as world champion in years gone by.

Gino was very glad to have his great friend back in the good graces of the company, and the two began to spend a lot of time together once again. Here they were, two guys who had helped put the company on the map, who had been selling out arenas together twenty years earlier, out there front and center, legends emeritus of the modern WWF. Of course, a big difference was that Gino had always been, for lack of a better term, a company guy who had found a way to become part of the office through loyalty. Bruno had never been the type to be a company guy—from the very beginning of his association with the McMahon family, back before he was even world champion, Bruno had kept the company at arm's length and was an island unto himself. And yet, despite that, the two men got along famously, and there was never anything to indicate any kind of distrust or awkwardness between them.

Bruno would turn out to be less committed than Gino had been to staying retired since, by the following year, he'd be back to wrestling again in addition to his commentary duties. Another difference that would eventually emerge between the two would be their reaction to the direction Vince was taking the company and the company culture growing up around him. There were things that Gino, while privately disgusted and disappointed, was willing to tolerate—but that would become increasingly difficult for Bruno to do over the three and a half years of his final run working for the McMahon family.

■

The same month as Sammartino's return to the WWF also saw the arrival of someone who would, in a very different way, play a role in Gino's career that would turn out to be just as pivotal. Raymond Louis Heenan had been in the business since he was twenty years old, back when his first employer, Dick the Bruiser, had bestowed on him the name "Pretty Boy" Bobby Heenan, in reference to the seminal wrestling manager Bobby Davis, original WWWF manager of Gorilla Monsoon. Despite his average size and unimpressive physique, Heenan was a natural in the ring and on the microphone. In Bruiser's WWA, he'd first settle into the role of an obnoxious wrestling manager who could bump his ass off when called upon to do so. It was in Verne Gagne's AWA in the 1970s that he first came to be known as "The Brain," managing Nick Bockwinkel to greatness as AWA world tag team champions with Ray Stevens and as AWA world heavyweight champion as well.

With the AWA being one of the prime companies being gutted for talent by the WWF, Heenan came on Vince McMahon's radar as a possible heel manager to finally fill the void left behind a year earlier by the loss of "The Grand Wizard" Ernie Roth. Heenan also came highly recommended by Hulk Hogan, who'd worked with him extensively as Bockwinkel's top challenger the year before in the AWA. Unlike other AWA recruits who were paid extra by McMahon to break their agreements with Gagne and jump ship, Heenan had insisted on doing business professionally, finishing out his agreed-upon dates for the AWA before finally making his first surprise appearance in the WWF at Madison Square Garden on September 22, 1984, as the manager of Big John Studd against his old rival Hogan. Despite his devious and craven wrestling persona, in reality, Heenan was a standup guy in the industry, who did business the right way and held others to a high standard. He was a man of solid character. Maybe this is why he and Gino were destined to become the greatest of friends.

Gorilla Monsoon was calling the action with Mean Gene Okerlund at the Garden for the debut of Bobby "The Brain" Heenan and would call many of his appearances going forward, as he accompanied early charges like Studd, "Dr. D" David Schultz, "Mr. Wonderful" Paul Orndorff and Ken Patera. On October 14 at a Brendan Byrne Arena show televised on the MSG Network, Bobby Heenan shared a broadcast table with Gorilla Monsoon for the very first time—albeit briefly—when he joined Monsoon and Lord Alfred Hayes as a guest commentator for Studd's match against S.D. Jones. It was a mere ten minutes, but clearly, Vince McMahon was listening that night.

■

Gino had already been establishing himself as a natural onscreen presence in his announcing duties, part of which had a lot to do with his familiarity with television production from his years working backstage. He'd worked closely with Dennis Dunn, the head of Intermedia Productions, the company that had produced all of Capitol's weekly television through much of the '70s and early '80s. According to long-standing company lore, Dennis had ingratiated himself permanently to the McMahons after saving three weeks' worth of TV video tapes from destruction when his car caught on fire in a freak accident. Now Gino found himself working with Dennis's son Kevin, who'd just graduated from Towson University in Maryland and had been hired by Vince as an associate producer. Gino and Kevin hit it off right away and remained close, demonstrating more than anything Gino's uncanny ability to get along with people most could not.

Another newly hired producer and director brought on board as part of the WWF's nascent television production unit was Kerwin Silfies, a director and producer for Channel 39, the public television station near Allentown from which the WWF had been leasing some television equipment. It was there that Dennis Dunn had gotten to know Silfies and recommended him to McMahon. Silfies, a wrestling fan as a kid who remembered seeing the fearsome Gorilla Monsoon on TV back in the '60s, was taken aback to discover that the very same man was now going to be his TV production colleague, as he recalled in a 2015 episode of *The Steve Austin Show* podcast: "I was shocked when this guy Bob kept talking in my ear, and I had no idea who he was, but he kept telling me, we gotta do this, we gotta do that, and so I found out that Bob was Gorilla Monsoon. I grew up hating him, and within six months of starting to do these shows, I absolutely loved Gorilla Monsoon. He helped me a lot."

Someone else who was helped out quite a bit by Gino in those early expansion days was Bret Hart, the twenty-seven-year-old son of Gino's old friend and mentor, Stu Hart. Bret had been one of three wrestlers brought on board the WWF—along with British grapplers the Dynamite Kid and Davey Boy Smith—when the company purchased Stampede Wrestling from Stu Hart in August 1984.[1] Vince's main goal was getting his hands on the Western Canadian TV contracts held by Stampede, but Bret would wind up being the one to perhaps benefit most from the deal in the long run. Bret had been barely out of diapers when Gino first worked the Calgary territory at the start of his career, but the first time he actually remembered getting to know him was in Puerto Rico. Now he found himself in unfamiliar environs, working for a man who'd just bought out his father, but it was Gino who became a friendly ally and a welcoming presence to the young man.

Gino fondly remembered the old days with Stu and enjoyed talking to Bret all about it from the very beginning of his time in the WWF, even allowing the newcomer to ride with him and Arnie Skaaland, who had been a groomsman at Stu Hart's wedding. "He took a shine to me," Bret remembers. "He really welcomed me in. And he loved my dad. He was a big influence on me, talking to me all the time." From the start, even when Bret began as a nondescript babyface, before forming the legendary Hart Foundation tag team the following year with his brother-in-law Jim "The Anvil" Neidhart, Monsoon would put Bret over every chance he got to call one of his matches. More often than not, he'd make sure to mention his famous wrestling family, parents Stu and Helen and the infamous "Dungeon" that he'd once learned about the hard way, which some even credit him with naming. It also didn't hurt that Bret was good in the ring—damn good, even back then. "He always appreciated my work and often complimented me or praised me on a match I'd just had, or one he just commentated on. And he would always say kind things to me, sometimes in front of the other wrestlers, but always in a nice way."

He'd also help out Bret when it came to money, usually giving him a little something extra when reimbursing him for travel expenses: "He was always really generous with the company's money. I don't know if that's a quality thing to say about him, but it was for me at the time . . . You weren't allowed to do that stuff, but Gorilla always did that for me. I always felt a little bit like he was a guy who was always looking out for me." Looking back on it, Bret attributes this kind of generosity to Gino's loyalty to the boys in general. He never forgot that he had been one of them: "He loved the wrestlers and the business more than he loved Vince McMahon and the office, and that was something that I always read between the lines about." Needless to say, for someone just starting out in the WWF, Gino was a great friend to have, and that relationship would eventually go a long way toward making Bret Hart not just a success in the World Wrestling Federation but one of the greatest stars the company ever had.

■

With Titan Sports providing weekly content for USA Network on Sunday afternoons (*All-American Wrestling*) and Tuesday evenings (*Tuesday Night Titans*), they next worked out a deal for a Monday night block, which would have major ramifications for the future of Gorilla Monsoon's broadcasting career, although not quite yet. Developed by McMahon and Nelson Sweglar, it was to be a different type of wrestling program format, set up as a kind of magazine show, featuring two hosts in a studio introducing and analyzing pre-recorded matches from house shows throughout the growing WWF circuit as well as from the WWF's weekend syndicated shows, but also featuring interviews and discussions between the hosts to further storylines and angles. The show would be called *Prime Time Wrestling* due to the novelty of seeing pro wrestling on TV in prime time during that era. It was a simple format, but one that hadn't really been tried with wrestling up to that point, and it would be highly influential on many programs that came after it.

The show would be taped at the studios of Sweglar's Video One Inc. in Baltimore, where *TNT* and other WWF studio material was already being taped. The first episode would air on the evening of New Year's Day, 1985. The original host of the show was Jack Reynolds, known to friends and family in Cleveland as Jack Rizzo, a longtime radio DJ and TV announcer who'd previously done some wrestling announcing for Eddie Einhorn's IWA and Pedro Martinez's NWF in the 1970s and had originally been hired by Vince McMahon to replace him as host of *All-Star Wrestling*. Joining Reynolds as the original co-host of *Prime Time Wrestling* was Jesse "The Body" Ventura, a colorful and charismatic wrestler who had first jumped over from the AWA the previous May. Vince originally had big plans for Ventura, intending to pair him up with

Bobby Heenan as his manager and slotting him into a big-money feud with Hulk Hogan that was just getting started when Ventura wound up hospitalized with a blood clot on his lung that threw a monkey wrench into his wrestling career.[2]

Fortunately for the Body, his gifts on the microphone exceeded his gifts in the ring, and Vince quickly realized he could channel that natural charisma and attitude to create the WWF's first-ever heel announcer.[3] Unlike the typical commentators that fans were used to, who acted as the surrogate for the viewer, defending righteousness and speaking out against the atrocities of the bad guys, Jesse would actually take the side of the villains, giving their perspective and rationalizing their actions from the point of view of one of wrestling's most notorious rulebreakers. Once again, it was a formula that would be copied forever after, but it started with Jesse Ventura, and his first chance to do it was on that first episode of *Prime Time Wrestling*. By the following week, he had also joined Reynolds as the new co-host of *All-Star Wrestling*, replacing the atrociously out-of-his-depth Angelo Mosca.

■

Gorilla Monsoon would eventually become the host of *Prime Time Wrestling*, but that was still a few months away. Although he'd been entrusted with monthly house show duties at several venues, he had yet to be given a commentating spot as host of any of the WWF's weekly programming. That would change in March, when he got the one assignment no one else really wanted, calling the action for *World Championship Wrestling* on TBS. Things had not been going well at all since the WWF took over the vaunted 6:05 Saturday night time slot, with viewers almost instantly flooding the station with complaints about the loss of Georgia Championship Wrestling and the drastic change in wrestling product. Part of that was also because Vince had immediately discontinued the popular tapings at the Techwood studio in Atlanta, instead turning the program into a stale recap show featuring a collection of pretaped matches that fans could already see on the WWF's regular programming. Clearly, once he'd gotten the time slot and swept GCW aside, McMahon had no intention of treating the show as a priority, instead putting all his focus on the expansion of the WWF's syndicated programming, which is where most of the eyeballs were in those days anyway.

But Ted Turner hadn't wanted the WWF on his network in the first place, and this only made it worse. By the beginning of 1985, he'd finally put his foot down, insisting that McMahon must produce an exclusive, dedicated show for *World Championship Wrestling*, and it must be recorded at the WTBS Studios. This version of the show would only run for five weeks and would be one of the strangest anomalies in wrestling history. Kicking off with the same iconic opening sequence and music that fans had been accustomed to from the GCW days, it would feature studio matches involving WWF talent, including perennial Georgia favorites like Les Thornton and Mr. Wrestling II, who'd been brought over with the GCW acquisition but were rarely seen anywhere else on WWF programming. With longtime GCW announcer Freddie Miller doing the interviews, Gorilla Monsoon stood at a brand-new studio set, introducing the matches and calling the action.

Taped on five consecutive Saturday mornings before a live studio audience, the show would feature a couple of important WWF highlights, including the debut of Ricky "The Dragon" Steamboat, newly arrived from Jim Crockett Promotions, and a special appearance in the Techwood studio from Hulk Hogan and Mr. T, the major movie and television star who had been brought in as an ally of the Hulkster during another MTV special that had aired from Madison Square Garden the month before, *The War to Settle the Score*. And short-lived though it was, those five weeks of *World Championship Wrestling* would represent the first time that Gorilla Monsoon was ever given the opportunity to host his own weekly WWF television program.

The TBS experiment had been one of the rare outright failures of Vince McMahon's national expansion plans. But it didn't matter in the long run, because he was already on to much bigger things. The reason the studio tapings of *World Championship Wrestling* didn't last long is that pretty much as soon as he found himself compelled to do them,

McMahon immediately started looking to get out of the deal and dump the TBS time slot altogether. It was a coveted property, and it didn't take long for an eager buyer to emerge in the form of Jim Crockett Jr., who hoped to get his regional, Carolinas-based wrestling product on that national cable outlet. A rueful and humbled McMahon would sell the time slot to Crockett for $1 million and, driven by his typical mix of ambition and vengeance, would use that money to help fund the ultimate gamble, an event that would cement the WWF's prominence in the industry and become the crown jewel in the company's 1980s explosion: *WrestleMania*.

■

The "Rock 'n' Wrestling Connection" had been picking up steam—the WWF already had Cyndi Lauper on its TV and, with the addition of Mr. T, had become just about the coolest thing around and more buzzworthy than ever. To capitalize on this, McMahon envisioned an event that would be thought of as pro wrestling's Super Bowl, which would truly make his company seem like the big-time major league of the industry. Like the last two Shea Stadium shows, it would be carried on closed-circuit locations in theaters, arenas and other venues, except this time, thanks to the WWF's growing reach, it would be available to fans in places all over North America. Plus, as an experiment, it would also be made available on an extremely limited basis through the medium of pay-per-view television, a technology that allowed fans to watch in the comfort of their own homes, which had been successful for boxing dating back a decade to the "Thrilla in Manila," but was pioneered for wrestling by Vince McMahon.

The date was March 31, 1985. The location, naturally, was Madison Square Garden. With this being the most important event the company had ever put on, it was vital that Vince be able to run things directly from backstage. For that reason, he chose not to host the event himself—that trusted position would be given to Gino. When *WrestleMania* kicked off, after the opening photo montage narrated by McMahon and set to

Phil Collins and Philip Bailey's "Easy Lover," it was Gorilla Monsoon, in tinted glasses, black tuxedo and ruffled blue shirt, who welcomed fans to "the wrestling extravaganza of all time." And standing alongside Gorilla for the very first time, not to be outdone in a sequined pink tuxedo, was color commentator Jesse "The Body" Ventura.

The twenty-three thousand live at the Garden that day, and the four hundred thousand others watching in closed-circuit locations throughout the United States and Canada were treated to a new kind of wrestling super-card. The team of Hogan and Mr. T, who had hosted *Saturday Night Live* as last-minute replacements the night before, joined forces to battle the evil incarnate of "Rowdy" Roddy Piper and Paul Orndorff. Cyndi Lauper was also there in the corner of Wendi Richter for her attempt to regain the women's championship. But T and Lauper weren't the only mainstream celebrities on hand: Muhammad Ali came back to work for McMahon, this time serving as an enforcer referee for the main event; Yankees manager Billy Martin was guest ring announcer; Liberace ostensibly served as "guest timekeeper" but was mainly there to kick up his heels with Radio City Music Hall's Rockettes. It was a true blending of sports and entertainment, hence Vince's new branding of pro wrestling as "sports-entertainment."

It was indeed, as Gorilla would himself describe it, "a happening." And Gorilla was right there at ringside, speaking to those hundreds of thousands of fans through it all. He'd been commentating on monthly shows at the Garden for a couple of years already, but this was different. And the fact that Jesse Ventura was with him for the first time made it even more special. This would be a very different dynamic from how he'd worked before. Unlike other partners like Pat Patterson, Lord Alfred Hayes or Mean Gene Okerlund, Ventura pushed back on Monsoon. He challenged him. They challenged each other. It was more adversarial but not to the point that it became distracting. Rather, they came off as two seasoned professionals who both knew the ins and outs of the ring wars but just had differing perspectives. Despite taking different sides, it was clear that they respected each other. Jesse would begrudgingly agree with Gorilla if it made sense, and Gorilla would do the same. There was chemistry and almost instant familiarity, exemplified by the way Ventura would insist on referring to his broadcast partner by his familiar name of "Gino," despite the fact that this name was not common knowledge to the fans who only knew him as "Gorilla."

WrestleMania was a rousing success and firmly thrust the WWF into the mainstream of 1980s popular culture right alongside Michael Jackson, Rambo, *Miami Vice*, Cabbage Patch Kids and the Rubik's Cube. It was essentially a "proof of concept" for the WWF as a viable, marketable media phenomenon. Before the spring was over, Vince would make a deal with NBC head honcho Dick Ebersol to kick off *Saturday Night's Main Event*, a sometimes monthly or bi-monthly late-night replacement for *Saturday Night Live* that put pro wrestling on national network television for the first time in thirty years. By the fall, there would be a Saturday morning cartoon show—not to mention ice cream bars, lunch boxes, action figures, T-shirts, posters and countless other bits of licensed merchandise that would contribute to one of Titan Sports' largest revenue streams. It was a totally different vision of what wrestling could be. And most importantly, as far as Gino and other doubters were concerned, it demonstrated that the WWF under Vince McMahon Jr. was going to be a blockbuster success beyond anything his father could have imagined. Gino's decision to stay on board had been the correct one.

For the national *Saturday Night's Main Event* network broadcasts, Vince made sure to put himself front and center, calling the action with Jesse Ventura. But make no mistake, just as he was at all important shows, Gino was there, manning the Gorilla position, directing traffic and communicating with Vince and Jesse via remote headset—the kind of technology he would've killed for back in the days when he would take off his glasses to signal to the referee that it was time to end a match. He would take a similar role at all the television events at which he wasn't the announcer. And even when he was at ringside calling the matches, he was still on the headset and would relay messages to the back whenever he could. There are even times when, if you watch closely enough, you can catch Gino relaying orders off-mic—directing a ring announcer to turn and face the hard camera, making sure a referee is in the proper position and so on. And he did so with the commanding presence of someone who'd been doing it longer than anyone.

•

After their successful partnership at *WrestleMania*, McMahon began teaming Monsoon and Ventura on commentary more often going forward. By April, they were working together on broadcasts from Maple Leaf Gardens; by May, they were calling shows from the Boston Garden, which had begun airing throughout New England and elsewhere on the NESN cable outlet. It was obvious that their chemistry was off the charts. By the summer, Vince had taken Jack Reynolds off *Prime Time Wrestling* and put Gorilla Monsoon in his place as the new host alongside Jesse Ventura, starting with the July 16 episode. Less than two weeks later, McMahon would do the same thing with *All-Star Wrestling*, making Monsoon and Ventura the new regular team. The handful of *World Championship Wrestling* episodes had been an experiment—now Vince was finally confident enough in Gino to position him on a long-term weekly program.

The move would reinvent Gorilla Monsoon for a whole new generation of young WWF fans who had begun tuning in all over North America. An unflappable defender of good, he really began to come into his own as the voice of the company for many. His keen command of human anatomy—both real and imagined—would be on full display as fans would grow accustomed to his descriptions of the "lower lumbar region," "lateral and collateral ligaments" and, of course, the "external occipital protuberance" at the back of the head. Well-worn clichés and colorful expressions had always been the stock-in-trade of wrestling announcers, but Gorilla Monsoon took them to a whole new level, employing an arsenal of classic euphemisms and phrases that remain associated with him to this day: It was always "a capacity crowd," with fans "literally hanging from the rafters" or "going bananas." Disreputable heels were regularly described as "fountains of misinformation," "snakes in the grass" or, as he would lovingly term his old friend Capt. Lou

Albano, "the biggest walking advertisement for birth control I've ever seen." Clichés they may have been, but they were also turns of phrase that he normally used in everyday life, which lent an air of conversational naturalism when he would speak them.

He called the matches with an easy kind of authority, conveying to viewers, without even having to go into detail about his own wrestling career, how knowledgeable he was. To the best of his ability, he called it like a sport, lending an air of believability to a patently unbelievable endeavor. His own credibility was on the line, and he knew that, which is why if a wrestler didn't have a hold quite cinched in just right, or had made a sloppy cover, he'd call them out on it—something that would be forbidden to younger announcers in later years, but that no one, not even Vince McMahon, would tell Gino not to do. For an entire generation of fans—and even aspiring wrestlers—he would reinforce the importance of "hooking the leg" to gain a pinfall, a common-sense concept now ingrained in the basics of wrestling psychology. He even became known for his regular critiquing of referees—a product of the very real frustration he had with the officials, who would often be assigned in those days by the state athletic commissions, even if, as Gorilla might put it, they didn't know a wristlock from a wristwatch. As he did behind the scenes, he held everyone to a standard of excellence in the ring and would readily praise those who met it.

Among the wrestlers who met and exceeded that standard was Bret "The Hitman" Hart, one half of the Hart Foundation tag team who was being given more of a chance to shine than ever. "If you really listen to him, he was reasonably accurate and honest," remembers Bret. "[He'd tell you] where it would hurt if you were in this hold . . . Gorilla was one of those guys that made it seem real all the time. He loved the business, and he loved guys that could really make it seem real." And the Hitman was one of those who made that part of the job easier for Gorilla. In fact, he was among the select few Monsoon would assign the highest praise, saying Hart possessed what he liked to call "excellence of execution." It was a phrase that Monsoon would reserve for select elite performers—assigning it to describe the likes of Ricky

Steamboat and Cowboy Bob Orton Jr. early on—but with Bret Hart, it would stick. And the reason it would stick was that Gorilla wanted it to. Before long, Bret and Bret alone was known as "The Excellence of Execution."

"It was a term that stuck in the dressing room," says Bret. "Gorilla was one of the first guys, even Jesse, too, who would always pump up my tires and say good things about me, even though I was just a mid-card heel at the time. For me, it was always a hidden nod of respect I wasn't necessarily getting at the time from everybody. I always got the sense that Gorilla respected the fine art of wrestling. Nobody loves a real master like the old-school guys, and he was one of them. He loved a great wrestling match, and he'd really let you know. In a lot of ways, he was one of my biggest fans. He was always saying something positive and defending me."

As with all great wrestling announcers—or sportscasters in general—Gorilla earned the trust of the viewing audience, which looked to him to tell it like it was and to be the voice of authority. And yet, as beloved as he was by many, and as enshrined as he would later become among those who grew up listening to him from their living room couches, his work was not without its detractors. Some wrestlers would complain about being buried on commentary by Gorilla, whether it was because he was pointing out the flaws in their application of holds or the weakness of pinfall attempts. Nevertheless, from his perspective, he was doing that to develop trust with the viewers and to call wrestling as a sports announcer. Baseball, football and basketball commentators wouldn't hesitate to call out a bad play, and neither would he. It was all in the service of selling pro wrestling as a real sport, which was the essence of kayfabe.

Bret Hart dismisses the criticisms off-hand: "Every wrestler thinks they're the greatest wrestler, fantastic workers and equal to everyone else . . . If Gorilla did take a few jabs at wrestlers for not picking up their style a little bit, I wouldn't have any objection. He certainly didn't do that in any of my matches . . . I would say to anyone that criticized him or had hurt feelings about something they did in the ring not being appreciated by Gorilla, maybe you should look back and revise your thinking and understand what an influence he was on everybody in the business."

These practices would also lead Gorilla to be regularly called out by a certain small but growing subsection of more smartened-up wrestling fans, who read insider newsletters like Dave Meltzer's *Wrestling Observer* and prided themselves on having more knowledge of the inner workings of the business than the average fan. Many of these fans, Meltzer chief among them, would groan at the very clichés and "Monsoon-isms" that his many supporters most enjoyed about him and critique him for what they saw as a sometimes arrogant dismissal of the hard-working athletes in the ring and the stories they were trying to tell.[4] In fact, on a record-setting six occasions, Gorilla Monsoon would win the infamous *Wrestling Observer Newsletter* Award for Worst Television Announcer of the Year, as voted on by the readers. Even the newsstand wrestling magazines, which Gino had always viewed askance anyway, would often knock him. But as deceptively loud as those criticisms could be to those who were plugged into them, the fondness felt toward him by the overwhelming majority of fans far outweighed them, as was readily demonstrated in later years when those criticisms would fade into the background and Gorilla Monsoon became lionized among the all-time great wrestling announcers, looked back on by fans today in the same way baseball fans remembers people like Vin Scully and Red Barber.

■

His official role in the company may have changed, but Gino was still looked to as a voice of authority even behind the scenes, always there to lend advice and relay important messages when needed. He was still very much a part of the office and a valued part at that. That much had not changed. If he saw something he didn't like, he wasn't afraid to let you know backstage, and not even Bret Hart was totally immune from that, as he points out when remembering a squash match at the Cap Centre when he and Jim Neidhart roughed up a preliminary wrestler who was refusing to sell for them, ending in a sloppy and embarrassing scuffle:

"It was noticeable to Gorilla in the back that we ended up roughing up this guy for real. We ended the match and came back to the dressing room, and he grabbed us as soon as we came back and chewed us out. He told us that we're professionals and there are better ways to do business. He was so right. He was one of the guys when he pulled you aside and chewed you out, you'd hang your head, and you didn't argue with him about it. He cared about the business."

Although things may have gotten off to a rocky start, the trust that Vince McMahon developed in Gino soon became implicit. Vince knew Gino was someone he could put his faith in, both from a product perspective and a business one. "You could see the respect all the time that Vince had for Gorilla," remembers Bret. "You always got the idea that Vince was like his apprentice. If Gorilla were to come up and say, that's a bunch of bullshit, don't do that, that's not the way to do things, Vince would heed the call. Gorilla was one of the few guys that he might actually listen to. But he didn't complain very often; I always remember him in a very friendly mood around Vince, and vice versa."

More than most could, Gino had found a way to politically navigate from the old company into the new company and remain just as protected. He was just as comfortable with the old-school clique of people like Arnold Skaaland and Freddie Blassie as he was with the new clique that was forming with the likes of Gene Okerlund, Lord Alfred Hayes and, of course, Bobby Heenan. He knew how to do business and had a good head on his shoulders as always—which couldn't always be said for the old-timers who sometimes had a hard time getting used to the new environment and the new man in charge. Lou Albano, for example, despite being among those that Vince Senior had made his son promise to take care of, would eventually be shown the door when his drinking and flagrant disrespect for the new boss simply became too much to deal with.[5]

And Lou's old tag team partner, the low-level lieutenant Tony Altomare, who'd been with the organization since the '60s, met a similar fate when he was caught with his hand in the till—a discovery made by Gino himself. "Back in the day, they used to carry that attaché case, and there'd be lots of money in there," remembers Tom Carlucci, who heard the story from Gino some years later. "Tony hit on hard times, and he robbed them. Gino found out, and they booted his ass." Gino had noticed that the figures weren't adding up, and it didn't take him long to determine where the money was going. "They finally figured it out, and they strung Tony along, and bam, Gino hit him, and Tony was not happy. And Gino was really pissed, too, because he'd put his trust in Tony."

■

Gino's loyalty was never in question, and as the landscape changed from the Capitol days to the Titan days, he remained an important bridge between the two worlds. But this loyalty would be put to the ultimate test in October of 1985, when Vince McMahon's ambitions perhaps went a little too far. Throughout the big expansion that was going on, one of the places Vince had yet to touch was Puerto Rico. He knew that Gino used to have points in the company and still had a strong relationship there with Carlos Colón and now Victor Quiñones as well. But none of that was known by Jim Troy, who booked an event there on behalf of Titan Sports, thinking he'd scored a major coup. The event was set up as a "bought show," in which a local promoter would pay Titan a set fee for the branding and the talent, then handle all the ticket sales, where the promoter would hopefully make their money back. The show was scheduled for October 19 at the Hiram Bithorn Stadium in San Juan, a regular stop for Colón's promotion. Vince assumed that it had all been approved by Gino beforehand, but nothing could've been further from the truth. In fact, Gino knew nothing about it until he saw the publicity for the show going out. Needless to say, he was furious.

Invading anyone else's territory was a dicey proposition, but in Puerto Rico, it could be particularly dangerous, and Gino knew that. "He was very upset because something bad could've happened on that night," explains Hugo Savinovich, who was especially caught in the middle because he worked for Carlos Colón but happened to be married to WWF women's champion Wendi Richter, who was coming to the island along with Cyndi Lauper as part of the WWF's show. "The right way would've been through Gino, running the show in partnership with the Puerto Rican office. That way, everybody would've made money." As it was, the booking led to major conflict, which put Gino in a very tough position. In response, Colón booked his own show for the same night, ten miles away at the Loubriel Stadium in Bayamón. A promotional war ensued, with the posters getting torn down by the opposing side and even stories of more direct intimidation tactics once the WWF crew made it to the island. "I believe that Hulk Hogan was threatened on that night," recalls Savinovich. "I think he was nervous and afraid, and he left the island as soon as he could." There was even a rumor that some of Colón's people had paid Troy himself a visit and hung him out a hotel window by his feet until Gino stepped in.

The plan was for the event to be recorded and released on VHS as a special home video production. But the result would be an unmitigated disaster, one of the biggest blunders of the WWF's expansion period. Adding insult to injury, or perhaps because Vince thought he'd be able to smooth things over, it was Gorilla Monsoon who was sent to Puerto Rico to be both ring announcer and ringside commentator. Gino did indeed meet with Carlos to explain that it was a one-time show and not a full-scale invasion, but even his diplomacy could only go so far. Colón could not be placated and stacked up his own card at Loubriel, booking himself in the main event against Abdullah the Butcher and bringing in other stars from his new partners at Jim Crockett Promotions, as well as other NWA territories. The whole mess even strained the WWF's relationship with Lauper, who was not pleased to find herself in the middle of an unpleasant wrestling war.

On top of everything else, it was pouring rain when the night finally came. A mere 1,200 fans turned up in a stadium that comfortably sat thirty thousand for wrestling, while across the island, Colón put fifteen thousand people in Loubriel Stadium. The WWF wrestlers anxiously slipped and slid around on the wet mat to get their matches over with as quickly as possible. Not even Culebra's own Pedro Morales, who went on last that night after Hogan, could save things, and when he realized that, he called an audible, abruptly going to the finish in the main event in just over a minute so everyone could just get the hell out of there. And through it all, Gino was there at ringside, spending most of the time huddled inside a plastic tent designed to keep the rain off all the television equipment, anxiously chain-smoking despite the loud protests of producer Nelson Sweglar, who could barely see the monitors through the clouds of smoke.

Needless to say, no official release of the Puerto Rico debacle ever came to fruition, and for the most part, it would remain locked away in the video vault for good. The company would never again return to Puerto Rico while Gino was alive and for several years after his passing. The incident would also do serious damage to whatever remaining ties Gino had with Colón, and the bitter feelings would take years to heal. Gino had assumed that it would be "hands off" when it came to Puerto Rico, but Vince's ambitions were proving to have no limits.

■

By the end of 1985, the wrestling war raged on all fronts. *WrestleMania* had tested the waters as far as pay-per-view television, but the first full-scale pay-per-view offering produced by Titan Sports would be *The Wrestling Classic*, presented November 7, 1985, from Illinois's Rosemont Horizon, a building once run exclusively by the AWA. The event would consist of a single-night tournament showing off sixteen of the WWF's biggest stars, most fairly recently acquired from other territories, as well as the only WWF pay-per-view singles match between WWF world champion Hulk Hogan and his arch-nemesis Roddy Piper. Just as they'd done at *WrestleMania* and had been doing weekly on *All-Star Wrestling*, Gorilla Monsoon and Jesse Ventura would be brought together again to call the action.

From that point forward, pay-per-view would become the company's biggest source of revenue and the new medium for fans to enjoy the WWF's most important events. It would begin a decade-long process of seeing the house shows that had once been wrestling's lifeblood become less and less relevant. And Monsoon and Ventura were also being solidified as the WWF's elite broadcast team—the one that was brought in when things really mattered most. Fans at the time would come to associate the Gorilla and the Body with the WWF on pay-per-view. As the company's pay-per-view schedule would increase to a few shows per year, they would be paired up on nine of those spectaculars over the next five years, including five of the first six annual *WrestleMania*s. Gorilla himself would have the distinction of serving as a lead commentator on the first eight *WrestleMania*s and, in total, would be featured as the lead commentator on twenty of the WWF's first twenty-five pay-per-view events over the next eight years—which suited McMahon perfectly, as it allowed him to run things from the back for these all-important extravaganzas.

For the inevitable *WrestleMania 2* on April 6, 1986, Gorilla and Jesse's talent would be split up, as there would actually be three different announce teams. The event would be spread out over three different cities across America in an ostentatious display of how vast the WWF's grasp was becoming: Vince McMahon would call the action from New York's Nassau Coliseum, while Gorilla Monsoon and Mean Gene Okerlund would do so from the Rosemont Horizon in the Midwest, with Jesse Ventura and Lord Alfred Hayes doing the honors out on the West Coast at the Los Angeles Sports Arena. The show was less than a critical success, and the pay-per-view audience would fall slightly short of what the closed-circuit audience had been for the first *WrestleMania*, but regardless, there was no sign of the momentum of the WWF slowing down. The expansion was nearly complete, and the rest of the territories were gradually dying on the vine.

WrestleMania 2 would also mark the last time Ventura would be seen in the WWF for four months. His high-profile presence on WWF television—especially *Saturday Night's Main Event* on NBC—had garnered the right kind of attention, and he'd been made an offer he couldn't pass up, to appear alongside Arnold Schwarzenegger in the action movie *Predator*, shooting that spring and summer in the tropical jungles near Puerto Vallarta, Mexico. The role had also come due to the negotiations of sports and entertainment agent Barry Bloom, whom Ventura had hired to represent him in a move largely unprecedented for a pro wrestling personality. It was a move that rankled McMahon, who enjoyed having total control over his talent—and McMahon was even more rankled to learn, thanks to the snitching of none other than Hulk Hogan, that Ventura had been trying to start up a labor union for the WWF talent, right around the same time.

■

Although Ventura would be back on WWF television by the end of the summer, McMahon would be more wary of him going forward and more aware of the need to have another effective heel announcer that he could depend on and trust in a key position. The man who would benefit from this turn of events was Bobby "The Brain" Heenan, who was offered a spot as the WWF's newest broadcast announcer—or "broadcast journalist" as he would describe it—starting in April 1986. He would immediately be paired up with Gorilla Monsoon in what would come to be one of, if not *the* most cherished and beloved broadcast team in the history of professional wrestling. It would mark the next great chapter in Gino's career, as well as the next great friendship of his life, and perhaps the greatest of them all.

In hindsight, putting them together was the most natural decision imaginable, as their personalities complemented each other so well. They had never crossed paths in the business before Bobby's arrival in the WWF in the autumn of 1984, but they had quickly discovered what kindred spirits they were, developing a close bond even before they first joined forces as an official team on the April 28, 1986, edition of *Prime Time Wrestling*. Three weeks later, Heenan also became Monsoon's permanent partner on *All-Star Wrestling*. Their chemistry and personal camaraderie were instantaneous, and it showed in how they worked together. Lifers in the pro wrestling business going back decades, and from the same generation, they shared so much in common. They both also happened to be consummate ballbreakers. It was a match made in heaven. "They both had the same outlook and view on humanity, where the majority of people are just fucking idiots," explains Bobby's daughter Jessica, who got to spend time watching them work firsthand as a kid, sitting in the control room with Vince McMahon and Kerwin Silfies. "And it's fun to make fun of those people. They didn't have patience for the stupidity, and they would also call people out for the dumb things they did."

Of course, even though the meticulous viewer could see through the façade, what the two of them conveyed through their onscreen relationship was anything but cordial. Gorilla and Bobby had a very different dynamic than Gorilla and Jesse. Whereas Monsoon and Ventura always seemed to show each other respect and gave the sense of being two equal peers, Monsoon and Heenan were as adversarial as it gets. It was also clear that Monsoon was the boss, while Heenan was the shifty, sniveling comic relief, always trying to get one over on him. It was Abbott and Costello. Bugs Bunny and Daffy Duck. Monsoon and Ventura were two alpha personalities who often disagreed on air, and Gorilla would never try to pull the things with Jesse that he could with Bobby. With the Brain, Gorilla had the perfect foil to play off.

Monsoon and Ventura were sportscasters. But what Monsoon and Heenan did together was something different. It was schtick. Yet pulled off to a degree that no schtick in wrestling had ever pulled off. They were genuinely and truly funny, with impeccable timing and formidable improv skills. For the first time in his career, Gino got to be in the position of being a comedy straight man. He got to do bits and engage in back-and-forth banter with someone who could give it right back to him. And he loved every minute of it. Before long, those recording sessions with Bobby, particularly for *Prime Time Wrestling*, would become his favorite part of the job. It was a spot that neither he nor anyone else could've imagined him slipping into. But it worked perfectly.

Unlike Ventura, who often agreed with Monsoon and would sometimes give the babyfaces their due, Heenan was completely and unapologetically in the corner of the heels. He would say the most outrageous and indefensible things to explain their behavior, which typically elicited from Monsoon a loud and hearty "WILL YOU STOP?"—a catchphrase response that became as much a part of their routine as Oliver Hardy's "Here's another nice mess you've gotten me into," or the exasperated outbursts of the Skipper from *Gilligan's Island*. And that's exactly what it was meant to be. Gorilla Monsoon and Bobby Heenan became professional wrestling's first, and still greatest, comedy team. And for the next seven years, they would make magic together, the memories of which to this day can bring forth a twinkle in the eye of those who were there to witness it.

Unsurprisingly, the smarts, who generally liked their wrestling serious and sports-like, would take issue with the schtick—with the very idea of mixing comedy and wrestling. But once again, history has judged the whole thing much more warmly, with the vast consensus being that Gorilla Monsoon and Bobby "The Brain" Heenan may have been the best to ever do it. The opinions of those who roasted them at the time are generally looked back on today with the same bewilderment as reviews panning *The Wizard of Oz* or the Beatles on *Ed Sullivan*.

Prime Time Wrestling had already been in existence for almost a year and a half before Monsoon and Heenan first linked up, and it would limp on for two years after they were eventually broken up as co-hosts. But really, all that most remember or care about today are the nearly five years that Monsoon and Heenan anchored the program, first at the Video One studio in Baltimore and later at Titan Sports' brand-new television studio facilities at 120 Hamilton Avenue in Stamford, Connecticut. Sweglar would produce the early episodes, with Silfies the director and Kevin Dunn as assistant director. The following year it would be Bruce Prichard who would step in as producer, and he began a close friendship with Gino as well. Taking over the unenviable role of corralling Gino and Heenan could be daunting, as they were known for constantly cracking each other up, and sometimes the funniest bits of all would wind up on the cutting-room floor.

Sweglar was once again impressed with Gino's ease in front of the camera as he took on the role of balancing comic banter with Heenan and introducing the many matches and segments that made up *Prime Time Wrestling*'s two-hour runtime: "You would have thought that someone who'd spent a number of years in the traditional wrestling world would have been ill at ease in a host position of a talk show, doing wraparounds and so forth. But that wasn't the case." It couldn't have possibly been further from the days of the raving and mute Manchurian Giant—the business had changed dramatically, but there he was, rolling with the punches, taking everything his job threw at him and making it work. And truth be told, Gino managed to get along with everyone, which made working with him very easy. "Gorilla even got along with Kevin Dunn," remembers Tony Chimel. "They were buddies. They liked to gamble together. Gorilla was the one guy that liked him."

■

These were the very good years. Gino had found his groove as a WWF television personality. Titan Sports was on a seemingly unstoppable upward trajectory. The man who loved to gamble had pulled off what was unquestionably the greatest gamble of his life. His agreement, which gave him one-and-a-half-times opening match money for every WWF live event produced, was really paying off in an era when the company was running close to a thousand shows per year—sometimes three per day. During the height of it, there were certainly more years where he saw upwards of $300,000 to $400,000 at a time when the average yearly American salary was about $20,000. To be sure, with the astronomical success of Titan Sports, he would have been making even more if he'd been able to hold on to his 20 percent of the company, but he was still making more than he had ever made as a wrestler in the days of the Capitol Wrestling Corporation. As always, he had managed to make the very best of an unfavorable situation.

As Titan Sports grew, the company made the move in the summer of 1986 from its cramped office park in Greenwich up four exits north on I-95 to 1055 Summer Street in the heart of downtown Stamford, the city in which it remains headquartered to this day. Around the same time, the Marella family was also embarking on a big move, leaving the waning township of Willingboro after nearly twenty years and relocating about six miles southwest to Moorestown, another South Jersey suburb. "He really didn't wanna move; he loved that house," Valerie recalls. "He said if he could've picked it up and moved it anywhere, he'd have done it. It was a great house. But he wanted to build his own house." With more money to spread around than ever, Gino envisioned something special, sitting on nearly two acres of land near the banks of Rancocas Creek at 56 Cove Road. It was a beautiful home he designed himself, with a fully finished basement that included his own office suite spanning the length of the house. Made for a man of prodigious size, it boasted double-wide stairways and eight-foot ceilings in the basement. "The builders said nobody does that," remembers Valerie. "He said, 'Who's writing the check? If you don't wanna do it, I'll find someone else.'" They did it.

In June of 1986, the family put together a big fortieth wedding anniversary celebration for Lenard and Connie, with the whole extended Marella clan getting back together in Rochester, with the exception of Sonny, who couldn't make the trip up from Texas. "That was very disappointing," remembers Gino and Sonny's sister Amy. "Because it would've been our last time all together." Not long after, on November 8, came Sharon's wedding, the planning of which Gino and Maureen had been agonizing over for months. It was the height of his fame and popularity, and he knew that many people from the business were going to be there. He wanted everything to be perfect. It would turn out to be a sumptuous affair, attended by multitudes of family members, as well as a cast of characters from the WWF locker room and television crew. There was a show that very day at the Philadelphia Spectrum, one of the only ones Gino would ever miss, and understandably so. Lord Alfred Hayes would take his place at Dick Graham's side that night. And Harley Race would have to do without the services of Bobby "The Brain" Heenan in his corner for his match against George "The Animal" Steele, just as "Mr. Wonderful" Paul Orndorff would have to do the same as he challenged Hulk Hogan the very same day in St. Louis. Because the Brain would be in New Jersey with his great friend on the day of his daughter's wedding.

Gino proudly held court, beaming as he walked Sharon down the aisle, resplendent in a blue-and-black tuxedo that most astute WWF viewers would recognize from television. Davey O'Hannon was also there for that opulent day: "We heard some kind of announcement or music, and out comes a parade of waiters, all dressed up, carrying . . . I can't even tell you how many prime ribs there were—the whole ones, not cut up. It was like a parade came out of the kitchen. It was a show! And I said, 'Leave it to Gino!'"

Presumably waiting to make sure they could attend their granddaughter's wedding, later that very same month, Gino's parents would move out to Las Vegas along with Amy, following her other sisters, Rosemary and Angela, who had already moved their families out there years earlier.[6] It would be a permanent move, and even though Gino would no doubt miss having his parents just one state away, it also gave him one more reason to go to Vegas—as if he needed it.

■

On the television side of things, the continued expansion of the company, combined with its ever-growing cash flow and desire to appear as big-time as possible, had led to the establishment of two new weekly programs at the end of summer, which only further benefited and spotlighted Gorilla Monsoon. Both of the WWF's long-running weekly shows, *Championship Wrestling* and *All-Star Wrestling*, which had been going since the '70s, would be retired, as would the concept of taping regularly in the same humble location. From now on, there would be two bright, shiny new weekly syndicated programs that would go on the road, taping in different major arenas across North America each time. It was an important step for a company leaving its Northeast origins further and further in the rear-view mirror. The A-show, *Superstars of Wrestling*, would be hosted by Vince McMahon along with Jesse Ventura and an ever more out-of-place Bruno Sammartino.

The B-show, *Wrestling Challenge*, would be hosted by Gorilla Monsoon, inexplicably joined for the first set of tapings by the unlikely duo of Ernie Ladd and "Luscious" Johnny Valiant before Vince came to his senses and reunited the regular *All-Star Wrestling* duo of Gorilla Monsoon and Bobby Heenan. With the exception of a nine-month period from

1989 into 1990, Monsoon and Heenan would host *Wrestling Challenge* together for six and a half years. Monsoon would continue to host the show, on and off, almost to the very end of its run in 1995. It would be at the announce desk of *Wrestling Challenge*, available on syndicated television in far more homes in those days than cable television shows like *Prime Time Wrestling*, that Gorilla Monsoon would be seen and heard by the widest audience for the longest amount of time, and what he would be best remembered for by the fans of the World Wrestling Federation during that period.

It was all building toward something, and that something would turn out to be the towering achievement of Titan Sports during the 1980s WWF boom: *WrestleMania III* at the Pontiac Silverdome in outer metropolitan Detroit. Vince McMahon running that territory, a relatively dead area for years, for his greatest pay-per-view extravaganza, was the perfect symbol for how massive the World Wrestling Federation had become. Buoyed by a titanic main event pitting WWF world champion Hulk Hogan against the newly turned André the Giant, with Bobby Heenan now in his corner, the event drew the largest crowd to ever witness professional wrestling live in North America. Although it was advertised, in typically inflated fashion, as 93,173, other reports have it somewhere in the seventy-to-eighty-thousand range. It may have set a new world indoor attendance record, but we can never be sure, as the real numbers were closely guarded. Add to that the approximately one million more people watching live on pay-per-view and at closed-circuit locations, and it was clear that the WWF was "What the World Is Watching," as the company slogan would proclaim.

It was also what many consider to be the finest hour of Gorilla Monsoon and Jesse Ventura as a broadcast duo. In every sense of the word, *WrestleMania III* was a gigantic show that acted as a true testament to how far the company had come and the incredible roster of talent that had been accumulated, which included the likes of Randy "Macho Man" Savage, Ricky "The Dragon" Steamboat, Jake "The Snake" Roberts, the Honky Tonk Man, the Hart Foundation, the British Bulldogs, Harley Race, the Junkyard Dog, Rowdy Roddy Piper, Adrian Adonis and many more.

And Monsoon and Ventura would add so much to what made the show great, with many of Gorilla's most famous soundbites coming from this exact broadcast—without a doubt, the most well-known and oft-repeated of which was his perfect summation of the Hulk Hogan / André the Giant main event, which he described as "The irresistible force meeting the immovable object." Sometimes referred to as the "Irresistible Force Paradox," it was by no means invented by Gino, being a phrase whose origins dated back to ancient Chinese philosophy and had been commonly used for centuries—in fact, Gino himself had used it in the past to describe similarly massive confrontations of "bohemoths," as he would pronounce the word. But on this occasion, it was more apropos than ever, and it's that clip, often paired with the visual of Hogan and André's epic stare-down, that lives on today in wrestling lore. And for those in the know, Gino's call on that legendary match possesses a whole other level of depth to it, because he'd been in the ring with both of them.

What made the match even more special for Gino was the fact that his son Joey had been chosen to be the referee. Assigning such an important match to him was a demonstration of how much confidence the company had in Joey as an official, just as it had in his father as a commentator. And although Jesse liked to rib Gorilla about the "incompetence" of Joey on air, since the family relationship between the two was never made public, the truth was that Joey Marella had become one of the WWF's most prominent referees, and his ascension was also an example of how the company was moving away from the ancient commission refs that frustrated Gino—and Vince—to no end and moving toward bringing referees in-house as company employees, getting everyone on the same page at last.

■

WrestleMania III was the turning point in the WWF's great war of expansion—the symbolic victory fully established that the company had gone truly national. And it was a sign to all the other promoters in all the other areas that this could no longer be denied or prevented. What remained of the once vast territorial system was in shambles. The Florida and Central States territories would soon be absorbed by Jim Crockett Promotions in a flailing attempt to match the WWF's national ambitions, soon resulting in bankruptcy and the sale of Crockett Promotions to Ted Turner. Bill Watts would see *WrestleMania III* as a breaking point, selling his UWF to Crockett at around the same time as well. World Class Championship Wrestling in Dallas was reeling from ever-compounding tragedy and loss that would make the company a shell of what it had been in the Von Erich glory days. The AWA was beginning to collapse from losing so much of its talent to the WWF. Dick the Bruiser's WWA would be reduced to running parking lots in Indiana. Memphis and Portland had found a way to run relatively undisturbed by hiding in the shadows in their little corners of the wrestling landscape. Dino Bravo and Gino Brito's Montreal territory, as well as Paul Boesch's vaunted Houston promotion, were about to fall under the thumb of Vince McMahon, the inevitable end result of more "promotional partnerships."

The wrestling war was, for all intents and purposes, over. Titan Sports had planted its chrome-logo flag from sea to shining sea. Crossing those seas would come next. Vinny's laughingstock of a dream was reality. And the old-timers, for all their bluster and bravado, were powerless to stop it. It was either get on board or get crushed. And sometimes, even the former didn't rule out the latter.

And as the World Wrestling Federation became more of a monolith, the product itself would continue to change, leaning more into the "sports-entertainment" aspects. It would become more sanitized, more homogenized. The use of blood would be more or less outlawed. It was a family attraction geared at children, and the presentation reflected that. Television production values were more polished than ever, as the big bucks the company was raking in could be seen on the screen. Live events were treated as a packaged touring attraction, with identical shows being presented in venues across most markets. And Gorilla Monsoon was very much a part of the TV product package. As that product became more cartoonish, more bombastic and over-the-top, even Gino's commentary evolved to meet that standard. Just as Vince himself had gone from the

1978 NWA Convention, Las Vegas Hilton: (Left to right) Willie and Lilian Gilzenberg, Loraine and Frank Tunney, Maureen and Gino. A visibly unwell Gilzenberg was secretly battling cancer at the time. He took ill days after coming home from the convention, and passed away several weeks later.

A young Vincent K. McMahon mediates between Muhummad Ali and Monsoon, in connection with their "impromptu" match on WWWF TV. This photo is believed to have come from a TV promo that did not make air.

NEW JERSEY ★★★

DAILY 🔳 NEWS

LARGEST CIRCULATION OF ANY PAPER IN AMERICA

120 Thursday, June 3, 1976

YANKEES BELT RED SOX, 7-2

Story on Page 102

A flabbergasted Gorilla Monsoon sees Ali enter the ring . . .

He quickly grasps the situation—and his worthy opponent.

Ali Goes to Mountain

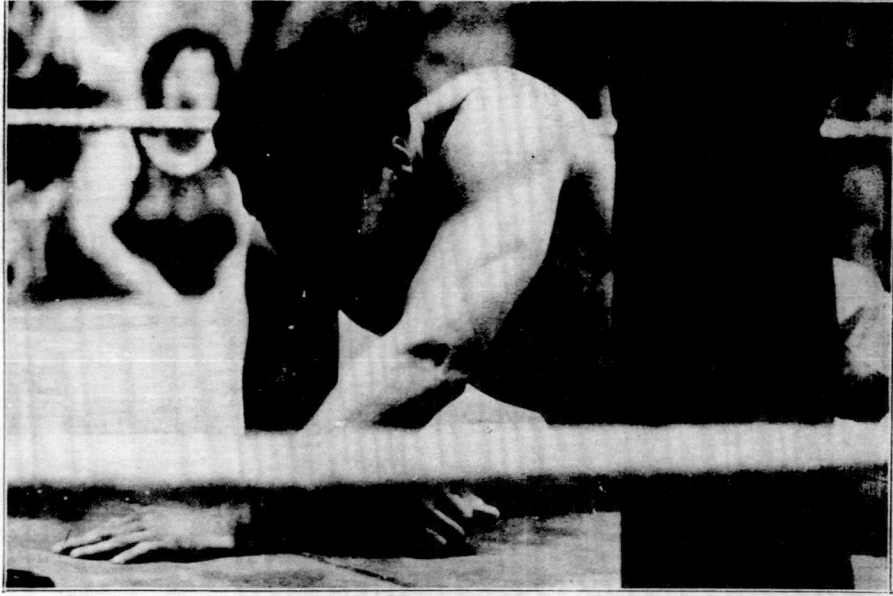

That widely-renowned hassler of rasslers, Muhammad Ali, found himself in Philadelphia the other night and, as often happens in Philly, time was heavy on his hands. Learning that Gorilla Monsoon, a 350-pound grappler, was in town, Ali decided to take him on as a warmup for his battle with Japanese wrestler Antonio Inoki in Tokyo later this month. The winner? Not Ali this time.

Ali gets an unaccustomed view of the deck. He's only been knocked down three—or maybe four—times in his career.

UPI Telephotos

AUTHOR'S COLLECTION

The back cover of the New York *Daily News* the morning after Ali clashed with Monsoon in Hamburg, two days before it aired on *Championship Wrestling*.

Vince Jr. and Gino appear on *Tomorrow* with Tom Synder, May 3, 1976, episode. Bruno Sammartino also appeared on the episode, which has not been seen since it aired.

Madison Square Garden—August 1, 1977: Gino serves as special referee as Superstar Billy Graham defends the WWWF heavyweight title against former champ Sammartino.

This Thing of Ours: Gino with fellow minority Capitol owner, the penguin-like Phil Zacko.

Wielding the notebook and pencil, Gino leaves the Gorilla position to escort Chief Jay Strongbow back to the locker room after a TV match.

Madison Square Garden—May 22, 1978: Trapped in the bear hug of the recently dethroned Superstar Graham, on the way to a double count-out. Semi-main event underneath Bob Backlund defending the title against Ken Patera.

André the Giant and Gorilla Monsoon strike a pose to help publicize their December 1978 boxing match in Puerto Rico. Taken backstage at the November 20, 1978, Madison Square Garden show, with referee Danny Bartfield standing between the two giants.

Wiseguys: Referee John Stanley, Pat Patterson, Lou Albano, Tony Altomare and Gino enjoy an evening out.

In front of the famous Mann's Chinese Theatre (originally Grauman's) during a 1980 family vacation in California. Left to right: Victor Quinones, Valerie, Joey, Sharon, Gino, Maureen and family friend Annie Capozzoli. Shortly after Gino's retirement from full-time wrestling.

Gorilla Monsoon, reborn as an erudite television commentator, takes his position at ringside.

Dick Graham and Gorilla Monsoon called the action together from ringside at the Philadelphia Spectrum on a monthly basis from November 1982 through September 1987.

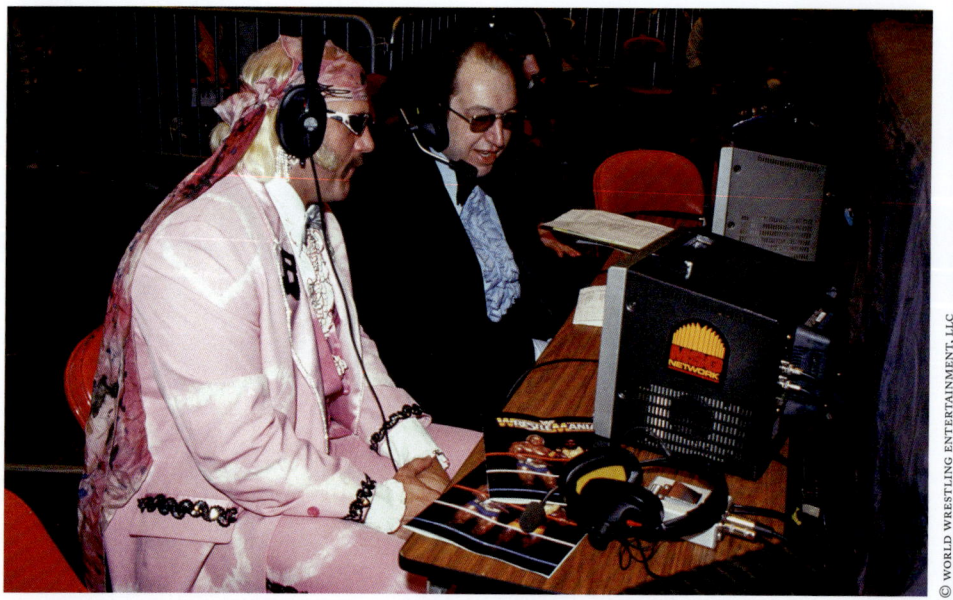

Jesse "The Body" Ventura and Gorilla Monsoon team up for the first time at the inaugural *WrestleMania*, Madison Square Garden, March 31, 1985.

Gino with sisters Angela, Rosemary and Amy at their parents' fortieth wedding anniversary party, June 1986.

Father of the Bride: Gino dances with Sharon on her wedding day, November 1986.

Bobby Heenan came off the road to be with his great friend on the day of his daughter's wedding. A favorite photo of Gino's.

Bobby "The Brain" Heenan and Gorilla Monsoon on the classic *Prime Time Wrestling* set at the Stamford TV studio, where they anchored the show from 1988 through the start of 1991, the last three years of their celebrated five-year run together as co-hosts.

While in Toledo, Ohio, for a *Prime Time Wrestling* and *Wrestling Challenge* taping on October 6, 1988, the Brain and Gorilla stop by for some shenanigans at Tony Packo's famous Hungarian restaurant. The wraparounds would air on the November 1 episode of *Prime Time*.

Bobby Heenan, Jerry and Barbara Brisco, Gino and Maureen, Cindy Heenan and nine-year-old Jessica Heenan together on their 1988 cruise.

"WILL YOU STOP?!" Monsoon berates Heenan during their first pay-per-view call, *WrestleMania VII* in Los Angeles, March 24, 1991.

Kicking back in the production office at Caesars Palace in Las Vegas for *WrestleMania IX*. Despite his jovial demeanor, Gino was struggling with health issues at the time.

Gorilla helped to pass the torch to Jim Ross in 1993, and they called three pay-per-views together on WWF Radio. Here they are at the Providence Civic Center for the 1994 *Royal Rumble*. Their commentary for the Razor Ramon/Irwin R. Schyster Intercontinental title match was simulcast on the television broadcast as well.

Old Friends: Backstage at *WrestleMania VIII* with (left to right) WWF President Jack Tunney, whose uncle Frank gave Gino his first big break; longtime Calgary promoter Stu Hart, for whom Gino also wrestled very early in his career; Arnold Skaaland, Gino's cherished friend and business partner (and best man at Hart's wedding); and Billy Red Lyons, Tunney's right-hand man in the Toronto office and one of Gino's early pals in the business.

October 1, 1994: Gino catches up with Pedro Morales (left) and Arnie Skaaland. All three were honored at the first East Coast Cauliflower Alley Club Reunion in Springfield, Massachusetts.

Civic Auditorium, Stockton, California—January 22, 1996: As WWF president, the former Manchurian Giant comes face-to-face with his 1990s counterpart, Vader, in a memorable angle on *Monday Night Raw*.

Iron Men: A longtime Bret Hart booster, WWF President Gorilla Monsoon stands proudly by the Hitman for his defense of the world title against Shawn Michaels (with manager José Lothario) at *WrestleMania XII* in Anaheim, California, March 31, 1996.

With his beloved grandsons, Joey and Gino, shortly after their birth in October 1996.

Last Public Appearance: Flanked by (left) "Bayonne Bleeder" Chuck Wepner and 1975 Golden Gloves champion Kevin Rooney, as ringside judges for the Bart Gunn/Butterbean Brawl for All match at *WrestleMania XV* in Philadelphia, March 28, 1999.

Kayfabe to the End: Gino's last New Jersey state license plate, still in the family's possession.

somewhat urbane Howard Cosell knockoff of the '70s to a roaring, bellowing, guffawing lunatic on the air, so Gorilla Monsoon ratcheted up the volume, intensity and even the tone of his voice, becoming less conversational and more impassioned in his pronouncements. Whether it was the result of a concerted effort and company-wide edict or just an organic byproduct of the "sports-entertainment-ization" of the WWF, it all contributed to the larger-than-life version of professional wrestling that the company embodied.

And yet, as he watched the business gradually transform into something he recognized less and less, there was a part of Gino that was uncomfortable with it all, that longed for the old days and merely tolerated the circus it was becoming, where what happened in the ring between bells seemed to be increasingly de-emphasized. He also seemed a bit dismayed at how, by leaning into the entertainment aspects, the company was moving the business away from the sports aspect, which was, in the end, the essence of the kayfabe code he'd spent his life protecting. "When the company was expanding so quickly and we were exposing it, when we became entertainment and were losing the legitimate factor of it, I don't know how much of that he could handle," explains Jerry Brisco, who sometimes shared that sentiment at the time, although no one vocalized it too loudly. "Gino always prided himself on being a big guy who could work really solid. He wasn't a novelty act. He was a guy that could go in there every night and work, unlike a Haystacks Calhoun, or guys like that. It was that old mindset." Still Gino did as he was asked to do, and more than almost anyone, focused all his energies toward selling that very product, even if he didn't always approve of it.

Gino was capable of evolving more than most of the old guard, and he chose to put his efforts into supporting and improving the product in whatever way he could, rather than allowing himself to be consumed by the negativity and bitterness that was turning so many of his peers into dinosaurs. Jimmy Korderas, a young referee who was making the transition from Jack Tunney's Toronto office onto the main WWF roadshow, remembers how valuable Gino was in those days as a guiding force: "He understood how to do wrestling on television. Yes, you have to project to the live audience. But at the same time, you have to play to the audience at home, because they're the ones you're trying to draw in. The people there have already paid. They're enjoying the live experience, but you're trying to sell it to a larger crowd now, watching on television." This was the reason that Gino would always famously stress that the commentator should, as much as possible, be watching the action on the monitor, not live in the ring itself, so that he could be calling what the television audience was actually seeing at all times. This approach became standard practice, adopted not only in the WWF going forward but throughout the industry.

Korderas also remembers the advice Gino would impart to him and the other referees about how to do their job effectively, something he was always a stickler for. He'd stress the importance, when refereeing matches for television, of "working the horseshoe," meaning that the referee should always be conscious of the hard camera fixed on the ring and move in an invisible "horseshoe" semi-circle behind the talent, so he was never blocking the camera's view of them. Mike Chioda, who was also joining the main referee crew at this time, echoes Jimmy's recollections of the valuable advice Gino offered: "He'd say, 'Look, Mike. The less the referee is seen and noticed, the more you're doing your job. Don't go out there and go into business for yourself. Don't oversell shit.'"

It also helped that Gino tended to have a more diplomatic approach than Vince, who was much more controlling and intense than his father had ever been and was known to browbeat talent and employees when they weren't giving him what he wanted. Perhaps it was because he no longer had an ownership stake, but Gino had softened his demeanor by that time and preferred a more tactful touch. "He never intimidated," Jimmy explains. "He was almost a father figure, for lack of a better explanation. He just had a kind heart to him. You could tell . . . It was the way he said things. He was trying to relax you, as opposed to making you nervous." This contrast in styles was typified by an incident that occurred at a television taping early in Jimmy's refereeing tenure, involving an eight-man tag team match with the Killer Bees and the Young Stallions on one side, and the Iron Sheik, Nikolai Volkoff, Sika and Kamala on the other. The match completely deteriorated, to the point that it couldn't be used for TV. "I looked horrible in it," Jimmy remembers. "I got buried completely. And when I got back to the Gorilla position, I got an earful from Vince. He was very intimidating." But as Jimmy was walking away, Gino called him over. "He said, 'I know how you feel right now. Try not to let it bother you. Listen to what he told you, try to learn from it. Think about what happened tonight, try to use it and move forward. Don't dwell on it too much, because it'll play with your mind.' He was trying to calm the situation and calm me down."

It was a counterbalance to Vince that the talent in general looked to Gino to provide. And as controlling as he could be with others, Vince was different around Gino. He gave him a wide berth and let him do things his way. He recognized his experience in the business and in producing wrestling television, both of which exceeded his own. Not to mention the relationship Gino had had with Vince's father, which loomed over everything. Above all, Gino remained one of the boys before he was part of the office, and that was something Vince had to accept. "He would tell me, 'I don't want to see you stooge on anybody,'" Mike remembers. "'If you have to stooge on somebody to enhance your position or your job, then you need to find another job, because you're not doing your job good enough.'"

■

Ironically, Gino's frustration with the commission referees would motivate him to help out in Titan Sports' growing efforts to free itself from the restrictions of state athletic commissions in general. A thorn in the side of pro wrestling promoters since time immemorial, the commissions imposed taxes on promotions that often amounted to no more than shakedowns and imposed the hiring of outside officials, doctors, announcers, timekeepers and other personnel who were often unqualified and were to be paid by the promotions, not the commission. And it was all part of maintaining the illusion that pro wrestling was a legitimate sport—an illusion that Titan seemed to be backing away from anyway.

Not every state had a commission, but one of the most prominent ones existed in Pennsylvania, where the company still conducted many of its events. When the Pennsylvania Athletic Commission held its next hearing on June 12, 1987, Linda McMahon and Bob Marella would be there to argue for the deregulation of professional wrestling in the Commonwealth of Pennsylvania. It was an easy decision to bring Gino along, not just because of his interest in deregulation but because of the clout he had with Pennsylvania state officials and how well he was known in those circles.

Even as he pointed out that wrestling was different from boxing in that wrestling was strictly entertainment, commissioner James Binns still insisted that regulation was required in order to maintain control and to protect the health and safety of the wrestlers (not to mention rake in those all-important tax dollars for the Commonwealth of Pennsylvania). "They're assigning people to our events that don't belong there," Gino complained to reporters, adding in typical fashion, "It helps to put a referee in the ring who knows the difference between a wristlock and a wristwatch."[7] Linda insisted that Titan Sports could supervise and police its own events without commission help and compared the WWF to live entertainment entities like the Ice Capades and the Harlem Globetrotters. However, what she came short of doing—and what it's hard to imagine Gino even contemplating doing—was admitting outright that the events she presented should be considered entertainment because they were performances with predetermined outcomes and not competitive sports. That admission appeared to be what was required before the commission would even consider deregulation. And that was a line that not even the McMahons were willing to cross, even to evade the costly taxes and fines of the commissions. At least, not yet.

Despite his unwavering support, there were certain lines that Gino was uncomfortable with crossing. Another was the line between business and family. He had always prided himself on making time for his wife and kids, for making Sundays and holidays special, especially proud and relieved by the fact that he had escaped so early in his career the grind of territorial travel and being constantly on the run, usually away from loved ones. But Vince McMahon was of quite a different mind, and didn't prize family above all else in the way that Gino did. For example, Vince's father had never booked shows on Christmas Day—while Christmas shows were common and even popular in some other territories, particularly in the South, it had never been a New York thing. But that would change under his son, as Christmas Day shows became part of the regular WWF touring calendar starting in 1984, his first full year in charge. He'd attempt this for three years in a row, including an annual Christmas show at the Cap Centre in Landover, one of Gino's regular haunts.

But Gino had long ago declared that he would never work on Christmas, and he held to that. It helped that the Cap Centre shows were no longer being televised, and so his services were less required. That was not the case, however, with a brand-new pay-per-view event that Vince was planning—not for Christmas but for another important family holiday, Thanksgiving. It was something that had directly to do with the wrestling war he was in the process of decisively ending. The last real rival standing was still Jim Crockett Promotions, the company that had used the 6:05 Saturday night TBS time slot Vince had sold them to turn their brand of wrestling into another nationally televised cable product. And now Crockett was also going to be testing the waters in pay-per-view, moving his annual *Starrcade* event to that platform in an attempt to fund his company's rapidly depleting coffers.

As it had been for the previous four years, *Starrcade* was slated to happen on Thanksgiving Day—a Crockett wrestling tradition that actually predated *Starrcade* to the '60s. In order to nip Crockett's new ambition in the bud, McMahon was prepared to step in with a killing blow: He would concoct a Thanksgiving pay-per-view of his own, the *Survivor Series*, which would run directly in opposition to Crockett's *Starrcade '87*. And more than that, he would strong-arm the cable systems that carried his pay-per-view events, stipulating that any system carrying *Starrcade* would not have the opportunity to carry *WrestleMania IV* the following year. Most cable operators chose the proven pay-per-view commodity, the World Wrestling Federation, over Crockett's unproven NWA brand. And on top of it, McMahon added the extra little barb of calling his *Survivor Series* "The Thanksgiving Tradition." Needless to say, *Starrcade '87* was a total financial disaster, and the WWF now had its second annual pay-per-view spectacular.

And so, thanks to Vince McMahon's ravenous competitive streak, Gino found himself having to break one of his cardinal rules. On Thanksgiving Day, 1987, he would not be home in Moorestown with Maureen, Valerie, Joey, Sharon and her new husband, Michael, enjoying turkey, stuffing, cranberry sauce and his favorite, peanut butter pie. Instead, he (and Joey) would be in Ohio at the Richfield Coliseum for *Survivor Series*. Gino was not pleased. And neither was the family. "We were all pissed off," recalls Valerie. "Because there was my dad and my brother, both gone for Thanksgiving. We didn't like that, but what were we gonna do?" As unhappy with the situation as he was, Gino did not let it come through in his work, sitting beside a pilgrim-attired Jesse Ventura to call the action live with all his usual enthusiasm. It was a classic show of professionalism from someone who was willing to do what he had to do to support the company. *Survivor Series* would continue to be held on Thanksgiving for the next three annual installments, and Gino would be there for all of them, pissing off his family each time. But they couldn't have been the only ones annoyed by the practice, as starting in 1991, the annual event would finally be moved off Thanksgiving.

It wasn't needed anymore anyway. The message had already been sent. *Starrcade* would never be held on Thanksgiving again, even when the annual show continued after Turner Entertainment took over Crockett Promotions and transformed the company into World Championship Wrestling, a new organization that would take its name from the very TBS program with which it had become so associated. By that point, it was all over but the shouting. Toward the end of the tumultuous 1980s, there was no one left to really challenge Vince McMahon for dominance of the industry, and there wouldn't be for years.

Gino's loyalty had been put to another test, and he'd passed. In the years ahead, it would be tested even further. He and his great compatriot Bruno Sammartino would choose different paths, and Gino would grow closer to Bobby Heenan than ever as the two weathered the storms around them with their typical humor and camaraderie. And through it all, the machine would keep on rolling.

CHAPTER 13

THE GORILLA AND THE BRAIN

"Will you stop?!"

As the 1980s closed, the wrestling industry had been utterly transformed. Titan Sports and the World Wrestling Federation stood strident across the entirety of the wrestling landscape, with everyone else fighting for the scraps. And now, with that wide, mainstream national audience in place, Gorilla Monsoon was becoming more than ever the comforting voice for all of it. The most sane man in the most insane show on television. And yet, somehow, he found a way to add to the excitement as well, getting more animated and bombastic than ever as he counteracted the ridiculousness of Bobby Heenan and occasionally, though they were being paired less often than before, the arrogance of Jesse Ventura.

"Please . . ." "Gimme a break!" "High unlikely . . ."

He always stood his ground and connected with fans because he felt the same way about the bad guys as so many of them did. Sometimes, he'd even go so far as to playfully invite viewers to head into the kitchen and make themselves a sandwich rather than watch some villain or another doing something reprehensible on screen—it would be hard to imagine

Vince McMahon allowing any of his other announcers that liberty. But make no mistake, Gino knew what his job was, and he worked tirelessly to get over the WWF product and all its top stars any way he knew how.

Chief among these, of course, was the star who had, just as much as Vince himself, made it all possible. The success of the WWF expansion could, at least to a significant degree, be laid at the yellow-booted feet of Hulk Hogan, and Gino always made sure to put him over to the moon every time he was out there. He never missed a chance to describe Hogan as "the greatest professional athlete in the world today," and his authoritative efforts on commentary absolutely contributed to building the aura and mystique of the Hulkster during this crucial period in the company's history.

In a way, the fortunes of the company had become so inextricably tied to Hogan that Vince would have trouble separating the two even when he wanted to. As the WWF world champion became more and more popular and enshrined in popular culture, he was also more in demand for other opportunities. He was also discovering, as Bruno Sammartino and others had discovered before him, that carrying the company on your back was exhausting work. The dependency on Hogan became clear when *WrestleMania IV*, the first *WrestleMania* to not feature Hogan as the world champion and in the main event, performed significantly less impressively, losing more than half the audience from the previous year's event. As Hogan stepped away to star in the Titan Sports co-produced motion picture *No Holds Barred*, a new world champion would be crowned in the form of Randy "Macho Man" Savage to at least keep the belt warm for Hogan for a year.

■

Despite the fact that, as Gorilla himself might have said, if you hanged Hulk Hogan for being a good actor, you'd be hanging an innocent man, the foray into motion pictures was just another sign of the dramatic growth of the WWF. Toward the end of the winter of 1988—around the time of *WrestleMania IV*, in fact—the company even unveiled its very own television production facilities, tucked away in a parking lot off the beaten path near downtown Stamford, just a stone's throw away from the corporate office. Gone were the days of having to go down to Baltimore to tape studio shows and record voice-overs. Now McMahon had his own dedicated staff on-site and owned all the equipment and everything else lock, stock and barrel—just the way he liked it.

The Hamilton Avenue studio would become a home away from home for Gino, for Bobby, for Gene Okerlund and for all the rest of the talent. And the production staff would become like a work family, many members of which still warmly remember Gino as a father figure to this day. Gino would happily make the two-and-a-half-hour drive up from New Jersey himself every couple of weeks, pulling his instantly recognizable Cadillac into the lot to go to work. It was a pleasure to do so, and a big part of that had to do with his ever-growing repartee with the Brain. In their deluxe new studio, they really got to spread their wings and would do their best work there on *Prime Time Wrestling* over the next three years. Additionally, a lot of that work would also take place at some of the remote locations where *Prime Time Wrestling* would begin shooting wraparounds now that the company had full control of its TV production. These remotes would be among the best segments the show ever produced, with Monsoon and Heenan truly in their element as masters of comic timing.

In fact, the very first true *Prime Time* remote had taken place back in November of 1987, during the transition period while the Stamford TV facilities were still being constructed. The World Wrestling Federation had rolled into Las Vegas for the first time earlier that year and now had returned for a pair of shows in both Vegas and Reno. Typically, Gino didn't go that far out on the road for house shows in those days, but it wasn't hard to convince him to come out to Vegas for a special *Prime Time* shoot that would feature him and Bobby sitting poolside at Caesars Palace. He got to see his family, plus throw some money around at the tables, and spend time working with his favorite broadcast partner, which was icing on the cake.

Around that time, hands-on production duties for the show passed from Nelson Sweglar to Bruce Prichard, Paul Boesch's former right-hand man, who had just come up from Houston after the WWF had completed the process of absorbing that great wrestling territory earlier in the year. Though only twenty-four at the time, Prichard would begin to play an important role in the company. Overworked and politically outmaneuvered, George Scott had departed as head booker the previous year to go and work for Fritz Von Erich in what was left of World Class Championship Wrestling, and Vince McMahon would rely more than ever on Pat Patterson and then Prichard to help him "book the territory."

True to form, Gino had been one of the very first to welcome Bruce aboard at a television taping in Worcester, Massachusetts, the previous April. Although initially intimidated by Gino, as many people could be, Bruce was taken aback by his kind nature and genuine helpfulness. It would be the beginning of a friendship that helped make the production of *Prime Time Wrestling* that much easier. Gorilla and Bobby never needed anything more than a run sheet and some suggestions—there was never a script, as the two pros would figure out the rest on their own. As Prichard would later say, producing Gorilla and Bobby was like a day off.[1]

■

Unfortunately, tapings at the new Stamford facility would start immediately after a scary episode for Gino, the beginning of ever-increasing health concerns for him, though he may not have realized it at the time. Health had been an issue ever since he'd first been diagnosed with diabetes back in his late thirties, but now that he had passed fifty years of age, the years of struggle were beginning to take more of a toll. He had always been a man of ravenous appetite with a notorious sweet tooth, and as anyone who's ever experienced life on the road can tell you, it wasn't always easy to avoid junk food and stick to a healthy diet. Not that he tried especially hard. And the heavy smoking that had continued unabated certainly did him no favors, either. In short, Gino was a man who believed in living life with no apologies. But the downside of that was the heart disease developing as a result of the worsening diabetes.

In mid-January of 1988, Gino suffered a cardiac episode that would later be recognized as a mild heart attack. It would be the first of several such events over the next few years, and it would put him in the hospital, then home on bed rest for the next few weeks. This would cause him to miss a string of important tapings. He had been scheduled to be lead announcer with Jesse Ventura for a new experiment known as the *Royal Rumble*,[2] set to be broadcast live on USA Network from Hamilton, Ontario's Copps Coliseum on Sunday, January 24, but had to be replaced by Vince McMahon. The following day, Vince would do the same for Gino at Madison Square Garden for that month's MSG Network broadcast.[3] Two days later, Gino would miss the *Wrestling Challenge* tapings from the Wicomico Youth & Civic Center in Salisbury, Maryland, which would impact the next three episodes of television. For the first of those episodes (February 7), Vince would join Bobby Heenan on commentary. Not long after, Gino had at least recovered enough to get himself back into the Stamford studio, so he could voice-over the other two episodes for which he hadn't been physically present. It was a sign of things to come and a wake-up call that Gorilla Monsoon was human after all.

Gino's absence had also forced Vince to sit in at the *Prime Time Wrestling* desk with Bobby Heenan for just one episode (February 1), and the near-total lack of chemistry or comic simpatico between the two (Vince wasn't exactly known for witty banter to begin with) only further emphasized how valuable the Monsoon/Heenan team was. Needless to say, everyone was pleased to see Gorilla back where he belonged the following week. The timing couldn't have been more perfect, either. The new TV studio would allow Gino to be more local and travel less often than before, which he was perfectly fine with at that stage of his career. And his body would continue to let him know that this was the right move as well. After nearly thirty years on the road, no one could ever say he hadn't earned the break.

Doing *Prime Time Wrestling* became an oasis for Gino, where he could relax and have fun with little pressure or responsibility. Larry Rosen, the audio engineer for those classic episodes, remembers the chemistry between Gino and Bobby, which derived from something very real: "What you saw on air was pretty much what they were off air. They were great friends. They were a little more laid-back than some of the crazier guys . . . They had regular home lives with kids and regular issues. They were family people first. Sometimes, Okerlund would get in the mix, and we could all go out at night. Gorilla and Bobby would join us occasionally, but they weren't as big a drinking and socializing crowd as me, Dunn, Okerlund, Alfred Hayes and anyone else who might have been in town." In his downtime between shots in the studio, Gino would take the time to talk with Larry and everyone else—about his family, about sports, particularly football and his beloved Philadelphia Eagles. "He had this great laugh," remembers Larry. "He was always even-keeled. I never saw him get angry with anyone."

The remote shoots for *Prime Time Wrestling* were especially enjoyable, and even more so if they happened to be really close to home. And the one that seems to be talked about most of all also happened to take place somewhere that Gino enjoyed going to regularly anyway: Atlantic City. What's most impressive about it is that it took place mere weeks after Gino had returned to work after his heart attack, which you'd never know. It was Monday, March 21, 1988—Gino and Bobby had just come from a *Wrestling Challenge* taping in Springfield, Illinois, the previous day, arriving in Atlantic City, where they were set to spend the next week in anticipation of *WrestleMania IV*, coming that weekend to Trump Plaza Hotel and Casino. The wraparounds would all be taped that very day and edited together for broadcast in the evening, featuring the two of them making their way around the hotel and casino.

In a knowing nod to his familiarity with the waterfront gambling mecca, much of the episode shows Gorilla buddying up to bellhops, waiters, security guards and other staff by name and even kicks off with the big man emerging from a stretch limousine and discreetly passing some cash to the valet like a true high roller. But the crowning achievement takes place on the casino floor at one of the blackjack tables. Kerwin Silfies had the idea to shoot some of the wraparounds while Monsoon pretended to play, but he was informed by the casino that this was against gaming commission rules. The only people allowed at the tables were people who were actually playing. Gino then informed them that it was no problem—he'd be happy to play for real.

What follows is truly amazing to behold. Astute viewers can watch closely and see that Gino is not only playing blackjack but winning almost every hand he plays. As he converses with the stoic dealer, with the pit boss, with Heenan, he can be seen discreetly tapping the table to signal the dealer for more cards and telling him when to stop, deftly playing with his hefty pile of chips like someone very used to being in that position. He does this all while simultaneously doing schtick with Bobby, hyping *WrestleMania* and introducing matches on the show, all without missing a beat. "You would have thought that this damn stuff was tightly scripted, and it was never scripted," Nelson remembers. "They had a way of improvising and supporting each other that was just incredible. Absolutely incredible." Larry remembers doing about ninety minutes' worth of takes while Gino played through it all. When they were finished and Larry informed him that it was time to move to the next shooting location, Gino refused. He was up $4,500 since he'd been sitting there and had no intention of stopping while he was hot.

By the time he was finished, he'd won eleven grand. As he got up to leave, he tossed four hundred-dollar chips on the table as a tip for the waitress. Sweglar leaned into Gino to ask if he'd like to share some with his executive producer, and as if responding to Bobby Heenan, he shouted back, "Get away from me! Not a chance!" For Gino, it was just another day in AC.[4]

■

It came off as a fun and carefree day for Gino, which it was, but what fans didn't fully grasp at the time was that it had come less than two weeks after one of his closest friends had a major falling-out with the company that would also end, for all intents and purposes, one of the great professional and personal relationships of Gino's life. Because, just before *WrestleMania IV* rolled around, after twenty-eight years of an admittedly rocky on-again, off-again partnership with the company, Bruno Sammartino walked away from the World Wrestling Federation for good and would never again have anything to do with the company during Gino's lifetime and for many years thereafter. More than just a parting of ways, it would mark the beginning of a bitter public war between Bruno and the company, particularly between Bruno and its owner, Vince McMahon. It was a crusade Gino could not follow, and in the end, he would be forced to choose his loyalty to the company to which he'd given his life over his loyalty to the man he had idolized like an older brother.

Bruno had reluctantly returned to the WWF back in 1984 in large part to try and help his son David's wrestling career, but that was never going to work out. David simply was not his father, and after a few months' push, it was clear that the company had no real plans to do anything big with him. At the imploring of Vince, Bruno himself had stepped back in the ring for a couple of years. But Bruno had finally put his foot down and hung up the trunks for good by the end of the summer of 1987, by which point David was being booked strictly against enhancement guys like Steve Lombardi, Barry Horowitz, Tiger Chung Lee and Terry Gibbs, and even that was just as a favor to Bruno. Finally, after a loss to rookie Steve Blackman at a high school gym in Watertown, New York, David took out his frustrations on a heckling fan, kicking him in the mouth and getting himself arrested for assault. Titan Sports fired him on the spot.

Bruno was six hundred miles away at a television taping in Winston-Salem, North Carolina, and when he found out the news, he promptly walked out and went home to Pittsburgh. With David done with the company, as far as he was concerned, he no longer had a reason to be there, nor did he have any desire to be. And since he was no longer even an asset as a drawing card in the Northeast, Vince let him leave. He didn't really need him anymore. And Bruno hadn't been with the company at the time when Vince's father had died, so he wasn't even included among those old-guard stalwarts Vince had been instructed to take care of anyway.

But there was more to Bruno's walking out than just David's termination. He'd lost interest in being a part of the company a long time prior, largely because, in his eyes, it was no longer the company that he'd worked for all those years ago. It had changed into something else, something with which he no longer wished to be associated. This made the decision to walk away that much easier for him. Simply put, Bruno was an old-school, honorable guy with a strict moral code and a strong proponent of clean living and family values. And he just couldn't reconcile those things with what he'd been seeing and hearing since he'd returned to the WWF. He'd held on for David's sake, but now he didn't need to. David had held out hope that his father would eventually return to the WWF's good graces, giving him a chance to get his career back on track. But Bruno refused.

Bruno was seeing the same things as Gino, not to mention Arnie, Freddie and the rest of those who had worked for the old man. But Bruno was deeply disgusted by all of it, and unlike Gino, who kept his disgust to himself, Bruno decided he could no longer tolerate it. The professional wrestling business had never exactly been a bastion of morality, and it had never exactly been populated by choir boys and Boy Scouts. There were certainly things that had gone on and been tolerated even in the halcyon days of Vincent James McMahon. But they largely paled in comparison to what had happened to the World Wrestling Federation by the mid-1980s. The entire culture of the company, fueled by a non-stop road lifestyle and a corporate mindset that mimicked much of what was happening elsewhere during that decade of excess, had morphed into a drug-fueled world of rampant sexual abuse and other misconduct.

All through the company's wild 1980s expansion, there had been a dark underbelly. All that success hadn't come without a price. Most noticeable of all was the extensive use of anabolic steroids—which, though not yet classified as controlled substances at this point, were being heavily abused by the overwhelming majority of the WWF locker room in an attempt to get the kind of comic book superhero bodies that Vince wanted. In Bruno and Gino's era, to be sure, there were guys like Superstar Billy Graham and Ivan Putski, but they had been the exception, not the rule. And as massive as Bruno was, he'd always prided himself on being completely natural and recoiled at the steroid culture that had taken hold around him. But beyond steroids, there was also the widespread use of hard drugs, chiefly pain pills and cocaine, which had become all but required in order to keep up with the insane seven-day-a-week schedule of crisscrossing the continent, which had taken hold during the expansion as well. It was a shock to those who still remembered the days when hard drinking was the worst substance offense on the road—and Bruno and Gino had rarely even partaken in that.

But there was worse than that going on, as stories had been spreading for years within the company of Terry Garvin, a former wrestler that Pat Patterson had brought in to be vice president of operations, creating a culture of systematic sexual exploitation of wrestlers looking for a break in the business, and far worse, of the young ring attendants and ring crew members, many of whom were underage. Patterson himself was even mentioned in rumors of widespread sexual harassment. And then there was Mel Phillips, the depraved ring announcer and head of the ring crew, whose penchant for young boys was practically an open secret, even predating Vince's takeover of the company. It had gotten so hard to ignore that Phillips had actually been fired in 1988 but was soon bafflingly brought back by the McMahons on the provision that he refrained from his reprehensible activities.

And presiding over it all, setting the very tone for this culture through his own combination of actions and inactions, was Vince McMahon himself. Rather than discourage the steroid and cocaine culture that had taken over, he had been one of its most enthusiastic participants. But beyond that, almost from the very beginning of his takeover, there had been other stories. Like the one alleging he had once helped get Jimmy Snuka off the hook for murdering his girlfriend in a motel room in a fit of rage. Or the accusations of sexual assault from referee Rita Marie Chatterton.

These were all rumors that had been making their way around for years and surely things that Gino had heard tell of. To someone like him, who'd been one of wrestling's straight arrows, it was taken with great dismay. Gino was someone who had never fallen into the more common pitfalls of the business—who had remained loyal to Maureen and abhorred the abuse of alcohol and especially of drugs. This was a man who, at the movies one night with Maureen, had nearly gotten into a fight with someone sitting in the back of the theater smoking a joint. One can only imagine what he had to sit still for in locker rooms and on the road during his years as a WWF commentator. But sit still he did. Yet despite the respect that Vince showed him, the behavior and the attitudes of which Gino was no doubt aware only further justified his position of always keeping at arm's length the son of the man who had once made him a partner.

Nevertheless, Gino was a loyal soldier, and he would remain a loyal soldier. To be clear, Bruno's decision to distance himself and call this behavior out was by far the exception, not the rule. That was simply the business mindset in those days, in some ways not that different from the code of organized crime: it was a world where you kept your head down, kept your mouth shut, and kept marching forward. Even Bruno himself had done that, up until the day they fired his son and he no longer benefited from doing so. And because of that ostracization, those within the company would eventually be forbidden from having anything to do with him, even those who had known and loved him for years. "Bruno's decision mentally affected Gino a lot, because they were so tight and had gone through so much together," Jerry Brisco remembers. "If they were in a town, you didn't see one without the other. So Bruno stepping aside really affected Gino in ways that a lot of us don't know. It bothered all of them, I saw it. It bothered Arnie, who was a great friend also. It really opened some eyes up there . . . This is our legend, this is our guy that brought us to the point where we were able to do what we're doing, and now he's stepping aside because of these issues. It made everybody do a double take in their thought process."

The two men who had headlined the territory for years and had rocked the Garden on seven occasions would hardly ever speak to each other again. And it was a sore spot for Gino, as is evidenced by the recollections of Tom Carlucci, who, like a true childhood fan who'd been watching since the 1960s, couldn't resist bringing it up: "Gino would never really talk about Bruno. Because I asked him, and you could tell. When Gino didn't want to talk about something, you didn't talk about it."

While Gino never took part in or condoned any of the rampant misconduct, and in fact, shared Bruno's shock at what their business was becoming, he would stop short of using his power to intervene. "I know that Gorilla had to be on the inside and getting all the inside dope on Terry Garvin," remembers Bret Hart. "He never seemed to address it, or let it show or reflect in his attitude. I think he still loved the business." Adds Carlucci, "Gino wanted no part of that crap. He could have probably managed it, but I guess he just turned the other way on it." As Bret surmised, in the end, Gino chose the business—and in that closed, carny world, that was pretty much what you had to do if you wanted to keep making a living in it. He chose his family over strangers. Now in his fifties and with a job for life at the highest level of his industry, he did not see the benefit of stepping out of line and getting himself blacklisted like Bruno. Aside from one year of teaching gym nearly thirty years earlier, the wrestling business was all he had ever known.

Far from the sweeping accountabilities of today, it was very much a closed business in those days, and you did what you had to do to get by and to cope with it. For some, like Gino, that coping included a generous dose of bleakly dark humor. Long before the scandals of Titan Sports became public knowledge in later years, attentive viewers might recall Gorilla Monsoon's occasional quips about the "Terry Garvin School of Self-Defense," a caustic inside reference to Garvin's harassment of wrestlers that went completely over the heads of fans at the time. This on-air ribbing would sometimes even extend to his good friend Patterson, whose sexuality was common knowledge inside the business but not outside of it. For his part, Patterson took the joking in stride and was often the first to laugh about it himself.[5] It was a very different time—in the wrestling business, in the entertainment world and in America. And perhaps the greatest sin Gino could be accused of was being a man of his time.

One thing that Bruno and Gino did have in common was they both had sons who were on the road with the WWF. Bruno had been relieved to get David off the road and away from some of the terrible influences that he saw. Gino was not as lucky. Joey was a young man in his twenties, spending hundreds of days per year as part of the biggest traveling party imaginable, and highly susceptible to those influences. "We were all scared, because he's on the road, and when he'd come home, we'd be out together, and I would see his behavior and know that that's definitely 'on the road' behavior," remembers his sister Valerie. "They didn't live in the normal world. It was an exclusive club." Joey was falling prey to all the things that Gino had wisely avoided during his years in the business, and it troubled him deeply to see. He had been reluctant and skeptical about getting his son involved in the business at all in the first place and seeing him go down this path was like watching a worst nightmare come true.

Emblematic of the drunken mischief that Joey was getting into on the road, not to mention the cruel ribbing and hazing that were pretty standard for the time, is the story of the Dynamite Kid—one half of the British Bulldogs tag team and one of the most ruthless and indiscriminate of ribbers—slipping something into Joey's drink one night, and then shaving his head and eyebrows while he was passed out. It was just the kind of thing Gino didn't want his son exposed to and that he'd been trying to shield him from. And the next time Gino spotted Dynamite at a taping, he gave him an earful. "He saw Dynamite and confronted him about it," remembers Ross, Bret's brother and part of Dynamite's extended family at the time. "He said, 'You don't do that to my son!' He was absolutely livid—even though Joey was probably going along with it, trying to show he could drink with everybody." Uncharacteristically quiet and nonconfrontational, Dynamite endured Gino's wrath and never gave Joey a problem again. But it was proof that on the road, no one was immune from this kind of hazing. Gino was pissed off not just that his son had been humiliated but that Joey's livelihood had been impacted, because he wouldn't be able to appear on television until his hair grew back.

Gino and the rest of the family were distraught over the stories they were hearing and the behavior they were seeing. There were a lot of tense family conversations—a lot of ultimatums given. For all they did know about, there were other things they didn't know about, and the not knowing made it even worse. "Some things got back to Gino, and he would get mad," remembers Joey's good friend Mike Chioda. "When Gino was pissed and spoke, you listened, man." Bret was also close to Joey, and was in a position to see a lot more than most: "There were some times when Joey was his own worst enemy . . . I was doing a lot of the same things, so I was right there a lot of the time." Like many a Titan employee of both the in-ring and outside-the-ring variety in those days, Joey wound up having to go to rehab and continued to struggle on and off with addiction. Gino continued to struggle with what to do with him, as Valerie recalls: "At the end of the day, my dad knew, here's my son, he's right out of high school, and what are his job skills? He can count to ten? You're not going too far with that. And there's nowhere else for him to go. I think he just looked away at some things and regretted it. We all did."

■

Gino received perhaps the grimmest reminder of the dark side of the business in the summer of 1988, when a specter from the past reared its head again in the form of Frank Goodish, better known as Bruiser Brody. Goodish had departed the WWWF in the winter of 1977, never to return. A decade later, the expanding company was seemingly bringing in anyone of value from territories far and wide. Among the most recent acquisitions had been Ted DiBiase and Hacksaw Jim Duggan of the Universal Wrestling Federation, Rick Rude from Jim Crockett Promotions and Jim Hellwig, who would go from World Class's Dingo Warrior to the Ultimate Warrior after walking through Titan's doors. It was a time of limitless opportunity for territorial veterans, but one name very conspicuous by its absence had been Bruiser Brody, who, if anything, had become a much bigger star since working for the McMahons.

One of the reasons often proposed as to why Brody was never brought in to the World Wrestling Federation for what surely could've been a big-money program with Hulk Hogan was his notorious heat with Gino from all those years ago. At the time, Brody had been a thorn in the side of the Capitol office in general, and once he'd finished up his program with Sammartino, they couldn't wait to send him packing. The story had always been that Gino had helped see to it that Frank would never again darken Capitol's door and opposed bringing him back even when Vince Junior took charge. As the territorial system dramatically contracted, Brody had managed to eke out an impressive living, jumping around to whatever places were left, including St. Louis, World Class, Florida, Memphis and the AWA. But he really found his fame and fortune in Japan, where he'd become one of the nation's most high-profile and well-paid *gaijin* superstars, first for Giant Baba's All Japan Pro Wrestling and later for Antonio Inoki's New Japan Pro-Wrestling.

The full reality of why Brody never turned up in the WWF is a little more complicated than just having heat with Gino. For one thing, Brody didn't particularly need the WWF since he had been thriving for years, charting his own renegade path. Additionally, there are believed to have been some preliminary talks about finally bringing in Brody to join the WWF's cast of characters sometime in late 1987, with Frank likely balking at Vince's suggestion of repackaging him as some kind of "Viking" character to fit in with the increasingly cartoonish and gimmick-heavy WWF roster.[6] There was also the fact that he had just re-signed with Baba after a stint working for Inoki that he'd come to regret. With a potential to make more than $10,000 per week by sticking with All Japan, Brody had even less inclination to rock the boat.

But no matter what hard feelings there had been between Frank and Gino, nothing could prepare Gino for what he discovered after returning from a trip to Vegas with Maureen on July 18, 1988. Joey came to the airport to pick them up and shared with them a shocking and sobering rumor that Frank Goodish had been murdered the day before in the locker room of Juan Ramon Loubriel Stadium in Bayamón, Puerto

Rico, Gino's old stomping grounds. The rumored perpetrator was José González, Frank's old nemesis from the WWWF days and a dear friend of the Marellas. As soon as they got home, Gino got on the phone with Victor Quiñones down in Puerto Rico and discovered, to his horror, that the rumors were true.

After a career spent often clashing with authority and rubbing promoters and bookers the wrong way, Frank had apparently pushed things too far with the wrong person—someone who had held a grudge against him for over a decade and now found himself in a position of power over him. "That was just the nature of Frank," remembers Hugo Savinovich, who also worked for the Puerto Rico office at the time. "He had had some close calls, and I was involved in a couple with him. Frank was fearless." In addition to still performing in the ring in Puerto Rico as the masked Invader, González had gotten in good with Carlos Colón and Victor Jovica, working his way into the position of head booker. His hatred of Frank was only compounded by professional jealousy, as Goodish seemed to be getting over like crazy in Puerto Rico, which González viewed as his home turf. "The Puerto Rican people identified with him," Hugo explains. "He was an ass-kicking rebel. He was so over, first as a heel and then as a babyface."

In addition to clashing with the promotion over money and other booking decisions, now Goodish was apparently close to having a position of power himself, as he was in the process of buying into the company. In fact, it has long been suspected, although never confirmed, that the points Frank was on the verge of buying comprised the 10 percent that belonged to Victor, which had been given to him by Gino. That was the last straw for González, who was also in a very dark frame of mind due to the recent drowning death of his young child—a daughter for whom Gino and Maureen had stood as godparents. According to reports that would later be shared by wrestlers such as Dutch Mantel and Tony Atlas, who were in the locker room, just prior to Brody's scheduled match with Danny Spivey, González had called Brody into the shower area, ostensibly for a quick private chat. There, the two men got into a physical struggle, which ended when José plunged a knife into Frank's abdomen. It was Tony who was first on the scene and spotted Frank lying prone on the floor with José standing over him, the bloody weapon still in his hand. And it was Victor who made the frantic call to a local radio station to broadcast the news on the air—a quick decision he made because he figured it was the easiest way to get an ambulance on the scene. Victor stayed with Frank for the hour it took the paramedics to get there through traffic as Frank bled out on the locker room floor. He would not survive the night.

Gino could not believe it. It was an unthinkable crime, committed by someone he had loved and in a place he loved, in spite of the unfortunate way things had turned out business-wise for him in the end. "There was nothing you could say to him to make him feel better," recalls Hugo, who also spoke to Gino about the news around the same time. "It was so sad." Puerto Rico had been a joyful place for him, and this harsh and cruel reality would taint that joy forever. Gino had witnessed firsthand how difficult Frank could be, but any anger he'd had toward Frank was completely overshadowed by the anger he felt toward José and the frustration he felt toward Colón and Jovica for failing to prevent such a tragedy.

He remembered how he and the others had dealt with Brody all those years ago in the WWWF, when they'd tried to control the situation as much as they could, make their money with him, pay him what he felt he was owed, and then send him on his way as soon as possible. Gino couldn't understand how Carlos could've allowed it to get so out of hand, especially since they should've seen trouble coming, knowing Frank and José's history. It was another black eye on the profession he loved. "It just hurt so many people, including the widow and their little boy," says Hugo. "But it also hurt the passion of a small nation, where wrestling was sacred . . . That night stole a lot of the innocence of our industry. And Gino was so sick from hearing about it, so sad and angry. Even today, I still don't understand why the heck it happened." An added layer that made it hurt Gino even more was that he was keenly aware of how Latino wrestlers were often treated and looked at in the business, and he had been one of those working to help change that. Explains Hugo, "Now they were given ammunition for the haters to say, 'You see? We were never wrong. These guys are killers.'"

Gino's relationship with Puerto Rico had already been strained, and needless to say, the whole situation would only make it worse. Even Victor regretted his decision to get involved with the office down there and found himself continually butting heads with Colón and Jovica, considering breaking away to get into business for himself. The handling of the Brody situation pushed him even further in that direction, especially the following year when González was totally acquitted in a sham of a murder trial in which Colón was accused of using his connections to make his head booker's problem go away. Alas, Mantel and others didn't even receive their subpoenas until after the trial had concluded. González walks a free man in Puerto Rico to this day.

It would all contribute to Victor getting out of the Colón organization entirely and setting up shop in Japan, of all places. He'd get hooked up with maverick Japanese wrestler-turned-promoter Atsushi Onita in a wild new project known as Frontier Martial-Arts Wrestling—a rogue group operating in the shadows of All Japan and New Japan that would provide a violent, edgy alternative for Japanese wrestling fans and turned out to be a perfect proving ground for a renegade soul like Victor Quiñones. Victor mastered the Japanese language and would wind up helping to launch the career of many an international star, although not all who worked with him would have pleasant things to say. The seed that Gino had planted was taking root in the business, but as it would turn out, Victor wasn't immune to the seamier influences of the industry, either.

Back home, Gino had his own double-header of loss to deal with. On September 16, 1988, his father, Lenard Marella Sr., passed away at the age of eighty-two after a full and happy life, which included the pride that came with twenty-five years of watching his son succeed at the highest level of his chosen business. Vince McMahon would once again fill in for Gino on *Prime Time Wrestling* as he went out to Las Vegas to be with his mother and his siblings for the services. Just twenty-two days after losing his father, Gino would lose his brother Sonny, who, at the age of fifty-four, finally succumbed to the damages of the rheumatic fever he'd had as a child, suffering a fatal pulmonary artery rupture in his home in Bedford, Texas. "His son Ken called me in the middle of the night and told me his father died," remembers Amy Marella. "I couldn't believe it. I thought, this can't be real. He had just had a physical one week before. He was in bed watching TV, started coughing, got up and went to the front door to get air, and by the time his wife got there, he was already dead." Vince graciously stepped in once more for another laugh-free episode of *Prime Time* while Gino hopped on another plane to the Lone Star State to pay his last respects to the brother he'd just seen at the previous funeral the month before.

■

Amidst all this tragedy, Gino clung to the things that brought him joy, and one of the chief sources in those days was his continuing and developing collaboration with Bobby Heenan. With the bright new set in place at the bright new facilities in Stamford, they really hit their groove. Their natural flow and interactions were such that a typical ninety-minute show could almost be shot completely in real time with little to no retakes. "I don't even know if they had a pregame chat," recalls Larry Rosen. "They knew the storylines. They would pick up on something, like the banana phone. Something would happen off-set. And they would just have this banter about it. That would become the theme of the show, and we'd just make it work." The shows were done almost like live television, with Gorilla and Bobby throwing to a match, and then sitting there and actually watching the match in real time, then cutting back to the studio.

The remotes became more common, more elaborate and even more entertaining, including a memorable episode in which Bobby interrupts Gorilla's fishing vacation. If there were *WWF Superstars* or *Wrestling Challenge* television tapings happening in a particular area, that would sometimes result in a *Prime Time Wrestling* location shoot, which is how Gorilla and the Brain wound up visiting the Kentucky Derby Museum; taking part in a slapstick-laden pretend western movie shoot at the historic Old Tucson film studio in Arizona;[7] getting into hijinks aboard a yacht, including Gorilla falling flat on his face amidst rough waters as both men did their best not to break character; or exploring the Busch Gardens amusement park in Tampa, where Bobby's wife, Cyndi, and daughter, Jessica, even got to take part in the fun, playing unsuspecting park patrons who get in a few digs at Bobby's expense, much to Gorilla's delight. The fun carried over into the studio as well. There would be a Halloween episode in which Gorilla would dress up as Brother Love, the Jimmy Swaggart–like televangelist character that Bruce Prichard had been portraying on WWF television, while Bobby would masquerade as "The Genius" Lanny Poffo.

One particular incident that especially stands out because it was not played for laughs took place on the January 16, 1989, episode—Gorilla Monsoon became part of the action for the first time in years. Heenan's former charge, "The Red Rooster" Terry Taylor, had been brought on the show, supposedly to hash out his differences with his former manager, with Monsoon acting as moderator. However, when the Brain takes a cheap shot and slaps the Rooster in the face, Gorilla tries to get in between the two men. It's then that Heenan's master plan comes to fruition, as his newest protégé, longtime WWF enhancement wrestler Steve Lombardi, repackaged as the scruffy Brooklyn Brawler, emerges from out of nowhere, blasts Gorilla Monsoon with a stool and then puts the boots to Taylor, as Bobby Heenan takes over the show.

The angle made the Brawler the first wrestler to put his hands on Gorilla Monsoon since the Big John Studd bodyslam contest of six years earlier, and certainly the first time such a thing had happened since Gorilla Monsoon had fully reinvented himself as the beloved and benign television commentator. In a subtle twist that hinted at the real-life camaraderie that existed between the two men despite their onscreen bickering, Heenan actually took it upon himself to apologize to Monsoon, who had been removed from the studio and "taken for medical attention," as fans were informed. On the next week's episode, Heenan and the recovered Monsoon have a heart-to-heart discussion in which Heenan reiterates his apology, while Monsoon insists he'll never trust the Brain again.

It was a surprisingly endearing exchange that added further dimension and life to their on-camera relationship.

That relationship only grew closer behind the scenes the longer they worked together, and they became quite social, even away from wrestling. Their families would get to know each other, taking vacations together each year, providing irreplaceable childhood memories to Bobby's daughter, Jessica, who recalls them fondly to this day. It also didn't hurt that Bobby's wife, Cyndi, just so happened to be Italian-American like Gino. Jessica remembers visits to the Marella home in New Jersey whenever the WWF was touring in the area. "My poor mother and poor Maureen," she laughs. "Because those two, how they were on screen was how they were all the time. I told my dad, you and Gino are better than Matthau and Lemmon." Of particular note is an ocean cruise taken by Gino and Maureen along with Bobby, Cyndi and Jessica. "They were inseparable," remembers Jessica of her dad and Gino. "I remember I came to the pool with mom, and Gino was sitting there in pants and a long-sleeve T-shirt, all in black, because he hated the sun." They were also joined on the trip by Jerry Brisco and his wife, Barbara.

Jerry had arranged the trip with a cruise line director who happened to be a huge wrestling fan, with all expenses paid. As part of the deal, Gino and Bobby had agreed to put on a comedy dinner show for the very fortunate passengers on board the ship. When asked if they had any script they'd be working with, Gino and Bobby politely informed the cruise directors that they never worked from a script. They just talked to each other, and magic would inevitably happen. "And they were a hit," recalls Jessica. "A huge hit." It would be the only known time that Gorilla Monsoon and Bobby "The Brain" Heenan would ever put on their own independent comedy show before a few hundred people on a cruise ship in 1988.

■

The Monsoon/Heenan announce team was front and center in those days thanks to *Challenge* and *Prime Time*, but the Monsoon/Ventura team would still come together for high-profile pay-per-view events, including the second and third editions of *Survivor Series* in 1988 and 1989, as well as the debut of the *Royal Rumble* on pay-per-view in 1989. And of course, there was *WrestleMania V*, held once again at Trump Plaza in Atlantic City, with a main event that gave Monsoon the opportunity to once again sing the praises of Hulk Hogan while Ventura indignantly railed against him, as the Hulkster finally regained the heavyweight crown from his former ally turned mortal enemy, the Macho Man. While Gorilla and Jesse continued to work beautifully together, and were consummate professionals who enjoyed working with each other, they didn't share the deep, real-life friendship away from the cameras that Gorilla and Bobby did. For one thing, Gorilla represented the office and often acted as a go-between for Vince McMahon, while Jesse, with his interest in unionization, always cast a wary eye toward management.

"They were completely different people," explains Larry Rosen, who worked with them both. "We didn't know that Jesse was gonna be a governor, but he was a political animal. He would always talk politics, and Gorilla wasn't like that at all. They were very, very different personalities. Jesse was colorful and a showboat and would be the center of attention, and Gorilla was more like, 'I'll be back here when you need me.'" This isn't to say that Monsoon and Ventura didn't get along, just that their relationship was different. And for the limited time they still had together, it still worked very well.

In later years, Ventura rarely spoke of his time working with Monsoon, but when he has, it has been reflective of a wonderful working relationship. In a 2022 interview for *Sports Illustrated*, he remarked: "With Gorilla and I, it was all chemistry. He was a wonderful man. Always respectful, an old veteran of the sport, he had a great sense of humor, he had great timing, and he understood what needed to be accomplished. My relationship with Gorilla was phenomenal, and it was that way all the way until his passing." Even more recently, in a 2024 appearance on *The Bill Simmons Podcast*, he said, "Gino was a dream to work with. You couldn't have asked for an easier, better tandem. I don't think Gino and I ever had a misunderstanding, ever."

But Jesse Ventura wasn't Gorilla Monsoon's only pay-per-view broadcast partner in those days. Perhaps the most unlikely of pairings occurred at the first installment of Titan Sports' third major annual pay-per-view event, *SummerSlam*, at Madison Square Garden on August 29, 1988, when Monsoon was paired up with a blast from his past, Superstar Billy Graham. Vince had always had a special fondness for the Superstar and had brought him back into the fold the previous year, hoping to stage a big comeback for the former world champion whose act had foreshadowed Hulk Hogan and much of the colorful 1980s WWF. But steroids had taken their toll on Graham's body, which had broken down to the point that he could no longer wrestle. He was briefly slotted as a manager for Don Muraco, but when even that was too physically demanding, Superstar Billy Graham became a short-lived commentary experiment.

After calling the action on MSG, NESN and PRISM for house shows in New York, Boston and Philadelphia, the Superstar was given the big stage with Gorilla for pay-per-view, and it was surreal. There they were, calling the action together in the very building where they had wrestled each other for the heavyweight title some eleven years prior. And just seven years prior, Gino had infamously declared the Superstar dead in his *Philadelphia Journal* column. Presumably, any hatchets had been buried by that point, but that certainly didn't help the commentary for *SummerSlam*, which was hampered by Graham's inexperience and total lack of chemistry with Monsoon. In just a few months, the Superstar would be gone for good from the WWF and ironically standing alongside Bruno as one of the company's two chief public detractors.

Another new partner who'd be paired up with Gorilla Monsoon, but would last a little bit longer, was Tony Schiavone. A former minor league baseball announcer from North Carolina, Schiavone had been with Jim Crockett Promotions as an announcer for years and had become especially known to wrestling fans for his co-anchor position alongside David Crockett on the nationally broadcast *World Championship Wrestling* on TBS after the WWF had ceded the show to JCP. A major shakeup had occurred at the end of 1988, when Turner

Broadcasting purchased Crockett Promotions. James J. Dillon, best known to Crockett fans as the leader of the Four Horsemen, had left the organization when the Horsemen were broken up shortly after the buyout and gone to work for Titan Sports as head of talent relations. It was Dillon who recruited Schiavone to the WWF, a move that Schiavone was only too happy to make rather than going to work for Turner Broadcasting in Atlanta.

In his new role in the WWF, Schiavone became part of a minor shakeup in terms of broadcast talent. Vince McMahon had always been keenly aware of aesthetics, and that went beyond just the wrestlers in the ring. He also had a bizarre, growing aversion to anything that resembled "old-school rasslin'," preferring to go in an ever newer, ever shinier direction. For a while, he'd been looking for young, well-put-together, professional announcers in an attempt to gradually phase out his cast of grizzled, older industry veterans. But it usually didn't work out, as those grizzled veterans were just so damn entertaining and beloved by fans. There had been Craig DeGeorge, who was later replaced by Sean Mooney. But while crisp and professional, neither man possessed the wrestling chops to hang with the likes of Gorilla Monsoon, Bobby Heenan, Jesse Ventura or Lord Alfred Hayes. Schiavone came with the professional broadcasting pedigree and look, as well as the legit pro wrestling credentials and experience.

The arrival of Tony Schiavone even led to Gorilla Monsoon and Bobby Heenan being split up on *Wrestling Challenge* for nearly a year, with Tony coming in as a new play-by-play commentator in July of 1989 and Gorilla taking on a secondary color commentator spot beside him. Gino didn't mind, as long as he got to keep doing *Prime Time Wrestling* with Bobby, which was his favorite job anyway. He enjoyed working with Tony and always took time to help him acclimate to his new surroundings and to a very different type of wrestling product. He got along well with him, just as he did with Mooney, another new, young announcer who benefited greatly from Gino's presence and wisdom. Schiavone would even take Monsoon's place with Jesse Ventura for two pay-per-view events during his year with the WWF, *SummerSlam '89* and the 1990 edition of the *Royal Rumble*. It appeared very much as though Vince McMahon was grooming Schiavone to be the WWF's new number-two announcer behind himself and maybe ease Monsoon into more of a supporting position. Rather than seeing this as a threat, Gino saw it as less work, which was fine by him, as long as he still got to do *Prime Time*.

And yet even though Gorilla and the Brain did continue to work together on *Prime Time*, the experiment in separating them went on over there, too, as Roddy Piper was brought in for a time as Monsoon's co-host starting in July 1989, when Bobby Heenan was given his own dedicated segment of the program, *The Bobby Heenan Show*. Intended to capitalize on Bobby's natural comic timing and sense of humor, it was a bizarre undertaking, part talk show and part variety show, with the Brain being surrounded by such eccentric peripheral WWF personalities as "Jamison," the company's disheveled answer to Pee-wee Herman, as portrayed by comedian John DiGiacomo, as well as the rotund Rosati Sisters—Vivian, Christine and Diane, three WWF superfans who had become recurring *Prime Time* cast members. It had its moments, but it didn't quite work, because Bobby was funniest when he was with Gorilla. It was their chemistry together that created the real comedy gold. Before the end of the year, sanity prevailed, and the Brain returned to the *Prime Time* desk, much to Gorilla's make-believe consternation.

Schiavone also didn't last beyond his one-year contract. Although he would later describe his year with Titan Sports and working with Gorilla Monsoon as the best year of his career, he was a Southern guy at heart—he and his family hated living in Connecticut. Plus, it didn't hurt that the chameleon-like Jim Barnett, who had recently switched sides from Vince McMahon to Jim Crockett and had helped orchestrate the sale to Ted Turner, reached out to Tony with an offer that he couldn't refuse. By the end of the spring of 1990, he'd be exactly where he originally didn't want to be, working for Turner Broadcasting in Atlanta, for the company that was in the midst of rebranding itself as WCW. But once he got a good look at what the Turner organization was actually doing to the company he'd once worked for, Tony immediately regretted the decision. Still, he'd always look back fondly on his time working with Gino.

Once Tony was gone, Gino was right back in his spot as lead commentator for *Wrestling Challenge*, with Bobby by his side once again. The first attempt to replace him was over. But it wouldn't be the last.

■

With the '80s ending and the '90s beginning, Titan Sports had gone from dominating North America to next fixing its gaze across the Atlantic Ocean to Europe. The company had first tested the water with cards in Italy and France as early as late 1987, and by 1989, the World Wrestling Federation would debut in the United Kingdom, where it would be met by a fan base just as vociferous as its American one, if not more so. With WWF programming being beamed into far more countries than that, Gorilla Monsoon and the rest of the cast of characters were now becoming known to an international audience.

Almost as if to put the most appropriate icing on the cake that was the decade of the rise of "sports-entertainment," it would be at a state senate hearing in Trenton, New Jersey, on February 9, 1989, that Vince and Linda McMahon would testify once and for all about the true nature of their product, describing it as "an activity in which participants struggle hand-in-hand primarily for the purpose of providing entertainment to spectators rather than conducting a bona fide athletic contest." It really wasn't anything earth-shattering, as the nature of professional wrestling became readily apparent merely by watching it, and the prearranged and choreographed aspects of it had been exposed time and time again in the press and elsewhere over the years going back at least to the 1930s and strongly suspected for decades before even that. But the major difference this time was that it was the purveyors themselves who were publicly admitting to the artifice after generations of folks in the business doing and saying whatever they had to in order to protect kayfabe.

It's not known if Gino was there at the hearing with the McMahons on that day, as he had been two years earlier when they were already trying to get the ball rolling in Pennsylvania. At that time, they weren't willing to go that far, but for the commissions, that was the price that had to be paid for deregulation. Other state commissions would deregulate afterward in similar fashion, meaning there would be no more need to put up with commission-appointed refs, ring announcers or timekeepers, which had been the bane of Gino's existence for years. More importantly, to Vince and Linda, it meant no more kickbacks and no more having to pay state taxes on television-rights fees the way competitive sports had to do. But even though some developments came out of it that surely pleased Gino, a part of it also hurt him, as it hurt most of those who had come up in the heyday of the code of kayfabe.

"Exposing our business like that was hurtful to *me*," remembers another of those code-protectors, Jerry Brisco. "And for a guy that went back ten years longer than I did, somewhere inside, it had to hurt him. He was a legit badass; he had to fight people. He had to convince people, not only physically but verbally, that what we do in our business is real. He fought all his life to convince people of that, and then all of a sudden, we're out there saying it don't matter, it's all a work."

■

As much as the 1980s would see the fortunes of Vince McMahon and Titan Sports experience a dramatic and meteoric rise, the 1990s would be a lot more complicated. Much of that decade was not a good time for the company at all, and it saw many struggles take place—from a creative standpoint, from a business standpoint and most certainly from a public image standpoint. The honeymoon period of the national World Wrestling Federation was over. Creatively, the earliest signs of stagnation were showing. The efforts of the company to propel Hulk Hogan into the stratosphere seemed almost like a curse, as they seemed unable to truly replace him when needed. The first serious attempt to do it came at *WrestleMania VI* on April 1, 1990, before sixty-seven thousand fans at the Toronto SkyDome, where the Hulkster did the honors for the Ultimate Warrior. But as popular as the Warrior was, especially with children, he was no Hulk Hogan and would never escape his shadow. In fact, the beginning of the gradual downturn of Titan's business occurred during the world title reign of the Warrior, which prematurely ended after nine months.

WrestleMania VI would also be the final time that Gorilla Monsoon and Jesse "The Body" Ventura would work together in the announce booth. By this point, Gorilla and Jesse were only working pay-per-views, and the Body wouldn't even make it to the next one, *SummerSlam '90*. In the weeks leading up to the event, Ventura got into yet another dispute with McMahon, this time over Ventura's participation in a video game that would use his name and likeness without the permission of Titan Sports. Jesse refused to cut Vince in on the action, and Vince showed Jesse the door. As independent-minded as ever, Ventura didn't mind. Later that year, he entered politics, getting himself elected mayor of Brooklyn Park, Minnesota. The following year, he successfully sued Titan Sports for back royalties. And one year after that, he debuted as a commentator for Vince's main rival, WCW.

Ironically, neither Jesse Ventura *nor* Gorilla Monsoon would call the action at *SummerSlam* that year.[8] In Gino's case, it was health-related once again. Over the years, his diabetes had worsened. As often happens with diabetics, his feet had become a source of worry, and doctors had been keeping a close eye, especially on the left foot, where a black blister had been developing. Eventually, it was determined that the left baby toe would have to be removed, along with a portion of the side of the foot. Maureen accompanied him to the hospital for the surgery. "It almost looked like a shark bite," she remembers. "After, he was coming out of the operating room, and I was standing there, and he said, 'Honey, they took my toe off.' I said, 'Oh, you never liked that one anyway.' The doctor looked at me like I was a nut . . ."

It was not long after that Gino graduated from oral medication to taking insulin shots. The recovery would keep him away from television for about a month, as he went through physical rehabilitation, spending a good deal of it in a wheelchair. "I had to take him to the hospital for treatment," remembers Maureen. "It was a lot of work, and he was mad because I had to do it, and he was helpless." The most important thing to Gino was that he didn't want anyone to see him walking with a cane, so he stayed away until he had learned how to walk properly without one. During his weeks away from the arena tapings and away from the TV studio, Vince would take his place on *Wrestling Challenge*, while Mean Gene Okerlund filled in as Bobby Heenan's foil on *Prime Time Wrestling*. When he finally was ready to return, the company wanted to send a limo to bring him back and forth from New Jersey to Connecticut, but he initially refused until Maureen convinced him to begrudgingly accept the offer: "I said, 'If they want you to work, you take it!' So he finally agreed to that. He always wanted to do things himself. But I said, 'You deserve it, so take it.'"

There was no question that at fifty-three years of age, and still a man of great size despite his trimming down post-retirement, Gino was beginning to slow down. Health issues would only continue to sap his will in the years to come, making it harder for him to travel and more of a challenge to get around in general. He also had more reasons to want to stay home starting in February 1991, when Sharon and Michael made him a grandfather for the very first time with the birth of their daughter, Kelsey. "He was such a great grandfather," remembers Maureen. "He would say, I'm gonna go see Kelsey. I would say how do you know Sharon doesn't have something going on today? He'd say, she can go do what she wants to do, I'll take care of Kelsey. That was him; he loved his grandkids."

■

Still, he wanted to continue to be a part of the WWF product as much as he could, and he was always a person of great perseverance. Monsoon and Heenan would continue to call the action together on *Wrestling Challenge*, and eventually, starting with *WrestleMania VII* in March of 1991, they would become a regular team for pay-per-view broadcasts as well, after a short-lived experiment that saw Gorilla teamed with Roddy Piper for *Survivor Series* on Thanksgiving 1990 and the *Royal Rumble* two months later. Roddy had been great in his earlier years as a heel commentator for *World Championship Wrestling* and *Mid-Atlantic Championship Wrestling* prior to coming to the WWF, but Roddy Piper the babyface announcer was far less of a success, and Gorilla worked much better with a heel to play off anyway.

But just before Gorilla Monsoon and Bobby Heenan were joined for their first *WrestleMania* call together, the team encountered a crushing change in course that neither of them wanted. After six years, five of them with the Monsoon/Heenan pairing, Vince McMahon was looking to completely blow up the format of *Prime Time Wrestling* and go in a different direction. Maybe he thought it was getting stale. Vince was someone who always had an eye to the new and the next and possessed a notoriously short attention span and capricious nature when it came to things like this. In fact, it was a miracle he had allowed Gorilla and Bobby to do their thing for as long as he had. Although millions of fans would've disagreed with him, perhaps Vince found the Abbott and Costello–esque comedy of Gorilla Monsoon and Bobby Heenan on *Prime Time Wrestling* to be just a little old-fashioned. But whether it was old-fashioned or not, what it also happened to be was highly entertaining and genuinely funny, which *Prime Time Wrestling* would never again be during the two more years it carried on.

On February 4, 1991, Gorilla Monsoon and Bobby "The Brain" Heenan sat behind the *Prime Time Wrestling* desk together for the last time. The interesting thing is, during that final episode, Monsoon would continually hype the new format coming in two weeks, but never mentioned that there would also be a new host. It's entirely possible that the original idea was for Monsoon and Heenan to continue together, but if so, that was another last-minute shift, as when the new format kicked off on February 18, it would be Vince McMahon as the new permanent host of *Prime Time Wrestling*, co-hosting with Heenan.

Taking cues from *Saturday Night Live* as well as the old *Tuesday Night Titans*, the new format would take the form of a talk/variety show, in front of a live studio audience, and with Lord Alfred Hayes as the emcee. After weak attempts at topical comedy and various misguided variety segments, along with the usual match and interview clips, it was clear very quickly that the magic was gone. Heenan's jokes fell flat without his beloved straight man, and for all the things that

Vince McMahon may be known for, a strong comedy sensibility was not among them.

It was the end of an era, which, relatively short though it was, is still the subject of fond reminiscence—not just by the viewers who watched it but by the people who worked on it. And for Gino and Bobby themselves, it was a heartbreaker. Nagging neck injuries were motivating Bobby to bring his managing career to an end and focus strictly on sitting at the commentary table, and it was right at that moment that he'd be losing the most enjoyable part of his job. And as far as Gino was concerned, hosting *Prime Time* with Bobby was something he could have continued to do for as long as he was physically able. Losing that gig was going to make his job overall just that much less fun, which was an ongoing trend anyway. Gino was a protected man. He didn't have to do any of this. He could've easily just cashed that guaranteed check and done next to nothing, like his pal Freddie Blassie had been doing for years from his cozy Stamford office after coming off the road as a manager due to his ravaged knees. But Gino was never that kind of guy. He wanted to contribute. And it had been nice to enjoy himself while doing so.

The winds were changing, and that went for a lot more than *Prime Time Wrestling*. Legal woes were brewing that would soon endanger the entire future of Titan Sports and test Gino's loyalty even further. For months, rumors had been swirling after the offices of Dr. George Zahorian, a longtime ringside physician the McMahon family had been using going back to the days of Allentown and Hamburg tapings, were raided by federal agents on suspicion of massive anabolic steroid prescription and distribution—suspicions which turned out to be well-founded. Steroids had just been recategorized as controlled substances under the jurisdiction of the Food and Drug Administration, and handing them out like candy was no longer going to fly under the radar. And when those federal agents discovered that Titan Sports and the many wrestlers under its employ were among the good doctor's most loyal and well-established return customers, it was clear a storm was coming that could potentially tear down everything McMahon had built. It would have been enough on its own to do serious damage, but it would turn out to be just a portion of a massive maelstrom of disaster for the company. Much of the unsavory stuff that had been swept under the rug for years would finally be brought out into the sun for everyone—most notably the paying public—to see. Gino was about to see the business he loved dragged through the mud like never before and the man to whom he'd given all his loyalty, despite loads of misgivings, at the center of it all.

CHAPTER 14

CHANGING TIMES, CHANGING ROLES

"Tonight, you flatter and honor me at this induction ceremony, and I appreciate it from the bottom of my heart. Because this is the pinnacle of my career, no question about it."

Despite the adage Gino would often repeat to his colleagues—"If you're not in this business for the money, you're a fool"—the fact was that Gino did indeed love the business very much and greatly enjoyed being a part of it. It was fun. But as the final decade of his life, the 1990s, rolled on, it was becoming less and less fun. There were many reasons for this. The company to which he had pledged his undying loyalty would become awash in ugly scandal. The glory days of the national expansion, when it seemed like they had a license to print money, would end, leading to a steep decline in Titan Sports' fortunes for the very first time. In other words, the financial gains, which had been the greatest incentive for Gino to go along with the sale of his shares in the first place, were not what they used to be. He'd been able to rationalize the dramatic changes happening to the business he loved, because at least it was making money. But now that wasn't even the case anymore, not to the degree it once had been. And this caused him to pay closer attention to his own personal displeasure at the direction the business was taking. On top of all this, there was his steadily deteriorating health, against which he struggled mightily as he sought to continue to be a contributing part of the team, even as his passion for the business slowly ebbed, along with his willpower to continue.

He would see his role diminished over time, as he was finally and gradually phased out of his broadcast spots in order to make way for new and younger faces. He'd lose his favorite broadcast partner and best friend, Bobby Heenan, to the competition. But the greatest loss of all would come in the most unspeakable tragedy he would ever endure, the untimely death of his beloved son, Joseph, only just coming into the prime of his life. It would be a blow from which he would never recover, casting a permanent shadow over his personal life and professional career. Whatever remaining spark he had for living and for the business was all but extinguished on July 4, 1994, along with Joey, as his greatest fear turned to stark reality.

And yet, it would also be a time when the company would honor him as one of its very first Hall of Famers. He would be appointed to the figurehead role of WWF president, a seeming nod to all he had contributed to the company over the years, and ascend to the firmament of all-time wrestling legends, even as his spirits sank into the depths of private despair. The more the decade rolled on, the more the business would change, going to places that he wasn't sure if even he could follow. But whether he could or not, it would eventually be his body that would make the decision for him. Because even a heart as big as Gino's couldn't hold out forever.

■

On the one hand, it looked as if the company was more prosperous than ever, especially when in May 1991, having outgrown the cramped downtown location on Summer Street, Titan Sports moved to the outskirts of Stamford into a four-floor gleaming cube of glass and steel at 1241

East Main Street that would come to be known as Titan Tower. There was no denying that things had come an astronomically long way from the shady Holland Hotel days. But still, looks were a bit deceiving. The summer 1991 trial of Dr. George Zahorian was one of the first big signs that there was trouble ahead for Titan, as it was only a matter of time before the domino trail led to Stamford. Sensing danger, and responding to the new classification of anabolic steroids as controlled substances, the company enacted its first steroid-testing policy, which was clearly more of a token gesture than anything else, given the gargantuan appearance that still characterized most top WWF stars, with the now "Immortal" Hulk Hogan, then in his third reign as WWF world champion, right at the very top of the food chain. It would take a good year and a half before the feds finally came knocking at Vince McMahon's door. It was an odd situation, to be sure, as the general public had assumed that most top professional wrestlers were on the gas for years anyway, and it had been an open secret within the company for at least a decade. Still, it was a problem that had the power to potentially shut Titan Sports' doors for good.

But even worse than that for the company's public image was what happened in early 1992, when the far darker secret of rampant sexual harassment and assault finally came to light thanks to Tom Cole, a former ringside attendant who came forward with his story. Others would follow suit with either personal stories or things they allegedly witnessed, including jilted former world champion Superstar Billy Graham, implicating several—including Vince's right-hand man Pat Patterson, but especially Terry Garvin and Mel Phillips, whose patterns of systematic abuse were shocking, particularly to a rather innocent early '90s fan base and general public that was decidedly unused to and unaware of the more unsavory aspects of pro wrestling's seedy underbelly.

Combined with the steroid debacle, it formed a formidable two-headed monster of scandal that threatened to swallow the World Wrestling Federation whole.

It was a tough time for anyone to be publicly associated with the company, especially someone with as sterling a reputation and as intact a moral compass as Gino possessed. Although he kept his mouth shut publicly, and didn't go the route of walking away from the company that his longtime friend Bruno Sammartino had taken, Gino was privately quite distressed and repulsed by the whole thing. "I'd say [his personal view on it] was the same as Bruno," opines Bret Hart. "I think he was disgusted and unhappy with some of the direction it was going in a lot of ways. But I think he was also very careful how he approached that. All that had started happening just when my big run was also happening."

In fact, the big singles push of Bret Hart that began around the same time was a major example of the company's desire to move in a different direction, as far as public perception. Gino had long touted Bret behind the scenes, as well as on commentary, as the highly skilled performer that he was, more than worthy of a major push and the attention of fans. He had seen Bret as someone the company should get behind, long before even Vince did. He worked a very different style from the typical WWF headliner—crisper, more athletic and grounded in old-school psychology. And although by no means a lightweight, he was a bit smaller than the Hulk Hogans and Ultimate Warriors that fans had gotten used to at the top of the card—in other words, he appeared to have a physique that was less alarmingly dependent on chemical enhancement. He was an excellent choice of someone to put on a pedestal at a time when the company was trying to get people's minds off steroids.

■

And so, after nearly seven years of Gorilla Monsoon singing his praises on television, the "Excellence of Execution" was started on his ascent up the card at the end of the summer of 1991. The Hart Foundation tag team had been broken up, and he'd been moved away from his more volatile and unreliable brother-in-law, Jim "The Anvil" Neidhart. At *SummerSlam '91* in Madison Square Garden, with Gorilla calling the action alongside Bobby Heenan and Roddy Piper, Bret defeated "Mr. Perfect" Curt Hennig in an instant classic to win the Intercontinental championship, his first singles title in the WWF. "That was a big part of the concerted effort to really get me over," Bret remembers. "And I did my best. Gorilla Monsoon was a big part of all of that, and I never forgot him for that." Monsoon had already set up the backstory and would continue to do so. Over the years, fans had learned about Bret's background thanks to his commentary. Thanks to him, the fans knew about the Hart family. About Stu Hart. About the infamous Dungeon in Calgary. Even about Bret's other brother-in-law, "The British Bulldog" Davey Boy Smith. "All of that had come out, thanks to the crumbs that Gorilla started from the beginning, giving people a curiosity about who I was. He said little things about me to keep my character alive when I was really just dying on the vine."

But the Hitman's days of "dying on the vine" were behind him, and Gino couldn't have been happier. At the following year's *SummerSlam*, live from London's Wembley Stadium in front of 78,927 fans—the largest verifiable crowd in company history up to that point—he and Smith would take part in the main event, this time with Hart losing the Intercontinental title to his brother-in-law in another classic. Unlike in 1991 however, it would be Vince McMahon calling the action with Bobby Heenan. Gino would not be present for that moment, due most likely in part to his health and a hesitance to do too much heavy traveling, especially since he had just flown over to the United Kingdom for two major WWF supershows, the *Battle Royal at the Albert Hall* in October 1991 and *UK Rampage* in April 1992[1]—with the latter being one of the only times he had ever had to be away from his family on Easter Sunday. However, Gino's son, Joey, did get to be a part of it, as he was given the important task of refereeing the Hitman/Bulldog encounter, just as he had for the Hogan/André match at *WrestleMania III* some five years earlier. "Joey was such a big part of the match," explains Bret. "He helped me talk to Davey all the way through it."

Bret continued to climb up the card, bouncing back from the Intercontinental title loss when, just two months later, he got the nod from Vince. They were putting the world title on him. The title by that time was in the unlikely possession of Ric Flair, the man who had literally embodied Jim Crockett Promotions and WCW, the greatest rival company to the WWF, for as long as McMahon had been waging his promotional wars. But just like nearly everyone else, he had come over in the end to kiss Vince's ring and was in the midst of his second reign as WWF world champion when Bret Hart scored a shocking win over him at, of all places, a television taping in Saskatoon, Saskatchewan. A serious inner ear ailment that had stricken Flair, plus McMahon's desire to crown a new face of the company who was the antithesis of Hulk Hogan, had led the WWF chairman to abruptly pull the trigger. It was a vindication of what Gino had been saying all along and what Vince had finally come around to—Bret Hart was a champion the company could be proud of.

■

And speaking of Ric Flair, it had been the Nature Boy's own anointment as WWF world champion earlier that year that had afforded Gorilla Monsoon and Bobby "The Brain" Heenan what is often regarded as quite literally their finest hour as a commentary team. The world title had been vacated, with the winner to be decided by the thirty-man over-the-top-rope match to be held as part of the 1992 *Royal Rumble* pay-per-view at the Knickerbocker Arena in Albany, New York. By that point, nagging neck injuries had forced Bobby to largely step away from ringside managing and focus mainly on commentating, but he had still been affiliated with Flair on WWF television and was rooting for him from the sidelines. That was the case in Albany, where Flair had been slotted as the third entrant out of the thirty-man field, forcing him to last one full hour before winning the match and staking his claim of becoming only the second man to hold both the NWA and WWF world championships, following none other than the original Nature Boy, Buddy Rogers.

The chemistry between Gorilla and Bobby was always off the charts, but it was especially so on that night. A nerve-wracked Brain could be heard shamelessly cheering his man on, agonizing over every setback, exulting in every advantage, anxiously insisting that everything must be "fair to Flair." And all the while, Monsoon was his perfect foil, seeming to take genuine pleasure in his broadcast partner's anxiety, criticizing his bold-faced support for the Nature Boy, while at the same time being forced to concede that Flair was doing something especially impressive by lasting the full hour, going through old foe after old foe, on his way to the ultimate victory, which he famously claimed "with a tear in his eye." It was the classic example of how the two old pros fed into each other and off each other. They never telephoned in a performance, but on that night in Albany, long-considered the greatest Royal Rumble match of all time, they really brought their A+ game. It was an all-time classic call.

Royal Rumble '92 was the pinnacle of the Monsoon/Heenan partnership, and it was also the peak of a unique streak that the two men enjoyed through 1991 and 1992. From *WrestleMania VII* through *WrestleMania VIII*, they would call six consecutive WWF pay-per-view events, which in addition to *SummerSlam '91* and *Royal Rumble* also included the 1991 *Survivor Series* and the one-shot special, *This Tuesday in Texas*. It was a feat that not even the Monsoon/Ventura team had achieved and established Gorilla Monsoon and Bobby Heenan, at least for a relatively brief window of time, as the new bona fide voices of the World Wrestling Federation on pay-per-view.

■

However, *WrestleMania VIII* would turn out to be not only Gorilla and Bobby's last *WrestleMania* together but also the final *WrestleMania* to feature Gorilla on television commentary at all, ending his perfect run as the voice of the annual franchise in its infancy years. Changes were coming. For one thing, Gino's original ten-year contract, which had been signed when the Capitol Wrestling Corporation had been sold, was coming up by the summer of 1992, which might have also been a contributing factor as to why he was not present for *SummerSlam* in Wembley that year. There was never a doubt that he would be continuing on with the company, but his role and position were temporarily at least in flux as his new deal was worked out. While Gorilla and Bobby continued together on the weekly *Wrestling Challenge*, at least for the moment, it would be Vince once again who joined Bobby in November for *Survivor Series '92*, the next pay-per-view after *SummerSlam*. Although he called the action each week on *WWF Superstars*, in those days, it was unusual for Vince himself to be calling the matches on pay-per-view, as he was typically focused on running the shows with an iron fist—another role he'd taken over from Gino long ago.

For some time, Vince had had the notion of finding a full-time replacement for Gorilla Monsoon, and that impetus had only increased as Gino's health had begun to falter. For the next *Royal Rumble* event at the start of 1993, Gorilla and Bobby would be once again reunited on pay-per-view, but it was only a stop-gap measure. As it would turn out, that event would be the last pay-per-view spectacular that the legendary duo would ever call together.[2]

As Gino got a little older, approaching sixty and with his health getting shakier, he'd rely more and more on Tom Carlucci, the WWF television producer who'd grow to become many things to him—a driver when needed, a runner, a confidant, a great friend, and a fellow ballbuster he immediately clicked with. Ironically, Tom had remembered Gorilla Monsoon from his days as the fearsome Manchurian Giant in the late 1960s, back when his dad had taken him at the age of seven to the Crystal Ice Rink in Norwalk, Connecticut, where he got to see Gorilla in the main event from a front-row seat. In those days, he hated and feared him and could hardly ever imagine that one day, many years later, he'd be riding around with him. When he first came to work for Titan Sports in 1988 in his late twenties, he'd been in the shipping department and remembered Gino pulling up to the warehouse in his black Cadillac Coupe de Ville with the K-FABE license plate, just the nicest guy in the world, always making time to chat with the guys filling the boxes. Just a couple of years later, Tom would make his way to the international television department, which really began their friendship and close working relationship in earnest.

Being close to Gino had its advantages, such as when he took Tom and his new bride, Michele, for a weekend at Caesars Atlantic City. Tom had invited Gino to his wedding, and when he couldn't make it, this was how he'd decided to make it up to them. Much of the time was spent hanging with Gino in the high rollers room, where he'd gotten himself into a $50,000 blackjack tournament, which he nearly won. He offered to take them to any restaurant they wanted, which turned out to be the Japanese steakhouse. They met up there with Gino at six o'clock sharp. There was a line to get in a mile long.

"Gino, we ain't getting in here."

"Tommy, watch."

Gino went over and approached the maître d'.

"Oh, Mr. M.! Yes, your table's right over here."

Needless to say, Tom was flabbergasted. But he shouldn't have been.

■

You wouldn't know it by Gino's wheeling and dealing in Atlantic City, but the early '90s was a period of some belt-tightening in the organization. There was a lot of attention on the company—and not the good kind. In damage-control mode, Vince had been making the rounds on TV talk shows like *Donahue* and *Larry King Live* to defend his company against the sexual abuse allegations, even locking horns publicly with the man who had once been his family's bread and butter and was now its harshest critic, Bruno Sammartino. It was very telling that Gino, who had long been put into action as the company's eloquent public relations champion and defender, even appearing with Vince and Linda back when they were battling to free themselves from the state athletic commissions, was now nowhere to be found. Even for a loyal soldier like Gino, that would've been asking a lot. So when McMahon put himself out there this time, he did so alone.

And things would only worsen, as in November 1993, the chickens finally came home to roost when McMahon and Titan Sports were indicted in a Brooklyn court on federal charges of conspiracy to distribute anabolic steroids. The feds had flipped Dr. George Zahorian, who had been convicted of steroid distribution two years earlier and subsequently helped prosecutors build their case against McMahon, while being listed as a cooperating, unindicted co-conspirator. "Gino stood tight with Vince, even when they were threatening to close our doors," remembers Tom. "We didn't get raises for four years when they wanted to shut us down."

As close as he remained behind the scenes, and although he was still a part of the show, by the time of the indictment, Gino had receded further from the spotlight than ever, and his professional career was in a very different place than it had been even a year earlier. During 1993, sweeping changes would take place. The first of these occurred with the cancelation of *Prime Time Wrestling*. By this point, it had been transformed into a roundtable discussion format, led by Vince McMahon with a host of guests, which would occasionally include Gorilla Monsoon but more often included Bobby Heenan. In a nod to his importance in establishing the show, Monsoon made a surprise appearance on the second-to-last episode for the symbolic task of taking down the *Prime Time* set for the last time. For the final episode on January 4, 1993, Vince McMahon was joined on an empty set by both Gorilla and the Brain, the two men who had created the show's greatest moments, for a look back at the show's history. It was an acknowledgment of their contributions, which even then had to be recognized as the period for which the show would be best remembered. But the show had run its course.

Replacing *Prime Time Wrestling* the following week in the Monday night time slot on the USA Network would be a very different kind of show for the WWF, one that would signal the way toward the future of its television product. In an attempt to begin breaking away from the standard canned format of marathon tapings recorded weeks in advance, not to mention in response to the steadily dwindling crowds at those tapings in major venues, *Monday Night Raw* would be typically broadcast live—completely unprecedented for the WWF's weekly television at the time—or recorded a mere week in advance. For its initial nine months, its home would be the intimate and historic Manhattan Center in New York City, an ornate Edwardian-era ballroom that seated only about three thousand and was something of a throwback to the Allentown and Hamburg days. It was pitched as the antithesis of the stodgy *Prime Time Wrestling* and other traditional WWF shows, an event where anything could happen and usually did.

And Gorilla Monsoon, who perhaps embodied the old-style television more than anyone, would be nowhere in sight. The comforting presence of the fatherly Monsoon was replaced by a barking and strutting Vince McMahon, accompanied by the intense color-explosion of Randy "Macho Man" Savage and fast-talking stand-up comic and *Imus in the Morning* radio personality Rob Bartlett, who'd been added to give the show a hip, edgy vibe, but came off as if he'd rather be on the 1:30 a.m. show at the Comedy Cellar than calling professional wrestling. After a few months, he'd be replaced by the funnier and better-informed standby Bobby Heenan. But other than rare appearances such as the March 15 episode, when Gorilla hosted the show alongside Heenan and Bartlett after a blizzard prevented McMahon and Savage from being there, Monsoon was kept away from the new program. Gino's discomfort while attempting to interact with Bartlett, who was doing an impression of the absent Vince for the entire show, only underlined how out of place he was in the new format.

■

With *WrestleMania IX* rolling around, Vince McMahon was finally looking to begin the true phase-out of Gorilla Monsoon from the WWF broadcast team. With Gino approaching his fifty-sixth birthday, and a decade on the mic and health issues creeping in, Vince felt it was time. And as long as they found him something to do, Gino didn't particularly object. He'd be paid either way, and the way he saw it, it was less work for him. Although there had been attempts to take him off the air in the past, this one would more or less stick.

Ironically, the man who was positioned to replace Gorilla Monsoon, lead WCW announcer Jim Ross, was in the midst of being phased out himself in favor of Tony Schiavone, who had returned to WCW after an abandoned attempt to have *him* be Monsoon's replacement. Ross had been launched in his announcing career by Gino's old travel buddy Cowboy

Bill Watts years earlier in the heyday of Watts's Mid-South Wrestling. He had been in a great political position when Watts was brought in to run WCW's wrestling operations in 1992—but Watts's abrupt ousting early the following year after making controversial, racially charged comments to a wrestling newsletter had left Ross exposed. Watts's replacement as WCW executive producer, Eric Bischoff, who'd been working his way up from being an on-air talent himself, favored reducing Ross's screen time. The writing was on the wall, and Ross opened a dialogue with Bruce Prichard, who brought his name to Vince McMahon as a possible new voice for the company.

With the demeanor of a mainstream sportscaster, a down-home sensibility and delivery honed in his beloved Oklahoma and an encyclopedic knowledge of wrestlers' athletic backgrounds, Jim Ross was a sharp departure from the commentators that had typically populated WWF broadcasts in the past. But although there would be significant bumps in the road, he represented the future of the company and would become just as much of a fixture of the company's television in years to come as Gorilla Monsoon had been in years past. "Gino's health was really not good at that time, so he was looking to be on the road less," explained Prichard in a 2019 episode of his podcast, *Something to Wrestle With*. "He couldn't drive at night anymore; he would stay over wherever he was. Commutes were more laborious for him. So he was relieved when J.R. came in. He felt, OK, Vince has somebody that can fill that spot, and I can relax a little bit now."

The first weekend of April 1993 represented a changing of the guard, with Gorilla Monsoon stepping away from both *Wrestling Challenge* and *WrestleMania* simultaneously. The March 28 episode of *Challenge* was the last time Monsoon and Heenan would sit beside each other in the broadcast booth. Next week's episode, aired the morning of *WrestleMania* Sunday, featured the two of them hosting the show from outside Caesars Palace in Las Vegas. Meanwhile, the matches were called in the studio by McMahon, Savage and the WWF's newest heel color commentator, Jerry "The King" Lawler, who'd been brought in as part of the company's new working relationship with the Memphis-based USWA, the last of the old-school wrestling territories left standing. It never took a lot to convince Gino to go to Vegas, but those wraparound segments would represent the final time he and Bobby would appear on *Wrestling Challenge* together.

Gino was in town for *WrestleMania* as always, of course, but not in the capacity that fans expected. When the show opened, Gorilla Monsoon was there, dressed in a resplendent toga and golden laurels in conjunction with the event's ancient Roman theme, welcoming viewers to the show as he always had. But then he said something unexpected: "There'll be a lot of firsts here at *WrestleMania IX*, and here's one of them—the latest addition to the WWF broadcast team, Jim Ross!" From there, Monsoon threw it to Jim at ringside, making his surprise first appearance in a toga as well. It was as literal and direct a passing of the broadcast torch as could possibly be envisioned.

Jim would be joined by Gorilla's now-former partner Bobby Heenan (making his way to ringside riding backward on a camel, of all things), along with Randy Savage. Meanwhile, Gorilla stayed in the back, conducting backstage interviews and hosting interstitial segments, but most of the time settling into his comfortable old spot at the Gorilla position, sitting next to Bruce Prichard, who had largely assumed much of the Gorilla position duties by that point. It was a full-circle moment and the first time Gino had ever been afforded the opportunity to man the position for the company's biggest show of the year.

The following weekend's episode of *Wrestling Challenge* would see Ross take over Monsoon's customary spot alongside Bobby Heenan. For the first time in eight years, Gorilla Monsoon was not in any regular, weekly broadcasting spot on WWF television. The transition was complete, and although even Jim himself would admit that there was no way anyone could replicate the chemistry of Gorilla and Bobby, the time had come for something new and different. Gino would still come into the TV studio every few weeks to record various segments for syndicated programming, as well as work with the new broadcast talent, which in addition to Ross included Todd Pettengill, the peppy New York City radio personality who'd been brought in to host *WWF Mania*, a new, more kid-oriented Saturday morning program. Plus, there was the added bonus of jaunting over to Kevin Dunn's office to get in on all the latest football action (an activity which didn't slow down in the least later in the year, once Kevin was finally put in charge of all television production, replacing Nelson Sweglar). It kept him involved, and he still enjoyed being a part of things. And now and then, when they still needed him in a pinch, he would come off the bench. To him, it was a winding down, a precursor to eventually going home to his family for the retirement he had most richly earned. Sharon and Michael had just given him a second grandchild, Kevin, and that family life was more rewarding than ever.

Like many, Jim Ross came to look at Gino as a father figure. For one thing, not everyone was as welcoming to the Okie, who was, to some, a literal embodiment of the competition. Ross had done his job so well in WCW that several among both the talent and production crew didn't immediately like or trust him. Unfortunately, this even extended to fellow broadcasters like Lord Alfred Hayes and Randy Savage, as well as important backstage figures like Chief Jay Strongbow, who likely viewed Jim as something of a mole in much the same way he'd looked askance at Jerry Brisco. But Gino didn't see it that way. He saw a man who respected the business and who had paid his dues over the course of nearly twenty years in it—not to mention being a protégé of Bill Watts, which no doubt carried weight with him. Gino felt that Jim had earned respect and made that clear to everyone else as well. Before long, everyone started to come around to Gino's way of thinking, and Jim would eventually become a welcome member of the television production family. Having Gorilla Monsoon in your corner went a long way.

■

And yet, ironically, it was Vince McMahon who remained unconvinced about Jim in the beginning. Although Jim had taken the traditional "Gorilla Monsoon spot" alongside Heenan and Savage for *WrestleMania IX* and the inaugural *King of the Ring* pay-per-view two months later, Vince seemed to lose confidence in his new lead announcer in record time, opting instead to take over the spot himself, with Jerry Lawler as his new regular foil. Jim wouldn't get another chance to call a WWF pay-per-view on television for over two years and didn't fully rejoin the team for three. The mid-'90s would be a rocky road in the company for Jim, although Gino never left his corner. In fact, they were teamed together for a new venture that was comparatively low-pressure: *Radio WWF*. Carried in syndication by an admittedly anemic number of radio stations, the service featured Ross as the host, with Monsoon as regular co-host for the first month, returning to the booth to call the big shows on radio with Jim, starting with *SummerSlam '93*.

Their next radio assignment together, *Survivor Series '93* in November, would be a momentous one, however, since it would be the final pay-per-view event called by Bobby "The Brain" Heenan. That night, Vince and Bobby would trade places with radio announcers Jim and Gorilla for one match, with Gorilla and Bobby reigniting their onscreen animosity once more for a brief moment as they crossed paths during the transition. Though played for laughs, it was intended to be foreshadowing, as growing "enmity" between the two real-life friends had even been played up on WWF television for a few weeks earlier. In fact, they had the chance to clown around together one last time on the November 6 edition of *Wrestling Spotlight*, a syndicated highlight show hosted by Monsoon, for a memorable yet almost-forgotten episode in which Gorilla catches the Brain rummaging through the WWF's TV studio and proceeds to gleefully torture him for the remainder of the show. It was all part of a plan that Bobby himself had come up with. Bobby was leaving the WWF. But he wanted to do it in the most memorable way possible.

As part of the tumultuous year of 1993, major shakeups were afoot. Vince was making conscious moves to distance himself from the company's 1980s heyday. Part of that was thanks to the associations with rampant steroid abuse, which led to Hulk Hogan finally parting ways with the company that summer after an epic nine-year run that had started out with him able to do no wrong and had ended with him as an albatross and liability for the company. But there was also Vince's desperate desire to always look to the future and his tendency to view the past as hopelessly outdated and old-fashioned almost as soon as it was in his rear-view mirror. Unfortunately, many of the old-school personalities who had become the faces of the company in the earlier era fell under that category. By the end of the summer, that included Mean Gene Okerlund, who immediately jumped to WCW, where his deep association with the WWF was seen as a positive by Eric Bischoff, whose strategy for overtaking the weakened WWF seemed to be to replicate it.

Naturally, Gino was completely safe from such housekeeping measures. But Bobby was not. In a move no doubt implemented to try and get him to quit, Vince offered to renew his contract with a 50 percent pay cut. Of course, this produced the precise outcome that Vince was looking for. Besides, as part of Turner Broadcasting, WCW offered deluxe employee benefits, including the kind of health insurance Bobby had never had and which he intended to use in order to deal with his largely untreated neck issues, as well as for his teenage daughter, Jessica. It was an easy decision to make from a business standpoint—but not from a personal one. Bobby loved being a part of the World Wrestling Federation and wished deep down that he didn't have to leave. Most of all, he loved working with, spending time with and traveling with Gino. To him, that association represented the pinnacle of his work for the company. And that's why when it came time for him to check out, it was important to him that Gino be part of it.

Vince had already more or less lined up a replacement for Bobby in the form of Jim Cornette, as the WWF's newest brash, loudmouth manager and overall heel heat magnet. Jim, the tennis-racket-wielding patron saint of the blue light special, also happened to be the owner and proprietor of Smoky Mountain Wrestling, the Tennessee-based independent that had just entered into a talent exchange program with the WWF. Bobby himself introduced him on *Monday Night Raw* in a memorable torch-passing segment, and Jim had gotten a brief opportunity over the next few months to spend time around one of his true idols in the business. "Bobby used to rave about Monsoon to me," remembers Jim. "They loved each other."

The November 29 *Monday Night Raw* tapings at the Westchester County Center in White Plains—a vintage Capitol Wrestling venue for the past thirty-five years and still Arnie Skaaland's building—was to be Bobby's last night in the company. When Vince afforded him the chance to decide how he wanted to go out, it was an easy decision: He wanted Gorilla Monsoon to throw him out. And so, during the broadcast, the seeds were planted. As Vince and Bobby called the action for the second half of the tapings that would encompass the December 6 episode, Bobby badmouthed Gorilla on-air, secure in his foolhardy confidence that Gorilla was far away in his New Jersey home. But of course, Gorilla was there. He was always there. And finally, at just the right moment, Gorilla Monsoon emerged from the curtain and stormed down to ringside to confront a shocked and dismayed Bobby Heenan, much to the amusement of a gloating Vince McMahon.

If you watch very closely, there are real tears welling up in the eyes of Bobby Heenan during the unforgettable segment, as Gino grabs him bodily and drags him away from the broadcast position, informing him that he's opened his big mouth for the last time and that he intends to take no more of it. The crowd erupts, and Bobby falls to his knees to beg, but Gorilla is having none of it. He drags the pleading Brain all the way to the back, where his purported belongings are apparently waiting for him. Gino kicks the back door of the arena open, tosses out Bobby's bags, and then tosses out Bobby himself, slamming the door behind him as the Brain flails around frantically, stolen hotel towels, plastic utensils and toilet paper spilling out of his bag and onto the street. Bobby offers one last farewell salute as the show goes to commercial. It's comical in the best Bobby Heenan way possible. But there's also real pathos and heartbreak here. An era is ending.

"Dad's the one that came up with that exit," confirms Jessica. "He insisted on it being Gino throwing him out. It had to be Gino. And it was very hard to shoot and very hard to watch—for us, for Maureen, even for the two of them when they went back and watched it. It was very symbolic, and it meant a lot. Dad wanted to make sure that he went out as best he could. And he wanted to get Gino over one last time."

Although Bobby could be heard during the segment pleading for anyone to give him a ride back to LaGuardia Airport, in reality, it would be Gino who'd give him that ride. The two men rode back to the airport hotel together that night and rode up the elevator together to the same floor, where both of their rooms were located. The doors opened, they both got out, and Bobby looked at Gino:

"Well, I guess this is it."

They parted ways and went to their respective rooms. Once there, Bobby noticed a fruit basket waiting for him. It was the perfect excuse. He got on the phone and called Gino's room.

"Hey, ya big ape. I got bananas over here. Why don't you come down?"

Gino came down the hall, and Bobby was waiting for him—with the bananas, of course. The two men wound up sitting in that hall for close to an hour. Crying together. Looking back on their incredible run and the fun times they'd had. Knowing it was now over.[3] The fans had always thought they hated each other—and they'd certainly just given them one more big reinforcement of that. But the truth was, they loved each other. And their separation meant that there was going to be a whole lot less to look forward to going into work each day, for both of them.

Gino knew that Bobby was headed to WCW, the enemy. Ordinarily, that would've meant communication and fraternization would be forbidden going forward. But not for Gino and Bobby. No one was going to tell either of them that they couldn't talk to each other anymore. That they couldn't be friends anymore. And Gino would be damned before he'd have to give up another dear friend the way he'd had to break off ties with Bruno. And so they made it a point to continue to speak on the phone with each other each week. To visit each other whenever they were in the same area. And to continue their tradition of family vacations together. Neither Vince McMahon nor Eric Bischoff had the power to stop that, nor would either of them have dared. It was a friendship that was bigger than the business.

The departure of Bobby Heenan meant that Gino was pressed into duty for the time being, temporarily replacing him on *Wrestling Challenge* alongside Jim Ross—only this time, he happily got to enjoy the more laid-back color commentary position while Jim did the heavy lifting on play-by-play. Even though they only initially worked two months together on *Challenge*, during those two months, Jim could see the fatigue that was setting in with Gino and some of his frustrations with the product at the time. In later years, he would recall Gino during some of those pretape voice-over sessions getting so annoyed and worked up about guys lazily phoning it in or doing things that didn't make sense to him during matches they were calling together. Jim would take him outside for a cigarette break behind the studio, just to settle him down and get him into a better headspace to do their job.

But Gino abruptly found himself with a new partner on *Wrestling Challenge* at the start of 1994, as Jim Ross was fired by Vince McMahon, just two weeks after suffering the first of what would be several attacks of Bell's palsy, a disorder that left his face partially paralyzed. Ordinarily, that would be the kiss of death for a television broadcaster, but Jim's talent and value to the business were such that he'd be back, eventually. For the time being, Gino was joined on the *Challenge* call by Stan Lane, a longtime friend and associate of Jim Cornette, not to mention one half of Cornette's two great tag teams, the Midnight Express and the Heavenly Bodies. Lane had come in as part of the working relationship with Smoky Mountain, having just retired from the ring and looking to transition into announcing. Gino remained with Stan for two months before another legendary veteran in much the same boat as Stan, Ted DiBiase, stepped in to join Stan and finally relieve Gino of what had always been a short-term measure anyway.

■

Perhaps it was Gino's obvious boredom and discomfort with the WWF product, in addition to some feelings of uselessness, that led him to take a shot at something quite different, which turned out to be one of the most bizarre and unexpected episodes of his career: *Bingo Break*.

After nearly a decade and a half of dealing with the whims and demands of Vince McMahon, not to mention the general lack of professional recognition that went along with it, Nelson Sweglar had departed his position as the executive in charge of television production at Titan Sports, ceding the spot to the keenly hungry and ambitious Kevin Dunn. He'd left Stamford and gone back to his native Baltimore, where he got it into his head to produce a new television series that would combine the daytime talk show craze with interactive gaming—specifically the game of bingo, which was and is a great cultural passion in the Baltimore area especially. Sinking a quarter of a million of his own money into it, he got the show lined up on WBFF FOX45 in Baltimore, where it would get a pilot run for three months, running a half hour every weekday morning before hopefully getting picked up for national distribution on the FOX Network.

Right away, Nelson had Gino in mind to host the show. "He had a good feel," Nelson remembers from his years working with him. "Nobody had to script anything for him. He knew what needed to be covered and how to cover it so that audiences at home saw what looked like a tightly prepared commentary." After checking with Vince, who had no problem with it and was likely pleased for Gino to have something to keep him occupied, he agreed. For the first time in a public forum, at least since turning to professional wrestling, he'd be using his actual given name, Bob Marella. "Gorilla Monsoon was a character," Sweglar rationalized. "Developed and staged for wrestling. Since this was *Bingo Break*, why not use his real name?"

The show was shot in a studio in Baltimore, set up in the typical style of *Sally Jessy Raphael, Live with Regis and Kathie Lee* or any other of the myriad shows of the type in production then. Gino was joined at the host's couch and coffee table by Caron Tate, a largely unknown actress and writer who'd just come off shooting, of all things, an episode of *Homicide: Life on the Street* alongside Robin Williams and a young Jake Gyllenhaal. There would be a variety of guests, including magicians, psychics and offbeat musicians, and even their own house band, a jazz quintet called the Dave Smith Five. True to its name, bingo numbers would be called out over the air, with viewers able to pick up the cards at local supermarkets and other businesses in order to play along at home and potentially win prizes. And the Bingo Master calling the numbers would be none other than Gino's old broadcast colleague Sean Mooney, who had himself moved on from the WWF some nine months prior.

In short, it was exactly as eccentric, odd and awkward as it sounds. Some of the comedy bits and other ideas were even lifted wholesale from *Prime Time Wrestling* and *TNT*. And as genial, welcoming and natural as Gino was, this would have been a tall order for anyone to pull off. However, the one great thing that did come out of *Bingo Break*, its one outstanding claim to fame, is that it featured the last onscreen appearance of Gino and Bobby Heenan working together. By early 1994, Bobby was already coming to regret his decision to go to WCW. Right off the bat, he'd been disappointed by the vast differences between his past employer and his current one: the lack of a cohesive operational structure, the utter chaos behind the scenes and what he perceived as an overall lack of professionalism. It was, as he'd later explain to the author, "like going from the major leagues to T-ball." When Nelson called him to see if he'd want to reunite with his old buddy for one day of taping in Baltimore as a guest on *Bingo Break*, Bobby jumped at the opportunity.

And so, there they were, for the April 1 episode, appropriately enough—a contracted WWF commentator and a contracted WCW commentator, sharing the same space on television, where all the chemistry and magic came back in a rush for one moment in time.[4] Although only seen on local television, it would be their final appearance together publicly. After it was done and Bobby got to share the spotlight one last time with his perfect straight man, he was back on a plane to Atlanta to continue locking horns with Tony Schiavone and Eric Bischoff. As for the entire *Bingo Break* experiment, needless to say, there would be no national pick-up, and the show would cease production after the April 15 episode. It was a brief chance for Gino to spread his wings a little bit, but now it was time to go back to what he knew best.

■

If he needed any reminder of just how perfect his combination with Heenan had been, it was his newest WWF broadcasting assignment, which began while he was also working on *Bingo Break*. Immediately after being replaced by Ted DiBiase on *Wrestling Challenge*, Gino was switched over to that old USA Network stalwart, *All-American Wrestling*, now in its dying days as a recap show. Following the departures of both Gene Okerlund and Bobby Heenan, Vince McMahon had been hosting the show himself, a duty he was more than happy to hand off to Gorilla Monsoon starting with the March 20 edition, broadcast remotely from the Madison Square Garden rotunda just prior to *WrestleMania X*, being presented there later that day. In fact, Gorilla would actually be seated ringside for that tenth-anniversary edition of the company's flagship show, back at the arena where it had started, calling the action with popular sportscaster and talk radio personality Chet Coppock for *Radio WWF*. Although the broadcast has not been heard or released since it first happened in 1994, that was the final time Gorilla Monsoon would call a *WrestleMania* in any form.

The following week, Monsoon was in the Stamford TV studio for *All-American Wrestling*, only this time joined by his new regular co-host Scott Levy, better known then as Johnny Polo. Although a fine wrestler in his own right, Levy had been brought in as a manager and had a natural onscreen presence and flair for comedy. The son of an accomplished journalist, and a college graduate with a stint in the Marines reserve under his belt, he was in the process of transitioning into a TV producer role when he was paired up with Gino. Right away, it seemed clear that they were trying to replicate the Monsoon/Heenan formula, with Polo as a younger, hipper stand-in for the Brain. They shot segments going bowling, playing golf and engaging in other shenanigans, but it was a far cry from the classic *Prime Time Wrestling* days of old. And the chemistry never quite gelled. "Gino would break balls a lot when he was with Johnny Polo," remembers Tom Carlucci, who produced the show. "He used to bust Johnny's balls about his hair, his clothes, everything, even when they were on camera. Johnny would call for us to cut, and Gino would go, 'What's wrong? I'm only making fun of his hair.' He would constantly do that. It wasn't going the way it was supposed to go."

It just wasn't the same. How could it be?

Polo was a part of what was being branded as the "New Generation" of the World Wrestling Federation, a movement to get away from the Hulkamania era of the company in favor of younger (and in some cases more natural-looking) talent. This was a result not only of the still-ongoing steroid trial but also because Hogan and others who had been faces of the WWF's national expansion of the 1980s were now migrating toward WCW as a full-scale war between the two companies was brewing. Benefiting from this new youth movement were wrestlers such as former tag team specialist Shawn Michaels, the Tony Montana–inspired Razor Ramon (aka Scott Hall) and most notably Bret Hart. In fact, *WrestleMania X* had been something of an official coronation of Hart as the definitive new face of the company, as he emerged at the end of the night once again the reigning WWF world champion. As the show closed, the ring had filled with jubilant wrestlers and other supporters of the Hitman, and included in that group was Gorilla Monsoon, who had left his spot at ringside to celebrate and give his blessing to the man he'd first met when he was just a little boy at the Hart home in Calgary.

The New Generation theme even extended to the McMahon family itself, with the occasion of *WrestleMania X* representing the official "coming of age" of Shane McMahon, Vince's twenty-four-year-old son, who had just gotten his communications degree from Boston University. In years past, Shane had done it all, from working in the warehouse to refereeing, but would now be an official part of the company's corporate structure, learning the ropes from his dad, as Vince had learned from his own father. Gino had always been fond of Shane, believing him to have a great future with the company, and no doubt considered the possibility that he might one day become the third generation of the McMahon family that Gino would work for.

■

Yet despite the push for the New Generation, there was still time to honor the greats of yesteryear, of which Gorilla Monsoon was decidedly one. While Vince McMahon had had no interest in celebrating the past when he was busy turning his company into a global powerhouse in the present, now that business was on a definite downturn, there was a certain warm, nostalgic appeal in paying tribute to those who had helped put his father's company on the map, and so was born the WWF Hall of Fame. A year earlier, it had been kicked off, appropriately enough, with just one inaugural inductee, the Eighth Wonder of the World, André the Giant, who had sadly passed away just weeks prior at the age of forty-six while in Paris to attend his father's funeral. Now, the first full class of inductees would be welcomed into the Hall. And when it came time to name these "first-ballot" choices—handpicked by Vince, of course—it was obvious to all that the name of Gorilla Monsoon would have to be among them.

And so, on the evening of Thursday, June 9, 1994, Gino found himself seated up on the dais at Baltimore's Omni Inner Harbor International Hotel as part of the first-ever WWF Hall of Fame banquet. His fellow inductees were people he'd known and loved in the business going back to the earliest days of his career, including his former business partner Arnold Skaaland, mentor and dear friend Bobo Brazil, "Classy" Freddie Blassie, Chief Jay Strongbow, James Dudley and posthumous inductee "Nature Boy" Buddy Rogers, the first WWWF world champion, who had indirectly given Gino his big break when Gino was chosen to replace him as the company's top heel once upon a time.[5]

It was a memorable evening, with the entire company on hand to honor those who had helped to build their business, a fact that was even more greatly appreciated now that that business seemed to have seen better days. Included in that appreciative throng were Maureen and Joseph, seated near the front for the auspicious occasion. Early in the night, Gino got the chance to induct his old friend and the erstwhile babysitter of his kids, Chief Jay Strongbow. For his own induction, it's entirely possible that Gino might have loved to have had Bruno Sammartino or even Bobby Heenan, two men with whom he'd been so closely associated at different points of his career but were both in exile from the company at the time. Nevertheless, bringing him to the podium that night was another excellent choice and cherished friend, in the form of Walter "Killer" Kowalski—his former United States tag team championship partner and the man who'd recognized his talent and helped bring him to Capitol Wrestling for the first time some thirty-one years prior.

Dressed in a plain, black-and-white tux, Gino was visibly humbled and appreciative as he accepted his induction. In a speech lasting a mere four and a half minutes, he shared some brief memories from his wrestling career, which included some gentle ribbing of other luminaries such as future Hall of Famer Pat Patterson and fellow inductee Bobo Brazil, whom he'd known from his very first night in the business in that Rochester War Memorial locker room back in 1960. And as he looked out at the gala audience in attendance and brought his speech to a close, he made sure in his inimitable way to take the opportunity to put over the current WWF roster, as well as to thank the person more important to him than any other:

> I feel very honored to be up here tonight with these esteemed inductees, and to look out there and see the faces of the new generation of wrestling stars to come, and see some very impressive individuals . . . And I look back over my career . . . and you saw some of the things I accomplished, but there are other things. I have three lovely children, a beautiful home—and being a professional wrestler, how do you have those things and do what I did? You have to have an awful lot of help. Well, I had an awful lot of help. I had someone to raise those children and take care of that home. And tonight, you flatter and honor me at this induction ceremony; and I appreciate it from the bottom of my heart, because this is the pinnacle of my career, no question about it. But not only tonight, but for the rest of my life, I will

honor and treasure the person that made it all possible: my wife, Maureen. Thank you very much.

With that, he saluted her and then took his place back at the dais, seated right between Arnie and the Killer. It was a moment that Maureen didn't know was coming but typified the transcendent relationship that they had shared for all those years. And she knew he meant every word he said, because she had lived it.

She turned with a smile over to Joey, obviously glad to be able to share the night with him. With his constantly being on the road as a referee, plus residing these days down in Florida, chances to spend time with him were few and far between. But what she couldn't have known on that night in Baltimore was that it would be the last day they would ever spend together. In just a few tragically short weeks, Gino, and the whole Marella family for that matter, would go from the highest of highs to the lowest of lows, and the grand Hall of Fame dinner would seem like another lifetime.

■

Despite the merry proceedings at the Hall of Fame, things were not at all what they seemed at Titan Sports. Tensions were running high, everyone was under the gun, and the shit, for lack of a better term, was about to hit the fan. The sex scandals, at least, had been largely put behind them, with Terry Garvin and Mel Phillips banished from the company for good, and Pat Patterson quietly rehired after several of his accusers recanted their stories and he was acquitted of wrongdoing by a private investigation firm. But the federal government's steroid case against Vince McMahon had been building for months, with the trial finally set to begin. There was a very real chance that the chairman would be going down hard, maybe even behind bars, and the fate of the company itself was hanging in the balance. He had even lined up Jerry Jarrett, owner of the USWA, to step in to fill his position should he have to go away. In a startling coincidence, Vince would also be going under the knife mere days before the trial to repair a herniated disc in his neck.

With legal and medical woes mounting and his presence required elsewhere, Vince was forced to step back from his duties as lead television commentator, leading Gino to have to step into the breach, just when he'd been happy to be stepping into the background. For the time being, until either Vince was off the hook or a suitable long-term replacement could be found, it would be Gorilla Monsoon as lead announcer for pay-per-view, for *Monday Night Raw*, even for *WWF Superstars*, where for the June 25 episode he worked play-by-play with Jerry Lawler as his color guy, the one and only time that would happen.[6] In the clutch, despite their complicated relationship, Gino's diminished interest and his disdain for the whole situation, it was Gino who was there for Vince when the chips were down.

Just ten days after the Hall of Fame, Gino was back in Baltimore for the 1994 installment of *King of the Ring*, manning the booth as lead pay-per-view commentator for the first time in a year and a half. It was a night doomed to be a dismal failure, producing what is often called the worst commentary track of any major wrestling company pay-per-view in history. On top of being out of practice himself on live commentary, Gino's partners on that night included Randy Savage, one of his least favorite people to work with, as well as Baltimore football legend Art "Fatso" Donovan.

A longtime defensive tackle for the Baltimore Colts, one of the greatest NFL players of the 1950s and an overall Baltimore sports legend, Donovan was to football what Yogi Berra was to baseball, parlaying his guileless charm and likable demeanor into a post-player public life that included numerous talk show appearances for the likes of Johnny Carson and David Letterman. But as Gino might have put it, he was in no way, shape or form prepared to call a WWF pay-per-view, which became painfully apparent mere minutes into the broadcast. As the story goes, there was zero preparation done, and it shows. Donovan is utterly confused throughout the broadcast, seeming to genuinely not know who almost any of the wrestlers are, in addition to being fixated on asking

CHANGING TIMES, CHANGING ROLES

everyone's weight. Savage, ever the perfectionist, is quite obviously irritated with Donovan, which only makes more difficult Gorilla's job of having to maintain some semblance of order through the whole mess. Everyone is thrown off their game, and even Gorilla is not immune, such as when he refers to Donovan as "Art O'Donnell." Although Gino was the least to blame of the three, it was what would have to be considered the ultimate low point of his broadcasting career.

In short, to a control freak like Vince McMahon, it was exactly his worst nightmare of what might happen if he was ever out of commission. It was the last time Gorilla Monsoon would be put in charge of calling any show of major importance.

As he would recall years later, Jim Ross received a call the very next morning from an exasperated Gino, looking to commiserate. "Did you see that shit?" was his rhetorical question. Of course Jim had, and he took pity on Gino for having to slog through something that was so clearly beneath his usual standards. At the same time, he also knew it was a ripe opportunity. Vince needed somebody to fill in for him, and if Gino wasn't up to it, perhaps he might be.

That night in White Plains, Gino pushed through, taking the lead announcer position alongside Randy Savage for the *Monday Night Raw* tapings, as planned. But perhaps owing to a conversation between Gino and Kevin Dunn, Dunn would soon get on the phone himself to Jim and offer him the spot on a short-term basis through the summer, which Jim accepted. While Vince was away, it would be Jim Ross filling in for him on *Raw*, on the *SummerSlam* pay-per-view, as well as on *WWF Superstars*, where for the first time, he was teamed up with Jerry Lawler, forming a broadcast duo that would one day become as beloved by fans as Gorilla Monsoon and Bobby Heenan themselves.

■

It was becoming clear that Gino wasn't quite the go-to guy he used to be. His backstage duties reduced, his role on the broadcast team minimized, he was beginning to fade into the background, and he had to come to terms with that. He wasn't having as much fun as he used to anyway, and the business just wasn't the same. But whatever passion for it he still had, whatever joy it still brought him, was about to be completely drained away and snuffed out, as he faced the irreparably defining tragedy of his life. After July 4, 1994, he would never be the same again.

There's no doubt that Joey Marella had been causing his family distress for some time. His partying lifestyle and the choices he'd been making had estranged him from his younger sister, Valerie, for one thing. "At the time, we were hardly even talking to each other," she recalls. "I think I knew more than anybody about his issues." She had chosen to keep quiet to her parents about much of what she saw, but they still knew. And it wasn't just issues of substance abuse. The rigors of the road and the grueling demands of the WWF touring schedule had been taking their toll, and Joey had been living it for over a decade by that point. For many of the men who chose that lifestyle in those days, disaster was always waiting just around the corner. And one night, Joey turned that corner.

Once Jim Ross was back in place, Gino had gotten to take a breath after that June 20 *Raw* taping in White Plains. But Joey got no such rest. The next day, he was off to Wilkes-Barre, Pennsylvania, for the *Superstars* taping, then the Mid-Hudson Civic Center in Poughkeepsie, New York, for the *Challenge* taping. From there, the boys broke up into "A" and "B" house show crews. The A-crew, headlined by Bret Hart and his youngest brother, Owen, flew to Toronto for a week of Canadian live events, while the B-crew, headlined by Razor Ramon and Kevin "Diesel" Nash, went out to California. Joey was part of the A-crew: From the 23rd through the 30th, they put on eight shows on eight consecutive days in Ontario and Quebec without a break. As soon as the tour was over, they flew into Newark Airport to get ready for three straight days of television tapings back on the East Coast.

The last day of this punishing run was Sunday night, July 3, at the Ocean City Convention Center right on the Atlantic in coastal Maryland. Three weeks' worth of *WWF Superstars* was being recorded that night. World champion Bret Hart was pulling double duty. On the one hand, it was a unique taping because a major angle was being kicked off. Bob Backlund, the last great WWF world champion of the pre-expansion days, had returned to the company nearly two years earlier, and on this night, after failing to connect with the modern WWF audience, he was going to have a total meltdown. Turning heel after suffering a defeat in a classic encounter with Hart that is often called the greatest match ever aired on *WWF Superstars*, Backlund trapped Hart in his infamous cross-face chicken wing before a stunned audience. Later that night, in a dark match intended to send that live crowd home happy, Bret defended his title a second time against his brother Owen. That would be the last match Joey Marella would ever referee. "As he was checking my fingers, he said to me, 'You're the best in the business, the best I've ever seen,'" Bret remembers. "I had that really stuck in my head when he died that night."

At the conclusion of the tapings, Mike Chioda and Tony Chimel, who were still on the ring crew at that point and had to break down the ring before they could leave, invited Joey to hang out and come stay with them for a bit at the house they had rented down the Jersey shore. They had all been on the road for seventeen days straight, and everyone was beaten to hell. But despite the offer, and despite the fact that Joey's parents lived right near there anyway, Joey was in a hurry to get back home to his new house in Tampa in time for the Fourth of July celebrations the following night. Because of sweeping budget cuts in what was shaping up to be the first money-losing year in company history, the travel department had instituted a cost-effective policy requiring WWF personnel to fly out from the same airport they'd flown in on—which meant that Joey would have to make the four-hour drive back to Newark Airport in the middle of the night to catch his flight in the morning.

Bruno Lauer, who worked for the WWF as the pipsqueak manager Harvey Wippleman, had a company rental car and was also flying out of Newark in the morning, and so Joey opted to travel with him. Needless to say, they were both dog-tired, but Joey volunteered to drive. Somewhere along the way, they stopped to eat, which made them even more tired.

Bruno was the first to fall asleep. Then, at about three in the morning, as their 1994 Dodge Shadow made its way up the New Jersey Turnpike between Burlington Township and Westampton, Joey fell asleep behind the wheel. In the most shocking irony of all, it was just as they were approaching Exit 5—the one closest to Gino and Maureen's home—when the car spun out of control in the left lane, careening through an opening in the concrete barrier of the median, designed to allow police and emergency vehicles to make U-turns on the highway. The out-of-control vehicle continued at full speed about ninety feet down a wooded slope, smashed into a tree on the driver's side, then continued another twenty feet before finally coming to a stop against another tree.

Though severely shaken up, Bruno had been saved by being in the passenger seat, sustaining only minor injuries, including a gash on his hand that required twelve stitches to close.

Joey was killed instantly.

Chioda and Chimel, on their own way home to Jersey from the tapings, passed the wreckage in the middle of the night, not knowing who or what it was. "I was in the back sleeping, Chimel was driving," Mike remembers. "He goes, 'Chioda, man, get up because our exit is coming up soon.' And there's about ten cop cars, ambulances and fire trucks . . . And we drove right on past it." Tony recalls the cops had closed some lanes, and everyone looking in that direction to see what was going on: "There were people and cars in the woods, but I didn't think anything of it." The next morning, they realized what they'd seen when Mike got a fateful call from Gino at about six in the morning: "He said, 'Mike, I got some really, really bad news, son. Joey passed.'"

Gino and Maureen had been in Atlantic City for the weekend. Before all the details were known, Sharon called them to let them know there had been an accident, and they rushed back home. "When we got home," remembers Maureen of that difficult morning, "I walked in the door and said, 'What hospital is he in?' And she said, 'Mom, he's dead.' I just couldn't believe it. It still hurts me." In the moment, shock and grief were mixed with anger. There were airports near to Ocean City, like Baltimore and Salisbury, that they could have flown out from. There were others they had passed on the way, like Philadelphia. It seemed so unnecessary, even reckless, to have forced him to go that far out of the way back to Newark, just to fly down to Florida. Some small solace was taken when the autopsy results came back and revealed there was nothing in Joseph's system. They could at least be assured that, in the end, it wasn't his demons that took Joseph away from them. But that modest comfort couldn't bring their son back.

Services were set for the morning of Friday, July 8, at Goes-Scolieri Funeral Home in Willingboro. Vince was in a courtroom on Long Island, trying to stay out of jail, and was unable to attend, but he was represented by Shane, who went with Bruce Prichard. The funeral itself was massive, with streets closed off from the funeral home to the church and then from the church to the cemetery in order to make way for the procession of cars. "I can't imagine what Gorilla or Mrs. Marella were thinking," remembers Tony, who was also there that day to say goodbye to his childhood friend. "When you've got to bury a kid, that's got to be the worst thing you can go through in life." More than anything, Mike will never forget seeing Gino on that day: "It was just one of the worst days of our lives . . . Gorilla was taking it hard. Real hard. Sometimes, you can't tell; well, with Gorilla, you could tell. I remember Mrs. Marella and Valerie and Sharon, and everybody was just crushed. We were all crushed."

At the graveside in Lakeview Memorial Park in Cinnaminson, Gino was despondent in the extreme. Not wanting anyone to leave, he invited everyone back to the house after services were over. As always, being in the presence of friends and family brought comfort, or at least in this case, as much comfort as was possible. The depth of his despair was all-consuming. He had known Joseph since he was practically a newborn baby, taken him on just as if he were his own flesh and blood, and proudly raised him into the man he was. The wrestling business had not been what he wanted for his son, but it's what his son wanted. He knew how tough and unforgiving the business could be. And now, his worst fear had become real. But once the initial anger subsided, Gino put aside any thoughts of blame. For better or worse, this was the life they had both chosen. And they had done so with eyes wide open.

In the days following the funeral, the family flew down to Tampa to Joey's place to sort out his things. There in the garage was his pride and joy, his 1990 Corvette ZR1. Gino asked Valerie if she wanted it, but she refused: "I said, 'I don't want this car. I don't want you to be having a good day, and then pull in the driveway and see that car. I don't want any part of it.'"

■

The psychological damage sustained by Gino would be permanent. "A big piece of him died the day Joey died," Prichard would explain years later.[7] "That was the moment, in a lot of ways, when he gave up." While he was trying to look after Maureen during such a terrible time, he also had himself to look after, and in that area, he fell far short. Diabetes doesn't take a break for grieving, and Gino quickly began to neglect his health as he simply stopped caring. "He really went downhill," recalls Maureen. "He wouldn't do anything that Joey liked to do. He wouldn't touch the pool table. We didn't have picnics anymore. Didn't go on the basketball court. We stopped playing racquetball, which we used to do on Thursday nights as a family."

The *All-American Wrestling* experiment with Johnny Polo came to an abrupt end, as did the show itself just a few weeks later.[8] For two months, Gino stayed away from the television studio, or anywhere else, for that matter. It was a slow progression back into the swing of things, with Kevin Dunn reaching out to him to try to gently coax him back. Meanwhile, *United States v. Vince McMahon* had gone the chairman's way, as federal prosecutors simply couldn't build a strong enough case against him to make anything stick. McMahon was getting back into the swing of things himself at a time when that was sorely needed. With his eye off the ball, the company had sunk to its lowest lows. On August 25, 1994, Madison Square Garden, the company's heart and soul for three and a half decades, was more than three-quarters empty, with just 4,300 fans on hand—the smallest crowd to ever attend a Garden show produced by the McMahon family, and the smallest wrestling crowd at the world's most

CHANGING TIMES, CHANGING ROLES

famous arena since 1949.[9] Although it would never get quite that bad again, the Garden remained more than half empty for WWF shows all through that year, and the next year. And when it came to the company's business, as went the Garden, so went the rest of it.

Arnie Skaaland was also seeing his company responsibilities dwindle, and he and his wife, Betty, spent lots of time with Gino and Maureen on weekends as Gino pulled himself out of his funk. The Gorilla Monsoon who returned to the studio at the start of September was a very different person, and it didn't take long for everyone to realize that. More somber, deflated. He could perk himself up when needed for work, but as soon as he was done, he would return to his morose state. There was little to none of the joking around between takes that there used to be back in the glory days. On the road for television and in the Northeast for local events, it was much the same. "He used to refer to us as the bookends," remembers referee Jimmy Korderas of Gino's nickname for him and Joey. "He would say sometimes he looks at me, and it reminds him of Joey. And I was both happy and sad to hear that."

Jerry Brisco remembers a darker side of a man who seemed to have lost his way in life completely, and whose behavior on the road was becoming far less characteristic: "He was hurting. Joey was his pride and joy and the guy that was going to take over his spot eventually. I wasn't around up north to see the full brunt of it, but I know he started drinking a lot then and started gambling out of control at that time. He'd kind of lost control for the first time in his life. His lovely wife, she's the one that pulled him back down and got everything straightened out." As always, Maureen was his rock, even when she was hurting just as badly as he was. But even her love couldn't completely save him from the despair and anguish that continued to engulf him.

■

After *SummerSlam*, Jim Ross had parted ways with the company once again, unable to work out a mutually agreeable contract extension. And so Gorilla Monsoon returned to *Wrestling Challenge* for what would be his final run as a regular commentator on domestic television, lasting from September through July of the following year. "He came in, and he was a little sad," remembers audio engineer Larry Rosen. "He said, 'I'm fine. We have work to do. Let's everyone do our job.'" For the first half of that period, he was teamed up with "The Million Dollar Man" Ted DiBiase, whose wrestling career had been cut short the previous year due to injury and had been transitioned into other outside-the-ring roles such as wrestling manager. But DiBiase became a classic example of a brilliant in-ring performer who struggled to translate that into other areas. Thankfully, Gino liked Ted and wanted to help him out, and especially to keep him off Vince's radar. Tom Carlucci, who was producing the show in those days, remembers it well: "We used to do voice-overs, but before every match, Gino would feed him lines. Because Ted was lost, he couldn't be as witty as he was live. I don't know why. Not everyone could be a good color commentator. But all that funny shit that DiBiase was saying, it was coming from Gorilla."

Tom and Gino became especially close during this period, and Tom would always look out for him, both in the studio and on the road: "When he would come in to do voice-overs, he'd call me up. He goes, Carlucc', get me some groceries. That meant lunch. He loved sausage and peppers on a wedge with melted provolone. He would eat anything he wanted. When we were on the road driving, we'd always go to Bob's Big Boy, wherever we were. He would get six round sausage links, hit them with paper towels just to get the oil out and eat that with some eggs." It was the doctor's worst nightmare, but Gino just didn't care anymore. He was going to do what made him happy.

The beauty of being Gino's driver was always the perks that came with it. Gino's gold Hertz card meant never having to wait in line for a rental car. And it had to be a Coupe de Ville every time, preferably black. It had to have a cassette deck because Gino brought his cassette tapes with him. There was Sinatra and Dean Martin—Tom remembers Gino recounting to him how he'd once met Dino in Atlantic City. But there was also Richard Pryor, whom Gino loved to listen to on those car rides with Tom. Gino's worsening vision, added to everything else, made Tom a necessity behind the wheel. But they made the most of it, and then some.

■

Less than three months after the loss of Joey, Gino put on a brave face and went with Maureen to the Sheraton Monarch Hotel in Springfield, Massachusetts, where the very first East Coast reunion of the Cauliflower Alley Club was taking place, and where he was to be the guest of honor. A fraternal order of veterans of both the boxing and wrestling ring, the Cauliflower Alley Club had been founded in the 1960s by wrestler and tough-guy movie star Mike Mazurki. By 1994, Mazurki was gone, and the president of the CAC was Gino's old friend and someone he looked up to earnestly, Lou Thesz. Also serving on the board and helping to organize the event was noted wrestling historian and journalist Tom Burke, as well as prolific New England promoter Sheldon Goldberg.

The CAC in those days was based in Studio City out in Hollywood and held a reunion of wrestling luminaries every year, where the old-timers could reunite with their pals, raise a glass and reminisce. Tom and Sheldon had been wanting to set up a reunion on the East Coast—partly to make it easier for the folks who lived on that side of the country, but also, in Sheldon's case, to try and establish some kind of working relationship with the most powerful organization in the wrestling business, Titan Sports. Most of the old guys detested Vince McMahon for the way he'd decimated and thoroughly transformed the business they'd known and loved, but Sheldon believed that the CAC couldn't survive forever on the older generation. It needed to attract younger members, and the way to do that, he felt, was by courting the World Wrestling Federation.

Sheldon reached out to his old friend and colleague Joe Perkins, a Titan board member whose associations went back to the old days and Vince's father. He asked about maybe getting Gorilla Monsoon and Arnold Skaaland to come out and be honored, and Joe helped to make that happen. Also being honored at the reunion were former WWWF world champion Pedro Morales and the great Ilio DiPaolo, which were two more enticements for Gino to come out.

The event was a heartwarming one for Gino, and a bit of a revelation. He (and Arnie, for that matter) had been inside the Vince McMahon bubble for a decade and had had little to no opportunities to mingle with their colleagues from the old days. "He was very gracious, very pleased," remembers Burke. "He said it was like a high school reunion, in the sense of all the guys that he had worked with all those years ago and hadn't seen." He lit up at the chance to rub elbows once again with the likes of Verne Gagne, Red Bastien, Tony Parisi and even lesser-known individuals like 1930s, '40s and '50s journeyman Jackie Nichols, whom Gino had known from back in the Missouri days of the early '60s, and later when he promoted Maine for Capitol Wrestling. Even former Boston promoter Abe Ford, who'd once tried to cross the McMahon office by booking talent out of Montreal, was there; but all bad blood was in the past. Gino was reverential to Gordon Solie, the master of ceremonies for the reunion, telling him how much he missed seeing him on television, where for years, the venerated announcer had been the voice of Georgia Championship Wrestling on TBS, as well as Championship Wrestling from Florida. Though still active with WCW, by that point, Gordon was being minimized in much the same way Gino was by the WWF.

"Gorilla was a delight," remembers Sheldon. "He was so loved and appreciated by all the people who were there . . . He was very touched that they made such a fuss over him. He enjoyed being around his contemporaries who were around when he was coming up." The board of the CAC also understood what a power broker Gino was and how getting close to him could also be the way toward getting some financial backing from Titan Sports. This could help them not just in the reunions, but more importantly, in the charitable work the group did to support wrestlers, boxers and even actors in need, which was and is its primary mission. He was invited to sit in on a board meeting that weekend, which he appreciated, although he made it clear that he really wasn't up to taking on an active role in the organization. Still, it felt good to be wanted.

His general demeanor was serious and even melancholy, as Sheldon remembers from their interactions. And he was much more candid and open than he would typically be in his official WWF capacity, not to mention wistful when he shared some of his true feelings. "He said that the aura that the business had when he was wrestling was gone... How it was rapidly becoming more of a corporate, organized enterprise, and that was antithetical to the way that he came up in pro wrestling. He was cashing in and was gonna take the money and pretty much keep his mouth shut. But if you asked him, he would tell you point blank it was not the same animal that it used to be."

That kind of honest circumspection, a far cry from the ballyhoo master most fans knew from television, was on display even in Gino's quiet ninety-second speech at the podium after being presented with his recognition plaque by Sheldon and Red Bastien:

> I want to thank this esteemed organization for this honor here tonight. Certainly, it's a pleasure to be in the company of such great superstars of yesteryear... In our generation, it was a tremendous attribute to know the difference between a wristlock and a wristwatch. I am deeply honored tonight, and I thank you all for this tremendous display of affection that I've had since I walked in this building... It's people like you who made it worthwhile to be part of this profession... I just want to thank you from the bottom of my heart for everything...[10]

Less in performing mode than he'd been four months prior at his WWF Hall of Fame induction, Gino enjoyed the evening, sitting with Arnie and Pedro and even Lou Albano, who was briefly back in Vince's good graces and had come up to support Gino—although the support might have been a little bit in the other direction once Lou had gotten a few too many drinks in him, as usual. It was an ingratiating experience, but the one and only time Gino would ever come out for Cauliflower Alley.

Nevertheless, it would sow the seeds of a healthy relationship between the CAC and the WWF, which has flourished to this day.

■

Despite his diminished enthusiasm, Gino enjoyed the company of friends very much in those days. He took solace in phone conversations with Bobby Heenan that would go on for hours, as they no doubt swapped stories of whatever bullshit they were having to contend with in their respective companies. They continued to try to see each other once a month if possible. Jessica remembers a particularly priceless occasion that would bring joy to the heart of any fan of Gorilla and the Brain. Gino had come down to Florida for a visit. After having dinner with the family, Jessica, still in high school, excused herself to go and catch a baseball game at her school and check out all the cute boys with her girlfriends. Sure enough, Gino and Bobby showed up and launched into an impromptu schtick straight out of *Prime Time Wrestling*, solely for the benefit of the lucky individuals at that high school baseball game. "They proceeded to do an Abbott and Costello type of play-by-play from the stands, as loud as they could," remembers Jessica. "They had everybody hysterical. And I'm sitting there thinking, 'Oh my God. Should I be embarrassed? Or should I be proud?'" Like always, Bobby could bring out the best in Gino.

Anything that could take his mind off his loss was welcomed. His diminished enthusiasm meant that his role as a commentator of any real consequence to the company was coming to an end. It was a job that required the kind of steady focus and passion that he just didn't have left to give anymore. In November 1994, at the *Survivor Series*, he served as Vince McMahon's color commentator, just as he had a dozen years earlier at the beginning of his broadcasting tenure. With the show taking place in San Antonio, Texas, Gino was a good sport as always, donning blue jeans, a giant belt buckle, a cowboy hat and a shirt and bolo tie that would've made Roy Rogers proud in connection with the event's western theme. Vince did the heavy lifting that night, and even

Gino couldn't completely hold back his sarcasm when calling some of the more outlandish New Generation antics, which on this particular evening included literal midget clowns. It would be the final pay-per-view call for Gorilla Monsoon.

He hosted his final *Monday Night Raw* on January 2, 1995, on a rare occasion when Vince had actually decided to go on a holiday vacation. He was joined by Shawn Michaels, out of action with a broken hand. It was also around that time that Jim Ross would finally be hired back for good and would even be granted a spot on Vince's booking team.[11] This time, he would stick around, which also meant that Gino could breathe a sigh of relief. Ross replaced DiBiase on *Wrestling Challenge* in April, reuniting with Monsoon for four months before Gorilla bowed out with the July 30, 1995, episode, his final appearance as a regular commentator on domestic WWF television. It was an on-location shoot—rare in those days of studio voice-overs—from the venerable Kiel Auditorium in St. Louis, where Gino had once battled the likes of Pat O'Connor, Stan Stasiak and Don Leo Jonathan in the early '60s. The last segment he would call on the show was a vignette introducing Jerry Lawler's new protégé, the wrestling dentist Dr. Isaac Yankem, DDS—the epitome of the mid-1990s WWF, if ever there was one.[12] With that, his last run on *Wrestling Challenge*, the show he'd launched, was over—as was his regular career as a WWF commentator.

But Gino's original deal with Titan Sports had called for him to always have a place on WWF television, so he wasn't about to disappear from WWF programming exactly. He was just going to take on a new role, which, despite its importance as far as the fans were concerned, would require less physical presence and less effort than being an announcer, certainly less than manning the Gorilla position. It would also be a nod to his status in the eyes of the fans and the company and a recognition of all that he had contributed—a natural progression for him as an onscreen persona. It would be a figurehead position, to be sure, but in the grand tradition of the company's greatest figurehead position. Gorilla Monsoon was about to be named president of the WWF.

CHAPTER 15

PRESIDENT MONSOON

"I'm not your son."
—Gorilla to Stone Cold Steve Austin, January 20, 1997

Since Vince McMahon Sr. had first established the World Wide Wrestling Federation as its own independent entity back in 1963, there had been a fictional president to preside over the fictional governing body and to obscure to the fans who was really in charge. On August 5, 1995, Gorilla Monsoon officially became the fourth person to hold that position. Due to his declining health, he would be the shortest-tenured WWF president of them all, but for a number of reasons, he would also be the one most fondly remembered by many fans. He would be a different kind of WWF president, putting his own unique stamp on the role. It would also give him a much-needed break from the rigors and demands of both the road and the broadcast booth. Those two years would also be his final phase as a contributing member of the company he'd been involved with in one form or another for more than thirty years.

Jack Tunney, the nephew of longtime McMahon family associate Frank Tunney and inheritor of the Toronto wrestling office, had been installed as

PRESIDENT MONSOON

WWF president in 1984 after Titan Sports moved in on Toronto and had held the position ever since, appearing now and then, usually in benign pretaped clips from his office, in which he'd issue some stoic proclamation or another that helped to move along the WWF's storylines and angles. But by the summer of 1995, Tunney found himself on the wrong side of the political tracks within the company. There were rumors that he had opposed the company's decision to get behind fellow Canadian Bret Hart as the new top guy. As the legitimate head of Titan Sports Canada, there were even rumors that he'd been embezzling company funds to help pay off some gambling debts. Whatever truth there might have been to any rumors, in July 1995, Titan Sports pulled the plug on its partnership with the Tunney family, citing financial losses as the reason for shuttering the Toronto satellite office entirely. It was an archaic deal anyway, made during an era when Titan Sports was expanding across North America and working out short-lived partnerships with whatever territories weren't being completely steamrolled. The partnership had run its course, and the organization would be directly running wrestling in Ontario going forward. Tunney was out.

It was perfect timing for Gino's appointment to fill Tunney's shoes. His spot on the broadcast team had been minimized over the past couple of years, as had his passion for it. Jim Ross was firmly installed as the new number-two commentator behind Vince. Gino's health was making it more difficult to be present all the time. Vince needed someone with authority, whom the fans would take seriously, and who had been firmly established as a force to be reckoned with in the WWF, and there was no one associated with the company who checked off all those boxes like Gorilla Monsoon. "He knew how to be believable in an authority role," remembers Jim Cornette, who, in his capacity as gadfly heel manager, would take the brunt of many a presidential decision from Monsoon. "Jack Tunney, he looked great sitting there in a suit. But it was almost like the episode of *Star Trek* where the leader of the planet is just sitting there, zombified, and they're piping in his voice." The fans had known Gorilla for years and considered him to be someone who had serious strokes anyway, which he did.

Certainly, Gino would've found a kind of humorous irony in taking on the position originally held by his old cohort Willie Gilzenberg, who'd been an elder statesman of the Capitol Wrestling Corporation when he'd first come on board as a greenhorn wrestler, and whom he'd later spend summer vacations with in Vegas for the NWA conventions. But Monsoon would be a different kind of WWF president than anyone who had preceded him. Although Gilzenberg had been president in name only, the reality was that he was a promotional partner in the organization; he had helped to found it, and he maintained a real office in Newark, New Jersey, where he presided over much of the wrestling in the northern portion of that state. His successor, Hisashi Shinma, was a real executive in New Japan Pro-Wrestling, and his placement in the role had been a crucial part of establishing the partnership between the Capitol office and New Japan. And of course, in addition to being a talking head on TV, Jack Tunney was the actual president of Titan Sports Canada and had been running the WWF's shows at the Maple Leaf Gardens for over a decade.

In contrast, Gorilla Monsoon was the first WWF authority figure to be really and truly a television character, and nothing more. Although he had once been a partner in the company, and remained a very respected and influential person there, Gorilla Monsoon as WWF president was really just a persona on a television show, playing the part of an authority figure for a few minutes onscreen for pretapes at the television studio; or, if he happened to be on hand for a television taping in the arena, coming out to make his momentous proclamation, then going backstage to hang out in the Gorilla position with Bruce Prichard and Pat Patterson, or to get back to playing cards with Arnie Skaaland. That's really all it was, and that's really all he wanted it to be.

■

However, on the actual corporate side of things, there was a bit of restructuring going on in the aftermath of the company's emergence from its legal and public relations nightmares of the early '90s. The added scrutiny had inspired Vince McMahon to try to run his business less like the carny mom-and-pop wrestling territory it had been and more like the honest-to-goodness corporate entity it pretended to be. A wave of new executives was brought in to help run things and create more of a layered company structure than before. Ironically, however, one of the new executives was someone right out of wrestling's territorial past, as well as an old friend of Gino's, in the form of Cowboy Bill Watts.

The Cowboy had been pushed out of WCW after a short-lived run as head booker, and Vince wanted to bring him in for the same type of role at Titan Sports. He had proven his booking acumen in years gone by, especially as the man behind Mid-South Wrestling / UWF from 1979 through 1987, and Vince had decided to try stepping back from the day-to-day booking responsibilities and handing over creative duties to someone he could trust while he focused on more big-picture issues as owner of the company and chairman of the board. And for three whole months, Vince actually committed to that idea. Gino and Bill had maintained a friendship over the years since their days making the towns together as tag team champions and sharing a condo complex in South Jersey, but they hadn't been around each other regularly since those days. "I got to spend some time with him again," remembers Watts of that brief window. "I had nothing but the highest regard for him. We didn't have any intimate talks when I went back there those three months. We just saw each other, and it was good seeing each other. But I was busy in the creative department, and he was doing what he had to do."

In the brief time he was there, Watts and McMahon started butting heads in short order, especially when it came to Vince's new golden boy, Shawn Michaels, and Michaels's best buddy, then-WWF world champion Diesel, both of whom Watts found insufferable. The Watts/McMahon relationship soured quickly, but thankfully, that had no effect on his friendship with Gino, who had largely taken himself out of the political equation by that point. Once Watts came to realize that McMahon's micromanaging urges could not be restrained and that he would never really be allowed to run things his way, he walked away—not just from Titan Sports but from the entire pro wrestling industry, for good.

For better or worse, Vince was never really going to willingly step away from running creative. He just didn't have it in him to do that. And his resolve to stay in full control was only further justified as the ongoing cold war with WCW began to turn very hot in the fall of 1995, thanks to the debut of *WCW Monday Nitro*. Spearheaded by WCW Executive Vice President Eric Bischoff with the blessing of Ted Turner, the show was created to run directly against *Monday Night Raw*, kicking off a bitter half-decade programming dustup that would become known as the Monday Night War. Rising from the ashes of Jim Crockett Promotions, WCW was the only other company able to pull off anything like the WWF's national expansion and was about to take full advantage of its rival's weakened state. The new show, aired on Turner's TNT cable channel, would be broadcast live every week; would feature a weekly program full of marquee, pay-per-view quality matches, a rarity in those TV squash-match days; and kicked off with the shocking appearance of Lex Luger, a former WCW headliner who had just finished up with the WWF the week before.

Shots had been fired across the Titan bow, and Vince McMahon needed to be front and center to lead the fight. He'd respond in kind, gradually transforming *Raw* into the WWF's answer to *Nitro*, along the way establishing it as the company's unquestioned primary show, where all the most important things would happen each week. *Wrestling Challenge* was put to bed for good, while *WWF Superstars* became more of a rehash show full of highlights and clips. The very nature of the WWF product began to change, becoming faster-paced and dependent on live programming, including the pay-per-view offerings, which had already gone from seasonal to monthly presentations.

And President Gorilla Monsoon became an important part of the product right from the start. The announcement of his position (originally described as "interim president," although the interim nature was eventually dropped) was first made, of all places, by Todd Pettengill on the August 5 edition of Titan's Saturday morning program, *WWF Mania*.

Right away, he was inserted into the top storylines, and unlike his predecessor, he took on a decidedly babyface bent. Whereas Tunney was often an aloof and frustrating figure to fans, sometimes seeming clueless as to the tactics of the bad guys and making rulings that only aggravated tense situations, Gorilla Monsoon was presented as a more no-nonsense fixer who was there to cut through the heels' nonsense and give fans what they wanted to see. It was a refreshing change of pace. The very same weekend as his appointment, he appeared on WWF television to announce the very crowd-pleasing Shawn Michaels / Razor Ramon ladder match for the Intercontinental title at *SummerSlam '95*, a rematch from their critically acclaimed encounter the previous year at *WrestleMania X*.

President Monsoon could be counted on to appear on television about once or twice a month, maintaining order and interjecting himself into the company's top angles of the time, usually acting as proxy for Vince McMahon, the guy who was really making the decisions that put the words in his mouth. And it wasn't always for a reason that made fans happy, such as when he had to strip Michaels of the Intercontinental title after Michaels had gotten trounced by a group of irate Marines in a real-life altercation outside a Syracuse nightclub. Other times, it did please fans, such as when he foiled the dastardly plans of a newcomer to the WWF, Hunter Hearst Helmsley, in his 1996 *Royal Rumble* match with wrestling garbageman Duke "The Dumpster" Droese.

■

That event also led to what is perhaps the best-remembered incident of Gorilla Monsoon's entire WWF presidency, because it saw the WWF debut of Leon White, better known as Vader—a dominant former WCW world champion whose arrival in the WWF was highly anticipated, and who was expected to run roughshod, just as he had for the competition. A former Los Angeles Ram and all-around mauler of the highest order, Vader was in some ways a modern-day answer to the Gorilla Monsoon of old: a gargantuan man who could move around the ring with alarming speed and dexterity, with similar dimensions of height and weight to the fearsome Manchurian Giant. Clearly, Gino saw something in him and recognized him as a potential main event monster heel for the company, just as Vince did. And so, when Vince proposed an idea to help get Vader over like gangbusters, an idea that would even involve Gino physically, he got on board. "It was obviously Vince's idea," remembers Jim Cornette, Vader's onscreen manager at the time. "But Gorilla was right with it, because he wanted to make a new monster heel. Because think about it; thirty years before that, he'd been in the same situation where somebody had to put him over as a monster. And he was so great with it."

There was also the little problem of Vader needing shoulder surgery, which the planned angle would also cover. It was a big deal and not something Gino was going to do for just anyone, especially pushing age sixty and already having heart problems. Aside from the Brooklyn Brawler incident on the *Prime Time* set in 1989, no one had put their hands on Gorilla Monsoon in thirteen years. Certainly not in front of a live audience. And especially not in the national era of the World Wrestling Federation, in front of fans in other parts of the country who had never even seen him in his WWWF wrestling heyday. The angle was to take place on the January 22, 1996, edition of *Monday Night Raw*, from the Civic Auditorium in Stockton, California. Cornette had his concerns: "I was afraid because I know they'd seen him as the announcer, but nobody out there . . . You would have had to tell them he used to be a wrestler, not an announcer. A lot of those people, they didn't know who Bruno was out there. I said, 'Boy, I wish we were doing it in Philly or Madison Square Garden, you know?' . . . I was afraid they wouldn't buy it, because he had to get some offense—it's Gorilla Monsoon, right? We can't just punk him out. He wouldn't have gone for that anyway."

Before the segment, they worked out exactly what they were going to do. Gino took the lead. It had to be believable, and with a man the size of Gino in there, it would. Gino talked, and Vader listened. "Honestly, even at that point, *maybe* Leon could have taken him [in a real fight], but he might have had trouble. So Leon's going, 'Yes, sir. No, sir.' Because it's fucking Gorilla Monsoon."

PRESIDENT MONSOON

The night before, during the Royal Rumble match, Vader had made a major splash in his debut appearance, eliminating several participants, then returning to the ring after he himself had been eliminated and tossing out some more hapless wrestlers until Monsoon, among others, had come out from the back to restrain him and escort him back to the locker room. The table had been set for a confrontation between Vader and the WWF president, and it happened after his *Monday Night Raw* match against Puerto Rican sensation Savio Vega, whom he crushed in three minutes. As Vader attempts to continue his assault on Vega, with Cornette goading him on, referees Jimmy Korderas and Jack Doan intervene, and both are wiped out, with Doan taking a powerbomb.

Next out is Gorilla Monsoon, to check on Doan in the ring and to read Vader the riot act. The two giants stand nose to nose with each other as Cornette implores his man to back down. The president instructs the ring announcer to declare that Vader has been suspended indefinitely. This enrages Vader, who gets in Monsoon's face again as Cornette's anxiety skyrockets. But Gorilla does not back down. He never backed down, nor ever showed any fear during his entire time as president, for that matter. Instead, he backs Vader into a corner, taking off his glasses, and tosses them to the mat as the excitement of the crowd mounts. (Cornette, in a moment of decency that pokes the tiniest of pinholes through the wall of kayfabe, quickly gets Gino's glasses out of the ring so they aren't crushed in the ensuing fracas, which would've rendered Gino blind for the rest of the evening.)

As Vader begins to turn on his own manager in a fit of fury, Gorilla goes back to check on Doan in the corner. Vader comes over and gives Monsoon a couple of shoves that would have sent a lesser man through the ropes and down to the floor. It's then that Gorilla Monsoon rises up, and for a shining moment, it's not 1996. It's 1976. It's not the Stockton Civic Auditorium anymore—it's Sunnyside Garden. Monsoon lays into Vader hard with three chops across the chest that stagger the big man. "He switched," explains Cornette, still in awe thirty years later. "He hadn't done anything physical in so long, and that's one of the things that made it . . . But he channeled it. When he fired up with those fucking chops, you saw for like twenty seconds or whatever it was, what he might have looked like thirty years before, doing that to Bruno in the Garden. And the people got with it."

Of course, in the end, the purpose of the angle was to get Vader over. When Gorilla makes the cardinal mistake of turning around to check on Doan one more time, Vader attacks him from behind with a big splash in the corner, and Monsoon goes down like a redwood. Vader drops an elbow on the fallen president as an apoplectic Vince McMahon screams on commentary: "That's Gorilla Monsoon in there! That's the president of the World Wrestling Federation!" Vader then takes it a harrowing step further, dragging Gorilla to the corner, ascending to the second turnbuckle and dropping down on him with his thunderous Vader Bomb finishing maneuver, until the cavalry—in the form of Shawn Michaels and Razor Ramon—runs in to chase off Vader and Cornette.

Living in Cancún by then, Valerie remembers sitting in a bar and being caught off guard when the whole thing unfolded on a television that happened to be tuned into *Monday Night Raw*. When she got back home, she had about twenty-five messages on her answering machine from people asking if her dad was alright. "I was worried about him, because even though he looked good at the time, I knew he was not well, and definitely not well enough to be doing that." But when she called him the next day to see how he was doing, he told her he was fine and to stop being a mark, so that was that.

Any concerns that Cornette or anyone else might have had about fans buying in, or Gino being able to hold his own, were, of course, unwarranted. "Leon didn't treat him like some of the other fodder that they fed him," Cornette points out. "It was very respectful, and he made sure to do a nice job of everything." The angle did what it was supposed to do, getting Vader over as the WWF's newest top-of-the-food-chain predator and an eventual threat to Michaels, who was set to win the world championship from Bret Hart at *WrestleMania XII*, where Gorilla Monsoon would once again be reintroduced as WWF president, after getting a nice two months off to sell the angle, during which Roddy Piper would briefly serve as interim president. Vader also got some time to tend to his much-needed surgery during his "suspension." Unfortunately, once he returned, he never quite reached the heights originally hoped for him. Although he didn't dare to pull anything on Gino, Vader had a reputation for being something of a bully who could rub people the wrong way, and when one of those people turned out to be the politically bulletproof Shawn Michaels, Leon's fate was sealed. But no one could ever say that Gino hadn't done all in his power to get Vader rolling in the strongest way possible. The idea of Gorilla Monsoon getting physically involved in an angle in those days was nearly unthinkable and left an impact that's still talked about to this day. He'd never do that for anyone again.

Gino's reintroduction at *WrestleMania XII* at Anaheim's Arrowhead Pond came just in time for him to proudly stand in the ring as the WWF president alongside Bret "Hitman" Hart, the WWF world title belt slung over his shoulder as he and Shawn Michaels received instructions from referee Earl Hebner for their sixty-minute Iron Man match in the main event. Gino had watched Bret grow and develop as a performer and an attraction for a dozen years in the company, so it was a gratifying moment. Of course, Gino was also there in his official capacity to facilitate the angle by which the title would change hands that night from Hart to Michaels—a contentious transition, to be sure. The Hitman and the Heartbreak Kid were oil and water, both positioned as the company's top guys in that era, locked in a very real dispute over who deserved the spot, neither man respecting the other enough to agree to do business amicably. It was always a struggle.

The rules of the Iron Man match stated that the winner would be the man who could achieve the most decisions—by pinfall, submission, disqualification and/or count-out—within the sixty-minute time limit. It was designed to placate both participants, giving them both a chance to shine against the other, but in typical fashion, the agreed-upon finish saw the entire one-hour period elapse without either man scoring a decision over the other, Michaels trapped in Hart's sharpshooter submission hold as the final bell rang. With the initial decision being a draw, the Hitman exited the ring with his championship intact, only to have WWF president Gorilla Monsoon emerge to insist that the match would have to go into sudden death overtime until there was a decisive winner, much to the champ's apparent consternation. Just a few minutes later, Michaels hit his superkick and pinned an exhausted Hart, making his "boyhood dream" come true (never mind that Michaels grew up in Texas wanting to be the NWA world champion, not the WWF world champion). It was a winding road to get to where they needed to get, but at least they wound up doing business in the end. It wouldn't always be so.

As Titan Sports continued trying to dig itself out of its hole, the wrestling war was heating up even more. Bischoff had already gotten older WWF stars like Hulk Hogan and Randy Savage to jump to WCW, but was now taking aim at its younger, current headliners, nabbing Scott "Razor Ramon" Hall and Kevin "Diesel" Nash in an astonishing power play. At the May 1996 Madison Square Garden show, both Hall and Nash had their final matches in the WWF, then had a farewell embrace in the ring with their running buddies Shawn Michaels and Hunter Hearst Helmsley, a character-breaking moment between supposed babyfaces and heels that infamously became known as the "Curtain Call." It was an unprecedented exposure of the business that naturally dismayed the old guard, not to mention the boss. "What Razor Ramon and Kevin Nash pulled at the Garden," recalls former Titan engineer Larry Rosen, "they completely broke kayfabe. I'm sure Gorilla was crushed by that."

It was just another example of a business moving on from what it had been. And there would soon be much more of that to come. By the middle of 1996, both Hall and Nash had joined WCW and were introduced as "invaders" from the WWF, forming a faction known as the New World Order that would be the core of an ongoing storyline that led to *Monday Nitro* pulling ahead of *Monday Night Raw* in the ratings on a weekly basis. For the first time, there was another company on the national stage that was supplanting the WWF as the premiere organization in the business. Gino himself shared in the ongoing frustration. "A lot of it was that he had seen the best of the best," explains Kevin Kelly, who joined the broadcast team in the middle of 1996 and sat for a bit under the Monsoon learning tree. "Generationally, it had started to trickle down and not be as good. As he was getting older, he lost patience with the things that weren't as good as he remembered them. The crowds were smaller. When he was calling it, every taping was packed, pay-per-views were packed. And then all of a sudden, they're in upstate New York or in Fernwood, in front of three hundred or four hundred people, taping *Raw*. It was tough."

Drastic measures were called for. Perhaps more drastic than Gino was comfortable with.

■

Steve Austin had been a solid mid-card workhorse in WCW, a wrestler with unlimited potential that Eric Bischoff had nevertheless notoriously seen fit to unceremoniously fire via Federal Express in the fall of 1995. Titan Sports had snatched him up shortly after, but it had taken half a year for him to finally hit his stride, transforming his look with a goatee, a shaved head and a leather vest and adding "Stone Cold" to his name. But the changes were far more than aesthetic; Stone Cold Steve Austin represented a seismic shift in how a top WWF attraction could talk or act. After defeating real-life born-again Christian Jake "The Snake" Roberts in the finals of the 1996 *King of the Ring* tournament, he grabbed the microphone, scowled and said "Talk about your psalms, talk about John 3:16 . . . Austin 3:16 says I just whipped your ass!" to the roaring approval of the Milwaukee crowd. It was like a bomb going off, signaling the eventual start of the ultimate scorched-earth strategy that would regain the WWF the top spot in the business and eventually put WCW six feet under: the Attitude Era.

The rise of Austin coincided with the rise of another individual that would have a decided impact on the changing creative direction of the company. Long Island native Vince Russo had parlayed a year as the host of a wrestling-themed radio show into a spot on the editorial team of *WWF Magazine*, and by 1996, he'd launched *RAW Magazine*, an edgier, grittier publication aimed at a more mature readership (the first cover featured a shot of Vader hovering over a fallen Gorilla Monson). The story went that one day, Vince McMahon called Russo up to a meeting in his executive board room, tossed a copy of *RAW Magazine* on the table in front of him and asked, "Can you make my show more like this magazine?" When Russo responded in the affirmative, he was made a member of the TV creative team. And within a year, he'd be head writer.

Gino was in the studio less than ever in those days, but Kevin Kelly still remembers getting to know him during that time, using the fact that his great-uncle was married to one of Gino's sisters-in-law as a means of introducing himself.[1] And even when he wasn't there, he was there, as Kevin remembers: "There were little reminders of Monsoon all over the TV studio. The big Gorilla-sized sport coat that was hanging on a coat rack right outside of the studio. Jill Clark in makeup had 'Gino makeup.' Little stuff like that. He had been there for so long and had done so much, and anybody that ever worked with him had good things to say about him and had Monsoon jokes and stories to break up the monotony of these long editing sessions."

Kevin himself was included in some of those stories early in his WWF tenure, such as one which he enjoys retelling of riding with Gino and Tommy Carlucci. They had stopped at a Cracker Barrel for breakfast, and Kevin was watching what he was eating and so asked if Gino wanted to split some food, which he did. However, the famished Kevin wound up eating all of it right in front of a stunned Gino, who remarked, almost as if he were responding to Bobby Heenan, "I thought you were watching your weight. You're eating like you're on death row!"

One rare usage of Gino in his commentator capacity during his WWF presidency occurred at the end of the summer of 1996, on the occasion of *WWF Superstars* finally leaving syndication after a ten-year run and shifting to the USA Network. A ten-year retrospective show was put together, and Gorilla Monsoon was enlisted to host it alongside yet another sidelined wrestler attempting to fill Jesse Ventura's original role as heel commentator, in this case, "Mr. Perfect" Curt Hennig. Shot completely in the studio, the odd episode even featured complimentary words from Monsoon on the career of Hulk Hogan, who by that point had not only been wrestling in WCW but had turned heel to become the leader of the New World Order at a time when the WWF was getting spanked in the battle between the two companies.

■

There was still always time for family and friends. On September 14, 1996, Gino and Maureen attended the wedding of the third generation of the McMahon family they'd spent time around, Shane McMahon, who married his childhood sweetheart, Marissa Mazzola, in Greenwich, Connecticut. At the time, Gino and Maureen were just a month away from becoming grandparents for the third and fourth time, with Valerie expecting twins. It was a difficult pregnancy, and Valerie had been scheduled for a C-section on Monday, October 21—which upset Gino, who had been scheduled to be in Fort Wayne, Indiana, for a marathon *Monday Night Raw* taping that day. Fortunately for him, the Friday night before the C-section was scheduled, after having dinner with her parents, Valerie's water broke. "I said, 'We should go now,'" she remembers. "He was ecstatic because he got to be there, and it worked out perfect. He got to be at the hospital." And then he broke down completely when Valerie told him what she'd decided to name the two boys: Gino and Joseph.

The following month, Gino got to be around dear friends once again for the third annual WWF Hall of Fame banquet, held at the Marriott Marquis in Times Square the night before the *Survivor Series* at Madison Square Garden. It was an especially great class of inductees, filled with individuals who had meant a lot to him throughout his career, including Baron Mikel Scicluna, whom Gino himself inducted; Capt. Lou Albano; Johnny Rodz; Pat Patterson; the Valiant Brothers, Jimmy and Johnny; company patriarch Vincent James McMahon; and Killer Kowalski, whom Gino might have enjoyed returning the favor for and inducting, but that honor was instead given to Hunter Hearst Helmsley, who had been a star pupil of Kowalski's wrestling school in Massachusetts in the early '90s. It was a welcome chance to remember the old days and reunite with old comrades, some of whom he hadn't seen in many years—like his former tenant Jimmy Valiant, whose daughters stayed at the Marella home in

New Jersey afterward for half a week before flying back home to be with their father in Virginia.

Sadly, it would be the last Hall of Fame ceremony held in Gino's lifetime. A year later, the company would be starting to regain momentum, and business, as Jim Ross might have said, was about to pick up. Vince McMahon once again became far more interested in looking ahead than in looking back.

■

Stone Cold Steve Austin was fated to be a major factor in business picking up, and as the Attitude Era began to take shape in the early months of 1997, his star was most decidedly on the rise. Although a heel at the time, his take-no-shit, unpredictable, intense persona was winning over the more mature fan base that the WWF was courting. They'd grown up with Hulk Hogan telling them to say their prayers and take their vitamins, but now they wanted someone to go out there and kick some ass, and Steve Austin was the man for the job. There was a plan in place to turn him babyface by *WrestleMania 13* that spring, while at the same time gradually turning his rival Bret Hart into a heel—a double-switch that would eventually be pulled off to perfection and set Austin on the road to becoming the company's number-one attraction.

Austin's growing popularity arose from the fact that he was the ultimate rebel, an anti-authority figure who needed a figure of authority to play off in order to make the whole thing work. Although it was no public secret that Vince was the real man in charge of Titan Sports, within the kayfabe world of the WWF, he had never been acknowledged as such and was merely presented as the lead television commentator. Thus, the responsibility of being Austin's first foil would fall to WWF president Gorilla Monsoon. And so Gino found himself thrust into the highly unlikely position of being in the chaotic mix involving Austin, Hart, Michaels and others during a time when the product was undergoing a drastic transformation. With Bret regularly airing his grievances in profanity-laced tirades on TV and Austin running roughshod over everything like a rabid dog, the World Wrestling Federation was suddenly becoming a very different place.

Some of that was coming from a desire to keep up with WCW and the edgier, more reality-based storylines they were implementing, but it was also due to the influence of Extreme Championship Wrestling, an independent Philadelphia-based outfit built entirely around an anti-establishment, mature-audience ethos. Russo had been keeping an eye on the goings-on there and was influenced by it in his own edgy approach to wrestling—not to mention the fact that ECW was, unbeknownst to most outside the business then, involved in a top-secret business arrangement with the WWF, with Titan Sports invested in propping up the group and using it as an unofficial talent exchange program as it had similarly done in the past with the USWA and Jim Cornette's Smoky Mountain Wrestling.

But while Gino had long been a Bret Hart booster and by all accounts had the utmost respect and admiration for Steve Austin as a performer—Austin being a hard-working old-school wrestler at heart who had come up in the dying days of the territories—there were also things about the new presentation with which he wasn't entirely comfortable, including the decidedly rough language being used. Now, Gino certainly didn't exactly have the vocabulary of a deacon in his everyday personal life, but language used privately vs. language used on television in front of fans and viewers was something totally different. But as always, Gino was a team player and did his best to be what Vince needed him to be.

For the first half of 1997, in the often overlooked final phase of his onscreen career, Gorilla Monsoon held his own, locking horns with Stone Cold. Most importantly to him, it kept him busy. On that handful of occasions, he never once flinched or backed down in any way, even as Austin screamed and yelled in his face and threatened bodily harm in his inimitable fashion. Unlike those who would come after him, Monsoon stood his ground, appearing not to be intimidated at all by the man who would come to be known as the Texas Rattlesnake. And despite all his bluster and the violent glint in his eye, Stone Cold would typically compromise and acknowledge Gorilla's authority in the end. During one particularly memorable backstage vignette on *Raw* from the Broome County Arena in Binghamton, New York, the two went literally nose to nose, screaming back and forth at each other, with Monsoon giving just as good as he got and eventually ejecting Austin from the building for his disruptive behavior, with Austin begrudgingly complying.[2]

It was a unique dynamic and one that Austin would only share for that brief time with Monsoon, as in later months and years, his character would grow to become too much for any authority figure to handle. But Gorilla Monsoon was someone fans had grown to respect, and they probably wouldn't have bought it any other way, not to mention the fact that Gino had never been made to look weak and wasn't about to start now. But for the Stone Cold character to really progress to the next level, he would need to be able to steamroll over everyone, and that just wasn't going to happen with Gorilla Monsoon. Not only would it have been untrue to his persona, but at that point, Gino simply wasn't capable of the level of physical involvement that would be required.

■

His health was declining fast. On top of that, he had never gotten over the loss of Joey, and never would. And as much as he was drawn to continue to work, being around the business was also a constant reminder. "I think he wanted to kind of get away because of the memory," explains Jerry Brisco. "Everywhere you go, people are gonna come up to you. And whether it's six months, eight months, a year afterward, somebody's gonna come up to you that didn't get the opportunity right after it happened, and pat you on the back and say, 'Hey, man, I'm so sorry about your son,' and all of a sudden, all the memories are right back on top of you." He was neglecting his diet, eating more uncontrollably than ever, with little to no regard for the diabetes and the serious heart condition that it had caused. "That was sad to see," Brisco continues. "Everybody felt for him. When a guy like that, that you respect so much, is hurting so bad, you have sympathy for it. We saw that Gino wasn't going in the right direction. Fortunately, he had a strong family support system around him, helping him get out of that nosedive."

And so, for his own sanity, he was gradually pulling away from a business that was continually less recognizable to him anyway. "I can't speak for him, but just from observation, maybe he was like a lot of us that didn't really buy into it 100 percent," Jerry speculates. "Maybe these kinds of things were getting to him. There was a lot of drinking and drugs going on at the time. I think he saw that. I don't think Gino could really understand the philosophy of a lot of these younger guys, the craziness that was going on—even though there was craziness going on during his era, too." But while a lot of that old-school craziness could be chalked up to booze, the drugs were what really bothered him, as he saw it get worse and worse over the years. He could see what was going on with a lot of guys in the locker room, and it had also touched his own life directly through the struggles of his son. The private part of him couldn't help but blame the business for that.

But in the end, like with so many old-timers, he wasn't going to truly walk away until his body forced him to. He may have succeeded in his pledge to never again step through the ropes as a wrestler, but that didn't mean the business didn't still have a hold on him. Nevertheless, in the summer of 1997, his body finally relayed the message. On the June 23 *Raw* from Detroit's Cobo Arena, Gorilla Monsoon would have his last real storyline involvement as WWF president, making his presence felt during a unique three-way encounter involving Hunter Hearst Helmsley, Goldust and Intercontinental champion Owen Hart—the WWF's very first Triple Threat match.[3]

Not long after, either at the very end of June or the very beginning of July, Gino suffered a massive heart attack, and this one nearly killed him. It would be thanks to the aforementioned family support that it didn't.

Valerie and the twins were living with Gino and Maureen at this point. She could tell her dad wasn't feeling well at all, but he refused to have her take him to the doctor to get checked out. One morning, she was up early with her mom, getting the boys' breakfast and getting ready for work, when she noticed her dad was nowhere to be found. The shower wasn't running, and she didn't spot him in his bedroom. Maureen went to the bedroom to double-check and let out a scream when she saw that Gino was lying on the floor, wedged between the dresser and the bed, and he didn't appear to be breathing. Val called 911 and, without any medical training, managed to perform CPR just well enough to get him breathing again in time for the ambulance's arrival. Doctors revealed that not only had it been a severe heart attack, but Gino had clearly sustained several silent heart attacks over the past few years that no one even knew about, although whether he had just been keeping them secret was anyone's guess. Remembers Gino's sister Amy, "My father would never go to the doctor. He would always try to hide it if he was in any kind of pain or agony. And I think my brother was the same way."

He had been doing his best to ignore his health as much as possible and keep pushing on, but this was not something he was going to be able to just bounce back from. As much as he was drawn to remaining a part of things, he would have to concede the hard fact that those days were behind him. Especially for the role he was being expected to play, he just simply couldn't do it anymore. The terrifying near-death experience was a wake-up call. The days of Gorilla Monsoon as a vital part of the WWF machine were over.

CHAPTER 16

"GOODBYE, MY FRIEND."

It was ironic, and more than a little tragic, that just as the company was returning to prosperity and rising from the ashes, Gino was fading away.

In the final years of the 1990s, as Titan Sports experienced a dramatic resurgence that would see it once again dominate the wrestling industry, day by day, week by week, month by month, Gino was less and less a part of it, to the point that the vast majority of fans had no idea he was still involved in any way. But perhaps it was for the best. This was a resurgence built on middle fingers and expletives, sexual innuendo and exploitation and liberal doses of cynicism, with wrestlers often seeming to spend more time standing in the middle of the ring airing their grievances like characters in a soap opera than actually wrestling. In short, it wasn't a business he related to much anymore.

His heart attack in the summer of 1997 put him down for the count like nothing had before. He got back up, but he never returned to being the Gorilla Monsoon fans knew and loved after that. For two years, he pressed on, trying to find ways to contribute if he could, but mainly lingering in the background like a ghost from wrestling's past. The Attitude Era brought a new crop of wrestlers, many of whom had not worked with him or witnessed him at his vital best, when the Gorilla position was truly his.

But even then, he could still be found—at local cards, some major television tapings and here and there still at the TV studio, where he was most beloved. For someone like him, who had been so driven throughout his whole life, it was impossible to just turn it off. And not even heart attacks, disillusionment and the loss of his son could totally extinguish that.

And when he finally did pass, it was mere days after his last voice-over recording sessions at 120 Hamilton Avenue. He did it until he quite literally could do it no more. Even when his heart wasn't in it anymore, he still did it. Because that's who he was. That was the drive and determination that had taken him to the top of his chosen field in the first place, and though diminished, those qualities never really went away until the very end.

■

Unable to travel like he used to, and the ravages of his health issues no longer easy to hide, the tough decision was made that he couldn't and shouldn't really be on television anymore. He just wasn't up to playing that crucial role of the WWF president and continuing to be a part of the company's most important angles. For that, they needed someone in better condition who could mix it up more with the talent in a way that he no longer could. But in order to get there, some loose ends needed to be tied up.

And so astonishingly, just a few weeks after the heart attack, Gino made his first television appearance, although a brief one, on the July 28, 1997, episode of *Monday Night Raw*, making the trip out to Pittsburgh to sit in with commentators Vince McMahon, Jim Ross and Jerry Lawler. In a rare moment of public sentimentality, Vince asked Jim, "Who is that fine young gentleman sitting next to you?" in reference to the man he had known since he was a teenager. The purpose of the visit was to announce that, as president, Gorilla would be "appointing" a troubleshooting commissioner to act on his behalf, "because I can't be everywhere at one time."

That commissioner would turn out to be Sgt. Slaughter, another major headliner from the WWF's past with a tough-guy reputation who had been working in a backstage capacity for the company since retiring from active competition in 1992. Sarge also happened to be eleven years younger than Gino and could even still get physically involved when called upon to do so. The ever-more-chaotic storylines being played out on TV called for a blustery stuffed-shirt type of foil, who could be made to look foolish in the face of brash anti-authority figures like Steve Austin and Bret Hart, as well as the newly developing faction of renegades that would come to be known as D-Generation X, spearheaded by Shawn Michaels and his junior partner Hunter Hearst Helmsley, who by that point was starting to go by the slightly edgier moniker of Triple H. Slaughter could be the butt of D-X's off-color jokes and pranks and could even put on the boots now and then, such as when he faced off with Triple H on pay-per-view that December. He was a different kind of authority figure in an age when the authority figure was meant to be a joke. Gino was never going to play that type of role, even if he was healthy.

One week after his appearance on *Raw*, Gino turned out for *SummerSlam '97* at the Continental Airlines Arena in East Rutherford, New Jersey. Ordinarily, he might have stayed in the background, but it was an auspicious occasion: Titan Sports' first televised event in his home state in eight years. The company had been wrangling with New Jersey legislators dating back to 1989 and those infamous kayfabe-breaking pronouncements in court, and now Governor Christine Todd Whitman had finally found a legal loophole to get things back up and running in the Garden State, a mainstay for the company since the 1950s. As Todd Pettengill interviewed the governor in the middle of the ring, WWF president Gorilla Monsoon was there to present her with a ceremonial WWF world championship belt as a token of gratitude, which she accepted with all solemnity. It would be the last time Gorilla Monsoon would be seen on WWF television for more than a year and a half.

It would also be one of the last appearances for Pettengill as a WWF broadcaster, and his replacement would make his pay-per-view debut that very same night as a backstage interviewer. Thirty-year-old Sean Coulthard had been a journalist and radio news correspondent for nearly a decade by the time he was hired to be the newest member of the

WWF's broadcast team under the stage name Michael Cole. The new career, which was just then kicking off, would eventually see him become every bit the voice of the company as Jim Ross, Vince McMahon and Gorilla Monsoon had been before him.

■

But other than those two high-profile appearances, Gino completely stayed away from work and from the WWF for a good half year, heeding his family's advice to rest and take it easy. Mike Chioda even came off the road himself for a little while just to help take care of him, driving him to errands around town. When they'd make one of his favorite stops at the Italian bakery, he always made sure to pick up a few things for Mike's mother as a sign of gratitude. At age sixty, he was settling into life at home in New Jersey with his family and trying to enjoy the fruits of his many years of labor as he could. He even took the time for lengthy phone calls to his extended family out in Vegas, including one recalled by Amy, in which he spoke with her son Robert (named for her brother), a six-foot-four teenaged giant with aspirations of getting into the business. Gino talked him out of it.

While he was away, the World Wrestling Federation continued to get crazier. Austin was getting hotter than ever, and when he laid out Vince McMahon himself with a Stone Cold Stunner at the first *Monday Night Raw* at Madison Square Garden that September, to the roar of the crowd, the new direction of the company began to crystallize. The days of Vince McMahon the friendly television announcer were soon coming to an end. Sgt. Slaughter was doing an agreeable job as commissioner, but to really heat things up, both Vinces—McMahon and Russo—were contemplating adding a dose of reality to the situation. And since McMahon was the actual boss in real life, there really was no better choice to be the ultimate foil for Steve Austin than him.

But whether McMahon was completely on board with jumping into the spotlight as a full-fledged wrestling heel or not, he was going to be thrust into that position almost without choosing to be, when that dose of reality got just a little too real the night of November 9, 1997, at the Molson Centre in Montreal. That night would mark the ignominious end of Bret "Hitman" Hart in the World Wrestling Federation, and in a manner in which Gino most certainly wouldn't have approved had he been around while the plot was being concocted and executed.

The details of the so-called Montreal Screwjob have been thoroughly explored and analyzed ad nauseum over the course of the three decades since it all went down, and no good can come of another autopsy in these pages. Suffice it to say that it was a highly unprofessional and unscrupulous way to do business, especially with a longtime headliner—even one on the way out. But it was also not without precedent in the cutthroat world of professional wrestling, even if most thought that such double-crossing chicanery had been left behind in the industry's carny past.

Looking back now, Bret goes so far as to say that Gorilla may have even done more than simply express private disapproval: "Gorilla was super respected by everybody, including Vince. If that had happened under Gorilla's watch, Gorilla would have said, 'That's not the way to do it, don't do that. That's a stupid way to handle it. Let me talk to Bret, let me handle it.' I just always felt if he'd been around, if Vince had walked over to him and said, 'This is what's gonna happen, we're gonna screw Bret Hart over, mum's the word,' Gorilla would never have tolerated it. I think that would've been a deal-breaker for him." Although it's impossible to say for sure, it was true that Gino had always been one of Bret's most ardent backers and backstage counselors and fully supported his ascension into the company's top spot some years earlier. How it ended was indeed unfortunate.

Bret promptly left the WWF for WCW and never saw or spoke to Gino again. He never got a chance to discuss the situation with him, although he always wanted to: "I always wondered what he would've thought. Maybe he would've been disappointed in me for being as difficult as I was." The week that it happened, he thought about calling Gino and talking to him, seeking out his counsel like he used to, to try and remedy the situation. Even just to find out what his feelings were on it. He never heard him speak about it, but Bret knew how Gino was. Bret had always been a loyal company guy, and Gino knew that. But Bret also knew that Gino was sick, and it wouldn't really be possible to speak with him in a meaningful way.

Much of the changes happening in the business at the time was also thanks to the internet, where fans were getting a greater glimpse behind the curtain than ever before, and where they could interact with one another and even with those inside the business with a kind of regularity and immediacy that had never before been possible. Whatever semblance of kayfabe had survived the 1990s was more or less annihilated by the new world of online communication. Far from being a true backroom dealing as it would have been in years past, the Montreal Screwjob played out front and center for fans to dissect and digest on the internet, and that meant the jig was up as far as Vince McMahon's involvement. Fans loved Bret and despised the company for what they felt it had done to him. Vince became the chief target of that derision, and instead of running away from it, he ran headlong toward it, embracing it, in the process turning himself into perhaps the most hated heel the company had ever had.

■

In January 1998, Gino took the plunge and reported to the television studio for work for the first time since the heart attack. It was determined that he would not need a heart transplant, and so he returned to Stamford to attempt to make himself useful. He was at least fifty pounds lighter than he had been since the last time they'd seen him, which took some getting used to. "It was sad to see him when he was so much smaller and older-looking," Jim Cornette admits. "But everybody loved seeing him, and he commanded instant respect, both from the old guard that knew who he was or the new guys because they'd grown up watching him on TV." At first, the company once again convinced Gino to have a limo come and ferry him back and forth, but that didn't last long, as he resented losing his freedom of movement. Pretty soon, he was back to driving his Cadillac in, parking it in the truck bay behind the building and heading right upstairs to place football bets with Kevin Dunn. Then

"GOODBYE, MY FRIEND."

he would come downstairs, do his voice-overs, get in his Cadillac, and head home. "He was woven into the fabric of that studio," remembers Kevin Kelly. "He was like the grandfather for everybody in that place. All those young twentysomethings fresh out of school, first job out of college, and they get to work with Gorilla Monsoon."

To be sure, he wasn't being placed in high-visibility positions anymore. In fact, not only was he not seen on TV, but he wasn't even heard by viewers in the United States. Instead, they found a more low-key spot for him, tucked away, where he could still contribute in his own way. At the time, the company's syndication package was in flux, with the focus turning almost exclusively to cable. But some of the old syndicated shows continued to be produced for international markets, and Gorilla Monsoon could be heard on those, calling the action for fans in Canada, the United Kingdom and other markets for international versions of secondary shows like *WWF Superstars* and *Shotgun Saturday Night,* with partners like Raymond Rougeau, Dr. Tom Prichard (Bruce's brother) and Michael Cole, who was being groomed for a regular commentary position on *Raw* and later the WWF's other weekly prime-time show, *SmackDown.* Gino wasn't there every week but showed up as often as possible and would occasionally even still be referred to on commentary as the WWF president. It was about as under the radar as you could get and still be on WWF television, but Gino, no longer the belting Gorilla of old, his voice noticeably weaker, summoned up as much of the old energy as he could to get the job done. "When he was around people, when he was working, he tried to be Gorilla Monsoon, the big friendly giant," Larry Rosen recalls. "But then he would let his hair down, so to speak, and at the end of the day, he would say things like, 'I don't know, Larr . . . I don't know . . .' Just that kind of attitude. It just wasn't worth it at that point."

■

The month of Gino's return to the WWF TV studio was the very same month that the company made national headlines when Stone Cold Steve Austin got into it with none other than special guest and former heavyweight boxing champ Mike Tyson on a live edition of *Raw*, as WWF officials filled the ring to get in between them. With Vince playing the exasperated boss fed up with Austin's anti-authoritarian antics, it was an electrifying moment that got everyone talking and lit a fire that lifted the WWF back to dominance in the television ratings war later that year. As Stone Cold was pushed all the way to the world title at *WrestleMania*, the Attitude Era came into its full bloom, and it's hard to even imagine Gorilla Monsoon calling some of that action, even on international recap shows—but he did.

With Bret Hart gone, Vince McMahon embraced his dark side, revealing it for all the world to see out in the open, as the Machiavellian "Mr. McMahon" character, locked in a power struggle with Stone Cold Steve Austin that dominated WWF television for the better part of two years and even saw Vince finally fulfill his youthful ambition of stepping through the ropes and wrestling. And why not? His father had done everything in his power to keep his son out of the business, then to limit his interactions in the business and most certainly to keep him out of the ring. But there was no one around to stop him now. In fact, the entire McMahon family had gotten into the act, with their family dynamics played out on television for ratings. "When my mom would see Shane and Stephanie and Linda and everyone in the ring," remembers Valerie, "She would say, 'His father is turning in his grave right now.' My dad was definitely rolling his eyes at a lot of the stuff Vince was doing toward the end."

It was a far cry from the stately President Gorilla Monsoon and his pronouncements from on high, and it's difficult to imagine what part Gino might have played in all this had he stayed healthy. Would Gorilla Monsoon have been the one taking Stone Cold Stunners? Or been asked to play the stooge in Mr. McMahon's evil corporation, as his fellow wrestling legends Pat Patterson and Jerry Brisco were enlisted to do? It's difficult to imagine Monsoon in that spot, and it's difficult to imagine the fans accepting him in it. Or more likely, was his presence an obstacle, and did his absence finally help to open the floodgates, allowing things to be taken to this level with more willing and physically capable parties?

Certainly, not even Patterson and Brisco themselves were completely on board with it, but they also understood that if something was working and doing strong business, you went along with it, and they were smart enough not to rock that boat. "I mean, I saw things that made me say, why do we have to do it like this?" explains Jerry. "And Gino was from a generation even earlier than me. So, what he was seeing was totally off the wall from what his entire career and life had been based on."

However, it was tough to argue with success, and that was what the company was experiencing in spades during that era, raking in money hand over fist for the first time in years and, by certain metrics, even becoming more successful than ever before. The business changes; it always has. Sometimes, it can pass you by, and Gino seemed finally to be suffering from a bit of that. And whether he liked it or not, he really wasn't in a position anymore where anyone was asking his advice anyway. "Those who knew him would go and sit and have conversations with him," remembers Kevin Kelly. "Not, 'Did you watch my match? Tell me what I could do better. What do I need to do to get over?' Those conversations weren't happening at that point. And that could have been some of the disconnect. You've seen so much over forty years, and now all of a sudden, your opinion doesn't matter. The newer guys only saw Monsoon as the announcer or the older guy sitting backstage. They didn't even make the connection. Why do we call it the Gorilla position? That guy over there, I think, knows a thing or two."

■

It's tough to pin down exactly what Gino was thinking during this period and how he felt about the drastic changes going on around him. And yet there are some clues. There are some anecdotes of conversations he may have had privately with others at the time. One of these happened to be with longtime Philadelphia sports writer Bill Lyon, with whom Gino had a long-standing relationship over the years thanks to his media connections in the City of Brotherly Love. While memorializing him after he passed away, Lyon would admit that Gino was "privately distressed" at what they had done to his craft and that he would talk about how, in his view, they had "perverted" it.

This attitude is backed up by a particularly poignant story that was related by Bill Apter, also on the occasion of Gino's passing.[1] The omnipresent wrestling journalist, who had known Gino for nearly thirty years, recalled how he'd been going through the motions for quite some time and how his heart just wasn't in it. Specifically, he remembered running into Gino backstage at a WWF show at the Atlantic City Convention Center in the summer of 1998. Bill was still working in his capacity as writer, editor and photographer for the London Publishing family of wrestling magazines, chief among them *Pro Wrestling Illustrated*. There had been a time when the outside wrestling magazines had been banned by Vince, but things had relaxed a bit, and Bill was back in the good graces for the moment. The relationship between the office and the wrestling magazines certainly had its ups and downs. There had even been a time long ago when Gino and Vince Senior had railed against Bill and his old boss, Stanley Weston, for running lurid "apartment wrestling" articles featuring scantily clad women rolling around on the floor in titillating pictorials. Ironically, all these years later, that had essentially become part of the WWF product itself. Times had indeed changed.

It was only a house show, but it was also only seventy-five minutes from Gino's home and a chance to hit up some of his old AC haunts anyway. Stone Cold Steve Austin was defending his WWF world title that night against Long Island's own Mick Foley, better known under his leather mask as Mankind. The fearsome Undertaker, whose debut at the 1990 *Survivor Series* had been memorably called by Gorilla, was facing his "brother" Kane, whom Gino first knew as the wrestling dentist Dr. Isaac Yankem. On the middle of the card was Triple H, challenging for the Intercontinental title against another star on the rise, Dwayne "The Rock" Johnson—the son and grandson of Gino's old friends Rocky Johnson and High Chief Peter Maivia, respectively. Bill recalled seeing many of the wrestlers hanging out in the back on a truck loading platform, laughing and joking as the boys always did—and then he spotted Gino, a few feet away in a dark corner, sitting alone on a television production crate.

"GOODBYE, MY FRIEND."

He was pale and tired, a far-off look in his eye, his mind elsewhere. But when Bill came over to say hello, he seemed to come to life.

"Gino, I never really got to say thank you for all the doors you helped open for me early in my career," said Bill. "I miss those classic matches with you and Bruno."

"Those were special days," responded Gino wistfully. "There is much more money in the business now, but it just does not match the aura of the sport we knew way back then."

Bill and Gino sat on the platform and talked for a bit about the wrestlers of years gone by, then exchanged a warm handshake. Bill walked away, heading toward the arena floor, but before he went in, he took one last look back at him sitting there, once again alone and quiet: "The man who used to scare fans and have great matches had become a lost soul in the current wrestling scene." Bill didn't realize it at the time, but he was saying goodbye to Gorilla Monsoon.

Nevertheless, despite the dramatic sea changes in the business, Gino could still count himself among those cherished legends of the company's past who remained highly respected and admired by the company, chiefly by Vince himself. In fact, Gorilla Monsoon was included, along with Fred Blassie, Killer Kowalski, Pat Patterson and Ernie Ladd, in a newly shot promo put together to glorify those legends as they passed the torch to the present-day stars of the Attitude Era. It was an emotional piece created by producer David Sahadi, who would later recall how Vince McMahon was reduced to tears during his initial viewing of it. Gino's inclusion in such a piece demonstrated that even then, he remained what he had always been: World Wrestling Federation royalty.

He embodied a moment in time, even if that moment was now in the past. And he still was a loyal company man, which is why he would never publicly share his critical opinions, especially when the company was doing so well. "I always got the sense that Monsoon had more to say, but out of respect to Vince, he didn't say anything," explains Kevin Kelly. "And I don't think Vince ever dared to ask. Gino was checked out. He wasn't getting paid to give his opinions anymore. But if you really got to sit down and talk to him and ask him about it, I'm sure that he would have said, no, I don't like this. Because yeah, I saw some of those eye rolls... He did not like the Attitude Era, per se. The vulgarity of the show." Jim Cornette is another one who remembers a bit of it as well: "If the Human Oddities walked by, or the *Howard Stern Show* people or whatever, there would be eye-rolling, in a jocular sort of way. But I think at that point, he knew that the horse had left the barn. And he was too professional [to complain]."

∎

But Gino still had strokes within the organization when needed, as could be seen when Titan Sports went into business with none other than Victor Quiñones. The 1990s had been a whirlwind decade for Victor that had seen him go from the junior partner Gino had set up in Puerto Rico to one of the most powerful, not to mention wealthiest, promoters and bookers in the business on a global scale. Not long after the Bruiser Brody debacle, Victor had parted ways with Carlos Colón over money disputes, opting instead to strike out on his own. His involvement with Atsushi Onita's Frontier Martial-Arts Wrestling had continued to develop his taste for what would eventually be termed hardcore wrestling—the wilder and bloodier, the better. He put down roots in Japan and was involved in the establishment of Wrestling International New Generations, or W*ING, as well as his own promotion shortly thereafter, the International Wrestling Association (not to be confused with the Einhorn group of old), which started in Japan before he attempted to bring it to Puerto Rico and go to war directly with Colón for dominance of the region. He was building strong relationships with powerful people in the business, including the Funks and the Savoldis, and amassing a fortune for himself.

Victor had just been getting started on his work in Japan when Joey had died, and as someone who had lived with the Marella family for years, it had hit him just as hard as any of them. Hugo Savinovich even recalls that it was partly Victor's encouragement during that period that had convinced Gino not to give up and to do his best to soldier on in the business, at least for a little while: "I don't think that it would have taken that long for him to make the decision that he didn't want to go through it anymore. He said to him, come on, don't give up, we need you. And that was a light that made him at least delay what eventually happened, when he just didn't want to go through it anymore."

Gino had taught Victor well. But Gino couldn't fully impart to him his decency and strength of character. On his road to success, the legacy Victor had been building for himself was much more complicated than Gino's. Although there were several Japanese wrestlers, including Taka Michinoku, Yoshihiro Tajiri and Kintaro Kanemura, who lauded Victor and who showed great loyalty to him, even stating they owed their careers to him, there were other situations and stories that painted a different picture. While working with Onita, he had shown extraordinarily bad taste in trying to capitalize on the murder of Brody, helping Onita put together a revenge angle involving Onita and José González, Brody's killer. Far worse than that were rumors circulating for years of Victor abusing his booking position to take sexual advantage of vulnerable young wrestlers. Specific accusations wouldn't fully come to light until accusers came forward many years later, but included sexual harassment, assault and favors in exchange for pushes. It was hard to even imagine that someone with those kinds of accusations against him could have been brought into the business and even partially raised by someone like Gino. "I think he wanted to [be like my dad], but I just think he couldn't," says Valerie. "I'm sure my dad heard about those things, but if my dad didn't want you to know something, you didn't know. It wasn't something that was discussed with the kids."

After establishing his IWA in Japan, Victor brought it to Puerto Rico thanks in large part to a working agreement arranged with the World Wrestling Federation. Victor was well-known in the company because of Gino and had even brought Taka Michinoku to their attention in 1997. As a courtesy to Gino, they listened to his pitch about working with the IWA, and that led to the short-lived endeavor known as WWF Latino, which included the creation of the Spanish-language TV program *Super Astros* with Savinovich and former news radio announcer Carlos Cabrera calling the action.[2] The agreement also included Titan Sports using the IWA as a developmental territory and talent exchange program, bringing in young Latino wrestlers while also sending down some established WWF superstars for co-promoted shows in Puerto Rico. The company had stayed away from the island for many years, again out of respect for Gino, but now things were very different.

Working with Savinovich and Miguel Pérez Jr. (another son of one of Gino's past associates) as well as Savio Vega, a WWF regular and former star for Colón's World Wrestling Council, Quiñones set up the IWA as the first real competition the WWC had seen after decades of uncontested control of Puerto Rico. For the first time since that ill-fated show back in 1985, WWF talent was being brought before the Puerto Rican fans, including many of the top acts of the Attitude Era, such as the Undertaker, Kane, the New Age Outlaws, the Hardy Boyz, Edge & Christian, Goldust and the Big Show. And it was all made possible thanks to Victor's connection to Gino. Through this partnership, the IWA was able to edge out the WWC as the premier wrestling promotion in Puerto Rico. And although Gino had long ago made peace with any trouble he'd had with Colón, for Victor, it was a sweet revenge to steamroll over the company he felt had burned him and Gino in the past.

The WWF Latino experiment was another example of the company working to tap into the Latino markets in the United States and elsewhere, as it had done so often in the past. But although the company pulled the plug on it not long after Gino's passing, it did lead to Savinovich and Cabrera becoming WWF mainstays as the regular Spanish-language broadcasters for all programming for years to come. And the working relationship between the WWF and the IWA would continue into the new century, at least for a time.

■

In coming to work for Titan in 1999, during those final months of Gino's life, Hugo was saddened, as many others were, to see him as he was then, compared to when Hugo had last been around him years before. "The Gino we saw at the end was like a skeleton of this true giant," he remembers. "I always compare it to Ernest Hemingway's *The Old Man and the Sea*, where eventually, after the fisherman catches the big fish, his hands are destroyed, and from the time he achieves his dream of the big fish, going from where he catches it to the port in Havana, the sharks eat it. I think that was like Gino with Joey's death. He had nothing to show because his baby was gone." Indeed, Gino had conquered the wrestling world, had done it all and come so far; yet along the way, he'd lost something so precious to him, and now he wondered if it had been worth it at all.

And yet even through 1999, he continued to persevere, at least for a while. On *Canadian Superstars*, he would take a back seat to Michael Cole and Tom Prichard, occasionally interjecting specific geographical references intended to appeal to the Canadian viewers. There was *International Sunday Night Heat* and other shows largely forgotten by anyone who wasn't watching them when they first aired. ("I don't even think they knew where they were sending it," jokes Cornette.) Even then, he would do his best to verbally joust with his co-hosts, especially Prichard, who had the unique distinction of being the last heel announcer Gorilla Monsoon would ever torment on commentary. In a 2021 shoot interview, Prichard, who was not prepared for how sharp Gino still could be, remarked: "Monsoon would just hammer me on commentary. Sometimes he'd have a thing that he couldn't leave alone, and if you threw something out in the water, he'd eat that and come after what was next. He'd make a smart-ass remark, and I'd think, I know he's working, but is he? . . . He was the same whether he was on camera or off; he was Gorilla Monsoon. If you didn't have a comeback, he'd hit you again. I'd be like, 'You're burying me here,' but that's just what he did."[3] His body may have been failing him, but his wit and his instincts never did.

Fans didn't realize that Gorilla Monsoon was still involved with the company at all, that he was still coming out for shows and for tapings, which is why it was a surprise to so many when he came out to take that final bow at *WrestleMania XV* in Philadelphia that year. In a way, it was a welcome sight, even though it only underlined how out of place he seemed on a card headlined by Stone Cold Steve Austin vs. The Rock at the peak of the Attitude Era. But it was also then and there that the general public became aware of his deteriorating condition and feared that he might not be around much longer.

Reaction online following *WrestleMania* was one of general concern for Gorilla. And that concern was certainly well-founded. Gino did not look like himself that night, and his alarming weight loss was in part due to the decision he'd already made by that point, that he was basically ready to die. He had made his choices, and there were consequences for those choices. His blood sugar was out of control, and doctors had advised him that kidney dialysis was the only thing that could save his life, or at least prolong it. Gino refused. "He wouldn't go on it," confirms Tom Carlucci. "He chose to die. I know this, we talked about it. He said, 'I'm not going on dialysis.' I said, 'Gino, they're gonna make you.' He didn't care. He said, 'I've lived the life I lived, and I'm still going to live it. That's not going to stop.' He set up everything for when he passed, for his family . . . The man chose to die. Think of that for a minute. Your demise is coming if you don't do this, and he didn't care. He lived life so full, that's what he did."

Not long after that *WrestleMania* appearance, the Marellas sold the big house in Moorestown. At six thousand square feet, it was just getting too big for them to take care of. Gino had loved to do stuff around the house, but when it got to the point that he couldn't do it anymore, he didn't want anyone else doing it. Valerie was planning to move out soon with the twins, and with Gino declining as he was, it was just time to downsize. They were having a new house built just fifteen minutes away in Mount Laurel, something smaller, with a bedroom on the main floor. They sold their Moorestown home pretty quickly, and the new owner was anxious to take possession right away. The new house wasn't ready yet, so in the meantime, they settled on a rental place, which coincidentally just happened to be back in Willingboro on Crestview Drive—the very same street where they had once lived and made all those memories back in the '70s and early '80s. "We were panicking; we had to find something quick," remembers Valerie. "My mom had beautiful bedroom furniture

"GOODBYE, MY FRIEND."

she didn't wanna give up that my dad had bought. She based every house we looked at on whether or not that furniture would fit, and it was huge furniture." It was meant to be a temporary measure, while they waited for the new home to be completed—but it started to become clear that Gino might not make it that long.

It was while they were staying at the rental house on the night of Sunday, May 23, 1999, that Valerie woke up her father with some terrible news. At the pay-per-view event that night, *Over the Edge* from the Kemper Arena in Kansas City, Missouri, Owen Hart, the youngest of Stu and Helen Hart's twelve children, had plummeted to his death on live television, the result of a botched stunt of the kind all too common in that reckless "can you top this" era of the Monday Night War. Gino had been a dear friend of the Hart family since before Owen was even born, and he had gotten to know the warm and good-natured young man over the course of the decade or so long as he had been with the WWF, having first met him back when the company was co-promoting shows with Stampede Wrestling in the mid-1980s. Gino began to weep immediately upon hearing the news. He knew all too well the feeling.

Gino took the news of Owen Hart's death very hard. In the days following the senseless tragedy, Stu and Helen Hart, along with Owen's widow, Martha, contacted Gino. Stu Hart spoke with Gino on the phone—two of the toughest men that pro wrestling had ever produced, both forced to grapple with losing a beloved son to the business. They explained that they were planning to bring a wrongful death lawsuit against Titan Sports—the incident, they argued, had been shoddily planned and executed, and Vince had made things even worse by controversially deciding to continue with the show, forcing his performers to go on with their matches after just having seen their fallen compatriot taken out of the building on a gurney. The situation had also driven a wedge through the Hart family, with some members choosing to side with Vince and the WWF, ostensibly to stay in the good graces of the industry's most important power broker.

Gino sympathized greatly with their plight, but when asked if he would be willing to break ranks and help them with the lawsuit, he had to draw the line. Remembers Valerie, "He said, 'I can't. I still work for this company. This is what you sign up for. This is your life on the road.'" Even then, at the end, Gino would remain loyal to the company to which he'd given his own life in a different way.

■

Up until almost the very end, until he literally couldn't do it anymore, Gino continued to come into the studio, or to local shows if he could. If they knew he was coming, they would organize a card game in advance for when he got there. The guys at the studio continued to get calls from him, looking for action on anything he could bet an over/under on. Into early September 1999, he was still coming in, with his final known commentaries recorded for episodes of the international airings of *WWF Superstars*.[4]

Mere days after his last recording session at the studio, on September 19, Gino suffered another heart attack and had to be hospitalized, first in Philadelphia, but then he was transferred to Cooper University Hospital in nearby Camden. The effects of the heart attack quickly caused his complications from diabetes to worsen. He knew he didn't have much time left. It was important to him that everyone was settled, and it was while he was in the hospital that the papers for the new, finished house in Mount Laurel finally came through. But Maureen wouldn't sign them. Gino knew that she didn't own anything in her own name and didn't work, so it was going to be hard for her to find a place on her own. "I'm not worried about that right now," Valerie remembers her saying. "We'll figure it out. But I don't want to go into that house without you." And they didn't.

Word spread throughout the industry of Gino's dire condition. Bobby Heenan had been making regular visits to Jersey since the last heart attack. His last visit had been several months before, and he'd been planning another, but wouldn't make it in time. Gino wasn't keen on hospital visitors, but Davey O'Hannon made it a point to call him: "I could tell that he was really down. The diabetes was insidious." One visitor was

Tom Carlucci, checking in on him on behalf of the company: "He told me he wanted me to know he appreciated everything I ever did for him. He said, 'I love you,' and I said, 'I love you too, Gorilla. This isn't the last time we're gonna see each other.' But it was."

He was in a dark place for those final days. His kidneys were shutting down, and he wasn't always lucid, but when he was, he was usually filled with despair. Maureen and Sharon would stay with him during the day, and Valerie would be with him at night. After about a week in the hospital, he asked the doctor how long it would take him to die if he stopped taking his medications. "The doctor said probably a day," remembers Valerie. "And he said, 'That's what I want to do.'" Maureen was firmly against the decision. "It's not that I want to leave you," he told her. "It's just that I can't take it anymore." That night, he explained himself to Valerie: "This isn't living. I haven't been living for a long time. I don't want to do this anymore. I love everybody. But I don't have to be here to do that. This is not a life. I just want to go and be with Joey."

On October 1, the doctors agreed to stop treatment, but the hospital would force them to release him if he wasn't being treated, so they had to keep moving him around from room to room as a stalling tactic to stymie the bureaucracy while they continued to keep him under observation in his final hours. But as always, his body just wouldn't quit. As opposed to what was predicted, one day turned into two, then three, and then four. "The hard part was every day when we would say goodbye, we thought that was goodbye," says Valerie. "And then the next morning, he would wake up, and he was so fucking pissed off, because he had to go through it all over again." He would call his grandchildren when he could, crying as he wondered, "Why am I still here?" Not even the doctor had an answer for that. Finally, on October 5, the hospital had to send him home.

It was about four in the afternoon on the day they got home that Valerie offered to cook for him: chicken and rice, one of his favorite dishes. She cried as she cooked in the kitchen, while he got situated in bed. But before she was finished, perhaps he changed his mind, or more likely just forgot, he instead asked for a peanut butter sandwich and an orange soda—his *real* favorite dish, truth be told. Valerie couldn't help but get annoyed, but Maureen laughed: "Give him his peanut butter." So she did. They had put him in Valerie's bedroom in order to give him more space and make it easier to tend to him. She settled down in the recliner next to him, intending to sit there with him through the night, but he insisted she get some rest.

"I'm home now, I'm here. Go to sleep, we'll start over tomorrow."

So she kissed him goodnight and went to go sleep in the living room. Maureen was sleeping in the main bedroom, with a monitor so she could listen in on him in the next room. She woke up early and checked on him and noticed that his breathing sounded strange. She went into the kitchen to make a cup of tea, and by the time she returned, he was gone.

At 6:15 on the morning of Wednesday, October 6, 1999, Robert James Marella, the mighty Gorilla Monsoon, died peacefully in his sleep with a smile on his face. He was sixty-two.

■

When word got out at the office later that day, it became a day of mourning. Everything stopped. Employees who were there that day can still recall the McMahons openly sobbing in the halls after hearing the news.[5] Down the road at the studio at the time, Kevin Kelly remembers the day: "Your influence on people is how they react when you die . . . People who weren't related to him, who didn't know him other than having worked with him, were brought to tears. We all cried about it. Tommy Carlucci, Chris Lawler, Jill Clark and her husband, Dan. They all had Monsoon stories." When Maureen called Bobby and Cyndi Heenan to let them know, a devastated Bobby couldn't even get on the phone. It took him another day before he could work up the strength to call Maureen back.

Obituaries poured out from newspapers and other news outlets far and wide for the next couple of days. The *New York Times* summed it up, describing Gorilla Monsoon as "one of the most famous athlete-entertainers ever to don tights and climb into the professional wrestling ring." Wrestlers he worked with were quoted in several places, most notable among them being Bruno Sammartino, his greatest in-ring rival, still connected to him

"GOODBYE, MY FRIEND."

in the public's imagination despite the fact that they hadn't spoken in years. In his hometown paper, the *Pittsburgh Post-Gazette*, Bruno looked back on their great 1964 time limit draw from Madison Square Garden and remembered Gino as "a gentleman and a good and gentle man." Jesse Ventura, who had moved on from the wrestling industry and was by then, quite surreally, one of the most high-profile politicians in the country, less than a year into his term as governor of Minnesota, released an official statement in which he said, "The loss of Gorilla Monsoon saddens me deeply. He was both a friend and a colleague, and I have many fond memories of the time we spent together."

The night after Gino's passing, before the usual chaos, *SmackDown* would open with a quiet tribute, narrated by Vince McMahon himself, who said:

> This week, one of the greatest men I've ever known, Robert James Marella, passed away at age sixty-two. He was celebrated and beloved worldwide as legendary superstar Gorilla Monsoon. To his friends, he was known simply as Gino. Gino had a gorilla-sized passion for life, this business and, more importantly, the people in it. Behind the scenes, he was a cornerstone in the World Wrestling Federation. Our thoughts and prayers go out to his wife, Maureen, and his entire family. With great sadness and heavy hearts, we say goodbye to Gino. A very special man who lived a very special life.

It was a windy and overcast Saturday when Gino was laid to rest, a rather warm day, especially for early October. A Catholic service was held at Goes-Scolieri Funeral Home in Willingboro, the same place where Joey had been memorialized just five years earlier. The place was mobbed with friends and family. The McMahons were all there, as well as Arnie and Betty Skaaland, Howard Finkel, Bruce Prichard and Jim Ross, and many other representatives from the front office and especially the television studio—even some faces from the past, like Nelson Sweglar. However, conspicuous by their absence were members of the current WWF roster at the time, the only two present being Savio Vega and Miguel Pérez Jr., there with Victor Quiñones, who had flown in from Puerto Rico. Some close to Gino were said to be upset by that, especially due to the fact that the road crew had been local all that week, with shows in New York and New Jersey. Flowers were sent by Steve Austin and Mark "Undertaker" Calaway, two of the company's biggest stars who were both off the road for the moment dealing with injuries.

Perhaps the connection to Gino just wasn't as strong with the younger guys as it had been among the guys of earlier generations, who did come out in force: Bob Backlund, Baron Mikel Scicluna, Rene Goulet, Johnny Rodz, Bugsy McGraw, the Savoldis and Dick Woehrle, to name a few. Included among the pallbearers were Shane McMahon, Victor Quiñones, Kevin Dunn, Tom Carlucci, Savio Vega and, as the two lead pallbearers, Davey O'Hannon and Bobby Heenan, who had flown up from Florida with Cyndi to be there.

As reporters and photographers swarmed behind a barricade outside, Deacon Jim Ayrer of Willingboro's Corpus Christi Church presided over the ceremony inside the funeral home: "Though I always knew he was a famous wrestler, my picture of him was of a man who was a fine father and husband . . . A big guy, a nice guy, a guy who was always kind and gentle with his family. Now he gets a chance to be with Joey again." Several made speeches, including Goulet, Woehrle and Ross, who noted how Gino had passed the torch to him as the voice of the WWF, and who called him "the most compassionate mentor that I ever had in the business." Jesse Ventura, who could not attend, sent a note that was buried with the casket.

As he wanted, Gino was buried right next to Joey at Lakeview Memorial Park in Cinnaminson. At the graveside, a highly emotional Vince McMahon gave the eulogy for the man who had once been one of his father's most trusted partners and friends, and who had grown to become that for him as well. He remembered the good times. The old days. He recalled the last time he saw him, which was, appropriately enough, beating Arnie Skaaland at cards at the TV studio. "To his friends, to his peers, he was known as a man who commanded respect," said the most powerful man in the wrestling industry. "He was generous, kind and a man who would literally give you the shirt off his back."

It was a full-circle moment. Their relationship had not always been such a close one, and Vince was the very man who had essentially muscled him out of his position in the company. But by the same token, he had followed his father's wishes to always take care of him and had also given him a platform to become one of the most beloved figures in wrestling history. In the end, Vince's affection and admiration for Gino was genuine. Their relationship had been contentious at times—more so than anyone knew—but that was also a long time ago. "As my dad got older, and maybe Vince saw him becoming vulnerable, he made amends with it," explains Valerie. "It did change. Not a lot, but you could see there definitely was a difference. I don't want to say he felt sorry for him, but he could see the decline, and he maybe gave in a little bit, not that that's really his nature. But for whatever reason, he did."

Of all Gino's friends and business associates, the one who took it hardest may have been Bobby Heenan, who was a wreck the whole day. At one point, he almost threw himself on the casket and had to be held back. At the end, after the services were all complete and most everyone had begun to disperse, Bobby and Davey remained.

"Bobby, I don't even want to leave," Davey said, as they both cried hysterically.

As Bobby stood over the grave of his former broadcast partner and dear friend, the man who had scolded him at the announce table all those years, whom he had driven nuts in front of the camera despite loving him away from it, he patted the casket.

"Goodbye, old buddy. Goodbye."

■

The wrestling world continued to reel, and thoughts of Gino were still keen in Bobby's mind two days later, when he had to return to the job that had been making him so miserable, flying down to Biloxi for *WCW*

Monday Nitro at the Mississippi Coast Coliseum. Despite the improvement in pay, the health benefits and all the other perks of working for the Turner organization, the past six years had been an increasingly terrible time for Bobby. The fun was long gone. He had felt disrespected and ignored by Executive Vice President Eric Bischoff. And although he had made a great friend among his new broadcast partners in Mike Tenay, that had not been the case with his main partner, Tony Schiavone. There was an antipathy between the two men that bled over into their work together. The fact was, they simply had zero chemistry. Try as he might, Bobby just couldn't rekindle any of the magic he'd created with Gino and other broadcast partners of the past. Tony didn't seem to know quite how to interact with him. When the Brain would fire off a typical one-liner, instead of the humorous "Will you stop?" of Gorilla Monsoon, Tony would just bark at him to shut up. Or even worse, ignore him.

The relationship between Heenan and Schiavone was already quite strained, and when Bobby came to TV that day suggesting they open the show with a heartfelt tribute to Gorilla Monsoon, it was not well received. For one thing, Gino had never worked for WCW, and it's believed that some within WCW viewed him as someone who represented the competition, a proxy for Vince McMahon. Bobby didn't see it that way, viewing Gino as someone who transcended companies and was universally beloved in the business. After all, many others at the show that day had worked with Gino in the past, including Bret Hart, Meng (King Tonga), Ric Flair, Curt Hennig and Lex Luger. It became a point of conflict as that evening's *Nitro* was being put together, with Bobby finally threatening to walk off the show if he wasn't allowed to say something about his friend. In later years, Schiavone would put some of the blame on Eric Bischoff, but the fact is that Bischoff was on hiatus from WCW at the time, having been relieved of his duties the month before. Schiavone had himself worked with Gino during his year with the WWF. He liked Gino a lot and had learned much from him. But he was now the head of the WCW announce team and was also responsible for directing traffic on the air. He was in a tough spot.

"GOODBYE, MY FRIEND."

As the show approached its live airtime, it was decided that Bobby would be allowed to say just a few words about Gino at the top of the show, but he had to make it brief. The show would open with its typical pyrotechnics and ballyhoo, with Tony Schiavone at ringside dutifully hyping up the next WCW pay-per-view before throwing it to a visibly shaken Bobby Heenan, solemnly looking down at the desk as he did everything in his power to hold it together.

"Before we start with tonight's action, Brain, there's something we both, but particularly you, have to say about our longtime friend Gorilla Monsoon."

Bobby lifted his head, his eyes red, his chin quivering, a far cry from the arrogant smart-ass fans were used to seeing. His words were simple, direct, and as heartfelt as any ever spoken on a professional wrestling broadcast.

"Gorilla will be sadly missed. He was one big, tough man. He was a decent, honest man. And we're all gonna miss him very much. And you know the pearly gates in Heaven? It's now gonna be called the Gorilla position. Goodbye, my friend."

In a business of illusion, those few seconds were about as real as it gets—one human being baring his soul and his pain in a brief moment of vulnerability. As Schiavone did his best to quickly move on and stomp right ahead into talking about the various matches and feuds to be featured on that week's show, Bobby still sat there shaken, choking back tears and summoning every ounce of professionalism he had to try to slam himself back into character. And the success he had in that regard, limited though it may have been, is a tribute to the consummate professional that he was.

It had been something, but nowhere near what he felt Gino deserved, and the manner in which it had been handled filled him with disgust. He would never forgive Schiavone for it. But at least he had gotten the chance to publicly share some of his feelings for his lost friend. To shed a tear for someone who had meant so much to him and to the business. And as those moments were broadcast live to millions watching at home, he was certainly not the only one.

CHAPTER 17

HISTORY HAS BEEN MADE

"I'd like to be remembered as an outstanding pro who put back into the business more than he took out."

We now stand a quarter century apart from the passing of Gorilla Monsoon. In some ways, his legacy has grown over time, as his memory is cherished by those who grew up with him or even around him. As Tiny Marella from Rochester who made national waves as the standout superstar from Ithaca College. As the singing Gino Marella, learning his craft in the territories. As the insidious Manchurian Giant who almost took the title from Bruno, then flipped the switch and carved his way into the hearts of fans. And perhaps most vividly these days, as the commentator who remains even now the voice of a specific golden era in the company known these days as WWE. Just as he was in life, Gorilla Monsoon remains one of the most universally beloved figures in wrestling history, with the very mention of his name usually bringing a smile to the faces of those who remember him.

He touched people. And not just the fans who watched him and listened to him but also the people who worked with him. In the intervening years since his passing, his reputation has even improved. He was a tremendous performer and entertainer both in the ring and on the microphone, and those who criticized him in his day never seemed to understand that it was the very things they criticized about him that were the things the fans loved so much. And over the years, as the voices of those who criticized him have been drowned out by the vastly outnumbering multitudes who adored him, the very notion of critiquing his work these days is tantamount to critiquing Arnold Schwarzenegger for being a bad actor, or Santa Claus for being gaudily dressed. That is to say, it misses the point entirely. Gorilla Monsoon the wrestler and Gorilla Monsoon the commentator embody everything that makes professional wrestling great.

■

In the years immediately following Gino's death, he continued to be memorialized and recognized by those who respected and admired him. As a testament to his pop culture ubiquity, in the year 2000, he was included in a select group of noted figures who had passed away the previous year, in a deluxe spread in the *New York Times Magazine* that also featured the likes of Mario Puzo, Shel Silverstein, Jim Jensen, Dusty Springfield, Frank De Vol and Lili St. Cyr. Ten years later, he was elected to the Professional Wrestling Hall of Fame and Museum, an institution spanning not just the WWE but all of wrestling history, and in which he was inducted by his great friend Davey O'Hannon. The following year, he made it into the George Tragos / Lou Thesz Professional Wrestling Hall of Fame, a subsidiary of the National Wrestling Hall of Fame in Waterloo, Iowa, that requires all inductees to have an accomplished amateur background.

The one major pro wrestling hall of fame that continually eluded him was the *Wrestling Observer Newsletter* Hall of Fame, in which, as of this writing, he has not only never been inducted in its thirty years of existence but was dropped from the ballot in 2015—no doubt the result of many years of his work being diminished in that otherwise esteemed publication and his general unpopularity among a certain mold of newsletter-reading fans. This is the only possible explanation for one of the most famous names in the history of the business, one of the most beloved announcers and one of the most crucial figures in the history of WWE itself being so glaringly omitted. In anticipation of the publication of this book and the inevitable reappraisals to follow, the *Observer*'s Dave Meltzer made known his intention to put Gorilla Monsoon back on the ballot this year, which may result in this omission finally being corrected by the time you hold this book in your hands.

For many years, longtime WWE employees would reminisce about Gino and continue to share stories about him. During *WrestleMania* week each year, a special Gorilla Monsoon memorial gin rummy tournament would be held, which no doubt would've tickled him pink. In 2007, when developmental wrestler Anthony Carelli was called up to the main roster and repackaged as a loveable and comical Italian babyface, he was given the ring name of Santino Marella—an inside reference that nevertheless demonstrated how fresh Gino still was in the minds of everyone.

■

Those years after Gino's death, as the company carried on into the twenty-first century, continued the trend of enormous change. Less than a year and a half after his passing, the WWF not only vanquished WCW but bought it, bringing a decisive end to the Monday Night War and to all the promotional wars incited by the company's initial national expansion. One year after that, due to a rare legal defeat by the World Wildlife Fund, the company was forced to change its name one more time and became known as World Wrestling Entertainment, taking one more step in the full transformation from pretend sports league to unabashed showbiz entity. At long last, Vince McMahon had attained the total and complete control of the wrestling industry he so longed for. And although in the intervening years other contenders would arise, like TNA Wrestling and All Elite Wrestling, WWE has remained the clear industry leader ever since.

And yet, the price of that evolution has been that the kayfabe Gino and others had prided themselves on for so long is now deader than dirt. To be sure, this was only the inevitable end result of a process that had begun long before, and Gino had long ago understood it. In fact, in that *New York Times Magazine* commemoration, he would be quoted on the topic of contemporary pro wrestling: "It's comic books . . . We were more serious. People really thought I was the Devil incarnate. Now it's all a joke." The quote was from 1990.

In today's internet wrestling world, Gorilla Monsoon is remembered, as many cultural icons are, in countless memes and references in miscellaneous hip-hop songs. Using artificial intelligence, he has even been brought back to life in the form of fictional "podcasts" created by real-life podcaster and ardent wrestling fan Joe Marotta, in which the simulated voice of Gino can be heard saying outrageously funny and seemingly out-of-character things which nevertheless resemble the kinds of things that would regularly be left on the cutting-room floor of the Edit 1 suite at the WWF television studio.

■

But naturally, those who most remember Robert Marella, the man, today are the members of the Marella family. His stepmother, Connie, passed away in 2003, as did his eldest sister, Rosemary, in 2010, but his sisters Amy and Angela reside in the Vegas area still. Sharon and Valerie remain in New Jersey, both happily married and both grandmothers, with Sharon's son, Kevin, the father of two young children, and one of Valerie's twins, the other Gino Marella, the father of a beautiful little girl.

A proud great-grandmother, Maureen Marella lived the rest of her long life surrounded by her loving family. She was also surrounded by the warm memories of her life with Gino, which sustained her over the twenty-five years she had to go on without him. The beautiful painting he bought her still hung in her home. Everywhere you looked, photos of the man himself. The Japanese-style bedroom set was still intact, as were the countless Japanese curios, ornaments and other pieces of décor—reminders of those many trips to the Far East. But most of all, she cherished the thirty-six years they spent together, during which they enjoyed one of the most loving and one of the most successful marriages the wrestling business ever saw. "I never get tired of people telling me how wonderful he was," she declared to kick off her first of several interviews for this book. "He was! He was! I haven't met the person to say anything bad about him. He was always there to help somebody or give something to them or whatever. He was Gino! He was very soft. If you gave him a Christmas card, he would cry." On February 16, 2025, after a lengthy illness, Maureen passed away at the age of eighty-five. She was laid to rest alongside her beloved Gino and Joseph.

Of Gino's many accomplishments, this may be the greatest one of all and the most elusive for a professional wrestler: He built a happy, healthy, thriving family that remembers him with fondness and love. The absence of Joey still hurts deeply even all these years later, but the warmth and strength of a solid family foundation remain, all the more so for having had to endure such a tragedy. And that's the direct result of Gino putting his family first, always. More than any match, title, house or payoff. The money, the success, the points on the territory, the sweetheart Titan Sports deal—all of these were just means to an end and not ends in and of themselves. From his own strong and healthy family foundation growing up, Gino understood the importance of that. How it's the only thing, in the end, that lasts.

■

And yet that family connection and love wasn't enough to save everyone. Victor Quiñones may have lived for a time as a part of that family and may have been treated as a son by Gino, but in the end, he chose a dark path from which there was no return. Devastated in the wake of Gino's passing, he had initially invited Valerie and her boys to come and live with him in Puerto Rico—an offer that she politely declined despite Victor's exploding wealth and lush living arrangements at the time.

The dawn of the century was a time of tremendous prosperity for Victor, with the IWA becoming the hottest wrestling sensation in Puerto Rico, thanks in part to the working arrangement with the WWF that continued to bring him all the top stars, including The Rock himself. "You go back and you look in that 2000 time frame," Kevin Kelly points out. "In relation to population, IWA Puerto Rico was drawing more people than any other promotion in the world. They were killing it on a night in, night out basis." By some accounts, Victor was making tens of thousands of dollars a week—but thanks to an extravagant lifestyle of lavish expenses, partying and drugs, he was often spending it just as quickly. The business partnership with WWE ended in 2002, partly due to IWA growing so successful it began to be perceived as a threat, but also for other reasons. "It seemed like a good idea at the time," Kevin explains. "But Puerto Rico was too far away. And there were too many temptations on the island. So, it wasn't the best place for some of our guys to be." Soon after, much to Victor's frustration, WWE started up a working agreement with Carlos Colón's World Wrestling Council, his chief rival—even bringing in Carlos's son Carlito in 2003 and turning him into a major WWE superstar for a time.

Victor continued to wheel and deal, working out arrangements with mainland companies like TNA and Ring of Honor, then both in their infancy, and even working with the Savoldis and others to bring the IWA to a significant number of local U.S. television markets for a while. But Victor became too caught up in his rock star lifestyle for any of it to be sustainable. And on top of that, the stories of Victor's sexual improprieties continued to grow as time went on. Perhaps the most high-profile of them involved David Flair, the son of Ric Flair, who had been sent down to Puerto Rico in 2003 by his dad to gain some valuable wrestling experience. He claimed to have experienced a level of sexual harassment and indecent exposure from Victor so traumatizing that it drove him from the entire wrestling industry for good.

Just over a year later, when WWE itself finally rolled into Puerto Rico for the first time in twenty years to present the pay-per-view event

New Year's Revolution, Victor showed up for the occasion at the José Miguel Agrelot Coliseum in San Juan to greet old friends and associates. He was confronted by an irate Ric Flair, who nearly got into a physical altercation with him on that day for reasons that were not apparent to most people there. It would be the last time Victor had any dealings with the company.

The *New Year's Revolution* show had been a tipping point. Enough time had gone by since Gino's passing that Vince McMahon finally felt comfortable once again dipping his feet into the waters of Puerto Rico, the bad memories of the disastrous 1985 show now also quite distant. This time, the show was a resounding success, and WWE has continued to return to Puerto Rico for a house show tour on an annual/biannual basis ever since. In 2023, they even taped an episode of *SmackDown* and staged another pay-per-view there for the first time in eighteen years. Both the WWC and the IWA continue to run there year-round. In 2014, Carlos Colón, Gino's old business partner, joined him in the WWE Hall of Fame.

But Victor Quiñones would not get to see any of that. Just a year after WWE's return to the island, on April 2, 2006, he was found dead in his home in Carolina, Puerto Rico, at the age of forty-six, the result of cardiac arrest brought on by a lethal mixture of alcohol and muscle relaxers. In the weeks that followed, many colleagues would celebrate him, to be sure, but there's no denying that the legacy he left behind is quite a muddier one than that of his beloved mentor. Victor learned the business side very well from Gino and was able to succeed at a high level like Gino did. But although he tried, Gino couldn't make him into the universally beloved and trusted human being that he himself was. Perhaps the life Victor led before he even crossed Gino's path had already done too much damage. Gino had managed to sidestep the many snares and vices that the business can throw at you at such a high level, and it was those very same snares and vices that consumed Victor. Gino's code of honor had prevented him from abusing his power over others, while Victor seemed to view that power as a license to indulge his darkest impulses. In the end, he became another cautionary tale.

As the Attitude Era came to a close and WWE's financial bonanza began to slow down a bit, just like clockwork, the company re-embraced nostalgia and brought back the Hall of Fame in 2004. For the first time, rather than the stars of his father's company, Vince McMahon would be primarily inducting some of the individuals who had been a part of the company under his own leadership from the 1980s period when he had been building the brand into a national powerhouse.[1] Both of Gorilla Monsoon's most revered broadcast partners, Jesse "The Body" Ventura—fresh off his term as Minnesota governor—and Bobby "The Brain" Heenan, were included among the inductees on March 14 at the New York Hilton in midtown Manhattan.

Bobby didn't quite look and sound himself that night, having just recently finished radiation treatment for mouth cancer that had been diagnosed two years earlier—but his razor-sharp humor and effortless charm were still there. Back in his element and relishing the chance to be in front of an audience again, he delivered one of the funniest, most engaging and most heartfelt induction speeches in the history of the WWE Hall of Fame. He held the crowd in the palm of his hand, with people doubled over in laughter and giving several standing ovations in what was the great pinnacle moment of his career, even introducing a tearful Cyndi and Jessica, as well as Jessica's new husband, John. He broke everybody's chops from the stage in classic Bobby Heenan fashion, while also looking back on his incredible career.

And yet, there was nearly no mention of Gino at all, even when he brought up *Prime Time Wrestling*. But that was for a reason. Bobby was there to make people laugh and to bask in his moment, and he knew that if he'd talked about Gorilla Monsoon and how much he'd meant to him, he simply would not be able to hold it together at all. And he was right. So he waited until the very end, just before he wrapped up, when he paused a moment, tears in his eyes as he said simply:

"Only one thing's missing. I wish Monsoon was here," and then blew a kiss heavenward.

It was one last hurrah for the sharpest wit the business ever produced. The cancer would maintain its merciless hold on Bobby, and just three years later, he'd need to have most of his lower jaw removed, cruelly robbing him of his greatest gift. But although his voice went away, his sense of humor never did, and he continued to make public appearances right up until his death in 2017.[2]

Over the years, the Hall of Fame would be a way for the company, or more specifically Vince McMahon, to work out the differences and bury the hatchets of the past. In 2006, for example, the wrestling world was shocked when Bret "Hitman" Hart went in, appearing publicly in a WWE setting for the first time since the Montreal Screwjob. Four years later, he'd make a full, short-term return to WWE television, even facing Vince himself in a match at *WrestleMania XXVI*, and he's continued to make appearances from time to time, much to the delight of so many current WWE roster members who grew up idolizing the man Gino termed "The Excellence of Execution."

But of all the surprise inductions, none was more unexpected than the headline inductee of 2013. Bruno Sammartino, the two-time former WWWF world champion and the foundational star of the entire company, had not had anything to do with it in twenty-five years when he finally agreed to accept the WWE Hall of Fame induction that he'd been consistently refusing since the thing began. After years of acrimony, the Living Legend had been persuaded by Paul "Triple H" Levesque, who by that point had become the son-in-law of Vince McMahon and was already making waves as a high-ranking executive in the company, positioning himself for a life after wrestling. Bruno enjoyed dealing with Triple H much more than the man he'd been holding his grudge against for so long, who was never known for his humility and ability to compromise. Convinced that the tawdry antics of the Attitude Era were far in the past and that the drug and steroid culture of the company had been at last reined in, not to mention being a man in his late seventies looking to secure a healthy inheritance for his children and grandchildren, Bruno relented at last.

On April 6, 2013, Bruno Sammartino main evented and sold out Madison Square Garden one last time, taking in the adulation of the thousands of fans in attendance who still loved him but had long ago given up hope that such a moment would ever happen. It was another full-circle moment in the very space where he'd defended his title dozens and dozens of times, including in the old version up on 49th Street, where he'd battled Gorilla Monsoon in seven epic encounters. And at the end of the night came the most surreal moment, when Bruno Sammartino and Vince McMahon stood together on stage, hand in hand.

Now back in his position as WWE's greatest emeritus legend of them all, Bruno continued to make appearances from time to time, sharing his memories and enjoying the respect of the company and the fans that he had so richly deserved, right up until his passing five years later at the age of eighty-two.

■

One by one, so many with whom Gino built the foundation, the old guard of the Capitol Wrestling Corporation, have left us. "Classy" Freddie Blassie, perhaps the most genuinely beloved by the McMahons, on account of a subversive personality and wicked sense of humor that most resembled Vince himself, retired to his home in Hartsdale, New York, and passed on in 2003. Arnold Skaaland, the last of the four CWC partners and loyal to the very end, passed on in 2007. Gino's mentor, tag team partner and dear friend Walter "Killer" Kowalski in 2008. The wild and uncontrollable Capt. Lou Albano in 2009. Angelo Savoldi, an associate of the McMahon family going back to the very beginning with Roderick "Jess" McMahon and the last survivor of the original inner circle, passed in 2013 at the age of ninety-nine.

Even those subordinates who knew Gino well and in some cases were brought into the company by him, the ones still around to tell the stories, are largely no longer there. The 2020 COVID-19 pandemic saw tremendous personnel cuts within the company that included Mike Chioda, Tony Chimel and Tom Carlucci.

The announcers who followed in Gorilla Monsoon's footsteps with the company have gone on to become beloved figures in their own right by later generations of fans. Following the phasing-out of Gino and the departure of Vince from the broadcast booth, Jim Ross, or good ol' J.R. as he's mainly known today, became the voice of the Attitude Era and beyond in WWE, creating a legacy that holds up to any of the all-time greats. He even spent years as the head of talent relations, filling the spot held before him by J.J. Dillon and Pat Patterson, becoming responsible for signing up decades' worth of future stars for the company. He was inducted into the WWE Hall of Fame in 2007 by Stone Cold Steve Austin and parted ways for good with the company in 2019, eventually finding a place with All Elite Wrestling, where he can still be heard calling the most important of the company's matches.

Meanwhile, Michael Cole, once the rookie announcer at Gino's side in the voice-over booth for international *WWF Superstars*, would go on to become the longest-tenured commentator in the history of the company. For twenty-eight years and counting, he has been calling the action week in and week out in one capacity or another—not only longer than Vince McMahon himself did it but nearly as long as the entire WWF commentating careers of Gorilla Monsoon, Jesse Ventura and Bobby Heenan combined. For generations of fans now, he has filled that all-important role of the trusted voice of the company, narrating their favorite moments. Adding to the impressiveness of the feat is the fact that he had to do so largely during an era when McMahon was known regularly to sit in the back on the monitors and scream orders into the headsets of his younger announcers throughout the entire show, seemingly making them into his figurative on-air puppets, speaking the words he would be speaking himself if he was still the one doing it. It was a level of neurotic micromanagement and unsettling intimidation that he would never have dared to try with the old-school guys—least of all with Gino. Because if he had ever tried to do it, that would've been the day that Gino took off his headset, went home and just let the money continue to roll in.

■

And then there's Vince McMahon himself. Perhaps never before in the history of the business has there been a more precipitous rise and fall of a major figure than that of the disgraced former owner and chairman of the board. Surviving the scandals and legal actions of the 1990s seemed to alter something in him, or perhaps liberate something that had always been there: a raw desire for power and control, seemingly unbound by societal norms the more that time went by. As with many corrupt men of power, he felt he had become impervious and untouchable and acted accordingly. And as the old guard died out one by one, as he was no longer beholden to even the ghost of his father in the form of his father's friends, he became more brazen than ever. There was no one around him to look up to anymore, no one for him to defer to or to speak to him with any level of experience or authority greater than his own. He was now himself the old man, the representative of the old guard, such as it was.

As this book is being put together, Vince finds himself embroiled in a legacy-destroying inferno of his own making, the result of years of behavior that seemingly have finally caught up to him. In a downfall similarly played out in public many times over in the era of "Me Too," he has become the target of numerous accusations from former employees involving rampant sexual abuse and millions of dollars of hush money payments from company funds, the most high-profile accusations coming from former WWE paralegal Janel Grant, whose legal team even released volumes of damning text messages and specific allegations detailing behavior of a most deeply repellent and heinously degrading nature, much of it in the alleged words of the chairman himself, for all the world to see. Never before had he been so openly exposed to the general public, and a subsequent multi-part Netflix documentary series, which he sought desperately to squelch, has dug the hole even deeper. With charges of sexual assault, rape and even sex trafficking, he came under federal investigation once again—the government taking another shot at catching the fish that first escaped the net thirty years ago.[3]

Faced with the reality of his own company attempting to push him out in the wake of the initial accusations, led by a board of directors that included his son-in-law Paul "Triple H" Levesque and his daughter

Stephanie, as well as WWE President (the real one this time) Nick Khan, he initiated one final Machiavellian gambit, forcing his way onto the board with his voting power, dismissing several members, and then installing himself once again as interim chairman. This allowed him to push forward with a deal to sell the entire company, which most for years had assumed would be going to Paul and Stephanie. But if he couldn't have it, then they weren't going to have it, either. In 2023, Vince McMahon brokered the sale of World Wrestling Entertainment, Inc. to the media and entertainment giant Endeavor Group Holdings, which merged it with MMA industry leader UFC to form the umbrella company known as TKO Group. At long last, after seventy years, the company had become another wholly owned property of the modern-day world of corporate media.

The company that Vince bought in that suite in the Warwick Hotel in 1982 for $1.7 million was sold to Endeavor forty-one years later for the price of $9.3 billion. Had Gino been allowed to keep his ownership stake, that portion alone would have been worth $1.86 billion.

Vincent James McMahon was certainly no angel when it came to business; no successful wrestling promoter ever was. But it's likely that today, he would not even recognize the man his son has become. And for Gino, who never quite warmed up to "Vinny" in the first place, who kept him always at arm's length, and who always saw through his bullshit, to see him today would no doubt be the most emphatic and disappointing of all reminders of why he viewed him the way he did. Vince always wanted to be like Ted Turner, and in a way, he finally succeeded, forced into resignation by a company he no longer controls. Today, Vince has divested himself of nearly all stock in the company. As the company does everything in its power to distance itself from the man who built it into what it is, as wrestlers and employees past and present scramble to come to terms with the legacy of a man both responsible for creating their very livelihoods but also for wreaking such widespread harm and toxicity, it is indeed a complicated and dizzying final act for professional wrestling's most historically significant figure. Gino managed to keep him close because it suited him. But Gino also appreciated some things Vince never did: that family comes first, before everything else. And that respect, both given and earned, is the hallmark of a man of honor. If money and power are all you seek, then that, at the very end, is all you're left with.

■

So what is the legacy of Gorilla Monsoon, of Bob "Gino" Marella, all these years later? When asked, he once said that his most lasting contribution was helping the construction of important buildings in his hometown in his youth, such as the University of Rochester, Rochester Institute of Technology and the headquarters of the Eastman Kodak Company. Certainly, from a wrestling point of view, the most tangible reminder of his continued presence would have to be the Gorilla position itself, so ubiquitous throughout not just WWE but the entire wrestling industry that it's usually abbreviated to simply "Gorilla." No longer just a simple buffet table with a couple of monitors on it, behind a flimsy curtain, the Gorilla position in WWE has become quite literally a part of the show, with its own dedicated and specially lit set, dutifully assembled backstage at every televised event, fully branded and manned by a multitude of people at any given time. It's regularly filmed during entrances and other backstage segments, a rarity once upon a time when it was the obscured holiest of holies.

And yet perhaps the Gorilla position has become so ubiquitous that it has taken on a life of its own, with some who came later not even fully grasping where the name came from, who the man was that it was named after, or his essential importance to the company. In her 2024 autobiography, Becky Lynch, one of the elite WWE performers and attractions of the past decade, described the Gorilla position in passing as having been named for "iconic backstage interviewer" Gorilla Monsoon. Time truly does erase all if we're not vigilant.

WWE, as it exists today, is almost completely unrecognizable from the company Gorilla helped to build. The revenue that it brings in is on a level that would've been incomprehensible to the pillars of the Capitol Wrestling Corporation, with cable outlets, television networks and streaming platforms paying billions of dollars just for the rights to broadcast WWE content—a far cry from the days when the company had to pay *them* to run the stuff. The ongoing *WrestleMania* franchise, now past its fortieth installment, packs in close to a hundred and fifty thousand fans over a two-night period each year, with attendance gates now measured in the tens of millions of dollars. In one night, a major WWE stadium show is known to gross more than several years' worth of monthly Madison Square Garden shows from back in the day. There is absolutely no doubt that in every measurable financial metric, WWE today is light years beyond anything Gino, Bruno, Zacko, Arnie or even the old man could have ever dreamed it could be.

In 2023, having long ago outgrown Titan Tower and its TV studio, WWE consolidated its global corporate headquarters into a new, sprawling, multi-building campus that sits alongside I-95 in the heart of downtown Stamford. For the first time ever, both the corporate side and the television studio share the same real estate, and the doors were finally closed for good at 120 Hamilton Avenue, where so many of Gorilla Monsoon's most memorable moments and calls were recorded.

In the wake of Vince's departure, Paul Levesque, whose first match in the WWF was called by Gorilla Monsoon back in 1995, has stepped up as the new corporate and creative face of the company—the only member of the McMahon family still directly involved in any way. And there is no doubt he has built a great deal of goodwill, crafting a product that has pleased millions of fans who access WWE content in ways previously unimagined. He has built bridges—even Jesse Ventura, Gino's old partner, was recently brought back into the fold thanks in large part to the downfall of his longtime nemesis and former boss.

The company is on fire these days, more profitable than ever, experiencing its latest boom and creating a product that is as thoroughly enjoyed by the fans of today as fans of previous generations enjoyed the wrestling that they knew. And yet, as with all progress, there is much that is also lost. Gone are the days of the glorified mom-and-pop organization stitched together by a patchwork quilt of promoters. Gone are the road trips Gino,

Bruno, Mario, Dominic and others would take from Jersey to Boston and back, filled with bottles of wine and salami and provolone sandwiches, with a stopover at Gino's house for a home-cooked piece of lasagna. In its place are transcontinental flights on private jets and giant tour buses with all the amenities. Gone are the fathers and sons and little old ladies paying five dollars for ringside tickets; the pitch darkness of the arena when the lights come down, and only the ring is illuminated under a halo of electric light; the deafening roar of the crowd providing the only entrance music that was ever needed. Today, Gino would have to put out his cigar before coming backstage, and the boys (and now, the girls) are far too busy on their smartphones and social media for a game of pinochle or acey-deucey. Despite all the glitz and glamor of the shiny, slickly produced product of today, there was a wild magic and a mystery to the wrestling that Gino knew, which have been utterly drained away in exchange.

These days, the name of Gorilla Monsoon seems to be heard less in WWE than it used to be. Ironically, the name of Bruno Sammartino, thanks to his reconciliation with the company, is mentioned much more often in historical reference, despite Bruno's many political and personal feuds with the McMahon family in contrast to Gino's unwavering loyalty. Nevertheless, what is still heard all the time, in historical retrospectives, in archival footage, in countless hype videos and documentaries, is the voice. Whether or not you're old enough to remember him, you can still regularly hear the unmistakable voice of Gorilla Monsoon, calling so many indelible moments featuring so many cherished matches and performers of the '80s and '90s.

And still, the most iconic of all those moments is the money shot from *WrestleMania III*. Hulk Hogan and André the Giant, face to face in the ring at the Pontiac Silverdome.

"The irresistible force meeting the immovable object!"

Gorilla Monsoon liked to reference those two things all the time. The irresistible force and the immovable object. And perhaps that's most fitting of all. Because throughout his career, and throughout his life, he was both.

ACKNOWLEDGMENTS

Taking a note from Gino himself at his WWF Hall of Fame induction, I acknowledge that the greatest thanks go first and foremost to my beloved wife, Jaimee, who, as always, is on the front lines when it comes to putting up with the crazy hours, the months of dedication, the constant old wrestling on TV and the endless conversations about Phil Zacko and Toots Mondt. Her support and understanding have helped make this book possible, as has the tolerance of that other wrestling hostage, my young son Peter, who made the supreme sacrifice of giving up video game time so that Daddy could go downstairs to work.

As referenced in this book's dedication, the cooperation and full support of the Marella family, more than anything else, took this book to another level. The value of their patience and generosity—with their time, with the memories they shared, as well as with access to priceless family photography—cannot be overstated. To the late Maureen Maurella, to Amy Marella, to Valerie Marella-Jankowski and her husband, Ed, I am eternally grateful.

To Bret Hart, who took the project seriously enough to graciously consent to penning the foreword. He dug deep into his heart and produced something very special, and I'm honored to have it attached to my work. I knew he was a badass thirty years ago as a wide-eyed fan, but this clinched it. Special thanks also go out to Bret's brother Ross for making the connection that made it possible.

This is my second book with ECW Press, and I continue to be impressed by and grateful for their tireless efforts to produce the best books available on professional wrestling and its rich history. Thanks to my great editor, Michael Holmes, whose praise and guidance mean more to me than I can say. Thanks to my superb copy editor, Peter Norman, whose suggestions made the book better. And thanks to the many others on the ECW team, including Victoria Cozza, Emily Ferko, Michela Prefontaine and Alexandra Dunn.

In addition to the Marella family on the photography front, I am thrilled and gratified to have the involvement of WWE on this project, something I was too cautious to even hope for. To the team in Stamford, including Amanda Guarino and my old work friends Frank Vitucci and Steve Pantaleo, my humble thanks. Also to the legendary George Napolitano, who came through with some jaw-dropping stuff, as always.

I always begin any book project with months of lengthy interviews, and in this case, those interviews formed the backbone of the story I wound up telling, and I couldn't have told it without the many conversations I had with the people who knew best. In addition to the previously mentioned individuals, these also include: Ken Patera, Bill Watts, the late Kevin Sullivan, Jim Cornette, Jerry Brisco, Gino Brito, Johnny Rodz, Tony Garea, Davey O'Hannon, Kevin Kelly, Bill Apter, Gary Cappetta, Mario Savoldi, Mike Chioda, Jimmy Korderas, Tony Chimel, Hugo Savinovich, Nelson Sweglar, Jeff Walton, Tom Carlucci, Tom Burke, Sheldon Goldberg, Matt Farmer, Michael Omansky, Jessica Heenan-Solt, Larry Rosen, Holly Gilzenberg, Dennis DiPaolo, Rich Kraemer and Curtis Raymond.

To my fellow author and friend, Keith Elliot Greenberg, who took the time once again to look over the manuscript and provide valuable and thoughtful critiques. Working with him has been my pleasure and honor for more than twenty-five years.

ACKNOWLEDGMENTS

To those who helped make all-important connections and introductions, including Jon Boucher, Brian Kunsman, Rick del Santo, Jill Clark, Jennifer Good, Pat Laprade, David Marquez, Scott Walton and Ben Czekanski (aka Benny Boombatz).

To those who provided valuable information, including Tim Hornbaker (for his incredible primary documents), Jim Ruehrwein (who compiled an indispensable Gorilla Monsoon match record), Greg Oliver and *Slam Wrestling*, Steven Johnson, Al Getz, Bertrand Hebert, Rich Schwantz (for his diligent research into the mysterious Inez More), Karen Dorosky-Mattice, Jesus M. Salas, Steve Anderson, and the members of the WWWF Kayfabe Network and WWWF/WWF 1970–1983 Facebook groups.

As an author whose prose stylings admittedly exceed his research acumen, I have openly walked on the shoulders of giants and have to acknowledge the crucial work done before me that provided a constant resource. I'm grateful to The Great Brian Last of the *6:05 Superpodcast*, as well as John McAdam of the *Stick to Wrestling* podcast (not to mention *STW* guest Craig Fair for his amazing Monsoon/Brody story), and John Arezzi's *Pro Wrestling Spotlight* podcast; authors and journalists Brad Balukjian, Josie Riesman and Evan Ginzburg; and the exhaustive materials made available by NYProWrestling.com, KayfabeMemories.com, WrestlingClassics.com, ProjectWWF.com, ArmDrag.com, and Richard Land's TheHistoryofWWE.com.

To Dr. Mike Lano, whose passing suggestion during a podcast interview lit the light bulb in my head and provided the inspiration for this book's subject.

And to the many others who supported the project in innumerable ways, including Joe Marotta, George Schire, James Romero and Rick G. Brooks.

APPENDIX

A GLOSSARY OF GORILLA-ISMS

CALLING THE ACTION
- "_____ and a beauty!": Insert name of wrestling move, often a dropkick or clothesline.
- "_____ City": Insert name of wrestling move. Survived in more recent years in Brock Lesnar's "Suplex City."
- "The bell is rung, and this one's underway!"
- "Close only counts in horseshoes and hand grenades."
- "double noggin-knocker": A move that involves smashing two people's heads together.
- "Excedrin headache number _____": Used to describe a blow to the head, in reference to 1960s and '70s commercials for Excedrin-brand headache medication.
- "Goodnight, Irene!": Used to describe holds that put wrestlers out cold, in reference to the title of a popular folk music record by the Weavers, which spent thirteen weeks at number one in 1950. Most notably became the actual name of Adrian Adonis's finisher.
- "He doesn't have that applied properly.": More often than not in reference to an abdominal stretch.
- "He just got his clock cleaned.": He got hit extremely hard.

- "He slipped out the back door.": He escaped the hold.
- "He went to the well one too many times.": He's tried the same move too often, and his opponent anticipated it.
- "He's busted wide open.": He's bleeding.
- "He's on rubber-leg street.": He appears to be on unsteady footing due to exhaustion or physical punishment.
- "I hope the ring has been specially reinforced for this one.": Typically said during matches involving two or more very large individuals.
- "The irresistible force meeting the immovable object!"
- "No love lost between these two."
- "nonchalant cover": A cover that doesn't involve hooking the leg.
- "That'll give you a negative attitude in a hurry."
- "That'll knock you right into the middle of next week."
- "Unloading with the heavy artillery"
- "You don't get paid in there by the hour."

GENERAL BALLYHOO
- "Batten down the hatches!"
- "The electricity is so thick you can cut it with a knife!"
- "Excitement personified!"
- "Jam-packed capacity crowd on hand!"
- "History has been made here!"
- "It's gonna be a happening."
- "Pandemonium has broken loose!"
- "The SRO lights went up early!": SRO = Standing Room Only
- "They are literally hanging from the rafters here!": It's so crowded that fans are figuratively—not literally—hanging from the ceiling.
- "This place has gone bananas!"

GORILLA'S ANATOMY
- "bleeding profusely"
- "breadbasket": stomach

- "cervical vertebrae"
- "external occipital protuberance": The back of the head.
- "ham hocks": Very large hands. Often reserved for André the Giant.
- "kisser": Face.
- "lateral and collateral ligaments"
- "lower lumbar region": The lower back.
- "Right in the solar plexus!": A kick or chop to the chest.
- "trapezius muscles"

PUTTING PEOPLE AND THINGS OVER

- "Excellence of Execution": Bret Hart.
- "The greatest professional athlete in the world today": Hulk Hogan.
- "He doesn't have any trouble getting a date for Saturday night."
- "It takes Greg Valentine fifteen to twenty minutes just to get warmed up."
- "The Mecca of professional wrestling": Madison Square Garden.
- "This is a main event anywhere in the country/world.": Very often less than true.
- "You don't get that way waiting for the bus.": A reference to the hard work it takes to stay in great shape.

REFEREES

- "Stick a fork in him, ref. He's done."
- "Come on, ref. Do something, even if it's wrong."
- "This referee leaves a lot to be desired."
- "You can count to a hundred.": A decisive pinfall.

TERMS FOR THE HEELS

- "The Benedict Arnold of the World Wrestling Federation": Used to refer to someone who's betrayed a trusted friend (notably "Mr. Wonderful"

A GLOSSARY OF GORILLA-ISMS

Paul Orndorff). A reference to the infamous colonial turncoat of the American Revolution.
- "The biggest walking advertisement for birth control I've ever seen.": Usually reserved for Capt. Lou Albano.
- "The Devious One": Mr. Fuji.
- "Folks, if you wanna maybe head into the kitchen and make yourself a sandwich, this might be a good time.": General disgust.
- "fountain of misinformation"
- "He ran off like a thief in the night."
- "snake in the grass"
- "miscarriage of justice": A bad call from a referee or other official.
- "One of them lies, and the other one swears to it."
- "Pearl Harbor job": A sneak attack, in reference to the December 7, 1941 Japanese bombing of Pearl Harbor during World War II.
- "The Walking Condominium": King Kong Bundy.
- "What a piece of work.": Gorilla keeping it clean for the kids. See also: "What a piece of garbage."

USUALLY RESERVED FOR THE BRAIN
- "Gimme a break!"
- "Highly unlikely."
- "I'll have you thrown outta here!"
- "Please . . ."
- "Will you stop?"
- "Will you be serious?"
- "You resemble that remark."

MISCELLANEOUS
- "barracuda": An undesirable woman. As in, "I've seen some of the barracudas you hang around with."
- "bo-hemoth": Mispronunciation of "behemoth."

- "Holy mackerel!"
- "If you hung him for being a good singer, you'd be hanging an innocent man."
- "Thanking the Man Upstairs": Thanking God.
- "This guy doesn't know a wristlock from a wrist watch."

NOTES

INTRODUCTION
1. Gorilla's tribute aired on just the seventh episode of the brand-new *SmackDown*.

CHAPTER 1
1. Chuck Wepner and Gorilla Monsoon are, in fact, two of three people who can make the claim of having been in the ring with both Muhammad Ali and André the Giant, the third being Antonio Inoki.

CHAPTER 2
1. Ironically, one of Faeto's claims to fame to this day is its delicious prosciutto, which might explain some of Gino's love of cured meats.
2. The *Perugia* was later requisitioned by the British and was eventually sunk by an Italian submarine during the First World War.
3. In American census reports just a few years later, Leonardo's birth year would be reported as 1908, which could have been to avoid

questions of the baby's citizenship, or to hide the possibility that his birth had preceded the marriage.
4. The heavily armored *San Giorgio* had a long life, being requisitioned by Mussolini for service in World War II, during which it was wrecked by British bombers at the Siege of Tobruk in 1941.
5. The site is now part of a condo complex.
6. Now the site of an enormous Family Dollar.

CHAPTER 3

1. The attending physician was Dr. Julius Rock, a young obstetrician just a few years out of medical school at the time.
2. Named for the first president of the University of Rochester.
3. During the Mother's Day 1992 episode of *WWF Wrestling Challenge*, Gino would pay an uncharacteristically personal tribute to Connie on the air, saying, "Mom, to you out there in Las Vegas, my love, my honor and my respect."
4. *Wilmington News-Journal*, February 15, 1982.
5. Later in life, Gino's singing skills would be called upon at functions like the weddings of family friends, with his sister Amy remembering how he—along with his brother and their father—sang at her wedding.
6. Gino would sometimes recall that on the ceiling of the gym read the words, "If you're reading this, you're not wrestling."
7. Her brother Dick was a teammate of Bob's as well, fullback for the football team.
8. *Democrat and Chronicle*, February 11, 1955.

CHAPTER 4

1. *Wilmington News-Journal*, February 15, 1982.
2. *Ithaca Journal*, December 6, 1956.
3. The May 19, 1956, edition of the *Ithaca Journal* describes an amusing scene, complete with photo, of "Tiny and Pals" in short pants,

NOTES

entertaining students at a school event to determine "the man on campus with the most beautiful legs."

4. *Ithaca Journal*, February 6, 1956.
5. "Recalling Monsoon Before He Was Top Gorilla," slamwrestling.com, July 21, 2011.
6. Recalled Marella to Andrew Wallace of the *Philadelphia Inquirer* on June 15, 1980, "I reached back like this for a wizzard (an arm lock) and drew him down across me and—crack! It just snapped." Note: The accurate name for the maneuver is "whizzer."
7. *Ithaca Journal*, February 13, 1959.
8. As Gorilla Monsoon, Marella would cross paths with both Woodin and Kaisy in the pro ranks. Woodin began his pro career as Tim Woods in the WWWF, meeting Monsoon in the ring on six known occasions in 1963 and 1964 and losing every time. As Billy White Wolf, Kaisy also lost his one and only singles match against Monsoon in Australia in 1968, but did manage a tag team victory two years prior, when he joined Pat Patterson and Ray Stevens to defeat Monsoon, Johnny Barend and Ripper Collins in Hawaii. It's doubtful that Gino took the fall in that one.
9. Adnan Kaisy, representing the San Francisco Olympic Club, took home the Greco-Roman title at 191 pounds.
10. Kerslake went on to win eight more Greco-Roman and freestyle championships and, as an engineer for NASA, helped to develop rocket propulsion in the 1960s.
11. McCann would go on to win a gold medal at the 1960 Summer Olympics and was inducted into the National Wrestling Hall of Fame in 1977.
12. March 10, 1960.
13. *Philadelphia Inquirer*, June 15, 1980.
14. *St. Joseph News-Press*, May 11, 1962.

CHAPTER 5

1. March 10, 1960.

2. "Hippodrome" was a reference to pro wrestling's showbiz antics and used as a code word meaning "staged," as opposed to a genuine "shooting" match.
3. February 14, 1960.
4. Many years later, in 1971, the WWWF would bring in the ancient Lopez for a handful of shots as a TV enhancement talent. With Marella producing those shows at the time, it's easy to imagine he might've been throwing a bone to the man, now at the end of his own career, who had put Gino over in his very first match.
5. Wrestlers becoming permanently known behind the scenes under previous pseudonyms isn't uncommon. To this day, WWE chief content officer Paul Levesque, aka Triple H, is commonly known as "Hunter" due to his earlier name of Hunter Hearst Helmsley. Mick Foley is often still referred to by friends as "Cactus" due to his earlier name of Cactus Jack. William Regal is often still called "Steven" from his days as Lord Steven Regal (his real name is Darren).
6. The eventual fate of Inez More-Marella is somewhat lost to time. In speaking with surviving relatives, it appears she eventually moved out west, ironically, and her whereabouts became unknown even to her own family. Some records indicate that she changed her first name to Kelly and eventually remarried, living out in California until her death in 2007.
7. That same application lists his home address as 190 Avery Street in Rochester, which was his parents' house—indicating that following the divorce, he may have moved back in with them for the time being.
8. May 11, 1962.
9. January 9, 1962.
10. Dr. Bill Miller also traveled from Omaha to Minnesota with Marella, but in Minnesota, he wrestled under a mask as Mr. M, the AWA world heavyweight champion at the time. It was not uncommon in those days for affiliated territories with different TV markets to be running different storylines with the same talent.

NOTES

11. On his podcast *Something to Wrestle With*, Bruce Prichard seemed to believe that Gino was incapable of growing a convincing mustache, which is why he stuck with the beard alone.
12. By winning the tournament, Kowalski advanced to the final match against top-seeded Rikidozan, who beat him two falls to one.

CHAPTER 6

1. That main event saw Kowalski and "The Shadow" (Clyde Steeves) upend Brazil and "Irish" Pat Barrett.
2. As told to the author in 2003.
3. Johnny Rodz would also do something similar when he went to California and became Java Ruuk.
4. July 28, 1963.
5. The fictional claim also gave McMahon and Mondt a chance to spitefully bury Rocca, who had had a falling-out with the company at the beginning of the year and was planning to boldly run opposition right across the East River at the Sunnyside Garden in Queens with the help of Carolinas promoter Big Jim Crockett.
6. Also wrestling that night in a one-off appearance, on loan from the Central States promotion, was a rookie Harley Race, just twenty years old and wrestling as "The Great Mortimer." He would return to the Garden fifteen years later as the NWA world heavyweight champion.
7. September 24, 1963.
8. *Bayonne Times*, October 2, 1963.
9. Bobby Davis was not present at Roosevelt Field in Gino's corner. At that time in his career, the manager was mainly making TV appearances only to talk up his protégés.
10. October 5, 1963.
11. The assailant was apprehended by police and taken to the fifth precinct for questioning before being released. He was never publicly identified.
12. *Pittsburgh Press*, December 24, 1980.

13. Gino cherished the win so much that he kept the medallions from his U.S. tag team title belt on permanent display at his home in later years.
14. In the September 21, 1980, edition of the *Philadelphia Journal*, Gino told a typically whimsical version of the story of how he'd met Maureen, explaining that they were both at a birthday party, and people were making fun of him for being unable to speak, with Maureen taking pity on the Manchurian Giant.
15. March 1, 1964.
16. Killer Kowalski vs. Don McClarity and Pedro Morales vs. Duke Miller.
17. An eighty-one-minute curfew time limit draw with Waldo Von Erich just three months later at the Garden.
18. *Scrantonian*, May 17, 1964.
19. Exceeded only by the Sammartino / Von Erich match of 8/22/64 (eighty-one minutes).
20. *Scrantonian*, May 17, 1964.
21. *Wrestling World*, June 1968.
22. Interview with Rod Luck, WWDB 96.5 FM in Philadelphia, March 15, 1983.
23. June 21, 1964. During the interview, he offered a candid assessment that included an early use of a phrase for which he'd later become well-known: "The people who watch us don't know too much about wrestling. On any given night, about 75% of the audience doesn't know a wristlock from a wristwatch. To them, it is a show."
24. Although Blassie was already a well-established star in the business, Gino helped give him the rub for Northeast fans, teaming with him in a bunch of tag matches, including October 19, 1964, at the Garden, where they defeated the team of Bill Watts and Don McClarity.

CHAPTER 7

1. Gino became close friends with Bockwinkel and always admired him, especially when he became AWA world champion. In one of Gino's newspaper columns, he put him over to the moon, going so

NOTES

far as to say that if a title unification round robin tournament were to be held, Bockwinkel would likely win out over both NWA world champion Harley Race and WWF world champion Bob Backlund and that he could probably also beat Bruno Sammartino. They got to spend some time together during Bockwinkel's tenure as a WWF road agent in 1987–89 and even called some shows together while Bockwinkel was being tried out as a color commentator.

2. Aileen Eaton's prominent accomplishments as a boxing promoter in the 1950s, '60s and '70s led to her posthumously becoming the first woman inducted to the International Boxing Hall of Fame in 2002.
3. Lenard and Connie had already become grandparents a few years earlier. Lenard's oldest child, Lenard Jr. ("Sonny"), and his wife, Zhan, had already welcomed their two children, Kenny and Susan, into the world.
4. Prior to 1963, the town had even been known as Levittown, as most of Levitt's developments would become known throughout New York, New Jersey and Pennsylvania.
5. Born Mario Fornini, Savoldi got his name from 1930s wrestling superstar "Jumping" Joe Savoldi, originally being presented as his younger brother.
6. Of course, with the New York market being as robust as it was, everything was relative, as the 5/15/67 Madison Square Garden show was still the highest attended of any of the seventeen different major pro wrestling events happening that day throughout the North American territories.
7. May 16, 1967.
8. In total, between the first run in 1963–64 and the second run in 1967–68, Philadelphia got ten Sammartino/Monsoon main events, more than any other major market.

CHAPTER 8

1. This particular configuration of Los Medicos included Tony Gonzáles, as well as Luis Hernandez, stepfather of Gino Hernandez.

2. That same card also featured a rare appearance from NWA world heavyweight champion Dory Funk Jr., who defended against King Curtis in the main event.
3. Wild Red Berry died four years later, on July 21, 1973, suffering a heart attack on his front porch after a game of golf. He had already had a stroke two years prior that took from him his greatest gift, his inimitable voice.
4. During his retirement in St. Louis in the 1970s, Toots was known to go out for regular lunches with his old friend and colleague, NWA president Sam Muchnick.
5. Interview with the author, 2003.
6. Nurnberg achieved his greatest wrestling success with a German gimmick as Kurt Von Stroheim, one half of the notorious Von Stroheims tag team.
7. Details vary. Gino himself would sometimes remember the attacking heel as Dr. Jerry Graham, which would've been impossible, since he was busy that day in Phoenix, getting into a drunken bar brawl and being arrested for burglarizing his dead mother's apartment. Some versions of the story feature Baron Mikel Scicluna or the tag team of Toru Tanaka and Mitsu Arakawa as Bruno's attackers.
8. As relayed by McMahon in his 2001 *Playboy* interview.
9. 1983 Rod Luck interview.
10. *Wrestling Shoot Interviews*, April 3, 2022.
11. As recounted in *Ringmaster: Vince McMahon and the Unmaking of America* by Abraham Josephine Riesman.
12. A fixture of (W)WWF job matches, this version of the Black Demon was journeyman wrestler Tiberio "Tony" Aurelio, who had wrestled in the South as Tony Nero, before donning the mask in 1970 and spending the last five years of his career in the WWWF.
13. The typically masked Spoiler had to wrestle with his face exposed, per the New York State Athletic Commission's archaic rule banning masked wrestlers.
14. Monsoon and Brisco took on Fuji and Tanaka for the tag team title at the Boston Garden on September 9, 1972.

NOTES

15. Although he got past Monsoon, Rivera would lose the title just four days later to Terry Funk.
16. Monsoon and Rivera were also joined by Black Gordman, the other half of the Americas tag team champions with Great Goliath.
17. This was a full three years before Georgia Championship Wrestling would get picked up nationally by Superstation TBS.

CHAPTER 9

1. Valentine would help to revolutionize Jim Crockett Promotions in the 1970s, as the company transitioned from a tag team territory to one based on hard-hitting, rugged singles competition, with Valentine and Wahoo McDaniel as its chief practitioners to start things off.
2. At the conclusion of the match, Tolos himself would be jumped in the ring by a chair-wielding Pak Song, who just a couple weeks later at the next Olympic Auditorium card would be the one to unseat Tolos as Americas champion.
3. This would be the only time that All Japan would present the MSG Series. It would later be picked up by New Japan, where it would eventually transform into what's now known as the G1 Climax.
4. Wrestling historian Evan Ginzburg described witnessing the match firsthand for ProWrestlingStories.com in 2023: "I will never forget them on their knees, chopping each other across the chest, selling like crazy, and feigning imminent collapse."
5. September 6, 1981.
6. Partly as a reward for the loyalty of the Vachons, Paul Vachon was granted a profitable run in the WWWF that lasted through most of 1975. This included a loss to Gorilla Monsoon on July 26 in Monsoon's first match at the Spectrum.
7. Gorilla Monsoon had been scheduled to take on Cowboy Bobby Duncum that night, but the match was cut for time.
8. While being interviewed on *Tuesday Night Titans* in 1985, Gino claimed that he'd been going down to Puerto Rico to wrestle for

twenty years. Jerry Brisco also corroborated that Gino had been wrestling there back when Eddie Graham was running it. No records of those matches have surfaced, however.
9. Ali famously idolized Gorgeous George, from whom he'd later claim to have taken much direct inspiration for his showmanship.
10. The fifteen-round fight would partially inspire Sylvester Stallone to write the script for *Rocky* at around the same time.

CHAPTER 10

1. *Philadelphia Daily News*, February 5, 1980.
2. Valerie also remembers an incident from one of these parties in which Ivan Putski inadvertently killed her pet hamster by feeding it beer, which only further fueled her father's antipathy toward him.
3. Brock Lesnar's 504-day reign as WWE Universal champion in 2017–18.
4. *Press of Atlantic City*, March 18, 1977.
5. The first Spectrum card to air on PRISM took place on April 2, 1977.
6. "Gorilla Monsoon—Remembering 'The Manchurian Giant,'" Pro WrestlingStories.com, October 25, 2023.
7. Although Toots Mondt had passed in 1976, Marella and Zacko were still making regular payments to his widow, Alma, in St. Louis for their shares, as agreed upon. They would continue to do so until the debt was paid off in 1979.
8. This was the match that Gino referenced during his WWF Hall of Fame induction speech, in which he humorously recalled how Patterson told André to "Let the little guy start."
9. Although many records have the match taking place in September 1977 (including WWE itself, which acquired the video of the match back in the '80s), the correct date is December 2, 1978.
10. Bruno wrestled Bob Morgan on February 20, 1980, in Lubbock for promoter Nick Roberts (father of Nickla Roberts, the future "Baby Doll"); then on February 21 in Amarillo, he teamed with his son David against Bob Morgan and Mr. Pogo; then came the chief

NOTES

attraction of the stint, a February 22 rematch with Superstar Billy Graham in the Sam Houston Coliseum.

11. Gino would do this again in February 1980, during the famous Larry Zbyszko heel turn against Bruno Sammartino on *Championship Wrestling*, when he came out to help the bloodied Living Legend, his former longtime foe.
12. Sika of the Wild Samoans was the father of current WWE main event star Roman Reigns.
13. Perhaps to give the feud more fuel to keep going around the circuit, the loss was a dubious one, as Hogan had clearly gotten his shoulder up before the count of three, despite the referee's count.
14. As told to Bruce Prichard (*Something to Wrestle With*, episode 140).

CHAPTER 11

1. Quiñones would claim in a 2003 interview with the Puerto Rican magazine *Lucha Libre* that Gino took him as his actual godson through the Catholic Church, but this was refuted in my interviews with the Marella family.
2. This was the same night of the famous Alley Fight between Pat Patterson and Sgt. Slaughter.
3. Troy was also the coach of the Cape Cod Buccaneers, the short-lived minor league hockey team owned by Vince and Linda, which played two seasons in the Cape Cod Coliseum.
4. Balukjian, Brad. *The Six Pack: On the Open Road in Search of WrestleMania*. New York, NY: Hachette, 2024.
5. Hornbaker, Tim. *Capitol Revolution: The Rise of the McMahon Wrestling Empire*. Toronto, Ontario: ECW, 2015.
6. Ibid.
7. On the same show, Chief Jay Strongbow and Jules Strongbow would wrestle the masked team of the Black Demon and his partner the White Angel, who almost certainly was Victor Quiñones.
8. Monsoon and Chuck O'Connor had faced off at least twenty times, including a December 18, 1972, match at Madison Square Garden

and a heated three-match series at the fabled Jack Witschi's Sports Arena in North Attleboro, Massachusetts.
9. As part of his ambitions to consolidate all his business ventures, McMahon would deny access to the outside wrestling magazines that had been giving the WWF free publicity for years. By the end of 1983, all outside photographers who didn't work for Vince McMahon were banned from shooting at the Garden and other WWF events.
10. Although details of Roth's death remain obscure to this day, Gino confided in some close to him that he believed it was related to drugs.
11. As told to the author in 2003.

CHAPTER 12

1. Stampede had been in a bad way thanks to a riot at the Victoria Pavilion that had gotten the promotion banned from Calgary for six months.
2. Ventura would be back in the ring by the beginning of 1985, but would never again be given a significant program, focusing instead on his announcing career. He would hang up his boots for good just before *WrestleMania 2*.
3. Although Ventura was the WWF's first heel commentator, Roddy Piper had been the first anywhere in the business, filling that role expertly on *Georgia Championship Wrestling* and *Mid-Atlantic Championship Wrestling* in the early '80s.
4. One common criticism involved Gorilla's insistence on "hooking the leg"—which some wrestlers felt sabotaged them since they claimed that road agents were specifically instructing them to only hook the leg after using their finishers.
5. One story has Albano slapping a teenaged Shane McMahon for mouthing off to him as being the last straw.
6. Angela had been the first to move out to Vegas during the '70s, when her husband's doctor suggested he move to a dry climate for health reasons. Rosemary came out to Vegas in 1981.
7. *Philadelphia Inquirer*, June 12, 1987.

NOTES

CHAPTER 13

1. *Something to Wrestle With*, episode 140.
2. Yet another counter-programming strategy, the *Royal Rumble* was a free basic cable special designed to sabotage Crockett Promotions' second pay-per-view attempt, the *Bunkhouse Stampede*, live from the WWF's stomping grounds at the Nassau Coliseum the same day. Needless to say, it was another abject Crockett failure.
3. The occasion would mark Vince's first time calling the action at the Garden since he'd taken over the company five years prior.
4. The episode would conclude with a beleaguered Brain pushing Gorilla along the Atlantic City boardwalk on a rickshaw, with Gorilla ordering him to take him down to "the old Steel Pier"—site of the shows he used to promote himself back in the late '70s.
5. From an unpublished portion of an interview with Patterson conducted by his biographer Bertrand Herbert: "I am often asked if I knew about the jokes and innuendo made about me on commentary back in the days by Gorilla Monsoon among others. It was just the boys ribbing me in good fun; it was never meant to be more than getting one over [on] me as a rib. Most of the fans back then would not get it anyways. We laughed about it like friends do."
6. Credence is lent to this story by the fact that three years later, Vince would saddle the Viking gimmick on John Nord, one of his last AWA acquisitions, turning him into the Berzerker, with a persona that featured a very Brody-like appearance and mannerisms.
7. Bobby recalled in a 2002 shoot interview that Gino was pretty annoyed at the Old Tucson shoot, which happened to take place on Super Bowl Sunday, meaning he couldn't watch the game.
8. Vince McMahon and Roddy Piper would take commentary duties for *SummerSlam '90*.

CHAPTER 14

1. With domestic business starting to flag, Titan Sports had been pushing heavily into the UK market, which was only just discovering its

product. This "UK golden era" of the early to mid-1990s provided the WWF with much-needed capital at a time when the brand had lost some of its luster with fans in the U.S. and Canada.
2. That particular Rumble would include as one of its thirty participants, of all people, Gino's old business partner Carlos Colón—with Gino infamously referring to the forty-four-year-old wrestler and twenty-seven-year veteran of the business as a "youngster," in what surely had to be a rib between old friends.
3. As described by Bobby in his 2002 shoot interview for RF Video.
4. Upon introducing himself to Tate, Bobby begins to say he is from the World Wrestling Federation before quickly correcting himself to say WCW. Whether a Freudian slip or typical Bobby Heenan ball-busting is anyone's guess.
5. Buddy would be posthumously inducted by his former manager Bobby Davis, who had also been Gino's first WWWF manager, and whom Gino likely hadn't seen since he walked away from the business many years earlier.
6. Gino most certainly didn't want to get stuck filling in for Vince on these shows, but his *Superstars* with Lawler is him at his least annoyed, as he has someone with natural comic chops to work with.
7. *Something to Wrestle With*, episode 140.
8. Todd Pettengill came to host the show in its final episodes, with Scott Levy self-destructing, getting himself fired from the company and heading over to Paul Heyman's ECW to reinvent himself as Raven.
9. The holder of the dubious record of smallest Garden wrestling crowd is the February 22, 1949, show presented by Toots Mondt, the first wrestling card at the Garden in eleven years. Not even Gorgeous George in his one and only MSG appearance could draw more than a dismal 4,197 that night.
10. Audio recorded by Don Laible and shared on the November 9, 2023, episode of John Arezzi's *Pro Wrestling Spotlight* podcast.
11. Ross would work on the booking team alongside Bruce Prichard and eventually Jim Cornette, with Pat Patterson taking less of a role, although he was still relied on for his fabled brilliance at developing finishes.

NOTES

12. Yankem, real name Glenn Jacobs, would later go on to much greater success as Kane.

CHAPTER 15

1. Kevin remembers the wedding from when he was a kid and his dad coming home with a Gorilla Monsoon autograph, saying, "You'll never believe who you're related to."
2. The previous night, the WWF had been in Gino's hometown at the Rochester War Memorial for a pay-per-view, marking the final time Gino would set foot in the building where he had had his first matches back in 1960.
3. ECW had for years been staging what were called "Three-Way Dances," which is where Russo undoubtedly drew inspiration for the Triple Threat concept.

CHAPTER 16

1. "Good-bye, Gorilla: A memory of a friend." Wrestleline.com, October 6, 1999.
2. *Super Astros* also brought Lilian Garcia to the WWF, who would quickly go from Spanish-language backstage interviewer to the company's new lead ring announcer for years.
3. *Wrestling Shoot Interviews*, November 12, 2021.
4. Those final episodes aired in the United States as the first few episodes of *WWF Jakked*, a new weekly supplementary show hosted domestically by Michael Cole and Kevin Kelly.
5. It had been a particularly rough week for the company, as just the night before at the *SmackDown* taping at the Nassau Coliseum, one of the wrestlers on the card, Darren "Droz" Drozdov, had sustained a catastrophic neck injury that would leave him paralyzed for life.

CHAPTER 17

1. One major exception to this was Superstar Billy Graham, who, after years of railing against the company, had returned to Vince's good graces, at least for a while.
2. In those later years, a fan at an autograph signing once presented Bobby with a Gorilla Monsoon T-shirt. He promptly blew his nose with it.
3. The federal case would be dismissed in February 2025, mere weeks before Vince's estranged wife, Linda, was sworn in as U.S. Secretary of Education for longtime McMahon family associate, and now U.S. president, Donald Trump.

BIBLIOGRAPHY

Arezzi, John. *Pro Wrestling Spotlight*. Episode 98. Alexander Media Services. 9 Nov. 2023.

Assael, Shaun, and Mike Mooneyham. *Sex, Lies and Headlocks: The Real Story of Vince McMahon and World Wrestling Entertainment*. New York, NY: Crown, 2002.

Balukjian, Brad. *The Six Pack: On the Open Road in Search of WrestleMania*. New York, NY: Hachette, 2024.

Blassie, "Classy" Freddie, with Keith Elliot Greenberg. *Listen, You Pencil Neck Geeks*. New York, NY: Simon & Schuster, 2003.

Burns, Will. "The Origins of the WWF." *Project WWF*. Jan.–Feb. 2021. https://projectwwf.com/2021/01/22/the-origins-of-the-wwf-part-one/.

Cappetta, Gary Michael. *Bodyslams! Memoirs of a Wrestling Pitchman*. Toronto, Ontario: ECW, 2005.

Fahey, Vince. *Kayfabe Memories*. Atom Designs, 2004. https://www.kayfabememories.com/.

Ginzburg, Evan. "Gorilla Monsoon—Remembering 'The Manchurian Giant.'" *Pro Wrestling Stories*. 25 Oct. 2023. https://prowrestlingstories.com/pro-wrestling-stories/gorilla-monsoon/.

Hornbaker, Tim. *Capitol Revolution: The Rise of the McMahon Wrestling Empire.* Toronto, Ontario: ECW, 2015.

Hornbaker, Tim. *Master of the Ring: The Biography of "Nature Boy" Buddy Rogers.* Gallatin, Tennessee: Crowbar, 2020.

Hornbaker, Tim. *National Wrestling Alliance: The Untold Story of the Monopoly that Strangled Pro Wrestling.* Toronto, Ontario: ECW, 2007.

Hornby, Fred, Scott Teal, et al. *The History of Professional Wrestling—Madison Square Garden: 1880–1999.* Hendersonville, Tennessee: Scott Teal, 2000.

Jares, Joe. *Whatever Happened to Gorgeous George?* London, England: Prentice-Hall International, 1974.

Johnson, Steven. "Recalling Monsoon Before He Was Top Gorilla." *Slam Wrestling.* 21 July 2011. https://slamwrestling.net/index.php/2011/07/21/recalling-monsoon-before-he-was-top-gorilla/.

Johnson, Steven, and Greg Oliver. *The Pro Wrestling Hall of Fame: The Heels.* Toronto, Ontario: ECW, 2007.

Kreikenbohm, Philip. *Cagematch: The Internet Wrestling Database.* 2001, https://www.cagematch.net/.

Last, Brian. *6:05 Superpodcast.* Episode 39. Arcadian Vanguard. 17 Mar. 2018.

McAdam, John. *Stick to Wrestling with John McAdam.* Episode 54. Arcadian Vanguard. 20 June 2019.

Meltzer, Dave. *Wrestling Observer Newsletter.*

Monsoon, Gorilla. "In this Corner: The Newspaper Archive." *Internet Archive.* 1978–81. https://archive.org/details/GorillaMonsoon/mode/2up.

Nulty, Mark. *WrestlingClassics.* 1998. http://wrestlingclassics.com/.

Prichard, Bruce, and Conrad Thompson. *Something to Wrestle With.* Episode 140. Westwood One. 1 Feb. 2019.

Riesman, Abraham Josephine. *Ringmaster: Vince McMahon and the Unmaking of America.* New York, NY: Atria Books, 2023.

Ring the Damn Bell. "The Rise of a Titan: Vince McMahon's Purchase of the WWF." 8 June 2021. https://ringthedamnbell.wordpress.com

/2021/06/08/the-rise-of-a-titan-vince-mcmahons-purchase-of-the-wwf/.

Rosado, Emmanuel. "Remembering Vitín: The Victor Quiñones Story." *Last Word on Sports*. 13 May 2018. https://lastwordonsports.com/prowrestling/2018/05/13/the-victor-quinones-story/.

Saalbach, Axel. *Wrestlingdata.com*. 2001. https://www.wrestlingdata.com/.

Sammartino, Bruno, with Bob Michelucci, et al. *Bruno Sammartino: An Autobiography of Wrestling's Living Legend*. Huntington, NY: Sub Entertainment, 1990.

Tanabe, Hisaharu. *Pro Wrestling Title Histories*. Puroresu.com. 1995. https://www.wrestling-titles.com/.

Walton, Jeff, with Scott Walton. *Richmond 9-5171: A Wrestling Story*. Los Angeles, California: JW Enterprises, 2004.

Entertainment. Writing. Culture.

ECW is a proudly independent, Canadian-owned book publisher. We know great writing can improve people's lives, and we're passionate about sharing original, exciting, and insightful writing across genres.

Thanks for reading along!

We want our books not just to sustain our imaginations, but to help construct a healthier, more just world, and so we've become a certified B Corporation, meaning we meet a high standard of social and environmental responsibility — and we're going to keep aiming higher. We believe books can drive change, but the way we make them can too.

Being a B Corp means that the act of publishing this book should be a force for good — for the planet, for our communities, and for the people that worked to make this book. For example, everyone who worked on this book was paid at least a living wage. You can learn more at the Ontario Living Wage Network.

This book is also available as a Global Certified Accessible™ (GCA) ebook. ECW Press's ebooks are screen reader friendly and are built to meet the needs of those who are unable to read standard print due to blindness, low vision, dyslexia, or a physical disability.

The interior of this book is printed on Sustana EnviroBook™, which is made from 100% recycled fibres and processed chlorine-free.

FSC
www.fsc.org
MIX
Paper | Supporting responsible forestry
FSC® C016245

ECW's office is situated on land that was the traditional territory of many nations, including the Wendat, the Anishinaabeg, Haudenosaunee, Chippewa, Métis, and current treaty holders the Mississaugas of the Credit. In the 1880s, the land was developed as part of a growing community around St. Matthew's Anglican and other churches. Starting in the 1950s, our neighbourhood was transformed by immigrants fleeing the Vietnam War and Chinese Canadians dispossessed by the building of Nathan Phillips Square and the subsequent rise in real estate value in other Chinatowns. We are grateful to those who cared for the land before us and are proud to be working amidst this mix of cultures.

ecwpress.com